# USING PC TOOLS DELUXE

## CHARLES ACKERMAN

ADVANCED
COMPUTER
BOOKS

**MIS:** PRESS

© 1990 by Management Information Source, Inc.

P.O. Box 5277
Portland, Oregon 97208-5277
(503) 282-5215

**Fifth Printing**

ISBN 1-55828-052-9

Printed in the United States of America

Clipper is a registered trademark of Nantucket Corporation.
CompuServe and EasyLink are registered trademarks of CompuServe Corporation.
Connection CoProcessor is a registered trademark of Intel Corporation.
dBASE III PLUS, dBASE IV, and MultiMate are all registered trademarks of Ashton-Tate Corporation.
dBXL is a registered trademark of WordTech Corporation.
DisplayWrite, IBM, IBM PC/XT, IBM PC/AT, PS/2, PC-DOS and Token Ring are all registered trademarks of
    International Business Machines Corporation.
Excel, Microsoft Works, Microsoft Word, MS-DOS and OS/2 are all registered trademarks of Microsoft Corporation.
FoxBase is a registered trademark of Fox Software, Inc.
HP-11C, HP-12C, and HP-16C are all registered trademarks of Hewlett-Packard Corporation.
InColor is a registered trademark of Hercules, Inc.
Lotus 1-2-3 and Symphony are registered trademarks of Lotus Development Corporation.
LapLink Quick Connect is a registered trademark of Traveling Software, Inc.
MCI Mail is a registered trademark of MCI, Inc.
NetWare is a registered trademark of Novell, Inc.
Paradox, Quattro, SideKick, SideKick Plus, and Sprint are all registered trademarks of Borland International, Inc.
PC Tools Deluxe is a registered trademark of Central Point Software, Inc.
R:Base is a registered trademark of Microrim, Inc.
SpectraFax is a registered trademark of SpectraFax Corporation.
VT52 and VT100 are registered trademarks of Digital Equipment Corporation.
WordPerfect is a registered trademark of WordPerfect Corporation.
WordStar is a registered trademark of The New MicroPro, Inc.
XyWrite is a registered trademark of XyWrite Corporation.

*To Rudolph Langer, Ph.D.,*

*whose daily moil proves that the best writers don't become authors.*

# ACKNOWLEDGMENTS

First of all, I would like to thank all the people at Central Point Software for being so courteous, enthusiastic, and helpful with this project. I've heard there's a tonic in the Pacific Northwest climate, and now I believe it.

When I started writing this book, there wasn't a single one on PC Tools Deluxe, the best-selling collection of DOS shell, desktop applications, and utility programs. Before this book was finished, Central Point Software had to set up a separate department simply to support all the books in progress. Through it all, they have been unfailing in their support, and this during an intense period of Beta product development.

Next, I'd like to thank Bob Williams, the publisher of MIS: Press, for agreeing to publish this book. An author always likes to extol the vision of his publisher—when they agree on a book idea. But Bob is an author himself, so there's no pulling the wool over his eyes.

Thanks also to Milan Moncilovich and Doug Snyder, my editors. I'm writing these acknowledgments last, just before I submit my manuscript—so we'll have to wait and see what they think of me. (I've always felt an editor should be given one page at the back of each book he works on to give expression to his sentiments about the effort.) And thanks to everyone else at MIS: Press who had a hand with this book.

# CONTENTS

# INTRODUCTION

P C Tools Deluxe is a family of programs for the IBM PC. It includes a DOS shell, a diverse range of disk utility programs, and a selection of desktop applications, such as a text editor, a clipboard, and a communications program. When you start to work with the programs, you will find them useful; when you have used them for a short time, you will find them indispensable. This book tells you all about PC Tools Deluxe.

I am writing this book because I have real affection for PC Tools Deluxe. It is the best implementation of a DOS shell and Desktop application programs presently on the market, and Central Point Software, the maker of PC Tools, continues to keep its product current.

This is a hands-on book. You're given step-by-step examples for every significant command in every PC Tools program. These examples are amply explained and illustrated.

There are three distinct parts to the PC Tools Deluxe program. The PC Shell manages your DOS files. The Desktop Manager executes most of your applied work. The Utility program files—including PC Cache, Mirror/Rebuild, and PC Backup—allow you to easily perform varied and necessary tasks, such as backing up your hard-disk files.

There are several problems with writing a book about such a diverse collection of programs. New users will require special guidance. Others will want to know all there is to know about one part of PC Tools and nothing about another part. Still others are familiar with most of the program already and will want to know more about the new, advanced features and how they can integrate the various programs into a working whole.

So the questions becomes: How do you write one book for everyone?

Because of the broad program array and the wide range of user learning requirements, I have served the topics like a smorgasbord, rather than dishing them up as a hodgepodge. This book is organized into four parts: The Tour, The PC Shell, The Desktop Manager, and The Utility Programs.

**The Tour.**  Chapter 1 describes the main programs and shows you how to navigate the menus and execute the commands by taking you on a quick tour of the Desktop Manager. It presumes that you have already installed the program, using the step-by-step instructions in appendix A.

**The PC Shell.**  Chapters 2, 3, and 4 teach you how to use PC Shell.  Chapter 2 teaches the interface and basic commands. Chapter 3 describes the menu interface in detail and different ways of configuring the PC Shell screen. Chapter 4 is devoted to the Applications pull-down menu and other ways of launching programs. For many people, chapter 2 will be all the exposure to the PC Shell they need. Only a minority of users will use PC Shell to the degree explained in chapter 4.

**The Desktop Manager.**  Chapters 5 through 16 describe the components of the Desktop Manager. The various modules—such as Notepads, Outlines, and Databases editors—are arranged in a way that supports an integrated education in what you can do in the Desktop Manager. Because most people will spend a great deal of their time in the Notepads editor, it comes first module. The Clipboard and Outlines modules follow immediately because they share much of the appearance and behavior of the Notepads editor. Chapter 16 describes how to use macros in the Desktop Editor.

**The Utility Programs.**  Chapter 17 describes the utility programs. These include Compress, which allows you to get the most out of your disk space; Diskfix, which analyzes, diagnosis, and fixes errors and incompatibilities on disks; Mirror/Rebuild, which allows you to rebuild lost and damaged data; and Undelete, which retrieves accidentally deleted files.

One appendix completes the book. It describes how to install the PC Tools Deluxe programs.

There is a method to this organization. On one hand, there is a flow from the more general features to the more specific. On the other hand, the chapters are modular; you can read them in any order and still gain benefit.  You can learn about any program or program features in the order you choose.

## Terminology

The following examples show how keyboard operations are represented throughout the book:

[Enter]      The Enter or Return key

[F1]         The first function key

[Ctrl]       The Control key

[A]          The letter A key

[⇑]          The Up Arrow key

You can enter either upper- or lowercase characters after the DOS prompt because DOS doesn't distinguish between the case of characters. For example, typing CHKDSK, chkdsk, or CHkdSk and pressing [Enter] all have the same effect.

To eliminate confusion, commands are shown in uppercase. For example, if I ask you to experiment with the DOS command CHKDSK, I will present it in the following way:

**Type:** CHKDSK

**Press:** [Enter]

When a program responds with a message, I will present the text in typewriter typeface (also called Courier):

```
This text appears in courier.
```

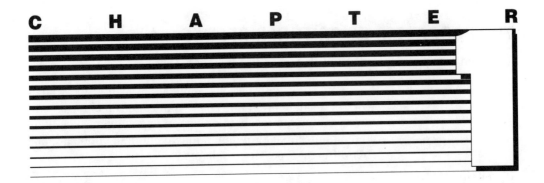

C H A P T E R 1

# A TOUR OF
# PC TOOLS DELUXE

This chapter is a quick tour of PC Tools Deluxe. On this tour you will gain experience using PC Tools by loading the Desktop Manager and learning how to use the basic program controls. Subsequent chapters will describe the Desktop Manager in detail and explore the other programs of PC Tools.

# THE PROGRAMS OF PC TOOLS DELUXE

There are nine principal programs that comprise PC Tools Deluxe:

**Desktop Manager**  Lets you work with various applications within the framework of a single program. These applications include an editor, an outliner, a database editor, an appointment scheduler, a communications program, a macro editor, a clipboard, and four different types of calculators.

**PC Shell**  Displays your disk contents in graphic windows and lets you perform all sorts of routine DOS commands—as well as some unique commands of its own—on disk files and the disks themselves.

**Compress**  Maximizes disk performance by defragmenting file sections and making more efficient use of disk space.

**Diskfix**  Fixes errors—including partition and FAT tables and lost subdirectories—on all types of disks. Also revives corrupted floppy disks with data.

**PC Backup**  Copies data files on a hard disk to floppy disks or tape.

**PC Cache**  Speeds up disk access time by storing frequently used information on a RAM drive.

**Mirror/Rebuild**  Protects you against data loss. Mirror builds files that save your disk information, and Rebuild uses that information to re-create data.

**PC Format**  Formatting program that lets you format hard and floppy disks to all available formats using a nondestructive method. This program should supplant your DOS format program, however, you can use the two side-by-side.

**PC Secure**  Protects selected data from prying eyes by encrypting, compressing, and hiding data.

All of these programs can work together or separately, depending upon what you want to do. They can be called programs, applications, or modules, and these names are used interchangeably throughout the book.

PC Tools Deluxe should be installed on your computer before you proceed with this chapter. If you haven't installed the program, read the appendix for more information.

## WAYS OF LOADING THE PROGRAMS

You can load the Desktop Manager and PC Shell programs two ways: as standard programs or as resident programs. There are advantages and disadvantages to each method. If you use the programs often while you're working with other programs, then you'll probably want to run them in *resident mode*. Resident mode allows you to interrupt your work in another program, pop the Desktop Manager or PC Shell up, work with it, then pop it back down again to resume your work.

However, running programs in resident mode causes computer conflicts, so the standard mode is also provided. Standard mode is how most programs for the IBM PC are designed to run: you load them from the DOS prompt. Running the Desktop Manager or PC Shell in standard mode should give you no conflicts, but you don't have the flexibility of popping in and out of the programs.

## RUNNING AS A STANDARD PROGRAM

To load the Desktop Manager as a standard program:

**Type:** DESKTOP

**Press:** [Enter]

When you load the program in standard mode, you might see a copyright screen. If it appears, press any key to remove it. Your screen should look like figure 1.1.

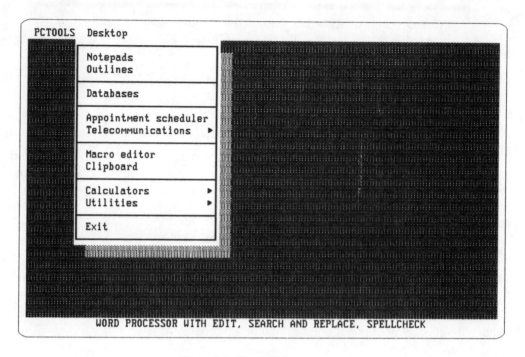

*Figure 1.1. The Desktop menu*

This screen is fairly simple. The top line shows you're working in PC TOOLS and the name of the only menu shows that you're working in the Desktop. This is the Desktop Manager main menu, which contains ten selections. The top selection, Notepads, should be highlighted. The bottom on the screen line shows the message: WORD PROCESSOR WITH EDIT, SEARCH AND REPLACE, SPELLCHECK. It defines the activities you can perform in Notepads.

You can check the activities provided in the other Desktop menu selections by pressing [⇓] and viewing the messages that appear on the bottom line for each selection. When you get to Telecommunications, you'll notice that another menu appears. This is called a *nested menu*. The nested menu under Telecommunications lets you select what type of communications with which you want to work. In addition to Telecommunications, there are two other nested menus off of the Desktop menu, each denoted by an arrow to the right of the Desktop menu selection.

When you've reached the bottom of the Desktop menu, pressing [⇓] or [Home] will return you to Notepads.

You may rarely need to use any program other than the Desktop Manager. If this is the case, you should probably load the program in standard mode. You might also want to change the name of the program file DESKTOP.EXE to something short and easy to type, such as D.EXE. Then you only need type [D] at your DOS command line and press [Enter] to load the Desktop Manager. You can change the file name using the PC Shell, as explained in chapter 2.

## FUNCTION KEY ASSIGNMENTS

When function keys have assignments in various PC Tools Deluxe screens, the assignments usually are noted at the bottom of the screen. The Desktop menu screen is the exception; the following three function keys work, but none of them are noted:

**[F1] Help**      Opens the general help screen.

**[F2] Index**      Opens the help index.

**[F3] Exit**      Exits the Desktop menu screen and returns you to your previous work.

You should explore the two functions that access help, [F1] and [F2], before you go further into the program.

## HELP

There are four major sources of help when using the PC Tools: the PC Tools manual, outside sources (such as this book), the online help (accessible with the function keys), and the designers of the PC Tools program. The latter can be contacted at Central Point Software via their technical support bulletin board. This chapter will describe how to access the online help. Chapter 13, "Using Telecommunications," describes how to contact the CPS bulletin board.

When you access help from a specific operation in a PC Tools program, the program senses where you are and what you're doing and presents help information specific to the operation. This is known as *context-sensitive* help.

Regardless of where you are in any of the PC Tools programs, you can access context-sensitive and interactive help at any time by pressing [F1]. For example, while you're viewing the Desktop menu (shown in figure 1.1), call up its help screen, which is shown in figure 1.2:

**Press:** [F1]

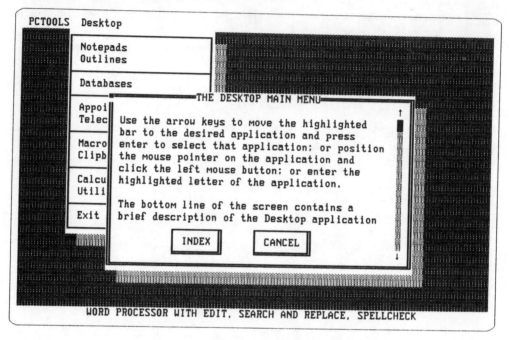

Figure 1.2. The Desktop main menu help window

The information in this screen tells you how to use help while viewing the Desktop main menu. To see the second half of the screen, press [PgDn]. Notice the vertical bar on the right side the window. This is called a *scroll bar*. The marker in it moves to show your relative position in a multiple-page window. If you're using a mouse, you can point to the arrow at the bottom of the scroll bar to move down, and you can point to the arrow at the top of the bar to move up.

A command at the bottom of the Desktop main menu help window will display a general index of all help subjects:

**Press:** [I]

This opens the general Help index, as shown in figure 1.3.

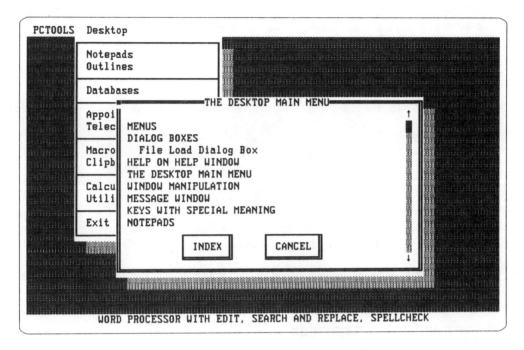

*Figure 1.3. The Desktop main menu help index*

You can press [PgDn] to scroll down through index entries, and you can press [PgUp] to scroll back up. Pressing [Home] will return you to the first entry, and pressing [End] will move you to the last entry. Unfortunately, the entries are not alphabetized. Notice how the scroll-bar marker shows your relative position in the help index.

To view specific help on an entry, highlight the entry and:

**Press:** [Enter]

To close any help window:

**Press:** [Esc]

Pressing [Esc] is the most common way for backing out of something. You can press [Esc] to close help, exit a module, and even quit the Desktop Manager.

If you accidentally press [Esc] too many times and exit the Desktop Manager, just type *DESKTOP* at the DOS prompt and press [Enter] to reload the program. To continue the tour, you should be looking at the Desktop main menu (shown in figure 1.1).

# ENTERING COMMANDS

The Desktop Manager and the PC Shell provide you with three ways you can enter commands:

**Key commands**    Pressing keyboard and function keys. This is easier for people who have memorized frequently used commands and who are good typists.

**Mouse controls**    Pointing to a menu selection and clicking the mouse button. This is easier for people who are accustomed to working with a mouse and who prefer visual control over their activities.

**Pull-down menus**    Highlighting a menu item and pressing [Enter]. This is easier for new users.

## Working with Key Commands

In all PC Tools programs, you can move around screens and menus and select commands using cursor keys (arrow keys, [PgUp], [PgDn], [End], and [Home]), letter keys, and function keys. You used cursor keys earlier to scroll through selections on the Desktop menu.

One way to use keys to open a menu item is to press the letter key that appears in a different color or in reverse video on the monitor. To open Notepads:

    **Press:** [N]

This opens the *NOTEPADS* dialog box, shown figure 1.4.

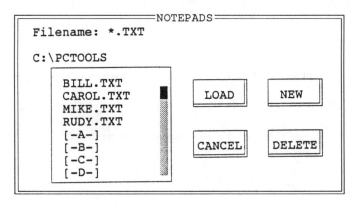

*Figure 1.4. The NOTEPADS dialog box*

A dialog box is so named because it carries on a dialog with you; it asks what file you want to use and what you want to do with the file. You then reply. In this example, when you select Notepads on the Desktop menu, the dialog box asks you to select the file you want to check or edit.

You will work with Notepads in chapter 6. For this quick tour, however, you should close the *NOTEPADS* dialog box:

**Press:** [Esc]

Only two commands on the Desktop Manager main menu are activated by a key other than the first letter of the command. The first is the Clipboard, which uses B, and the second is Exit, which uses X.

You'll find that pressing letter keys to move around menus can be very helpful. You might have to memorize a few irregular commands, such as [B] for Clipboard, but after using them a few times, they'll become habit. Menus respond quickly; you can press letter keys as fast as you can remember them. After becoming familiar with the menu structure of PC Tools, you'll go whizzing through menus to the exact command you want to use.

Take a closer look at other menus in the Desktop Manager. Move the highlight bar over *Utilities* using an arrow key. First take a look at the definition for this command on the bottom line of your screen. When the Utilities selection is highlighted, the definition should read: SET HOTKEYS, CHANGE SYSTEM WINDOW COLORS, ASCII TABLE. This means you can use this selection to set hotkeys, change system window colors, and view a representation of the ASCII table. Now open the nested menu:

**Press:** [Enter]

Figure 1.5 shows the dialog box that displays the four utilities that you can use.

```
┌──────────────────────────────────┐
│        UTILITY PROGRAMS          │
├──────────────────────────────────┤
│ Hotkey selection                 │
│ Ascii table                      │
│ System menu/window colors        │
│ Unload PCTOOLS Desktop           │
└──────────────────────────────────┘
```

*Figure 1.5. Utility Programs*

The first command on the Utility Programs, *Hotkey selection,* should be highlighted. To select this command:

**Press:** [Enter]

This opens a third menu, which looks like figure 1.6.

```
┌════════ PCTOOLS Desktop Hotkey Selection ════════┐
│                                                   │
│  DESKTOP HOTKEY: <CTRL><SPACE>                    │
│                                                   │
│ CLIPBOARD PASTE: <CTRL><INS>                      │
│                                                   │
│  CLIPBOARD COPY: <CTRL><DEL>                      │
│                                                   │
│ SCREEN AUTODIAL: <CTRL><O>                        │
│                                                   │
└═══ 9:41 am ═══════════════════════════════════════┘
```

*Figure 1.6. PC Tools Desktop Hotkey*

As soon as this menu appears, another menu name *Window* appears on the top menu bar next to the label *Desktop.*

Hotkeys will be explained later in this book. For now, return to the desktop menu:

**Press:** [Esc] until you are at the Desktop menu

## Using a Mouse

The Desktop Manager, like most of the PC Tools programs, provides you excellent control using a mouse, a track ball, or similar device. Of course, to be able to use a mouse, your computer must be installed with a mouse and a mouse driver. The latter is a disk file that comes with the mouse you purchase.

The mouse cable is connected to a serial port, and the mouse driver is activated each time you boot your computer. Occasionally, when you've installed a mouse and you try to use modem communications (which also needs to be connected to a serial port), you might experience some conflicts. This might require that you either reconfigure your system or disable the serial device you don't want to use.

If your mouse is installed correctly, you should see the mouse pointer somewhere on the screen when you load the Desktop Manager. You move the pointer around by sliding the mouse on your desktop or by rolling the track ball.

To select a menu command using the mouse, place the pointer anywhere on the command line within the borders of the menu and press either the left or right mouse button. The pointer doesn't have to be precisely on any of the letters of the command name to select the command.

To use your mouse to open the *NOTEPADS* dialog box:

**Select:** Notepads

**Press:** [Left button]

When the *Notepads* dialog box appears, four commands specific to mouse control appear on the right side of the dialog box: Load, New, Cancel, and Delete. To select any of these, place the pointer on the box containing the command you want to execute and press [Left button]. Use your mouse to exit the *NOTEPADS* dialog box:

**Select:** Cancel

**Press:** [Left button]

This returns you to the Desktop menu. Another good example to work with is the Help index you looked at earlier (figure 1.3):

**Press:** [F1]

You can use your mouse to scroll down through the index by placing your pointer on the down arrow at the bottom of the scroll bar on the right side of the window and pressing [Left button]. Similarly, you can scroll back up by placing your pointer on the up arrow and pressing [Left button].

You'll find scroll bars throughout the Desktop Manager modules, as well as arrows and other features you can use with your mouse to open, close and resize windows.

To initiate commands, this book only will use keyboard and menu commands because only a minority of PC users have a mouse. However, a mouse is so easy to use you will have no problems using one.

## Using Pull-down menus

The PC Tools Deluxe programs are intensively menu driven. You've seen the Desktop menu and menus nested in the Desktop menu. For a more detailed example, take a look at the Clipboard menu system (shown in figure 1.7). When you're viewing the main menu, open your Clipboard module window:

**Press:** [B]

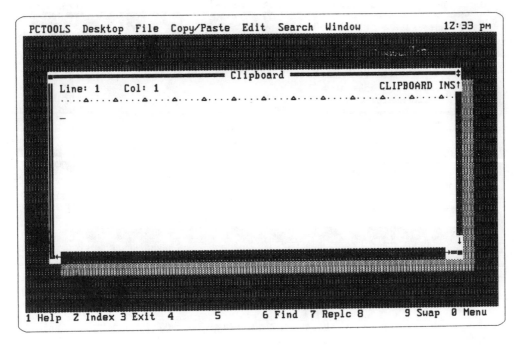

*Figure 1.7. The Clipboard window*

When the Clipboard window appears, you'll find six names of pull-down menus you can use in the Clipboard: Desktop, File, Copy/Paste, Edit, Search, and Window. To open a pull-down menu, press [Alt] or [F10] and the key that matches the first letter of the menu you want to open. To open the Desktop menu:

**Press:** [Alt]-[D]

When the menu's open, it will look like figure 1.8.

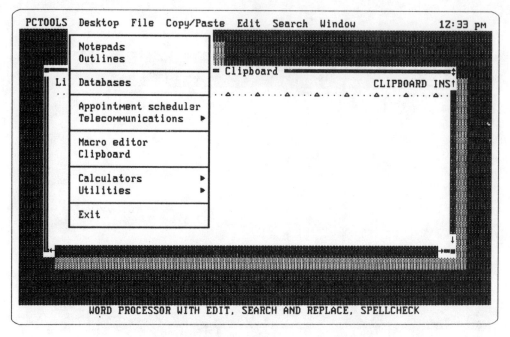

*Figure 1.8. The Desktop menu open in the Clipboard*

Don't be concerned with the details on this or any of the other Clipboard menus until you start working with this module in chapter 7. To close any pull-down menu:

**Press:** [Esc]

Another example is to open the Search menu:

**Press:** [Alt]-[S]

This provides you with two commands: Find and Replace. To open the Find menu:

**Press:** [Enter]

To close that menu and return to the Clipboard screen:

**Press:** [Esc]

> You can press either [Alt] or [F10] to activate the top menu bar. When you press those keys, you'll notice the first letters of each pull-down menu name change color or shade. I prefer to use [Alt] because I can hold that key down with my thumb.

The Desktop and Window pull-down menus are available in the nine applications you can access from the Desktop menu. Each module then provides other menus unique to the work you can do in the module. Since you're already familiar with the Desktop menu, take a look at the Window menu, which lets you change the way windows appear on your screen. First, return to the Desktop menu. Then open one of the calculators:

**Press:** [C]

**Press:** [Enter]

Now open a second module.

**Press:** [Alt]-[D]

This opens the Desktop menu. Select the Clipboard again (this relieves you of having to go through a dialog box):

**Press:** [B]

Now open the Window menu in the Clipboard:

**Press:** [Alt]-[W]

Your screen should resemble figure 1.9.

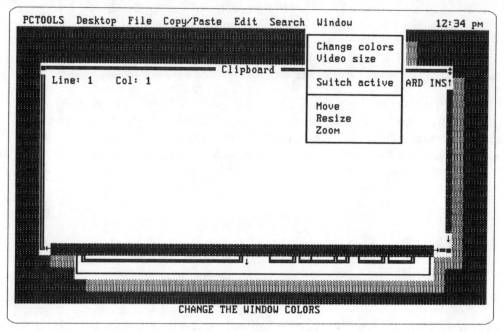

*Figure 1.9. The Window pull-down menu*

What you've done is open the algebraic calculator, overlay it with the Clipboard, then open the Windows pull-down menu. You're given six selections on the Window menu:

**Change colors**    Opens a palette that lets you select colors and intensity for various features on the current screen.

**Video size**       Switches you between 25-line standard display and 43-line VGA/EGA display.

**Switch active**    Switches you between active windows. This selection shows only when you've opened two or more windows.

**Move**             Moves the current window to another location on your screen.

**Resize**           Changes the size of the current window.

**Zoom**             Expands the current window to occupy a full screen or reduces the window to its previous size.

Pressing [Alt]-[Spacebar] opens a shortcut box that lets you resize or move the current window directly. You might want to experiment with these settings.

To switch back to the calculator window:

> **Press:** [S]

This selects Switch active. To switch back to the Clipboard window:

> **Press:** [F9]

This function key does the same thing as the *Switch active* command on the Window pull-down menu.

To set the display colors on your monitor, open the Utilities nested menu and select *System menu/window colors:*

> **Press:** [Alt]-[U]-[S]

This gives you a palette that looks like figure 1.10.

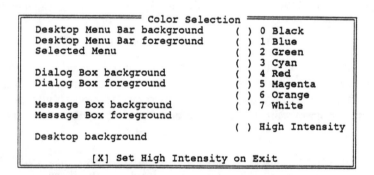

```
═══════════════════ Color Selection ═══════════════
Desktop Menu Bar background        ( ) 0 Black
Desktop Menu Bar foreground        ( ) 1 Blue
Selected Menu                      ( ) 2 Green
                                   ( ) 3 Cyan
Dialog Box background              ( ) 4 Red
Dialog Box foreground              ( ) 5 Magenta
                                   ( ) 6 Orange
Message Box background             ( ) 7 White
Message Box foreground
                                   ( ) High Intensity
Desktop background

        [X] Set High Intensity on Exit
```

*Figure 1.10. The color selection dialog box*

What colors you want to use is a personal decision. You'll find that the default color settings are suitable to begin with, but I prefer a blue background, red foreground, and white characters set to high intensity.

### Exiting the Desktop Manager

When the Desktop Manager is loaded as a standard program; you can exit it in two ways:

1.  Press [Esc] to back out of whatever you've loaded onto your screen.

2.  Return to the Desktop menu and select *Exit*.

# RUNNING AS A RESIDENT PROGRAM

The second way you can load PC Tools Deluxe is as a *resident* program. This is a nickname for TSR, or terminate-and-stay resident. This means that the program is first loaded into RAM and then terminated, but a portion still resides in RAM. The beauty of running a program resident mode is that you can pop it up whenever you need it. For example, if you're working in dBASE and you want to write a letter, you can pop up the Notepads editor, write the letter, then pop Notepads down again and return to your work in dBASE.

The ability for the PC Tools programs to go resident is one of their most marvelous features. I run both the Desktop Manager and the PC Shell in resident mode most of the time. That way, they're always at hand when I need them.

Watch out when you have PC Tools programs and other programs loaded as resident. Running several TSRs at the same time can cause memory conflict, which leads to problems when you try to run in. If this happens, you should juggle the order in which the programs are loaded to determine what combination lets them cooperate the best.

If you run any PC Tools programs in resident mode and you also want to run SideKick or SideKick Plus, you must load the PC Tools programs first. The SideKick programs insist on being loaded last. If you try to load any PC Tools programs resident after loading SideKick or SideKick Plus, you'll get an error message. To clear the conflict, you'll have to unload the SideKick program first, load the PC Tools programs, and then reload SideKick or SideKick Plus.

To load the Desktop Manager in resident mode:

**Type:** DESKTOP /R

The last part of this command, /R, is called the *IR switch*. In addition to the /R switch, there are other switches you can use for the Desktop Manager which you will learn later.

**Press:** [Enter]

When the Desktop Manager is fully loaded as a resident program, it will display a message window on the screen and return to the DOS prompt. The message looks like figure 1.11.

```
              PCTOOLS Desktop (tm)
         Personal Computer Desktop Manager
                   Version 6.0

    Copyright (c) 1988-1990  Central Point Software, Inc.
                 All rights reserved
         544 Kbytes free    15 Stackable windows

    To activate PCTOOLS Desktop, press <CTRL><SPACE>
```

*Figure 1.11. The Desktop Manager loaded as a resident program*

The bottom two lines of this screen provide valuable information that is not shown when you load the program in the standard mode. The line above the bottom line shows how much memory remains in your computer and how many windows you can open. The bottom line shows which keys are configured as the hotkeys. Hotkeys are keys that you press to activate a command. The Desktop Manager shows <CTRL><SPACE> as a hotkey (if the hotkeys haven't been reconfigured). This means that when you press [Ctrl]-[Spacebar] at the same time, the Desktop Manager is activated, or popped-up, regardless of what else you're doing:

**Press:** [Ctrl]-[Spacebar]

As the Desktop Manager pops up, you'll see the following message:

LOADING DESKTOP OVERLAYS. PLEASE WAIT.

In a few moments, your screen should again look just like figure 1.1. You can explore some of the menu selections if you want to. Program control doesn't vary between modes of operation.

In resident mode, you can exit the Desktop Manager three ways:

1.  Press [Esc] to back out of whatever you've loaded onto your screen.

2.  Return to the Desktop menu and select Exit.

3.  Press [Ctrl]-[Spacebar], which pops down the program. When you do this, you've terminated only your use of the program; it still lies in memory waiting for you to pop it back up.

You cannot load the Desktop Manager, or any other PC Tools program that can go resident, in both resident and standard modes at the same time. If you forget, and try to load the program a second time, either in the same or different mode, you'll get an error message (if you're lucky) or a conflict (if you're not). Whenever TSR programs conflict, you'll probably have to reboot the computer.

## SWITCHING BETWEEN STANDARD AND RESIDENT MODES

Switching from standard mode to resident mode is not difficult. All you have to do is exit the program in standard mode and reload it with the /R switch.

If you want to switch from resident mode to standard mode, you'll first have to unload the program from memory. You can either use a menu selection or run the KILL.BAT program.

To remove the Desktop Manager from your computer's memory, first pop up the program:

> **Press:** [Ctrl]-[Spacebar]

To open the Utilites menu:

> **Press:** [U]

To select and execute the *Unload PCTOOLS Desktop* menu command:

> **Press:** [U]

In a moment, the program will be unloaded from your computer's memory. To perform this procedure more quickly, you can press [Alt]-[Spacebar] at the same time and then press [U] twice.

If you get an error message that the program can't unload because other TSR programs have blocked it's exit, you'll have to pop down the Desktop Manager, unload the other programs, and then unload the Desktop Manager.

You can also unload the Desktop Manager program from memory using a batch file program supplied on the PC Tools program disks. This program is called KILL.BAT, and it runs a program called INKILL.BAT that unloads all PC Tools programs currently resident in memory. When the Desktop Manager is loaded as resident and the DOS prompt is displayd, implement this program as follows:

**Type:** KILL

**Press:** [Enter]

## HOW THE PROGRAM FILES WORK TOGETHER

You might be interested in the way the program files work together. The main part of the Desktop Manager program runs from the DESKTOP.EXE file. You load this file into your computer's memory when you type DESKTOP and press [Enter], both in standard and resident mode. The most frequently used features of the program are in this file, such as the editor that serves the Notepads module.

The Databases module runs from a separate file called DBMS.OVL. The file extension (.OVL) identifies this as an overlay file. This means it is loaded into your computer's memory only when you need to use the Databases module. The various calculators—such as the FINCALC.OVL and HEXCALC.OVL file—and the spelling checker in the Notepad all run as overlay files.

Using overlay files lets the master program swap code into and out of memory, giving you more flexible use of your computer's memory. There's some delay in swapping files into and out of memory; the delay is small, but you should keep that in mind when you load the Desktop Manager with any memory switches.

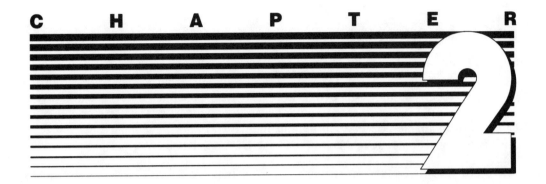

# USING PC SHELL

A *shell* refers to a graphical user interface and increased functionality that provides greater control over DOS, Microsoft's disk operating system for the IBM PC family of computers. The basic purpose of a shell is to make working with an operating system easier.

## ABOUT PC SHELL

Microsoft has been slow to upgrade its DOS. Only with version 4.0 did they include a graphical user interface. This opened the door to independently designed shell programs for DOS. Avid users stepped in where Microsoft declined to tread, and a variety of DOS shells began to enter the market in the mid-1980s. There are now many DOS shells available and they all exhibit their own minor advantages, but the PC Shell is the most complete and comprehensive DOS shell available.

There are several features that make the PC Shell remarkable. The single most important feature is its ability to go resident. This lets you work with DOS without leaving another program. Regardless of how often you access DOS, you probably work with other programs more frequently, making the ability to go resident very important.

The PC Shell also provides an extensive range of commands you can use to manage and work with your disk files.

While working in the PC Shell, you can:

- Work in a graphic-windowed environment
- Change the user level to suit your skills and needs
- Use all popular DOS commands more easily and use the original commands on the DOS command line
- Use more commands than are provided in DOS
- Use keyboard and mouse controls
- Recover inadvertently deleted files
- View a wide variety of file contents in their original format
- Launch outside applications, such as WordPerfect, dBASE, Lotus, and the PC Tools utility programs
- Access Desktop Telecommunications to send and receive e-mail and fax transmissions
- Work with standard network-compatible DOS functions on Novell's NetWare and IBM's Token-Ring networks
- Customize and configure the shell environment to your own needs, either temporarily or permanently
- View information about your current computer system configuration
- View the location of specific files on a screen map

• View a display of current memory usage

Believe it or not, a complete list would be much longer than this. However, don't be intimidated; everything will be explained in the next three chapters.

# LOADING AND QUITTING PC SHELL

The PC Shell can be loaded in both standard and resident mode. The mode you use determines the way you enter and exit the program.

## Loading and Quitting in Standard Mode

Standard mode refers to the way most programs are loaded. They can be accessed only from the DOS prompt. To load another standard program, you must quit the first program and load the second.

If you want to load PC Shell in standard mode, you use the following command at the DOS prompt:

**Type:** PCSHELL

**Press:** [Enter]

You'll see messages indicating that the system area and disk tree are being read. The screen then appears with the copyright notice overlaying it. To begin working in the PC Shell:

**Press:** any key

> You can insert the command PCSHELL in your AUTOEXEC.BAT file if you want PC Shell to appear each time you boot your computer.

When you load PC Shell in standard mode, you use the maximum amount of memory for the program, which means that you'll have the quickest program response. To exit PC Shell when it has been loaded in standard mode:

**Press:** [Esc]

You'll be prompted to confirm whether you really want to exit. To confirm and return to the DOS prompt:

**Press:** [Esc]

You should use PC Shell in standard mode only when you will be using it for an extended period of time, such as when you copy files from the hard disk to a floppy or tape backup, compress files, and do other routine DOS housekeeping chores.

## Resident Mode

Resident mode refers to the ability of the PC Shell to reside in your computer's memory and to be called up whenever you need it. You can pop up the shell using hotkeys, work in PC Shell, then pop it down and return to your previous work. The PC Shell will reside in your computer's memory, ready to be popped up the next time it is needed. As explained in chapter 1, this type of program is called a TSR program.

To load PC Shell into memory:

**Type:** PCSHELL /R

**Press:** [Enter]

The /R switch means "load as resident." When loaded in resident mode, PC Shell first displays a sign-on screen that looks like figure 2.1:

```
┌─────────────────────────────────────────────────────────┐
│                      PC Shell (tm)                        │
│              DOS shell and disk utilities                 │
│                       Version 6                           │
│                                                           │
│       Copyright (c) 1985-1990 Central Point Software, Inc.│
│                    All rights reserved                    │
│                    529 Kbytes free                        │
│                                                           │
│  To activate PC Shell, press <CTRL><Esc>                  │
└─────────────────────────────────────────────────────────┘
```

*Figure 2.1. The PC Shell sign-on screen*

This message remains on screen when the system returns to the DOS prompt. It gives you the name and version number of the program you're working with, copyright information, and the amount of memory that remains free after loading PC

Shell. It also tells you the hotkeys you would use to pop the program up and down. This last message can be particularly important. It ensures that you will always be able to find the meanings of your hotkeys.

> You can insert the commands for loading PC Shell in resident mode into your AUTOEXEC.BAT file. If you load the Desktop Manager and PC Shell from your AUTOEXEC.BAT, you might want to use the following series of commands.
>
> @echo off
> pcshell/rl
> desktop/rs
> cls
>
> The /rl and /rs switches define memory use. You'll learn about them in the next section.

Once the PC Shell has been loaded into memory, you can pop it up and use it, or you can load another program either in standard or resident mode. (If you load the Desktop Manager in resident mode after PC Shell, you'll be able to access PC Shell from a command on the Desktop main menu.)

To pop up the PC Shell:

**Press:** [Ctrl]-[Esc]

The PC Shell program reads the system area and tree structure just as when loaded the program in standard mode. It takes a little longer than usual the first time you load it, because it has to read the current data and setup. PC Shell then saves this information to a file called PCSHELL.TRE, which it refers to each time you pop it up. Therefore, you might want to pop up PC Shell each time you load it resident, just to refresh PCSHELL.TRE.

Even though you can pop up the PC Shell over another program, you shouldn't do this when the other program is in the middle of an operation, such as saving a file. TSR programs override whatever else is going on, and if you're saving a file, the save operation is stopped immediately. In most cases, saving will resume when you pop the TSR program back down, but it is possible that the operation will go haywire. You could lose some or all the data in the file.

To exit the PC Shell when in resident mode:

**Press:** [Ctrl]-[Esc]

You can also press [Esc] twice, or [Esc] once and [X] once to exit the PC Shell. Once popped down, you return to whatever you were doing before you loaded it—the DOS prompt, another program, or the Desktop main menu.

## Tradeoffs in Resident Mode

Using PC Shell in resident mode involves some tradeoffs in memory and load precedence.

The PC Shell is sensitive to other resident programs. You can use it with other TSRs, but there are exceptions. You can't install PC Shell after loading SideKick or SideKick Plus. These insist on being the last to be loaded.

In some cases, two TSR programs will use the same hotkeys. When you press the hotkeys, both programs try to grab the controls, and you'll probably end up with a memory conflict that requires you reboot your computer. PC Shell allows you to reconfigure the hotkeys that control the program, but you should avoid using conflicting TSR programs.

Precedence in loading also applies to precedence in unloading. Since DOS can't tolerate a hole in memory, you have to unload resident programs in precisely the opposite order in which you loaded them. This subscribes to the LIFO rule: last in, first out. You can always remove all PC Tools programs that have been installed resident by running the KILL.BAT program.

Every program you run uses some RAM. This means that DOS can be severely constrained by the 640-kilobyte limit for RAM. It's easy to run into *RAM cram*—running out of RAM and having to unload a program to make room for another.

PC Shell isn't immune to this occasional requirement, but the program has been designed so you can adjust the amount of memory it uses. You can use as little as 10 kilobytes or as much as 255 kilobytes. The amount of memory used by PC Shell can be adjusted by loading the program using various switches.

## Using Switches

There are seventeen switches you can use when loading the PC Shell program. Some are available only in resident mode, and others can be used in both standard and resident modes. Some switches can be used together, while others are mutually exclusive. Most switches use letters that serve as a reminder for what action the switch performs. For example, the /R switch loads both the PC Shell and the Desktop Manager into resident mode.

Switches available in PC Tools are:

*drive***:**     This is single letter designating the active drive. It specifies which drive becomes active when PC Shell is popped up. For example, typing PCSHELL D: and pressing [Enter] makes the D drive active. Once working within PC Shell, you can switch active drives using shell commands. This switch can be used for both standard and resident modes and with other switches.

**/A###**     Determines the *active memory size* for PC Shell above 225 kilobytes. This switch lets you fine tune the exact amount of computer memory so you can squeeze in other programs. The amount of resident memory used by the shell, when not active equals the setting you specify (in kilobytes). For example, /A245 would use 245 kilobytes of RAM.

**/BW**     Sets the *black-and-white video mode,* which provides a better screen display when using a color card with a monochrome monitor.

**/DQ**     Saves the current memory map for an application when PC Shell pops up. DQ stands for *Disable Quickload.* Loading PC Shell with this switch takes extra time, but ensures that nothing will be lost when you return to your previous application. You should use this switch only if you experience problems exiting PC Shell to return to your previous work.

**/FF**     Disables the suppression of screen snow on CGA display monitors. The program normally tries to suppress snow, but this can slow down the redraw rate for your screen display, particularly when you scroll through data or move through screens by pressing [PgDn]. To remember this switch, refer to it as *Free Flicker.*

**/F#**     Lets you assign a specific function key to serve as the second hotkey. For example, /F1 makes the hotkeys [Ctrl]-[F1], and /F2 makes them [Ctrl]-[F2]. You can use this switch only when loading the program in resident mode.

**/LE**     This switch stands for *Left Exchange.* It is designed to accommodate left-handed mouse users by exchanging the functions on the left side of your mouse with those on the right side.

**/IM**        This switch stands for *Ignore Mouse*. It can be used to disable the mouse if it is an early model or otherwise incompatible with the way PC Shell interprets mouse commands.

**/IN**        This switch stands for the *INColor card*. It runs PC Shell in color mode if your computer uses the Hercules InColor video card. If you use an InColor card and load PC Shell resident without activating this switch, PC Shell will be displayed in black-and-white. If you load PC Shell standard, its normal colors will be displayed without using this switch.

**/O*drive:***    Determines which drive to store the three files PCSHELL.OVL, PCSHELL.IMG, and PCSHELL.THM. These are temporary swap files PC Shell uses to store information on disk and save RAM regardless of whether the program has been loaded in resident or standard mode. If you don't specify a drive, the default drive containing the PC Tools program files is used. You should use this switch if you've created a RAM drive with enough room to accommodate the files. For example, if your RAM drive is D, use the switch /OD. The more RAM you use, the less disk space you need. The disk space required for the four memory variables in resident mode are:

   **/RT**    *Tiny* mode: uses 439 kilobytes of disk space for the three files if PC Shell is hotkeyed from DOS. If hotkeyed from another application, it uses 653 kilobytes.

   **/RS**    *Small* mode: uses 505 kilobytes for the three files if hotkeyed from DOS; otherwise 371 kilobytes.

   **/RM**    *Medium* mode: uses 338 kilobytes for the three files if hotkeyed from DOS; otherwise 434 K bytes.

   **/RL**    *Large* mode: uses 234 kilobytes for the three files regardless of where you hotkey it.

**/PS2**      Reconfigures your mouse setting, if necessary, when you are working with Microsoft Windows or on an IBM PS/2 computer.

**/350**      Configures your display for VGA mode with 350 lines on your screen. The results you see vary, depending upon your type of display monitor, even if it subscribes to the VGA mode.

**/R**         Loads the PC Shell in resident mode and lets you specify one of four memory usages. The less memory you use for PC Shell, the more you have for other uses; the more memory you use, the quicker PC Shell responds.

**/RT**      Loads the PC Shell into *tiny* use of memory (approximately 10 kilobytes of RAM). This is the default setting (same as /R) if you don't specify another value.

**/RS**      Loads the PC Shell into *small* use of memory (approximately 88 kilobytes of RAM).

**/RM**      Loads the PC Shell into *medium* use of memory (approximately 120 kilobytes of RAM).

**/RL**      Loads the PC Shell into *large* use of memory (approximately 225 kilobytes of RAM). Refer to the /A### switch for more information about how you can fine tune memory usage in the large setting.

**/TR#**      This switch stands for *Tree Read*. It determines how often PC Shell should read the current tree structure on disk and save it to the file PCSHELLD.TRE (where D is the disk drive letter containing the file). PC Shell uses the information to display the tree structure in the Tree List window. For example, using the switch /TR0 tells PC Shell to read the disk tree structure each time the program's loaded. Other numbers serve as the number of days between reads; that is, /TR1 reads the disk every day, /TR2 reads the tree every other day, and /TR7 reads the tree once a week.

All of these switches control the way PC Shell appears and behaves on your computer. Depending upon your computer configuration, some switches might be necessary, others recommended, while others will have no effect at all.

You can type switch characters using any combination of uppercase and lowercase characters.

Whenever you use mutually exclusive switches, the command line is parsed from the right to the left so that only the last switch takes effect. For example, if you load PC Shell using the command *PCSHELL /RL /RS /RM,* PC Shell will be installed resident using the medium amount of memory. The /RM switch was the first memory allocation switch to be parsed, and fixed memory allocation. The /RS switch was the second to be parsed, and the /RL switch was the third, but the feature they both work with had already been allocated.

If you use the PC Shell in resident mode—and I strongly recommend that you do—the most crucial switches are those that control memory size, the /R and /A### switches. The four /R switches allow you to load the program conveniently using one of four preset memory configurations. The /A### switch lets you adjust how much memory PC Shell occupies in the large setting.

> I load the Desktop Manager using the small memory setting and I load the PC Shell using the large memory setting, because quick access to DOS is important to me. Rarely I have to unload PC Shell and reload it using less memory, but this is easy to do.

## THE PC SHELL SCREEN

When PC Shell is loaded and active, it looks like figure 2.2.

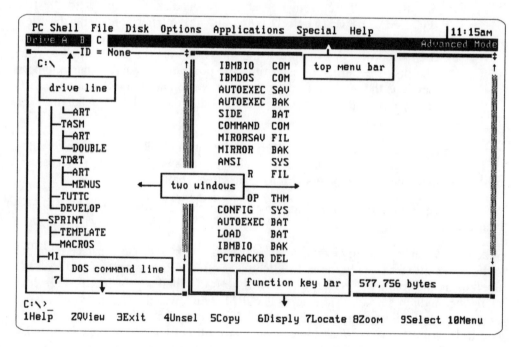

*Figure 2.2. The five primary features of the PC Shell screen*

32

The default level of operation is Advanced, indicated in the upper-right corner of your screen. This screen is chock-full of features. In its default appearance, there are five primary groups of features:

**Top menu bar**      The top line displays the name of the program (PC Shell), six pull-down menus, and the current time.

**Drive line**        The second line from the top shows the letters of installed drives detected by PC Shell, with the active drive highlighted.

**Two windows**       Taking up the largest part of your screen, the left window shows the current tree structure. The right window shows the current directory file contents.

**DOS command line**  The second line from the bottom shows the familiar DOS prompt, which allows you to type DOS commands when you prefer.

**Function key bar**  All ten function keys have assignments in the PC Shell.

Take a look at each feature as you learn how to navigate around the screen.

## THE TREE AND FILE LIST WINDOWS

The PC Shell presents you with a graphical user interface (GUI) driven by key and menu commands. Much has been made about GUIs recently, and if you've worked with DOS at all, you know how handy they can be.

Two windows show on the default PC Shell screen: a slim one on the left and a wider window on the right. The left window is called the *Tree List,* because it shows the directories on the current drive in a tree-like structure. The bottom line of the Tree List window shows the amount of unused space on the current drive.

The right window is called the *File List* and shows the list of files in the directory that is highlighted in Tree List window. The bottom line of the File List window shows the number of files in the current directory and how much space they occupy.

Only one window can be active at a time. The active window appears with a double-highlighted border. To toggle back and forth between the left and right window:

**Press:** [Tab]

To move around within a single window, use the arrow keys, [PgDn], and [PgUp].

To select a different directory and its file contents on the current disk, make the left window active. Then press [⇓] or [PgDn] to highlight the directory you want to use. The file contents for this directory will appear in the right window.

When you press [PgDn] in the File List window, you'll move to the bottom of a short list of files (if they only form one column). If the list is longer, you'll move to the file name at the top of the second column. Pressing [PgDn] again moves you to the top of the third column. Pressing [PgDn] a fourth time begins to move you in screens of file names. This can be a little disconcerting at first, but soon you find it a helpful series of movements. The [PgUp] key moves you upwards in the same way.

## Viewing Different Disk Drives

The drive line is the second line from the top of your screen. This shows the label *Drive* and the letters of installed drives PC Shell detects on your computer. On my computer, drives A, B, and C are available (see figure 2.3), but if you use many different drives, the letters can stretch across most of this line.

You can view the file structure on other disks by pressing [Ctrl] and the letter key that matches the drive letter you want to use. For example, to view the file structure on disk A:

**Press:** [Ctrl]-[A]

In order for this command to work, a disk must be in the drive to which you want to switch.

Notice how the drive letter A changes to reflect the new disk drive being viewed. Notice also how the disk file information beneath the window changes.

You can also view the file structure of two disks simultaneously on this screen.

**Press:** [Ins]

This should open a duplicate set of left and right windows, one set above the other, as shown in figure 2.3.

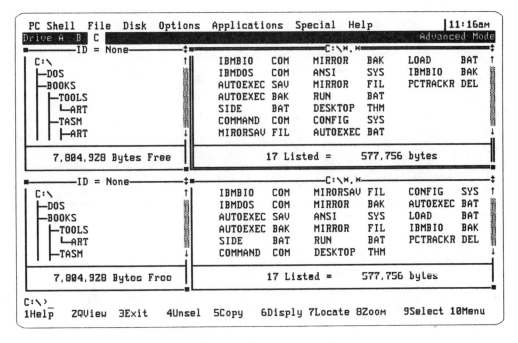

*Figure 2.3. PC Shell showing two sets of windows*

You switch between pairs of drive windows the same way you switch between windows for one drive:

**Press:** [Tab]

You can keep on pressing [Tab] to walk through all four windows. You can press [Shift]-[Tab] to walk backwards through the windows. This way, regardless of which window is active, only one key is needed to switch to the other windows.

You can see the usefulness of viewing two pairs of windows when viewing the contents of two different drives. First, make the lower pair of windows active. Next, display the contents of the disk in drive A in this set:

**Press:** [Ctrl]-[A]

The lower set of windows displays the contents of the disk in drive A while the upper set continues to display the C-drive contents. Your screen should resemble figure 2.4.

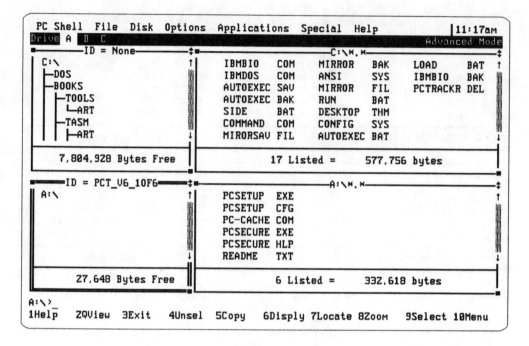

*Figure 2.4. PC Shell showing contents of two different disks*

You can press [Tab] or [Shift]-[Tab] to switch back and forth between the upper- and lower-disk displays. Two things change when you do this: the active-disk letter for the drive and the directory contents information.

You can close and open the inactive set of windows using the [Ins] and [Del] keys. To close the inactive set of windows:

**Press:** [Del]

To open the closed display:

**Press:** [Ins]

If you don't want to close a display, but instead just want to take a better look at the contents in the active window:

**Press:** [F8]

This zooms the active window to full-screen size. Pressing [F8] a second time returns you to the previous display. Working within a single window, you should practice pressing [Tab], [Shift]-[Tab], [Ins], [Del], and [F8], as well as your cursor keys, [PgDn], and [PgUp]. You will often use these keys; the sooner you memorize them, the more comfortable you'll make your work in PC Shell.

# THE DOS COMMAND LINE

You're given direct access to the DOS command line on the second line from the bottom of your screen. The cursor will be blinking after the DOS prompt when the PC Shell screen appears in the default configuration. The current path that shows in the active window will always be reflected in the DOS prompt.

Whenever the DOS command line is showing and you type character keys, the characters will appear next to the DOS prompt. This lets you access DOS commands that are familiar to you.

Try a few simple DOS commands:

**Type:** VER

**Press:** [Enter]

PC Shell will tell you its freeing memory to run the command, then it will run VER, the DOS command that checks the current version of DOS. The PC Shell screen will disappear, the version number will be displayed, and then the PC Shell screen will reappear. You might want to try this with the DOS command DIR, too.

If you don't see a DOS reply, check the current setting for Background Mat.

**Press:** [Alt]-[O]-[C]

Make sure the setting for Background Mat. is turned OFF.

If you intend to use commands on the DOS line frequently and read responses from the screen, you'll want to close the left window so you can view the replies from DOS.

**Press:** [Alt]-[O]

This opens the Options pull-down menu. Don't pay too much attention to this menu right now, just select the *Tree List Window* command:

**Press:** [T]

The left window should disappear. Now you're ready to run some commands and view DOS replies. You can also close all windows by selecting the *Hide Window* command on the Configuration pull-down menu.

If you leave the PC Shell while the Tree List window is turned off, you'll be asked whether you want to save this change to the configuration or cancel it. You shouldn't change the default configuration of PC Shell until you've become familiar with its default appearance:

**Press:** [C]

## Configuring the DOS Command Line

If you find you don't need the DOS command line, you can use that extra line to display one more line of information in the windows by turning the DOS command line off. To do this:

**Press:** [Alt]-[O]

This opens the Options pull-down menu. To select Setup Configuration:

**Press:** [C]

The arrow to the right of this command shows that the command leads to another menu. It doesn't have a title, but it's called the *Setup Configuration* menu.

**Press:** [C]

This selects DOS Command Line and toggles the feature off. The extra line is added to the bottom of the closest window or windows.

You can also replace the DOS command line with a list of shortcut key assignments. These commands comprise the second tier of the most popular commands you'll probably use in PC Shell. (The first tier is assigned to the function keys). You'll find out more about shortcut keys in the next chapter.

### Command History

An internal record is kept of the previous 15 commands you've typed and executed at the DOS command line. This lets you access previous commands and reinsert them on the DOS command line. This way you won't have to retype often-used commands.

After you've typed several commands, you can move back through the list and then forwards again looking for the command you want. To move backwards through the list, press [Ctrl]-[⇐]. To move forward through the list, press [Ctrl]-[⇒]. Practice using this feature now:

**Type:** DIR

**Press:** [Enter]

**Type:** VER

**Press:** [Enter]

**Type:** CHKDSK

**Press:** [Enter]

When the last command has finished running, you can re-enter the CHKDSK command this way:

**Press:** [Ctrl]-[⇐]

You don't execute the command until you press [Enter]. To access a command you executed before CHKDSK:

**Press:** [Ctrl]-[⇐]

You'll see VER appear. If this is the command you want:

**Press:** [Enter]

The VER command is executed just as if you typed it in.

To repeat the CHKDSK command:

**Press:** [Ctrl]-[⇒]

When CHKDSK appears on the DOS command line, you can execute it, you can look for other commands, or you can type a new command.

# THE FUNCTION KEYS

The fifth and last feature in the PC Shell screen can be found on the bottom line of your screen. This is the display of ten function keys and the commands assigned to them:

**[F1] Help**    Opens the first help screen for the PC Shell. The help file is called PCSHELL.HLP.

**[F2] QView**   Opens the *Quick* viewer showing the contents of the selected file. You can view and move through file contents using viewer, but you cannot edit the file.

**[F3] Exit**    Exits PC Shell and returns you to the previous screen and application.

**[F4] Unsel**   Unselects all selected files.

**[F5] Copy**    Opens the *File Copy* box, which begins the process of copying a file to a different location.

**[F6] Disply**  Opens the Display Options menu, which lets you select various ways to display file names in the *File List* window.

**[F7] Locate**  Opens the *File Locate* box, which lets you specify the parameters for the file name you're looking for. You can use DOS wild cards.

**[F8] Zoom**    Toggles the active window between full screen and the current size.

**[F9] Select**  Opens the *File Select* window, which lets you select a range of file names in the File List window based upon some common characteristic of their file names.

**[F10] Menu**   Activates the top menu bar so you can work with the pull-down menus. This is similar, but not identical, to pressing [Alt]. When you press [F10], the top menu bar remains active until you use a menu or press [Esc]. When you press [Alt], the menu remains active only while you hold [Alt] down.

You can reassign commands to most of your function keys if you want to customize them for your own use. This is described in the next chapter.

## Using the Default Function Key Assignments

The ten commands assigned to the displayed function keys are most frequently used when working with DOS files in the PC Shell. The Copy key [F5] is the only function key that corresponds to an actual DOS command: it does the same thing as the in DOS COPY, XCOPY, and DISKCOPY commands. The other function keys are only available in the PC Shell; they help you work with DOS commands on a refined basis. Learning these commands will make working in the PC Shell many times more effective than working directly with DOS. Remember, you can always fall back on your DOS knowledge by using the DOS command line in the PC Shell.

## Help

The [F1] key lets you access context-sensitive help in all the PC Tools programs. To view its effect in PC Shell, make the *Tree List* window active. Then:

**Press:** [F1]

This shows you help in the *Tree List* window, as shown in figure 2.5.

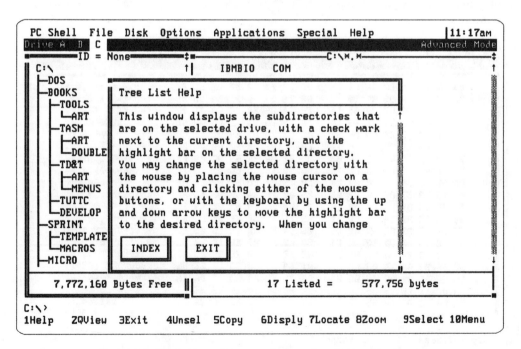

*Figure 2.5. The help window popped open when the Tree List is active*

To see more information:

**Press:** [PgDn]

To access help information about any aspect of PC Shell, press [I]. To view help information specific to a certain item, highlight that item and press [Enter].

You can close any help screen by pressing [X] for EXIT, or just press [Esc].

## Taking a Quick View

Viewing file contents quickly is a handy procedure when you want to refer to that file without loading it into the program that created it (such as dBASE, WordPerfect, or Lotus 1-2-3).

To view the contents of a file quickly, highlight the file name and press [F2]. You can view the contents of a wide variety of file types in their native formats. PC Shell has four types of generic viewers that display text, spreadsheet, database, and binary data on your screen.

For example, highlighting in my root directory and pressing [F2] causes my screen to resemble figure 2.6.

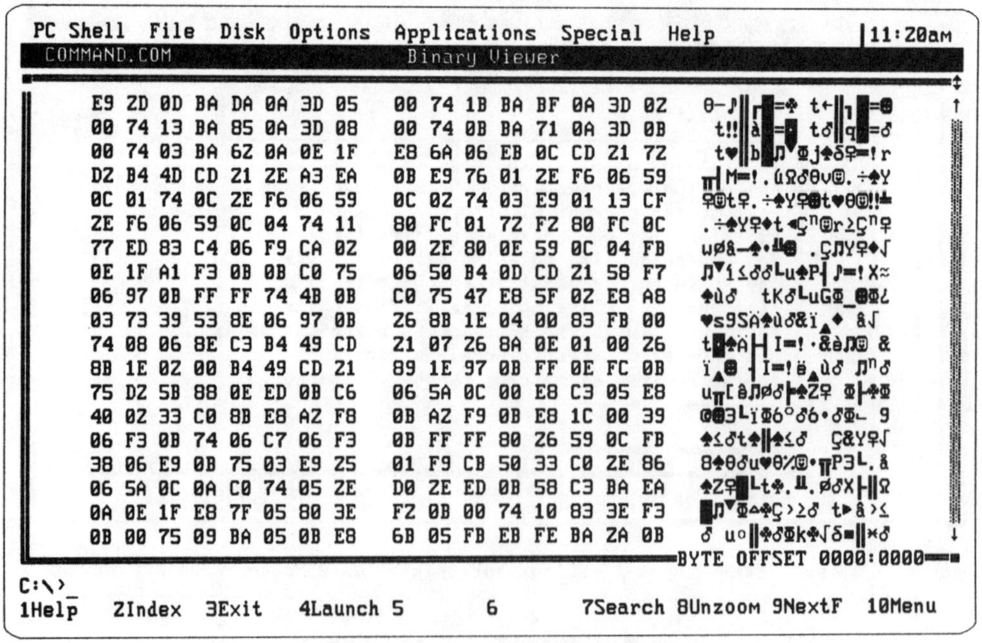

*Figure 2.6. COMMAND.COM in the Binary Viewer*

If I highlight my dBASE database file on publishers and press [F2], my screen looks like figure 2.7.

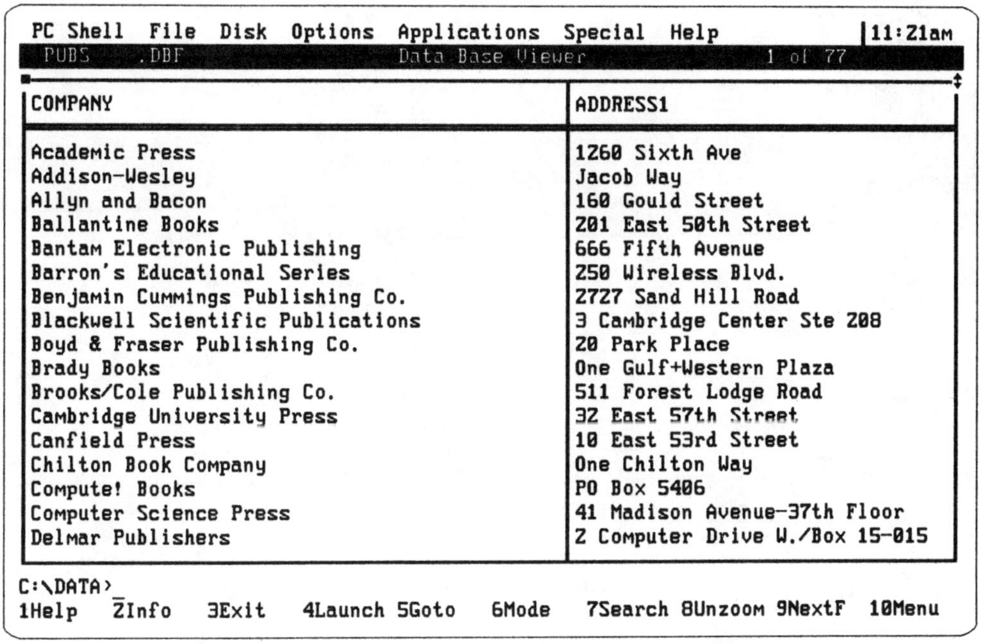

```
 PC Shell  File  Disk  Options  Applications  Special  Help        |11:21am
  PUBS     .DBF                 Data Base Viewer            1 of 77
 ┌──────────────────────────────────────────────────────────────────────┐‡
 │COMPANY                               │ADDRESS1                         │
 ├──────────────────────────────────────┼─────────────────────────────────┤
 │Academic Press                        │1260 Sixth Ave                   │
 │Addison-Wesley                        │Jacob Way                        │
 │Allyn and Bacon                       │160 Gould Street                 │
 │Ballantine Books                      │201 East 50th Street             │
 │Bantam Electronic Publishing          │666 Fifth Avenue                 │
 │Barron's Educational Series           │250 Wireless Blvd.               │
 │Benjamin Cummings Publishing Co.      │2727 Sand Hill Road              │
 │Blackwell Scientific Publications     │3 Cambridge Center Ste 208       │
 │Boyd & Fraser Publishing Co.          │20 Park Place                    │
 │Brady Books                           │One Gulf+Western Plaza           │
 │Brooks/Cole Publishing Co.            │511 Forest Lodge Road            │
 │Cambridge University Press            │32 East 57th Street              │
 │Canfield Press                        │10 East 53rd Street              │
 │Chilton Book Company                  │One Chilton Way                  │
 │Compute! Books                        │PO Box 5406                      │
 │Computer Science Press                │41 Madison Avenue-37th Floor     │
 │Delmar Publishers                     │2 Computer Drive W./Box 15-015   │
 └──────────────────────────────────────┴─────────────────────────────────┘
 C:\DATA>_
 1Help   2Info   3Exit   4Launch 5Goto   6Mode    7Search 8Unzoom 9NextF  10Menu
```

*Figure 2.7. A dBASE database file in the Data Base Viewer*

If the file you're viewing contains more characters than can fit into one screen, press [PgDn] or [PgUp].

Table 2.1 shows the four viewers and the types of files you can display in them.

*Table 2.1. Four quick viewers and associated files*

| Binary Viewers | Text Viewers |
|---|---|
| .ARC files | ASCII files |
| .BIN files | .BAT files |
| .COM files | Desktop Notepad |
| .EXE files | DisplayWrite |
| .OVL files | Microsoft Word |
| .PAK files | Microsoft Works |
| .PCX files | MultiMate |
| | MulitMate Advantage |
| **Database Viewers** | Lotus Symphony |
| Clipper | WordPerfect 4.2 |
| dBASE | WordPerfect 5 |
| dBXL | WordStar (all) |
| Foxboase | XyWrite |
| Lotus Symphony | |
| Microsoft Works data | **Spreadsheet Viewers** |
| Notepads Database | Excel |
| Paradox | Lotus 1-2-3 (all) |
| R:Base | Lotus Symphony |
| | Microsoft Works |
| | Mosaic Twin |
| | Quattro |

## Exiting the PC Shell

You can exit PC Shell three ways:

1. Press [F3] and then [X] to confirm your intention to exit.

2. Press [Ctrl]-[Esc], the same two keys you pressed to pop open PC Shell in resident mode. This is the quickest method if you're working in resident mode. If you're working in standard mode, you have to confirm your intention to exit by pressing [X].

3. Press [Esc] and then [X] confirming that you want to exit the program.

## Selecting and Unselecting Files

Selecting files lets you work with a group of files at the same time, such as when you want to copy or delete more than one file in the current directory. You can select one file at a time or you can select a group based upon some common characteristic of their file names. To select one file at a time, move your cursor over the file name in the File List window and press [Enter]. This places the file name in reverse video (or a different color, depending upon your screen) and inserts a number to the left of the file name.

As an example, when I mark my AUTOEXEC.BAT and CONFIG.SYS files in my root directory, my screen looks like figure 2.8.

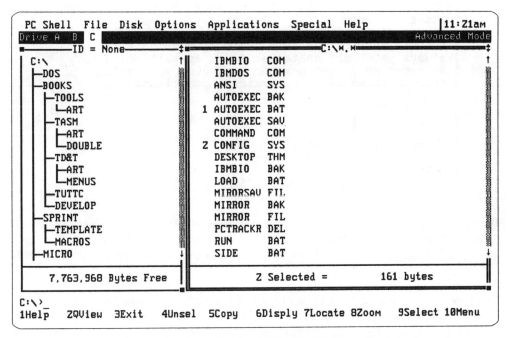

*Figure 2.8. My AUTOEXEC.BAT and CONFIG.SYS selected in that order*

As soon as you select a file, your cursor moves down one file name. You can continue selecting files in this way.

Use [F9] to select files that share a common characteristic in their file names. Any of the DOS wild cards can by used when specifying selection criteria. For example, to specify the criteria:

**Press:** [F9]

This opens the *File Select Filter* window, which looks figure 2.9.

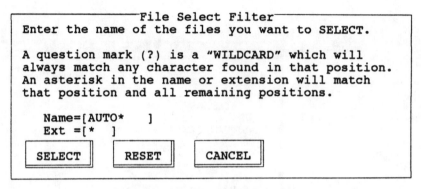

*Figure 2.9. The File Select Filter window*

When this window first appears, asterisks will show in both fields for Name and Ext. In figure 2.9, I've already typed in AUTO*. I will use these characteristics to select all the files in the current directory (in this case, my root directory) that begin with AUTO.

You type the common characteristics of the file name in the Name field and the characteristics for the file extension in the Ext field. Once you've entered the characteristics you want to use, begin the selection process:

**Press:** [Enter] twice

Notice that SELECT is highlighted; it then executes. In a moment, the selected files appear in the *File List* window, as shown in figure 2.10.

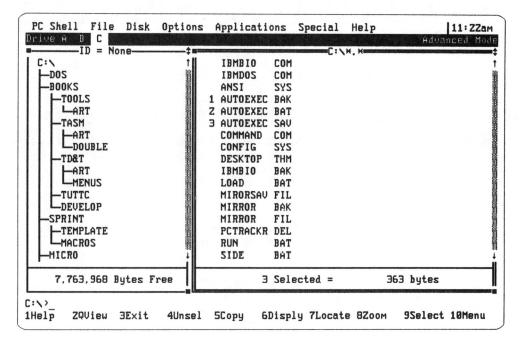

*Figure 2.10. A group of file names beginning with AUTO\* selected*

You can reselect a group of file names by pressing [F9], then pressing [Tab] to highlight RESET, and then entering a new group of characters.

You can unselect a group of currently selected files by pressing [F4].

## Copying Files

You can copy a file two ways:

1. To a different directory or disk using the same file name

2. To the same directory using a different file name

An example of the first method is copying a file from your hard disk to a floppy disk. An example of the second is making a backup copy of the original file in the same directory.

The basic procedure for copying files is to select the file or files you want to copy, press [F5] to begin the copy process, select the destination, then complete the copy. If you're copying it to the same directory, you must also rename it.

### Copying One File to a Different Location

To copy a file to a different location using the same file name, first highlight or select the file name you want to copy. Then, select the destination drive and directory. Finally, execute the copy.

For this example, move your AUTOEXEC.BAT file to another directory.

> **Highlight:** AUTOEXEC.BAT

> **Press:** [F5]

This opens the *File Copy* box, which looks like figure 2.11.

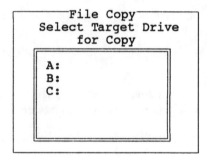

*Figure 2.11. The File Copy box*

The A: drive letter is highlighted by default, which lets you copy files to a floppy disk quickly. To copy the AUTOEXEC.BAT file from the root directory on hard drive C to the DOS directory:

> **Press:** [C]

This opens a box that asks you to select the location of the files to be copied. PC Shell will first read your system areas to make sure it's working with your current directory structure, then make the *Tree List* window active. (You can cancel the copy by pressing [Esc], [C], or pointing to CANCEL.)

To move the highlighting over your DOS directory name in the Tree List window:

**Highlight:** DOS

**Press:** [Enter]

This selects the directory that will receive the file copy. The contents of DOS (or whatever directory you use) are displayed after the copy so you can double check.

If a file with the same name already exists in the destination, you'll be warned and asked what to do. A second *File Copy* box will appear as shown in figure 2.12.

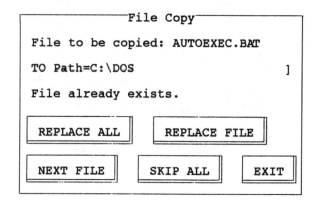

*Figure 2.12. A second File Copy box*

In figure 2.12, the *Replace All* option is highlighted by default, which assumes that you want to update the file name presented at the top of the box.

To replace the existing file with the new copy:

**Press:** [Enter]

### Copying One File to the Same Directory

You can also copy a file to the same directory as long as you change the file's name. To make a backup of AUTOEXEC.BAT in the root directory and call it AUTOEX-EC.BAK:

**Highlight:** AUTOEXEC.BAT

**Press:** [Enter] twice

This begins the copying process and selects the current directory as the destination. PC Shell will display the box shown in figure 2.13.

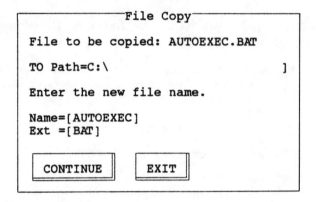

```
┌─────────────────File Copy──────────────────┐
│                                             │
│ File to be copied: AUTOEXEC.BAT             │
│                                             │
│ TO Path=C:\                             ]   │
│                                             │
│ Enter the new file name.                    │
│                                             │
│ Name=[AUTOEXEC]                             │
│ Ext =[BAT]                                  │
│                                             │
│   ┌─────────────┐   ┌──────────┐            │
│   │  CONTINUE   │   │   EXIT   │            │
│   └─────────────┘   └──────────┘            │
└─────────────────────────────────────────────┘
```

*Figure 2.13. The File Copy box making a backup*

You need to change at least one character in the file name or its extension. After changing a character:

> **Press:** [Enter]

> **Type:** BAK

> **Press:** [Enter]

As a precaution, you'll be asked to confirm the new file name.

To complete the copy:

> **Press:** [Enter]

You could also press [C] or point at COPY to complete the copying.

You should now have two files with the same name in your root directory: the original (AUTOEXEC.BAT) and the new copy (AUTOEXEC.BAK).

### Copying Several Files

If you want to copy more than one file at the same time, select the files you want to copy and then press [F5]. For example, to copy both AUTOEXEC.BAT and CON-

FIG.SYS and their backups AUTOEXEC.BAK and CONFIG.BAK to the DOS sub-directory, highlighting all four files. Once they've been highlighted:

**Press:** [F5]

**Press:** [C]

**Press:** [Enter]

**Select:** DOS

**Press:** [Enter]

When copying more than one file at the same time, a window monitors the progress of the series, which looks like figure 2.14.

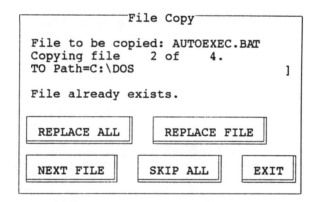

*Figure 2.14. The File copy box when copying more than one file*

You might not see this box for very long; it freezes in place only when another file of the same name is in the destination.

When you copy more than one file, the options in this box become important:

**Replace All**    Replace all files selected for copying and copies over any same-named files in the destination.

**Replace File**   Replaces the single file whose name appears at the top of the box.

**Next file**      Ignores the current file and moves to the next selected file name in the sequence.

**Skip All**        Skips all remaining selected file names and returns you to the PC Shell screen.

**Exit**        Exits the file copy procedure.

If you start copying files using a single window zoomed to full-screen size, each window you work in will appear in full-screen size.

If you start the copying while in the Tree List window, you can move only the currently highlighted file from the current directory.

If you start File Copy while you're using a four-window display, that is, you're viewing the Tree and File Lists for two different directories or disks, you'll be asked to confirm whether the second or inactive set of windows should serve as the target destination, as shown in figure 2.15.

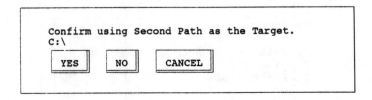

*Figure 2.15. The File Copy confirmation box*

You don't have to use the second path as the target, although it might make the copying process easier to follow.

## Rearranging the Display of File Names

The arrangement of individual file names in the *File List* window can often be crucial to your work with the files. To rearrange the display of the file names:

    **Press:** [F6]

This opens the *Display Options* box, shown in figure 2.16.

```
┌──────────────Display Options──────────────┐
│  Display Options:          Current Options:│
│                              Name          │
│       ( )  0 Size                          │
│       ( )  1 Date                          │
│       ( )  2 Time                          │
│       ( )  3 Attribute                     │
│       ( )  4 Number of Clust               │
│  File Sort Options:        Current order:  │
│       ( )  5 Name               Name       │
│       ( )  6 Ext                Ascending  │
│       ( )  7 Size                          │
│       ( )  8 Date/Time                     │
│       ( )  9 Ascending                     │
│       ( )  A Descending  ( ) B No Sort     │
│    ┌──────┐  ┌──────────┐                  │
│    │  OK  │  │  CANCEL  │                  │
│    └──────┘  └──────────┘                  │
└────────────────────────────────────────────┘
```

*Figure 2.16. The Display Options box*

Press the number corresponding to the type of arrangement you want to view. Some settings work well together, such as Name/Ascending or Date/Descending. Others won't, such as Name/Ascending and Ext/Descending.

Once you pick the sort order you want to use, the option names will show on this screen and *OK* will brighten up. Pressing [Enter] accepts the new order and closes this screen. You'll see the file names in the current File List window displayed in the new order.

## Locating Files

Locating files is extremely important when you work with hard disks that contain thousands of different files, particularly files with similar names or even identical names in different directories. To quickly locate a file, you need to know only a part of its file name, which will become the specifications of the file you're trying to locate.

To locate files with similar specifications (shared file-name characteristics):

**Press:** [F7]

This opens the *File Locate* box, shown in figure 2.17.

```
┌─────────File Locate─────────┐
│ Specify File Name(s)      ▓ │
│ dBase III Files           ▓ │
│ Mail Files                ▓ │
│ Fax Files                 ▓ │
│                           ▓ │
│                           ▓ │
│                           ▓ │
│                           ▓ │
│                           ▓ │
└─────────────────────────────┘
```

*Figure 2.17. The File Locate box*

Your list of file-name types might be longer. The top selection lets you search through all file names. The various application types let you narrow your search to files specific to those programs.

### Searching Through All File Names

You can search through all files on a disk by selecting the top item Specify File Name(s). To do this, when the *File Locate* window appears:

**Press:** [Enter]

This opens a box that lets you specify the range of file names to search for, which looks like figure 2.18.

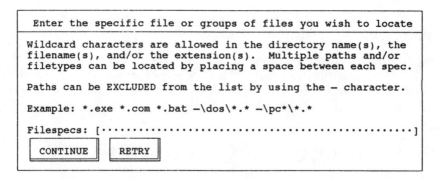

```
┌──────────────────────────────────────────────────────┐
│   Enter the specific file or groups of files you wish to locate │
│                                                        │
│  Wildcard characters are allowed in the directory name(s), the │
│  filename(s), and/or the extension(s).  Multiple paths and/or │
│  filetypes can be located by placing a space between each spec. │
│                                                        │
│  Paths can be EXCLUDED from the list by using the — character. │
│                                                        │
│  Example: *.exe *.com *.bat —\dos\*.* —\pc*\*.*        │
│                                                        │
│  Filespecs: [·······································]   │
│  ┌──────────┐  ┌───────┐                               │
│  │ CONTINUE │  │ RETRY │                               │
│  └──────────┘  └───────┘                               │
└──────────────────────────────────────────────────────┘
```

*Figure 2.18. The file specification box*

You'll find the cursor at the beginning of the field for *Filespecs*. This is where you type the characters you want to use to narrow you're search for file names. You can include the DOS wild cards * and ?. You're also given an additional wild card, the dash (-). Wild cards can also be used to specify directories to be searched.

For this example:

**Type:** AUTO*

**Press:** [Enter]

This opens a box that lets you search for specific characters in the range of files you've specified. The box looks like figure 2.19.

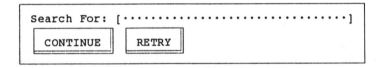

*Figure 2.19. The Search for box*

Type the characters that you want to search for. For this example, skip the *Search for* box:

**Press:** [Enter]

When the search is complete, the screen displays the list of files as shown in figure 2.20.

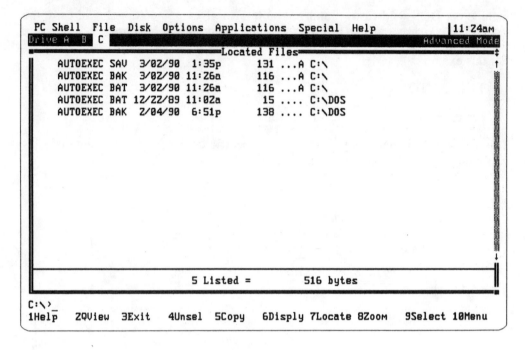

*Figure 2.20. List of AUTOEXEC.\* files located*

You can also specify particular file names. For example, to specify all files in my DATA directory that begin with P:

**Type:** DATA\P*.*

**Press:** [Enter] twice

This skips the *Search for* box and begins the locate procedure. In a moment, the Located Files screen appears and is shown in figure 2.21.

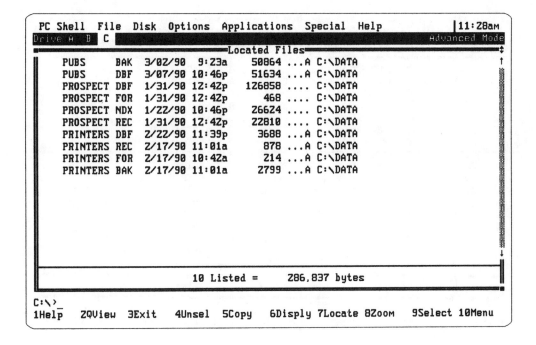

```
 PC Shell  File  Disk  Options  Applications  Special  Help        |11:28am
Drive A  B  C                                                  Advanced Mode
                              Located Files
     PUBS     BAK  3/02/90  9:23a    50864 ...A C:\DATA              ↑
     PUBS     DBF  3/07/90 10:46p    51634 ...A C:\DATA
     PROSPECT DBF  1/31/90 12:42p   126858 .... C:\DATA
     PROSPECT FOR  1/31/90 12:42p      468 .... C:\DATA
     PROSPECT NDX  1/22/90 10:46p    26624 .... C:\DATA
     PROSPECT REC  1/31/90 12:42p    22810 .... C:\DATA
     PRINTERS DBF  2/22/90 11:39p     3688 ...A C:\DATA
     PRINTERS REC  2/17/90 11:01a      878 ...A C:\DATA
     PRINTERS FOR  2/17/90 10:42a      214 ...A C:\DATA
     PRINTERS BAK  2/17/90 11:01a     2799 ...A C:\DATA
                                                                    ↓
                     10 Listed =      286,837 bytes

C:\>_
1Help   2QView  3Exit   4Unsel  5Copy   6Disply 7Locate 8Zoom   9Select 10Menu
```

*Figure 2.21. Files in C:\DATA filtered for P*.*.*

This shows my database and associated files (such as dBASE indexes) that begin with the letter P.

Once you get the feel for locating files, you'll soon find the process becoming second nature.

### Searching Through Specific Program Names

To look for files of a specific type, press the highlighted letter for the type you want. For example, to find a dBASE III file:

**Type:** [B]

As before, you're given the chance to specify file-name characters. Skip this box:

**Press:** [Enter]

PC Shell will now locate every dBASE file on the current disk, which means every file that ends with .DBF. When the list of acceptable file names is assembled, PC Shell displays it in a Located Files window, which looks like figure 2.22.

```
 PC Shell  File  Disk  Options  Applications  Special  Help        |11:29am
Drive A  B  C                                                    Advanced Mode
                              ═Located Files═                                ↕
    PUBS      DBF  3/07/90 10:46p    51634 ...A C:\DATA                       ↑
    LIST      DBF  3/06/90  2:01p   926011 ...A C:\DATA
    TEMP      DBF  3/05/90  1:34p      386 ...A C:\DATA
    SUBS      DBF  2/25/90 11:59p    25531 ...A C:\DATA
    CONTACTS  DBF  2/05/90  7:22p     6074 .... C:\DATA
    BOOKFAIR  DBF  2/04/90  9:27a     3884 .... C:\DATA
    COMP      DBF  2/24/90 12:19p     4954 ...A C:\DATA
    DIST      DBF  2/20/90  2:49p     1600 ...A C:\DATA
    FOREIGN   DBF  2/22/90  8:59a    23838 ...A C:\DATA
    PROSPECT  DBF  1/31/90 12:42p   126858 .... C:\DATA
    SIG       DBF  1/22/90  9:06a    11261 .... C:\DATA
    STORES    DBF  1/30/90  9:36p     1870 .... C:\DATA
    DISTS     DBF  2/20/90  2:51p     1600 ...A C:\DATA
    PRINTERS  DBF  2/22/90 11:39p     3688 ...A C:\DATA
    WARE      DBF  3/08/90 11:03a    22564 ...A C:\DATA
    SERIALS   DBF  2/11/90  2:27p      495 .... C:\DATA
    COMPUTER  DBF  2/23/90 12:12a     8034 ...A C:\DATA                       ↓

              28 Listed =   2,198,870 bytes

C:\>
1Help   2QView  3Exit   4Unsel  5Copy   6Disply 7Locate 8Zoom   9Select 10Menu
```

*Figure 2.22. The first screenful of all .DBF files*

Each line shows the file name found, the date and time of file creation or last save, the size of the file in bytes, which of the four attributes are set (the A or archive bit has been set for two of my database files), and the path that leads to the file. The bottom of the window shows the number of files found and their total byte size.

If the search found more files than can fit in one screen, you can scroll through the list by pressing [PgDn] and [PgUp].

You can work with files in this screen the same way you work with files in the standard PC Shell screen. This means you can move, copy them, and delete them, as well as view their contents and attributes. Basic procedures remain the same in both screens. The function keys are displayed on the bottom line with the same assignments. All of them are active except [F7] Locate. If you've switched on the DOS command line or shortcut key list, these too will show and be active.

You could have used the *File Select Filter* box to narrow down the search for specific dBASE file names so that each dBASE file name that is scanned will appear at the bottom of the PC Shell screen.

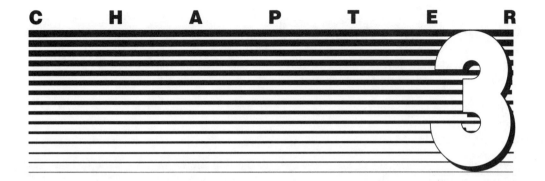

# THE MENU INTERFACE OF PC SHELL

M enus are one of the easiest ways for working with data that is presented visually. You can access most of the commands in the various PC Tools Deluxe programs through pull-down and pop-up menus. Pull-down menus appear under menu labels on the top menu bar. Pop-up menus appear when you select certain menu commands or press other keys—such as function keys or hot keys—to activate commands.

# WORKING WITH MENUS

To work with pull-down menus, you first activate the top menu bar, then you select the menu with which you want to work.

To activate the top menu bar:

**Press:** [Alt] or [F10]

When you press either of these two keys, notice that menu names on the top bar get bright, indicating that they menus can be used. While the top menu bar is active, you cannot use any other command in PC Shell.

There's a small difference between pressing [Alt] and [F10]. When you press [Alt], the top menu bar is active only for the time you hold down the [Alt] key. As soon as you release it, the top menu bar becomes inactive. However, when you press and release [F10], the menu bar remains active until you press [F10] again.

Once the top menu bar is active, you can pull down any menu either by pressing the letter key corresponding to its name or by highlighting the menu name using the arrow keys and then pressing [Enter]. Once a menu is open, you can scroll through the entire selection by pressing [⇑] or [⇓].

Once you've opened a menu, you select a command the same way you selected the menu: either highlight the command and press [Enter] or press the letter key assigned to the command, which appears in bold. If you use PC Shell often, you will soon find that pressing letter keys is the fastest way to move.

The six pull-down menus you can use in PC Shell and their three submenus are shown in figure 3.1.

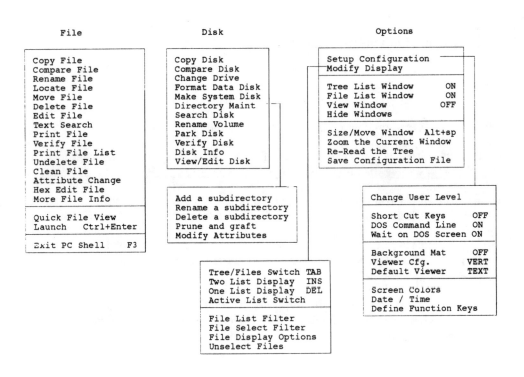

```
      File                    Disk                    Options

Copy File              Copy Disk              Setup Configuration
Compare File           Compare Disk           Modify Display
Rename File            Change Drive
Locate File            Format Data Disk       Tree List Window      ON
Move File              Make System Disk       File List Window      ON
Delete File            Directory Maint        View Window           OFF
Edit File              Search Disk            Hide Windows
Text Search            Rename Volume
Print File             Park Disk              Size/Move Window  Alt+sp
Verify File            Verify Disk            Zoom the Current Window
Print File List        Disk Info              Re-Read the Tree
Undelete File          View/Edit Disk         Save Configuration File
Clean File
Attribute Change
Hex Edit File          Add a subdirectory     Change User Level
More File Info         Rename a subdirectory
                       Delete a subdirectory  Short Cut Keys       OFF
Quick File View        Prune and graft        DOS Command Line     ON
Launch    Ctrl+Enter   Modify Attributes      Wait on DOS Screen   ON

Exit PC Shell    F3                           Background Mat       OFF
                                              Viewer Cfg.          VERT
                       Tree/Files Switch TAB  Default Viewer       TEXT
                       Two List Display  INS
                       One List Display  DEL  Screen Colors
                       Active List Switch     Date / Time
                                              Define Function Keys
                       File List Filter
                       File Select Filter
                       File Display Options
                       Unselect Files
```

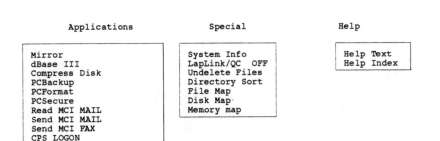

```
    Applications              Special               Help

Mirror                 System Info           Help Text
dBase III              LapLink/QC   OFF      Help Index
Compress Disk          Undelete Files
PCBackup               Directory Sort
PCFormat               File Map
PCSecure               Disk Map
Read MCI MAIL          Memory map
Send MCI MAIL
Send MCI FAX
CPS LOGON
```

*Figure 3.1.  Pull-down menus in PC Shell*

There are six pull-down menus in the PC Shell:

**File**          Lets you work with individual or selected files in various ways.

**Disk**          Lets you work with disks in various ways.

**Options**        Lets you change the way the PC screen looks and behaves.

**Applications**  Lets you access a wide range of popular application programs, if you've installed them on your disk.

**Special**       Lets you use seven special commands, including deleting a group of files and unloading PC Shell from your computer's memory.

**Help**         Lets you view the help screen specific to the active feature or the procedure you're using, or open the help index. You can also open specific help screens by pressing [F1].

The commands under the Disk, File, Options, Special, and Help menus will be discussed in this chapter. The commands on the Applications pull-down menu will be described in chapter 4.

## THE HELP MENU

The Help menu gives you two command choices: Help Text or Help Index. These are the same two commands you can perform by pressing [F1] and [F2]. When you press [F1], the program gives you help information pertinent to the task you are trying to perform. When you press [F2], you're given a list of items, from which you can select one that you want to learn more about.

## THE FILE MENU

The File pull-down menu lets you work with disk files in a variety of ways. In some cases, you can only work with individually highlighted files. With other commands, you can work with both single files or groups of files. The File pull-down menu contains 19 commands:

**Copy File**     Copies a single file or selected files to another location. Same as pressing [F5], described in chapter 2.

**Compare File**  Compares two files to see if they are identical.

| | |
|---|---|
| **Rename File** | Renames the highlighted file or globally renames a selected group of files. |
| **Locate File** | Locates files with similar characteristics. Same as pressing [F7], described in chapter 2. |
| **Move File** | Moves a file from one location to another. |
| **Delete File** | Deletes a single file or a group of selected files. |
| **Edit File** | Opens the PC Shell editor and lets you change the contents of a file. |
| **Text Search** | Searches for files containing a specific string of text. |
| **Print File** | Prints a single file or group of files to your printer or a disk file. |
| **Verify File** | Verifies the integrity of a file. |
| **Print File List** | Prints a list of all file names in the current File List window. |
| **Undelete file** | Begins the undelete process. |
| **Clean file** | Cleans the highlighted file or group of selected files from the disk by overwriting the data. |
| **Attribute Change** | Changes the attributes for a file. |
| **Hex Edit File** | Lets you view and edit the hexadecimal display of a file's contents. |
| **More File Info** | Displays more information about a file, such as path, attributes, most recent file access date, file length or size in bytes, number of clusters occupied by the file, starting cluster number, and the number of files in the current directory. |
| **Quick File View** | Opens the most appropriate of four file viewers and displays the contents of a file. Same as pressing [F2], described in chapter 2. |
| **Launch** | Exits the PC Shell temporarily and loads a separate applications program. You can also press [Ctrl]-[Enter] to duplicate this command. Launching files is described in the next chapter. |
| **Exit PC Shell** | Exits the PC Shell and returns to whatever you were doing before you entered it. You can also press [F3], or [Esc] and then [X] to exit the shell. |

Most of these commands are self-explanatory. Highlight the file or files you want to work with, open the File pull-down menu, select the command you want to use, and PC Shell will walk you through a simple list of instructional windows that tell you want to do. However, five of the commands on the File pull-down menu require a bit more elaboration.

## The PC Shell Editor

The PC Shell has a simple editor that lets you view and edit the contents of various types of files. To use the editor, highlight or select a file in the File List window, then open the File pull-down menu and select the *File Edit* command. For example, to view and edit the AUTOEXEC.BAT file:

**Highlight:** AUTOEXEC.BAT

**Press:** [Alt]-[F]-[E]

You'll be asked whether you want to edit the file, create a new one, or cancel this command. To edit the file:

**Press:** [E]

In the future, to edit an existing file, just press [Alt]-[F]-[E]-[E] in quick succession. Your screen changes should resemble figure 3.2.

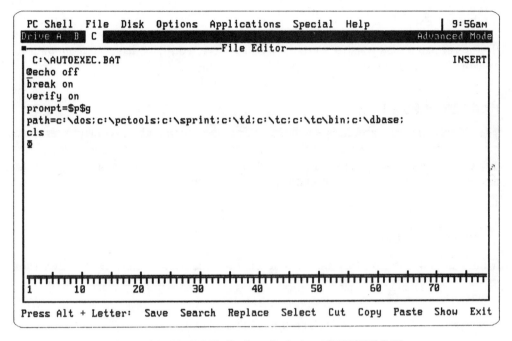

*Figure 3.2. The PC Shell editor displaying AUTOEXEC.BAT*

This is a simple screen to work with. You can move your cursor using the arrow keys, insert characters using the character keys, and delete text by pressing [Del] or [Backspace]. You can move down through screenfuls of text by pressing [PgDn] and [End]; you can move up by pressing [PgUp] or [Home]. The hour-glass figure at the bottom of the file marks the end of the file. You can work in either the *insert* or *overwrite* modes. When you're working in insert mode, the label INSERT will show in the upper-right corner and your cursor will change to a block shape.

The menus at the top of the screen are unavailable, but you can use the nine commands on the bottom line by pressing [Alt] and the highlighted letter of the command you want to use.

The *Cut, Copy,* and *Paste* commands use a clipboard available only to the PC Shell Editor. This clipboard is different than the Desktop clipboard or the hotkey clipboard (which can accessed throughout the PC Tools programs by pressing [Ctrl]-[Del]). The Editor clipboard works only for the current file; when you exit the Editor, the contents of the clipboard are lost. This means you *cannot* use it to transfer characters from one file to another. You can, however, use the hotkey clipboard to transfer character between files.

To exit the PC Shell Editor:

**Press:** [Esc]

If you've made changes that weren't saved to disk, you'll be asked if you want to save or abandon them; otherwise, you'll return to the PC Shell screen.

## Printing Files

The *File Print* command uses the DOS redirection command, so your printer must have the capability to handle DOS ASCII files directly. If you're using a PostScript printer, you'll have to print the file to a separate printed disk file first, then read the disk file into a PostScript editor that supports your printer.

To begin the print:

**Press:** [Alt]-[F]-[P]

If the file you're trying to print has one of four extensions: .$$$, .BAK, .COM, or .EXE, you'll be given an error message. Otherwise, you can print files with all other extensions.

This opens the *File Print* box, which looks like figure 3.3:

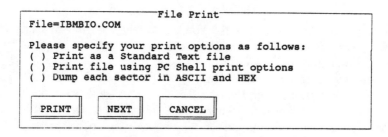

*Figure 3.3. The File Print dialog box*

Select the option you want to use by pressing the appropriate letter key: [P] for printing as a standard text file, [O] for using printing options, and [D] for dumping the file as hexadecimal and ASCII code. Once you've selected the way you want to print the file, begin the print:

**Select:** PRINT

**Press:** [Enter]

The highlighted file or selected files will begin to print immediately, unless you've selected the second option. If you want to print according to special options, you'll have to set them in a second File Print menu, which looks like figure 3.4.

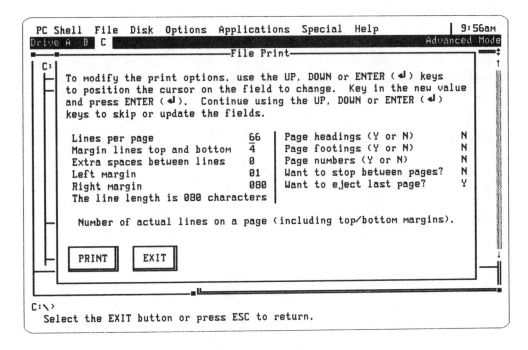

*Figure 3.4. The PC Shell File Print options menu*

These are the same options you can use in the Page Layout menu of the Desktop Manager. Each format setting will be defined as it is highlighted (more information about printing text files is given in chapter 6). When all the settings are as you want them:

**Select:** PRINT

**Press:** [Enter]

Printing begins. If you're printing more than one file, move to the next one by selecting NEXT. You can exit printing by pressing [X].

## Changing File Attributes

You can change one to four file attributes using the *Attribute Change* command on the File pull-down menu. Just highlight the file or select the files whose attributes you want to change, then:

**Press:** [Alt]-[F]-[A]

This open the *Attribute Change* window. When I select all the files in my root directory and open this window, my screen looks like figure 3.5.

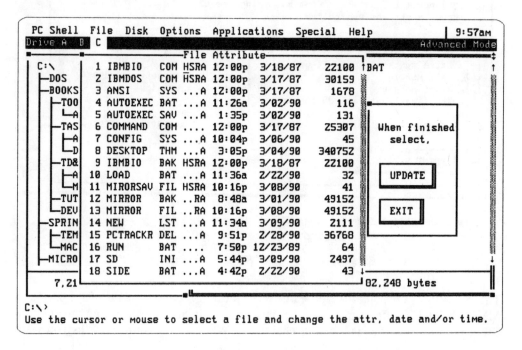

*Figure 3.5. The File Attribute window*

You're given the usual file information in this window, including file size and time and date of last change. The four attributes, or bits, you can change are:

**H** The hidden bit hides the file name from the standard DOS command DIR. However, you can still see hidden file names in the PC Shell File List window.

**S** The system bit shows whether the file is necessary to run your disk operating system or DOS.

**R**   The read-only bit shows that you can only read the file contents; you can't write over the file with changes.

**A**   The archive bit shows if the file has been changed since the last time it was backed up. This bit is switched off whenever you backup the file using DOS BACKUP, PC Backup, or another backup program.

To change one or more attributes, open the *Attribute Change* window. You'll find your cursor blinking under the space reserved for the first attribute H. To switch any attribute on or off, just press the letter of the attribute. For example, if A is on and you want to switch it off, press [A]. To switch it back on, press [A] a second time. You can only change attributes when the two commands on the right side of the window, UPDATE and EXIT, are not highlighted.

Once you've made the changes you want to save, press [Tab] to select UPDATE, and then press [Enter]. To cancel changes, highlight EXIT and press [Enter].

## Using the Hex Editor

The PC Shell hex editor displays file contents in two modes at the same time: hexadecimal and ASCII codes. If you know what you're doing, you can change the contents of a file by making changes to either the hexadecimal or ASCII displays.

> The only difference between the PC Shell hex editor and the PC Shell text editor is the way each displays data. In fact, on both editors the data is stored on disk in binary form, a series of 1s and 0s. The editors must first translate this binary data to the form they've been designed to display.

You can select several files in a group and view their contents sequentially. To view the contents of a file in hex, highlight or select the file, open the File pull-down menu, and select the command *Hex Edit File*. For example, to view the contents of COMMAND.COM in hex:

   **Highlight:** COMMAND.COM

   **Press:** [Alt]-[F]-[F]

My screen changes look like figure 3.6.

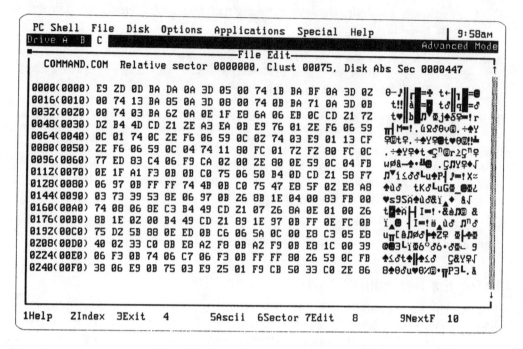

*Figure 3.6. The PC Shell Hex Editor screen*

If the function key [F6] has been assigned to hex, press it to make your screen look like figure 3.6.

You can't use any menus in this screen, but you can use these function keys:

**[F1] Help**      Opens the help screen specific to the hex editor.

**[F2] Index**     Opens the help index specific to the hex editor.

**[F3] Exit**      Closes the hex edit screen and returns you to the PC Shell screen.

**[F5] ASCII**     Displays the data in ASCII code in a full screen window.

**[F6] Sector**    Lets you move to a specific sector for the file.

**[F7] Edit**      Displays the cursor and lets you edit the data on screen. Watch out when you do this. You should know what effects your changes will have before you make them.

**[F9]  NextF**     Displays the contents of the next file in the selected group.

To switch to the full-screen ASCII display, which resembles figure 3.7:

>   **Press:** [F5]

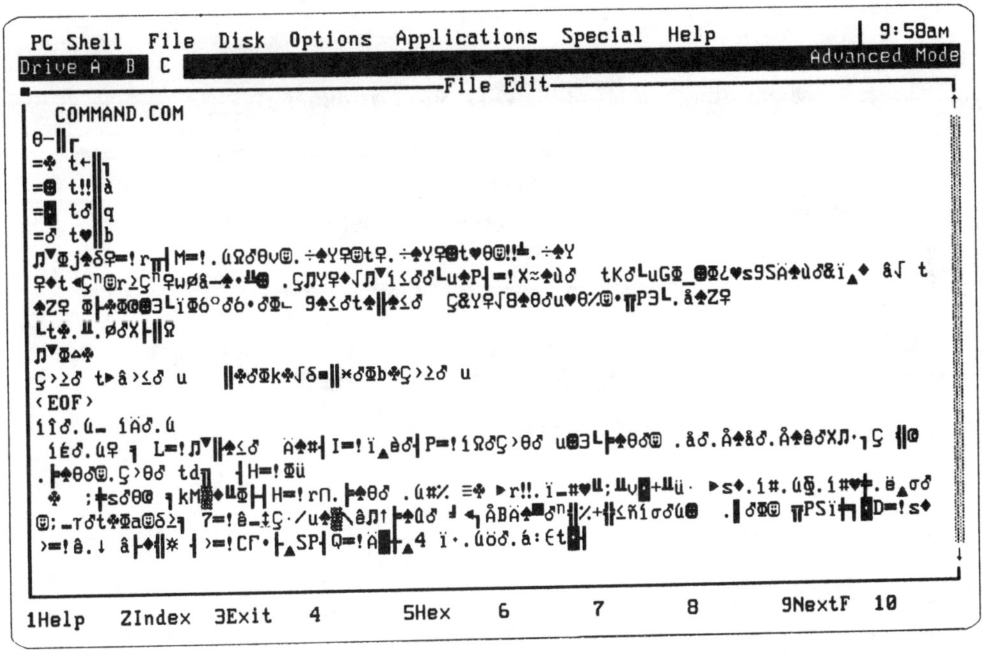

```
 PC Shell  File  Disk  Options  Applications  Special  Help        | 9:58am
 Drive A  B  C                                                 Advanced Mode
■─────────────────────────File Edit─────────────────────────────────┐ ↑
 |   COMMAND.COM                                                     |
 | θ─‖ r                                                             |
 | =♦ t←‖ ❘                                                          |
 | =❾ t!!‖ à                                                         |
 | =█ tδ‖ q                                                          |
 | =δ t♥‖ b                                                          |
 | ♫▼◻j♠δ♀=!r┬┐M=!.◖Ω∂θυ◙.÷♠Y♀θt♀.÷♠Y♀θt♥θθ!!▲.÷♠Y                   |
 | ♀♦t◄Ç"◻r⌐Ç"♀u♦å─♠•‖◙ .ÇΩY♀♦√♫▼í≤δδ▲u♠P┥=!X≈♠�❘δ  tK∂ᴸuGΦ_◙Φ∠♥s9SA♠❘δ&ï▴♦ &√ t |
 | ♠Z♀ ◻▐♦◻θ◙❸3ᴸ┐ï◻6°δ6•δ◻◻─ 9♠≤δt♠‖♠≤δ  Ç&Y♀√8♠θδu♥θ╱◙•╥P3ᴸ.å♠Z♀  |
 | Lt♦.▥.♀δX┤‖Ω                                                       |
 | ♫▼◻♠♦                                                             |
 | Ç>≤δ t►å>≤δ u    ‖♠δ◻k♦√δ■‖×δ◻b♦Ç>≤δ u                            |
 | ‹ EOF ›                                                           |
 | íî δ.◖─ íåδ.◖                                                      |
 |   íɛδ.◖♀ ┐ L=!♫▼‖♠≤δ  A♠#┤ I=!ï▲åδ┦P=!íΩ∂Ç>θδ u◙❸ᴸ┡♠θδ◙ .åδ.Â♠♠δ.Â♠åδX♫·┐Ç ‖◙ |
 | .┡♠θδ◙.Ç>θδ td┓┐ ┤H=!◻ü                                            |
 |  ♦  :┡sδθ◙ ┐kM█♣♠◻M◻♣H=!rΠ.┡♠δδ .◖#╱ ≡♦ ►r!!.ï_#♥◗;▥▥υ█─▥▥ü· ►s♦.í#.◖§.í#♥┡.ë▴σδ |
 | ◙;_┬δt♠◻a◙δ⌐┐ 7=!å_♦Ç·╱u♠█åΛ┦♠❘δ ◢┦ ◄ÂBA♠█δ"▥╱┼‖≤Ñíσδ◖◙  .┦δδ◙ ╥PSï┭┦◻D=!s♦ |
 | >=!ë.↓ å┡♦‖× ┦ >=!Cᴦ•┡▲SP┦ Q=!å█┡▴4 ï·.◖δδ.å:Et█┤                 |
 ■─────────────────────────────────────────────────────────────────┘ ↓
 1Help    ZIndex  3Exit    4       5Hex    6       7       8       9NextF  10
```

*Figure 3.7.  Full screen ASCII display*

This screen removes the hex code display and shows a little more file information in decipherable language. You can switch back and forth between these two views of a file by alternately pressing [F5].

## Deleting Files

New files are created and old files are deleted on a regular basis by even the most casual user. You can delete files and subdirectories in the PC Shell four ways:

1.  Highlight a single file name (or select a group of file names), press [Alt]-[F]-[D], then walk through the steps for deleting files. This executes the *Delete File* command on the File pull-down menu.

2. If the shortcut keys are showing, highlight the file (or select the group of files you want to delete), press [T], and walk through the deletion process.

3. If the DOS command line is showing, type DEL followed by the file name on your DOS command line, and press [Enter]. If the path of the file to be deleted is not the current path, you must specify its path or switch to that directory before you execute the delete.

4. To delete a subdirectory, use the Delete subdirectory command under the Directory Maint submenu off of the Disk pull-down menu.

> When you delete a file, only the first character is stripped from the file name. The data still remmains on disk and can be recovered, as described in the section, *Undeleting Files and Directories.*

The most common way for deleting files in the PC Shell is to highlight a single file or select multiple files, press [Alt]-[F]-[D], and delete the files.

For example, if you want to delete AUTOEXEC.BAK:

**Highlight:** AUTOEXEC.BAK

**Press:** [Alt]-[F]-[F]

This opens the *File Delete* box, shown in figure 3.8.

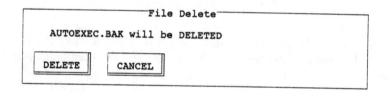

*Figure 3.8. The File Delete Box*

The name of the file you're going to delete should appear in the box. If it doesn't, press [C] to cancel the delete. If the correct name appears:

**Press:** [Enter]

This selects the default reply DELETE. File names in the File List window will move up to take the place of the deleted file.

To delete a group of files, select each file name first, then begin the delete process. This opens a more detailed version of the *File Delete* box, as shown in figure 3.9.

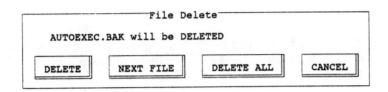

*Figure 3.9. The File Delete box for a group of files*

The name of the first file in the group will appear in the box, along with four options:

**DELETE**          Deletes the displayed file.

**NEXT FILE**       Does not delete the displayed file and moves on to the next file name in sequence.

**DELETE ALL**      Deletes all selected file names rapidly. If the series is a long one, you can stop the process by pressing [Esc], but all files deleted up to the point will remain deleted (unless you undelete them).

**CANCEL**          Cancels the group delete and returns you to the PC Shell screen.

## Undeleting Files and Directories

There are times when you delete a file by mistake. Throughout all the incarnations of DOS, you have never been able to recover a deleted file, but PC Shell fills this gap with a fine undelete feature. With PC Shell, you can begin undeleting accidentally deleted files five ways:

1. Press [Alt]-[F]-[U] and use the Undelete File command on the File pull-down menu.

2. Press [Alt]-[S]-[U] and use the Undelete Files command on the Special pull-down menu.

3. If the shortcut keys are showing, press [U].

4. If the DOS command line is showing, switch to the directory that contains the files you want to undelete, type UNDELETE, press [Enter], and follow the procedure for undeleting files.

5. Gather disk data into a file you create and save this file to disk.

The first thing to do after you accidently delete a file is DON'T DO ANYTHING ELSE. When a file is deleted, the data remains on disk, DOS just ignores it. You can still resurrect the deleted data if you haven't written over it with new data. Even if you have saved something since accidently deleting a file, not all is lost. However, your chances for successfully resurrecting deleted file data diminish with the more new data you save.

You're in good shape if you've loaded PC Shell as a resident program so you can pop it up immediately over your current work. This prevents data from being written to disk automatically if you're working in a program with a timed-autosave feature, such as the Notepads module.

> Because undeleting files and directories is so important, you might want to reassign the Undelete function to a function key. The method for doing this is described in the section *Reassigning Function Keys* in chapter 5.

To undelete a deleted file or subdirectory, go to the directory where the original file or directory existed, then begin the undelete process:

**Press:** [Alt]-[F]-[U]

This opens the *Undelete confirm* box, shown in figure 3.10, which lets you make sure you're working in the right directory.

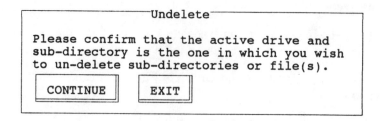

*Figure 3.10. The Undelete confirm box*

> If you want to use shortcut key assignments, first turn shortcut keys on:
>
> **Press:** [Alt]-[O]-[C]-[K]
>
> Now you can select the Undelete function, which is assigned to the letter key [U].

To continue with the undelete process:

**Press:** [Enter]

This opens the *Undelete* window, which looks like figure 3.11.

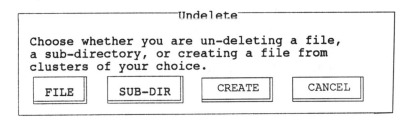

*Figure 3.11. The Undelete window*

The *Undelete* window gives you four options for undeleting files and subdirectories:

FILE          Recovers a single deleted file that hasn't yet been overwritten with data. You should use this option if you've just deleted a file and you're fairly sure the data hasn't yet been overwritten. You can always start with this option, and if it doesn't work proceed to CREATE.

SUB-DIR     Recovers a deleted subdirectory. Follow the same steps for deleting subdirectories as you do files, except select SUB-DIR instead of FILE.

CREATE       Assembles segments of data on your disk that you want to make into a file. This is a more complicated procedure than FILE recovery, but it allows you to resurrect part, or even all, of a deleted file that has been overwritten.

CANCEL      Cancels the undelete.

For the first example:

**Press:** [F]

This opens another version of the *Undelete* box, as shown in figure 3.12, which asks you to specify the method you want to use.

```
┌──────────────────Undelete───────────────────┐
│                                              │
│  "Delete Tracking" records exist. You may    │
│  un-delete by the "Delete Tracking" method   │
│  or by using the DOS directory.              │
│  ┌─────────────┐  ┌─────────────┐ ┌────────┐ │
│  │ DEL TRACK   │  │   DOS DIR   │ │ CANCEL │ │
│  └─────────────┘  └─────────────┘ └────────┘ │
└──────────────────────────────────────────────┘
```

*Figure 3.12. Another version of the Delete box*

There are three methods you can use to undelete an item:

**DEL TRACK**  This is a sophisticated process provided by PC Shell and works more effectively, but a bit more slowly, than the DOS method in locating and resurrecting all data for deleted files. Whenever you delete/files, information about the file is saved to a file in the root directory called PCTRACKR.DEL. This is the information you use to undelete files.

**DOS DIR**  This works more quickly, but less effectively, than Delete Tracking. You might try this method first for a quick pass.

**New file**  This lets you create a new file with its own name that will contain data from the disk. You walk through sections of the disk, view data, and decide what you want to save.

### The Delete Tracking Method

To select Delete Tracking:

**Press:** [T]

This displays a list of all deleted files and subdirectories in the current directory for which the Delete Tracking process has kept a record, as shown in figure 3.13.

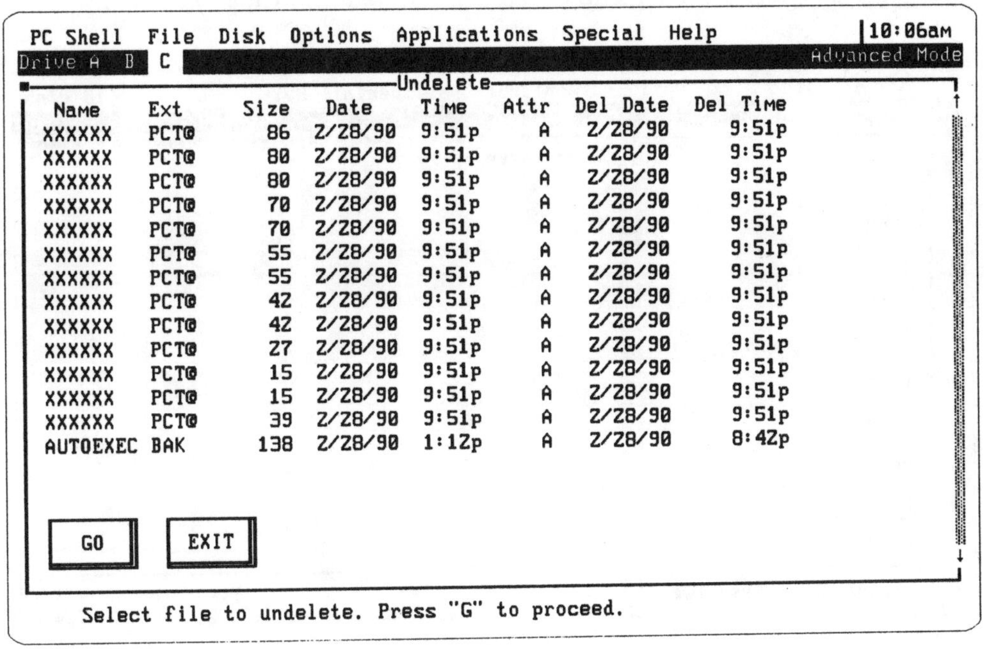

```
 PC Shell  File  Disk  Options  Applications  Special  Help       |10:06am
Drive A  B  C                                                    Advanced Mode
■                               ─────Undelete─
  Name    Ext    Size    Date     Time    Attr   Del Date   Del Time        ↑
  XXXXXX  PCT@     86   2/28/90   9:51p     A    2/28/90     9:51p          ▓
  XXXXXX  PCT@     80   2/28/90   9:51p     A    2/28/90     9:51p          ▓
  XXXXXX  PCT@     80   2/28/90   9:51p     A    2/28/90     9:51p
  XXXXXX  PCT@     70   2/28/90   9:51p     A    2/28/90     9:51p
  XXXXXX  PCT@     70   2/28/90   9:51p     A    2/28/90     9:51p
  XXXXXX  PCT@     55   2/28/90   9:51p     A    2/28/90     9:51p
  XXXXXX  PCT@     55   2/28/90   9:51p     A    2/28/90     9:51p
  XXXXXX  PCT@     42   2/28/90   9:51p     A    2/28/90     9:51p
  XXXXXX  PCT@     42   2/28/90   9:51p     A    2/28/90     9:51p
  XXXXXX  PCT@     27   2/28/90   9:51p     A    2/28/90     9:51p
  XXXXXX  PCT@     15   2/28/90   9:51p     A    2/28/90     9:51p
  XXXXXX  PCT@     15   2/28/90   9:51p     A    2/28/90     9:51p
  XXXXXX  PCT@     39   2/28/90   9:51p     A    2/28/90     9:51p
  AUTOEXEC BAK    138   2/28/90   1:12p     A    2/28/90     8:42p

   ┌────────┐  ┌────────┐
   │   GO   │  │  EXIT  │                                                   ↓
   └────────┘  └────────┘

       Select file to undelete.  Press "G" to proceed.
```

*Figure 3.13. The Undelete window showing deleted file names*

To undelete AUTOEXEC.BAK:

**Highlight:** AUTOEXEC.BAK

**Press:** [G]

If a file with the same name exists in the same directory, you'll be asked to enter a new name or exit the undelete procedure. You can exit this screen by pressing either [Esc] or [X].

The series of steps that brought you to this point are intricate, but can be summed up this way: *Press: [Alt]-[S]-[U]-[C]-[F]-[T]*

### The DOS DIR Method

If you want to use the DOS DIR method, when asked what method you want to use to undelete:

**Press:** [D]

This opens a modified version of the PC Shell screen, as shown in figure 3.14.

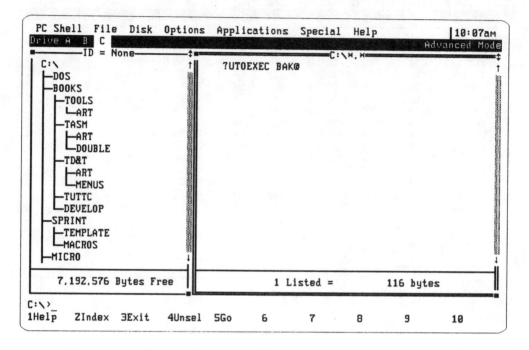

*Figure 3.14. DOS DIR undelete screen*

The results shown here were displayed right after the results shown in figure 3.13, which shows you that the Delete Tracking method is more effective than the DOS DIR method.

### Creating a New File

If neither Delete Tracking nor DOS DIR works, or you're sure some of the data you want to recover has been overwritten, you should select the CREATE option on the second *Undelete* window.

**Press:** [R]

This opens a box asking you to name the file that will be created to hold the data you want to recover, as shown in figure 3.15.

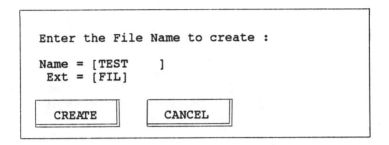

Enter the File Name to create :

Name = [TEST    ]
 Ext = [FIL]

CREATE         CANCEL

*Figure 3.15. The File Name create box*

Type the name and extension you want to use:

**Press:** [Enter]

This opens an undelete editing screen showing the first block of data on your disk, as shown in figure 3.16.

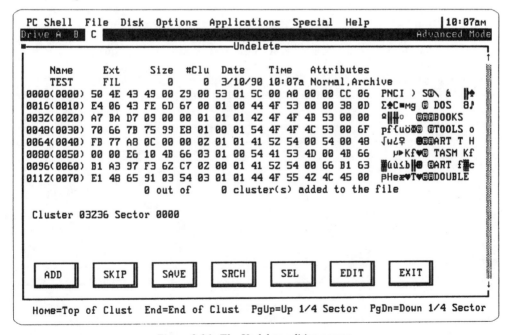

*Figure 3.16. The Undelete editing screen*

The bottom of this screen gives you the following controls:

**ADD**  Adds the data displayed in the screen to the file you've created.

**SKIP**  Skips the data in the current screen and moves to the next screenful.

**SAVE**  Saves the file you've created to disk. Remember, that while saving makes the file permanent, you might write over some data you want to resurrect but haven't yet found.

**SRCH**  Searches for the next occurrence of characters, which you specify in the screen shown in figure 3.17.

**SEL**  Lets you select a different cluster to work with.

**EDIT**  Lets you edit the characters on screen before you save them to your file.

**EXIT**  Exits the Undelete editing screen and return to the PC Shell screen.

**Home=Top of Clust**  Moves you to the top of the current cluster.

**End=End of Clust**  Moves you to the end of the current cluster.

**PgUp=Up 1/4 Sector**  Moves you up one-quarter of a cluster, or one screenful. Same as pressing [PgUp].

**PgDn=Down 1/4 Sector**  Moves you down one-quarter of a cluster, or one screenful. Same as pressing [PgDn].

Figure 3.17 shows the *Undelete search* screen.

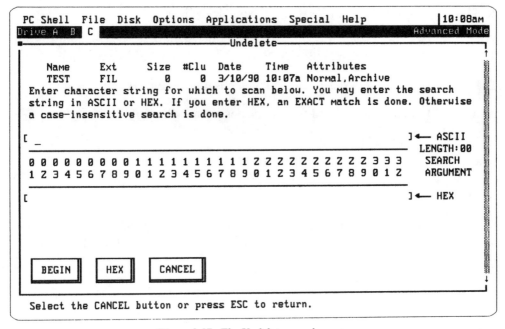

*Figure 3.17. The Undelete search screen*

Resurrecting data by accumulating quarter sectors can be tedious, but it can spare you the trouble of creating the data from scratch.

## Undeleting From the DOS Command Line

You can also undelete files by running the Undelete program from the DOS prompt. This is a stand-alone program run by the disk file UNDELETE.EXE. You run the program by typing the file name and pressing [Enter]. Nine switches will adjust the behavior of the Undelete program:

/?          Displays two help screens printed below. Same as /HELP switch.

d:          The drive where you want to undelete files.

path        The file path you want to undelete, for example, BOOKS\TOOLS\ART.

file specs  Specifications for the file name or names you want to undelete. You can use the DOS wild cards ? and *.

**/HELP**    Displays two help screens printed below. Same as /? switch.

**/LIST**    Lists the deleted files that can be undeleted.

**/DT**    Uses the Delete Tracking method to undelete files. This employs information recorded in the file PCTRACR.DEL in your root directory.

**/DOS**    Uses the DOS delete method which is quicker but less effective.

**/ALL**    Undeletes all deleted files in the designated directory.

For example, to find help information:

    **Type:** UNDELETE /?

    **Press:** [Enter]

You'll be asked to press [Enter] a second time to see the help information, which is presented in two screens. The complete list is printed, as shown in the following:

```
The following are the recognized parameters for PC Shell - Stand-Alone
Undelete

 V6.0

UNDELETE x:\path\filespec /HELP /DT /DOS /LIST /ALL

All parameters are optional.

"x:" is the drive letter where the deleted files can
     be found. If absent, the current drive will be used.
"\path\" is the path where the deleted files can be found.
     If absent, the current path will be used.
"filespec" qualifies which deleted files to use. "*.*"
     indicates all files. DOS globals (* and ?) can be
     used. If absent, *.* will be the default.
"/HELP" will cause this message to be displayed.
"/DT" indicates that only the Delete Tracking file is
     to be used.
"/DOS" indicates that only the DOS directory is to be
     used. /DOS and /DT are mutually exclusive.
"/LIST" will only produce a list of all the available
     undeleted files. That which is listed is controlled by
     any and all of the previously listed options except
     /HELP.
"/ALL" requests automatic
 of all specified files.
     Each file will be undeleted, in turn, without user
     prompting. If undeleting files from the DOS directory,
```

a special character will be assigned for the first
position of the filename. A different character will
be used if a duplicate filename already exists. The
characters that will be used, in order, are
"#%&-0123456789". If none of these characters provide
a unique name, the letters A to Z will be used.

The /LIST option should be used first to verify all
the files that UNDELETE will attempt to recover.
It is possible that two apparently unrelated files
occupied the same clusters at different times. Your
results will depend on the order of undeletion. Care
should be exercised when using the /ALL option to
keep track of the activity. It would be wise to print
out the results with CTRL-PRTSC. Do NOT use
redirection. You may overwrite files you are trying
to undelete.

```
C:\>
```

The best way to start out is move to a directory where you want to undelete some
deleted files.

**Type:** UNDELETE

**Press:** [Enter]

This loads the program, runs a check on deleted files in the current directory, and
gives you something like the following information:

```
C:\TEST>undelete

PC Shell - Stand-Alone Undelete  V6.0
(C) Copyright 1990  Central Point Software, Inc.
Unauthorized Duplication Prohibited.

Directory: C:\TEST
File Specs: *.*

    Delete Tracking file contains    6 deleted files.
    Of those,    0 files have all clusters available,
                 2 files have some clusters available,
                 4 files have no clusters available.

    DOS Directory contains   89 deleted files.
    Of those,    0 files may be recovered.
```

```
Using the Delete Tracking file.

   ** PCSHELL   CFG      1089  2/28/90   9:51p  ...A  Deleted:   2/28/90
9:51p
All of the clusters for this file are available.
Do you want to recover this file? (Y/dele}
```

This means that the file PCSHELL.CFG which I copied to TEST, can be undeleted. All you need to do to confirm the recovery is:

**Press:** [Y]

The file is now undeleted. You will be walked through subsequent deleted file names and asked if you want to delete each file in turn. If you don't want to be prompted this way, use the /ALL switch when you load the program.

When the Undelete program runs across a file it can't undelete, you'll see this message:

```
None of the clusters for this file are available.
The file cannot be recovered. Press any key to
continue.]
```

## Cleaning Files

Cleaning a file means wiping all the file data from the disk. This makes sure that no residual data remains that someone else might try to recover. To make sure no one recovers the data, you should clean the file instead.

To clean a file, use the *Clean File* command on the File pull-down menu. For example, to clean the file AUTOEXEC.BAK from your root directory:

**Highlight:** AUTOEXEC.BAK

**Press:** [Alt]-[F]-[N]

This opens the *File Clean* window, which looks like figure 3.18.

```
┌───────────────────File Clean───────────────────┐
│  Clean File Setup Information:  Enter NEW values or│
│  use DEFAULTS to CLEAN file information from disk. │
│                                                    │
│  Replacement HEX Value : [F6]   Use U.S. Government│
│  Number of Cycles : [01]        standards?  [N]    │
└────────────────────────────────────────────────┘
```

*Figure 3.18. The File Clean window*

There are three settings in this window you can change. The hex value refers to the hex character that will overwrite the file data. The hex character F6 shows up as a colon with a dash through the middle. You can use another character by typing it in. The number of cycles refers to the number of times the file data is overwritten. Setting the clean method to U.S. government standards refers to an overwrite character pattern of 0/1 repeated three times.

You can use three function keys when this window is open:

**[F1] Help**       Opens the help screen for cleaning files.

**[F3] Exit**       Closes the *File Clean* window and returns you to the PC Shell screen.

**[F5] Accept**    Accepts the values you've entered into the three settings and cleans the file accordingly.

# THE DISK MENU

The Disk pull-down menu lets you work with the following 12 commands:

**Copy Disk**          Makes an identical copy of a floppy disk. Same as the DOS DISKCOPY command. All you do is select the source and target drives, insert the appropriate disks in the selected floppy disk drives, and begin the copy.

**Compare Disk**      Compares two floppy disks and reports back on any mismatched data. Select the source and target drives, insert the disks, and execute the command.

**Change Drive**      Changes the current drive. Same as pressing [Ctrl] and the drive letter.

**Format Data Disk**  Formats a floppy disk as a data disk. No system files will be placed on the disk.

**Make System Disk** Formats a floppy disk as a system disk and places system files on the disk so you can boot from the disk.

**Directory Maint**   Opens a submenu giving you five commands specific to working with directories.

**Search Disk**        Opens the *Disk Search* window, which lets you type up to 32 ASCII characters. Searching for ASCII characters is not case specific. PC Shell will then look for these characters through all areas of the current disk and display each match it finds in sequence. You can also search for hex characters by pressing [F9] when the Disk Search window appears. Now any characters you type will be entered as hex code, which *is* case specific. The matching ASCII characters to your hex code will also be displayed.

**Rename Volume**      Renames the volume or disk name.

**Park Disk**          Parks your hard disk read/write heads over a safe track on the disk. You can also execute this command from the DOS command line by typing PARK and pressing [Enter].

**Verify Disk**        Verifies that all the data on the current disk is readable. PC Shell will display its progress through the data portion of the disk it is verifying and alert you to bad data.

**Disk Info**          Opens the *Disk Information* window for the current disk, which looks like figure 3.19.

```
┌─────────────────Disk Information──────────────────┐
│ Volume Label None                                  │
│                                                    │
│   31,812,096 bytes of total disk space.            │
│    4,175,872 bytes available on volume.            │
│      100,352 bytes in      5 hidden files.         │
│   27,416,576 bytes in  1,126 user files.           │
│       98,304 bytes in     40 directories.          │
│       20,480 bytes in bad sectors.                 │
│          512 bytes per sector.                     │
│            4 sectors per cluster.                  │
│           17 sectors per track.                    │
│       15,533 total clusters.                       │
│       62,288 total sectors.                        │
│        3,664 total tracks.            ┌────────┐   │
│            5 sides.                   │  EXIT  │   │
│          733 cylinders.               └────────┘   │
└────────────────────────────────────────────────────┘
```

*Figure 3.19. The Disk Information window*

**View/Edit Disk**     Lets you view and edit any sector of the current disks. You can find more information on this command below.

## The Directory Maintenance Submenu

The Directory Maint submenu provides the following five commands for working with directories:

**Add a subdirectory**      Creates a directory below the current directory marked in the *Tree List* window.

**Rename a subdirectory**      Renames the directory highlighted in the *Tree List* window.

**Delete a subdirectory**      Deletes the directory highlighted in the *Tree List* window.

**Prune and graft**      Moves the contents of an entire directory to another location.

**Modify Attributes**      Changes any of the four attributes (H, S, R, or A) assigned to the current directory.

## Viewing and Editing a Disk

You can use the *View/Edit Disk* command on the Disk pull-down menu to view and edit any portion of a disk. This is useful when you're working with a hard disk. To open the *Disk Edit* screen:

**Press:** [Alt]-[D]-[E]

Your screen should change to look like figure 3.20.

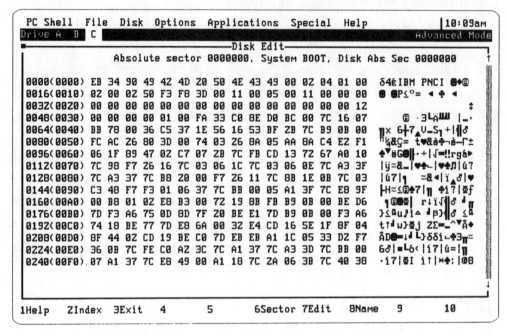

*Figure 3.20. The Disk Edit screen*

The top of the screen shows the disk location you're viewing in absolute sector and area. You can view half a sector, or 256 bytes of data, in the *Disk Edit* screen.

You can see three columns of data in this screen. The left column shows what's called the *offset location* within each sector. The middle column shows the disk data in hexadecimal notation. The right column shows the disk data in ASCII.

You can use six function keys shown at the bottom of this screen:

**[F1] Help**    Opens the help screen specific to the *Disk Edit* screen.

**[F2] Index**    Opens the help index specific to the *Disk Edit* screen.

**[F3] Exit**    Closes the *Disk Edit* screen and returns you to the PC Shell screen. Same as pressing [Esc].

**[F6] Sector**    Lets you select a precise sector to view and edit.

**[F7] Edit**    Displays the cursor and lets you edit the displayed data. While you edit data, you can use the current commands of [F1], [F2], and [F3]. The [F5] function key lets you save changes you make, and [F8] lets you switch between the hexadecimal and ASCII displays.

**[F8] Name**    Displays the name of the sector you're viewing.

Editing data directly to disk has its risks. When you edit file data, you can't do much damage except to your own data; but if you edit the boot or FAT areas, you could destroy important data DOS needs for working with your disk. Don't make any changes to those areas, unless you know exactly what you are doing.

# THE OPTIONS MENU

The Options pull-down menu providing the following 10 commands let you change the way PC Shell looks and behaves.

**Setup Configuration**    Opens the Setup Configuration submenu.

**Modify Display**    Opens the Modify Display submenu.

**Tree List Window**    Toggles the *Tree List* window on and off.

**File List Window**    Toggles the *File List* window on and off.

**View Window**    Toggles the *View* window on and off.

**Hide Windows**    Toggles all windows on and off.

**Size/Move Window**    Changes the size of the current window or moves the window to a new location on your screen. You can also press [Alt]-[Spacebar].

**Zoom the Current Window**    Toggles the currently active window between full-screen and its previous size.

**Re-Read the Tree**    Rereads the directory configuration for the current disk and redisplays the tree diagram in the tree list window. The information is saved to a file called PCSHELL.TRE.

**Save Configuration File**    Saves the current configuration of PC Shell to a disk file called PCSHELL.CFG. Using this command, you can save any changes you've made. You can also save them when you exit the shell, or you can cancel them.

Setup Configuration and Modify Display open menus of their own, described in the following sections.

## The Setup Configuration Submenu

The Setup Configuration submenu provides the following nine commands:

**Change User Level**    Changes the user level to beginning, intermediate, or advanced. It controls the display of certain commands in three of the pull-down menus, effectively limiting you to a range of commands based on your skill and confidence level. This command also lets you configure PC Shell only as an application launcher.

**Short Cut Keys**    Toggles shortcut keys on and off. There are twelve shortcut-key assignments.

**DOS Command Line**    Toggles the DOS command line on or off. This line can be blank or display either the DOS command line or the shortcut key assignments. Working with the DOS command line is described in chapter 2.

**Background Mat**    Toggles the background matte on or off. When off, you can view features displayed beneath the active features of the PC Shell, such as windows, menus, and boxes.

**Viewer Cfg.**    Toggles the viewer window in a horizontal or vertical display on and off. Database information is often better viewed in vertical display, while text information is often better displayed in horizontal mode. Experiment with each setting to determin which mode suits you.

**Default Viewer**    Selects the default viewer when a file can't be categorized by PC Shell. The text viewer that is selected by default is usually the best.

**Screen Colors**          Opens the master screen color palette listing the various screen features, colors, and intensities you want to assign.

**Date/Time**              Opens the *Set Date and Time* box.

**Define Function Keys**   Redefines assignments to seven function keys displayed on the bottom line of your screen.

All of these settings are optional and depend on your preferences and the type of work you do in PC Shell. You should experiment with various settings, particularly the shortcut keys, to see how you like them.

### Changing User Levels

You can select one of three levels to work with: beginning, intermediate, and advanced. The level you select determines how many commands will appear on the File, Disk, and Special pull-down menus. You can only use a menu command when it appears; the higher the level you use, the more commands are available.

Regardless of which level you select, all commands on the Applications menu are always available. You can, however, lock out all other menus, except the Applications menu, if you want the PC Shell to be used only as an applications launcher.

> I suggest you base the level on your confidence level and not on your skill level. I preferred starting out in the Advanced Mode, even though I wasn't familiar with all the commands in the PC Shell. I don't like being limited in what I can do, and I enjoy exploring commands I'm not familiar with.

To switch between user levels:

**Press:** [Alt]-[O]-[C]-[U]

This opens the *Change User Level* box, which looks like figure 3.21.

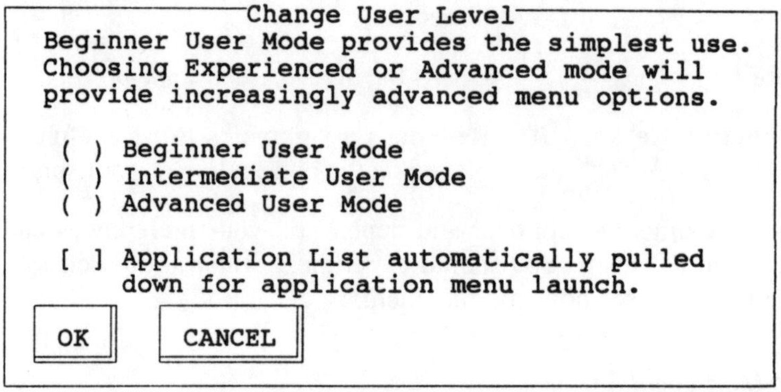

```
┌──────────────Change User Level──────────────┐
│ Beginner User Mode provides the simplest use.│
│ Choosing Experienced or Advanced mode will   │
│ provide increasingly advanced menu options.  │
│                                              │
│    ( ) Beginner User Mode                    │
│    ( ) Intermediate User Mode                │
│    ( ) Advanced User Mode                    │
│                                              │
│    [ ] Application List automatically pulled │
│        down for application menu launch.     │
│ ┌──────┐  ┌──────────┐                       │
│ │  OK  │  │  CANCEL  │                       │
│ └──────┘  └──────────┘                       │
└──────────────────────────────────────────────┘
```

*Figure 3.21. The Change User Level box*

You can select a new level by pressing the key that matches the first letter of the level. For example, if you're using the default Advanced User Mode and want to switch to Beginner User Mode:

**Press:** [B]

To implement this selection:

**Press:** [O]

The new level becomes effective immediately. Check this by opening the File menu. In the Beginner's level, you should see only seven commands on the File menu.

After making any change to the PC Shell, the Beginner's level will remain effective until you change it again or until you try to exit the PC Shell. That's when you'll be asked whether you want to make the change permanent. PC Shell will display the box shown in figure 3.22.

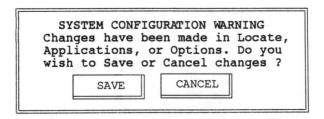

```
┌─────────────────────────────────────────────┐
│ ┌───────────────────────────────────────┐ │
│ │     SYSTEM CONFIGURATION WARNING        │ │
│ │   Changes have been made in Locate,     │ │
│ │   Applications, or Options. Do you      │ │
│ │   wish to Save or Cancel changes ?      │ │
│ │                                          │ │
│ │    ┌──────────┐   ┌──────────┐          │ │
│ │    │   SAVE   │   │  CANCEL  │          │ │
│ │    └──────────┘   └──────────┘          │ │
│ └───────────────────────────────────────┘ │
└─────────────────────────────────────────────┘
```

*Figure 3.22. The System Configuration Warning box*

Saving the change copies it to PCSHELL.CFG on disk.

If you're operating in standard mode and quit the program without saving changes, they won't be effective the next time you load the program. If you're operating in resident mode, changes remain in effect the next time you pop open PC Shell, but you'll get the same request to save or cancel changes the next time you try to quit PC Shell. This will continue to happen until you actually quit PC Shell.

Canceling changes removes them from PC Shell in both resident and standard modes. Each time you load PC Shell into memory, it will display the configuration as recorded in PCSHELL.CFG.

### *Using Shortcut Keys*

Shortcut keys are letter keys that have been assigned to the ten most frequently performed features in PC Shell. In the default mode, these key assignments are turned off. To turn them on:

**Press:** [Alt]-[O]-[C]-[K]

This feature is displayed in the same position as your DOS command line. You can't view both shortcut keys and the DOS command line at the same time. Toggling one on automatically toggles the other off.

To execute a function assigned to a shortcut key, just press the highlighted letter of the command. For example, to copy AUTOEXEC.BAT to AUTOEXEC.BAK:

**Highlight:** ΛUTOEXEC.BAT

**Press:** [C]

Select the drive and directory you want to copy the file to. If it's in the same directory (as in this case), you'll be asked to give the file a different name. This file-copy procedure is the same as the one you follow when you press [F2] or [Alt]-[F]-[C].

The following ten shortcut key assignments are provided and cannot be changed:

**Copy**      Begins the file-copy procedure. This command is described in chapter 2.

**Move**      Moves a file from one location to another.

**Delete**    Opens the *Delete file* box (described in chapter 2).

**Rename**  Renames a file. Opens the *File Rename* box, shown in figure 3.23.

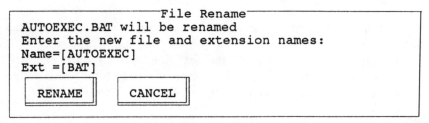

*Figure 3.23. The File Rename box*

To rename a file, type the new name, press [Enter], type the new extension (if necessary), and press [Enter] twice.

**View**      Views a file in its native format using one of the program viewer.

**HexEdit**  Views a file in hexadecimal display.

**Find**      Finds a file or files that contain the specified character string by opening the *Text Search* box, shown in figure 3.24.

```
┌─────────────Text Search─────────────┐
│  Enter case insensitive text to search for:   │
│     [···························· · ·]          │
│  in 1 file.                                    │
│                                                │
│  Search:                 If found:             │
│  ( ) All files           ( ) Select file and continue │
│  ( ) Selected files      ( ) Pause search      │
│  ( ) Unselected files                          │
└────────────────────────────────────────┘
```

*Figure 3.24. The Text Search box*

To search for text, simply type the characters you're looking for, select the way you want the search-and-find to behave, and press [Enter].

**Print**      Opens the *File Print* box, shown in figure 3.25.

```
┌───────────────────File Print──────────────────┐
│ File=AUTOEXEC.BAT                              │
│                                                │
│ Please specify your print options as follows:  │
│ ( ) Print as a Standard Text file              │
│ ( ) Print file using PC Shell print options    │
│ ( ) Dump each sector in ASCII and HEX          │
│                                                │
│  ┌─────────┐  ┌─────────┐  ┌──────────┐        │
│  │ PRINT   │  │ NEXT    │  │ CANCEL   │        │
│  └─────────┘  └─────────┘  └──────────┘        │
│                                                │
└────────────────────────────────────────────────┘
```

*Figure 3.25. The File Print box*

Printing as a standard text file filters for ASCII characters only. You can set PC Shell print options as shown in figure 3.4. You can also dump each disk sector first in ASCII, then in hexadecimal characters.

**Locate**     Finds files that match your specifications (described in chapter 2 for the function key [F7] Locate).

**FileEdit**   Opens the PC Shell file Editor, which lets you view and edit the contents of a text file.

**Undelete**   Recovers files that have been accidentally deleted.

**Zoom**       Toggles the currently active window between full-screen size and small size.

Copy, Delete, and Locate are duplicated in the default function key assignments.

### Using and Configuring Viewers

To view a file, just highlight its name and press [F2]. For example, to view the contents of your AUTOEXEC.BAT:

**Highlight:** AUTOEXEC.BAT

**Press:** [F2]

My screen changes to look like figure 3.26.

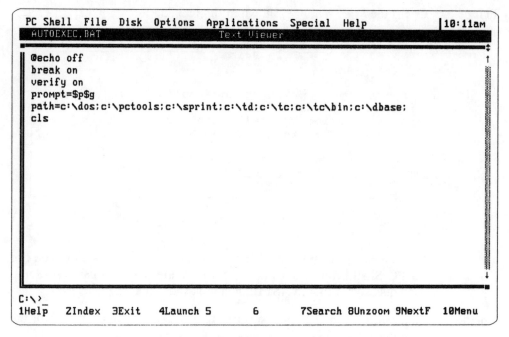

*Figure 3.26. Text Viewer displaying my AUTOEXEC.BAT*

This file uses the Text Viewer, which appears at the top of the view screen. The name of the file you're viewing appears on the right side of the same line. The function key assignments change when you open a viewer. The following assignments appear for the Text Viewer:

**[F1] Help**　　Opens the help screen specific to the Text Viewer.

**[F2] Index**　　Opens the help index for the Text Viewer.

**[F3] Exit**　　Closes the current viewer and returns you to the PC Shell screen.

**[F4 ] Launch**　Loads (launches) the file you're viewing, if it's a program file. Opens the *Run File* box, which looks like figure 3.27 when viewing the contents of WP.EXE (the program file for WordPerfect).

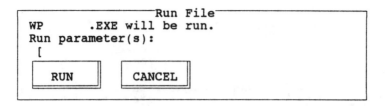

```
┌──────────────Run File──────────────┐
│WP        .EXE will be run.          │
│Run parameter(s):                    │
│  [                                  │
│  ┌───────────┐   ┌───────────┐      │
│  │   RUN     │   │  CANCEL   │      │
│  └───────────┘   └───────────┘      │
└─────────────────────────────────────┘
```

*Figure 3.27. The Run File box*

You can specify parameters before loading the program. You'll be told if the file does not have a .COM, .EXE, or .BAT extension, or if the file has not been assigned to an application for launching. Launching files is described in the chapter 4.

**[F7] Search**   Opens a box that lets you search for a character string.

**[F8] Unzoom**   Switches the viewer to half screen. The [F8] key function then becomes Zoom, which you press if you want the viewer to switch back to full-screen.

**[F9] NextF**   Displays the contents of the top of the next selected file.

**[F10] Menu**   Activates the top menu bar.

You can reconfigure the default viewer that appears on your screen when PC Shell can't figure out the type of file you want to view.

### Changing Date and Time

You can change the time displayed in the PC Shell window and in other applications running in your computer, including the Desktop Manager.

To open the *Set Date and Time* box, shown in figure 3.28:

**Press:** [Alt]-[O]-[C]-[T]

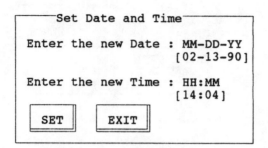

*Figure 3.28. The Set Date and Time window*

To change the date, type in the new digits, making sure to enter zeros where appropriate. Press [Enter] to set the date, then type in the new time. To set the changes, press [Enter] or [S].

### Redefining Function Keys

Function keys are usually assigned the most frequently performed functions within a program. In the PC Shell, there are ten default assignments.

You can configure seven of the ten function keys in PC Shell to access different commands if you find you use them more frequently than the default commands. For example, you may move files more often than you copy them, in which case you may wish to substitute file move for file copy, or for file select.

To redefine one or more of your function keys:

**Press:** [Alt]-[O]-[C]

This opens the Setup Configuration submenu. To open the *Define Function Keys* box, shown in figure 3.29:

**Press:** [F]

```
                    ┌─Define Function Keys─────────────────────────┐
            Current Settings:              Available Functions:
     F1 — Not Changeable       Help
     F2 — Quick File View      Qview    ┌─────────────────────────────┐
     F3 — Not Changeable       Exit     │ Copy File          Copy     │
     F4 — Unselect Files       Unsel    │ Move File          Move     │
     F5 — Copy File            Copy     │ Compare File       Compar   │
     F6 — Delete File          Delete   │ Rename File        Rename   │
     F7 — Locate File          Locate   │ Locate File        Locate   │
     F8 — Zoom Current Window  Zoom     │ Delete File        Delete   │
     F9 — File Select Filter   Select   │ Edit File          Edit     │
     F1O- Not Changeable       Menu     │ Search File        Search   │
                                        └─────────────────────────────┘
```

*Figure 3.29. The Define Function Keys box*

Current Settings, on the left side, shows three columns: the ten function keys, their current assignments as displayed on your screen, and the actual command that has been assigned to each one.

Available Functions, on the right side, shows the top eight descriptions and matching commands from a list of 61 functions you can assign to seven of your ten function keys. (You also cannot assign [F11] and [F12], because these keys make peculiar calls to the BIOS.)

The basic procedure is to highlight the function key you want to reassign on the left-side, then scroll through commands on the right side and pick the one you want to use.

Use the Update, Cancel, and Reset keys—shown on the bottom line—for shortcuts when you begin to reassign keys often.

The three keys you can't reconfigure: are [F1] for help, [F3] for exit, and [F10] for menu. You'll find them marked as Not Changeable followed by the command permanently attached to them. You can assign these commands to other function keys also.

When the *Define Function Keys* box first appears, you'll see the following line highlighted:

```
F2 Quick File View    QView
```

You can select which function key you want to reassign by highlighting it using the [⇑] and [⇓] keys.

For this example, change the assignment for [F4] from Unselect Files to Undelete Files:

**Highlight:** [F4] Unselect Files    Unsel

**Press:** [Tab]

This highlights the border of the *Available Functions:* window. Now scroll through the list of commands:

**Press:** [PgDn]

Because there are many command choices, you might want to page down through the list for a quick first look. Eight presses will take you to the bottom of the list. Unfortunately, this list is not arranged in alphabetical order, but follows the order of the commands on the PC Shell menus. To insert the menu description and command for [F4]:

**Highlight:** Undelete Files    Undel

**Press:** [Enter]

This switches you back to the *Current Settings:* window. The *Define Function Keys* box should now look like figure 3.30.

```
┌─────────────────Define Function Keys──────────────────┐
│          Current Settings:            Available Functions: │
│  F1 — Not Changeable        Help                          │
│  F2 — Quick File View       Qview    ┌──────────────────────┐│
│  F3 — Not Changeable        Exit     │ Re-Read the Tree    TreeRd││
│  F4 — Undelete Files        Undel    │ System Info         SysInf││
│  F5 — Copy File             Copy     │ Undelete Files      Undel ││
│  F6 — Delete File           Delete   │ Directory Sort      DSort ││
│  F7 — Locate File           Locate   │ File Map            FMap  ││
│  F8 — Zoom Current Window   Zoom     │ Disk Map            DMap  ││
│  F9 — File Select Filter    Select   │ Memory Map          MMap  ││
│  F1O- Not Changeable        Menu     │ Search File         Search││
│                                      └──────────────────────┘│
└────────────────────────────────────────────────────────┘
```

*Figure 3.30. The Define Function Keys box*

To exit the *Define Function Keys* box:

**Press:** [Esc]

To make your changes permanent:

**Press:** [S]

Now you'll return to the PC Shell screen. You should be able to see the new assignment after F4—Undel. If you find you don't like this assignment, you can always change it back, assign it to another key, or assign another function to [F4]. When you exit the PC Shell, you'll be asked again if you want to save or cancel the changes you made, either to function keys or any other configurable feature in PC Shell.

You can assign any of the 62 commands listed in table 3.1 to any of the seven configurable function keys in PC Shell.

*Table 3.1. All assignments for function keys*

| Command | Code | Command | Code |
|---|---|---|---|
| Active List Switch | Switch | Make System Disk | System |
| All Windows Toggle | AllWin | Memory Map | MMap |
| Attribute Change | Attrib | Modify Display | ModDsp |
| Background Mat | MatBak | More File Info | Info |
| Change Drive | ChgDrv | Move File | Move |
| Change User Level | Level | One Tree/File List | 1list |
| Compare Disk | DComp | Park Disk | Park |
| Compare File | Compar | Print Directory | PrintD |
| Copy Disk | DCopy | Print File | Print |
| Copy File | Copy | Quick File View | Qview |
| Date / Time | DatTim | Re-read the Tree | TreeRd |
| Default Viewer | DfView | Rename Volume | DRenam |
| Define Function Keys | Fkeys | Rename File | Rename |
| Delete File | Delete | Screen Colors | Color |
| Directory Maint | DMaint | Search Disk | DSrch |
| Directory Sort | DSort | Search File | Search |
| Disk Info | DInfo | Setup Configuration | Config |
| Disk Map | DMap | Short Cut Keys | SCutKy |
| DOS Command Line | DOSCmd | Size/Move Window | SizMov |
| Edit File | Edit | Switch Tree/File | Tab |
| Exit PC Shell | Exit | System Info | SysInf |
| File Display Options | Disply | Tree List Window | TreeW |
| File List Filter | Limit | Two Tree/File List | 2list |
| File List Window | FileW | Undelete Files | Undel |
| File Map | FMap | Unselect Files | Unsel |
| File Select Filter | Select | Verify Disk | DVerfy |
| Format Disk | Format | Verify File | Verify |
| Help Index | Index | View/Edit Disk | DEdit |
| Hex Edit File | HedEdt | View Window | ViewW |
| Launch | Launch | Viewer Cfg. | ViewCg |
| Locate File | Locate | Zoom Current Window | Zoom |

These commands are listed in alphabetical order, not the order in which they appear in the *Available Functions:* window. The order that each command appears in the window is listed after the command. This number doesn't appear anywhere; just use it as a general indication of position.

## The Modify Display Menu

The Modify Display Menu controls the way the PC Shell screen is displayed on your monitor. It provides the following eight commands:

**Tree/Files Switch**     Switches activity between paired tree and file-list windows. Same as pressing [TAB].

**Two List Display**     Opens two sets of tree and file-list windows. Same as pressing [INS].

**One List Display**     Opens only one set of tree and file list windows. Same as pressing [DEL].

**Active List Switch**     Switches active windows. Same as pressing [Tab] or [Shift]-[Tab].

**File List Filter**     Opens the *File List Filter* window, which lets you select file names with common characteristics that will be displayed in the file-list window.

**File Select Filter**     Opens the *File Select* window, which lets you select file names with common characteristics. This is the same procedure performed by default function-key assignment [F4] Select (described in chapter 2).

**File Display Options**     Opens the *File List* window, which lets you select or highlight a group of files in the file-list window with similar file name characteristics.

**Unselect Files**     Unselects all selected files in the active window. Starts the same procedure as when you use the default function-key assignment [F9] Unsel.

Four selections on the Modify Display menu let you change the way file names are displayed or appear in the *File List* window: File List Filter, File Select Filter, File Display Options, and Unselect Files. Two of these, File List Filter and File Display Filter require further explanation.

To display a list of file names with similar characteristics only in their file names, use the File List Filter.

    **Press:** [Alt]-[O]-[O]-[L]

This opens the *File List Filter* box, shown in figure 3.31.

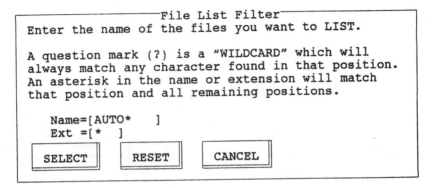

*Figure 3.31. The File List Filter box*

In this example, I've specified AUTO as the first four characters of all the file names I want to display. You can use the DOS wild cards * and ? to modify the file name selection. When I select this list, my screen changes to look like figure 3.32.

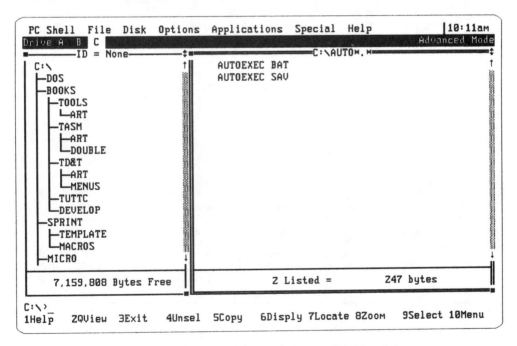

*Figure 3.32. All AUTO*.* files displayed in my File List window*

You can use the Display Options menu to change the order in which all displayed file names appear:

**Press:** [F6]

To arrange file names in alphabetical order:

**Press:** [5]

**Press:** [Enter]

## THE SPECIAL MENU

The Special Menu provides various display maps and graphical settings for special features:

**System Info**          Displays incidental information about the current disk. You can see what this information looks like in figure 3.33.

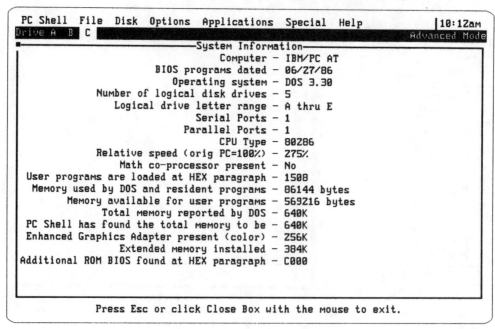

```
PC Shell  File  Disk  Options  Applications  Special  Help        |10:12am
Drive A  B  C                                                     Advanced Mode
■─────────────────────System Information──────────────────────
│                        Computer - IBM/PC AT
│              BIOS programs dated - 06/27/86
│                 Operating system - DOS 3.30
│          Number of logical disk drives - 5
│            Logical drive letter range - A thru E
│                       Serial Ports - 1
│                     Parallel Ports - 1
│                         CPU Type - 80286
│          Relative speed (orig PC=100%) - 275%
│             Math co-processor present - No
│ User programs are loaded at HEX paragraph - 150B
│ Memory used by DOS and resident programs - 86144 bytes
│      Memory available for user programs - 569216 bytes
│          Total memory reported by DOS - 640K
│ PC Shell has found the total memory to be - 640K
│ Enhanced Graphics Adapter present (color) - 256K
│            Extended memory installed - 384K
│ Additional ROM BIOS found at HEX paragraph - C000
│
│      Press Esc or click Close Box with the mouse to exit.
```

*Figure 3.33.  The System Info display*

| | |
|---|---|
| **LapLink/QC** | Toggles LapLink and Quick Connect on or off. |
| **Undelete Files** | Undeletes files you've deleted accidentally. |
| **Directory Sort** | Resorts the directories as directed by the *Directory Sort* box, shown in figure 3.34. |

```
┌─────────────Directory Sort─────────────┐
│                                         │
│  Choose Sort Field:                     │
│   ( )  1   By Name                      │
│   ( )  2   By Extension                 │
│   ( )  3   By Size                      │
│   ( )  4   By Date/Time                 │
│   ( )  5   By Select Number             │
│                                         │
│  Choose Sort Method:                    │
│   ( )  6   Ascending                    │
│   ( )  7   Descending                   │
│   ┌─────────┐   ┌──────────┐            │
│   │  SORT   │   │  CANCEL  │            │
│   └─────────┘   └──────────┘            │
│                                         │
└─────────────────────────────────────────┘
```

*Figure 3.34. The Directory Sort box*

| | |
|---|---|
| **File Map** | Opens a map of the current disk and locates the highlighted file locations, as shown in figure 3.35. |

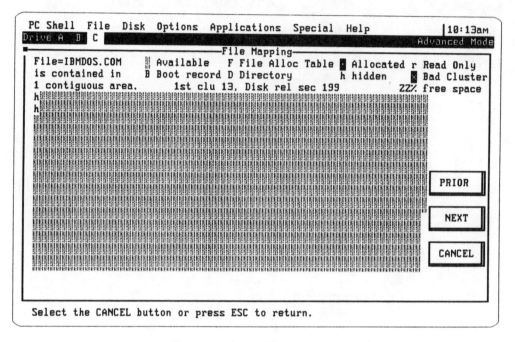

*Figure 3.35. The File Map display*

**Disk Map**             Displays a map of the current disk, as shown in figure 3.36.

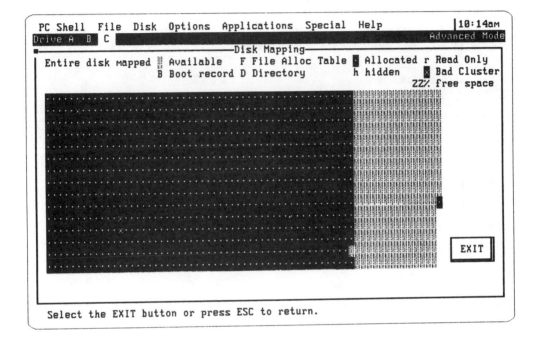

*Figure 3.36. The Disk Map display*

**Memory map**           Displays the way your computer's memory is currently being used.

You can view the current memory usage of your computer's RAM memory using the Memory Map command on the Special pull-down menu. This displays the way memory blocks have been used by DOS for the system and various programs. When you select this command, you open a window that lets you select one of four ways to view your memory usage, which looks like this:

```
Select mapping technique:
   ( ) 1 - show only program memory blocks
   ( ) 2 - show only program memory blocks with "hooked" vectors
   ( ) 3 - show all memory blocks
   ( ) 4 - show all memory blocks with "hooked" vectors
```

Press [⇑] or [⇓] to highlight the degree of detail you want to view, then press [Enter].
Whenever I use this command, I like to view all hooks to memory, and so my screen
looks like figure 3.37.

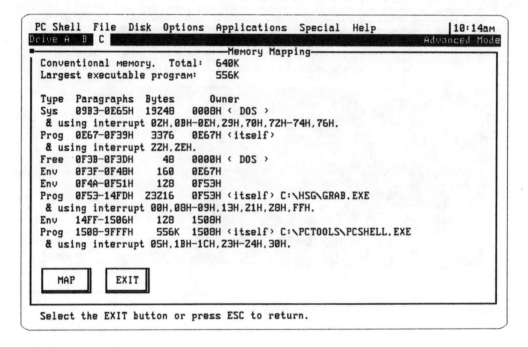

*Figure 3.37. The Memory Map display*

You have to know how programs hook into memory to make much sense of this
screen.

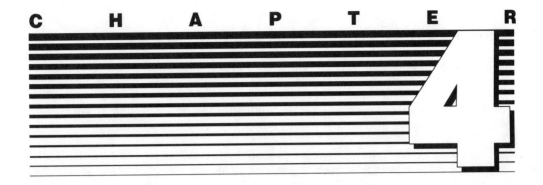

C H A P T E R 4

# USING APPLICATIONS
# IN PC SHELL

Application programs are those that apply themselves to a specific task. Both the PC Shell and Desktop Manager are application programs: the PC Shell applies itself to management of your DOS environment and the Desktop Manager applies itself to routine business chores, such as writing letters, arranging your schedule, making calls, and calculating figures.

For PC Shell, the term *application* means any program that runs in DOS and ends with the file extension .EXE, .COM, or .BAT. These refer, respectively, to executable, command, and batch files. Most application programs, such as those for Lotus 1-2-3 and WordPerfect, run from .EXE or .COM files. These files contain machine code instructions compiled by the manufacturer of the program. Batch files are simple ASCII text files that DOS processes as commands.

# WAYS OF LOADING APPLICATION PROGRAMS

You can load application programs four ways while working in PC Shell:

1.  From the PC Shell Applications pull-down menu. The menu must display the program name (or the name you use to identify the program) and be configured correctly to locate and run the program files.

2.  From the *File List* window by either highlighting a file name and pressing [Ctrl]-[Enter], selecting Launch on the File pull-down menu, or double-clicking Launch with your mouse. To load the application, you can load the *original* program file or you can load a file *created* in the application program.

3.  From the Binary Viewer while viewing the program file or from another viewer while viewing a file created by the program.

4.  From the DOS command line. (This method was described in chapter 2, when you worked with the DOS command line in the PC Shell).

If you've never used PC Shell before, then you probably use the fourth method: entering the command from the DOS command line. The first three methods are specific to PC Shell and will be discussed in this chapter in turn.

# THE APPLICATIONS MENU

The Applications pull-down menu in the PC Shell will vary in appearance from one user to the next, depending upon what programs are on the users' hard disks. When the Applications menu appears for the first time (just after installing PC Tools Deluxe using PCSETUP), the menu reflects the programs that are present on your hard drive and recognized by PCSETUP. The installation program searches the hard disk for the more popular program files; it then installs each program name and launch parameters in the Applications menu.

For example, after I installed my version of PC Tools Deluxe, my Applications pull-down menu looked like figure 4.1.

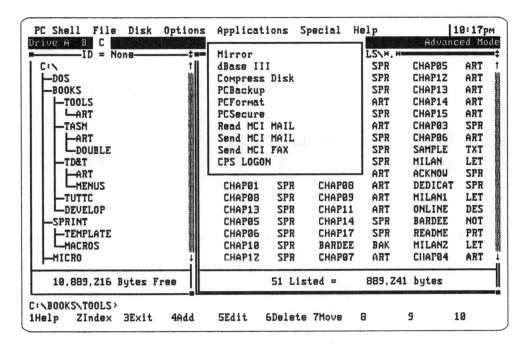

```
 PC Shell  File  Disk  Options  Applications  Special  Help          |10:17PM
 Drive A  B  C                                                  Advanced Mode
 ━━━━━━━━━ID = None━━━━━━━━━━╪══  Mirror                    LS\×,×━━━━━━━━━━━━╪
   C:\                         ↑  dBase III                  SPR   CHAP05   ART ↑
     ├─DOS                         Compress Disk             SPR   CHAP12   ART
     ├─BOOKS                       PCBackup                  SPR   CHAP13   ART
     │  ├─TOOLS                    PCFormat                  ART   CHAP14   ART
     │  └─ART                      PCSecure                  SPR   CHAP15   ART
     ├─TASM                        Read MCI MAIL             ART   CHAP03   SPR
     │  ├─ART                      Send MCI MAIL             SPR   CHAP06   ART
     │  └─DOUBLE                   Send MCI FAX              SPR   SAMPLE   TXT
     ├─TD&T                        CPS LOGON                 SPR   MILAN    LET
     │  ├─ART                                                ART   ACKNOW   SPR
     │  └─MENUS                    CHAP01   SPR   CHAP08     ART   DEDICAT  SPR
     ├─TUTTC                       CHAP08   SPR   CHAP09     ART   MILAN1   LET
     │  └─DEVELOP                  CHAP13   SPR   CHAP11     ART   ONLINE   DES
     ├─SPRINT                      CHAP05   SPR   CHAP14     SPR   BARDEE   NOT
     │  ├─TEMPLATE                 CHAP06   SPR   CHAP17     SPR   README   PRT
     │  └─MACROS                   CHAP10   SPR   BARDEE     BAK   MILAN2   LET
     ├─MICRO                    ↓  CHAP12   SPR   CHAP07     ART   CHAP04   ART ↓
 ┌──────────────────────────┐┌──────────────────────────────────────────────┐
 │   10,889,216 Bytes Free  ││      51 Listed =        889,241 bytes         │
 └──────────────────────────┘└──────────────────────────────────────────────┘
 C:\BOOKS\TOOLS>
 1Help   2Index  3Exit   4Add    5Edit   6Delete 7Move  8       9       10
```

*Figure 4.1. My default Applications pull-down menu*

WordPerfect and dBASE III PLUS were already present on my disk when I installed PC Tools Deluxe. The other program names—such as Mirror, Compress Disk, PCFormat, PCBackup, and PCSecure—are utility programs that come with PC Tools Deluxe. (The utility programs are described in chapter 17).

Notice how your function-key assignments change when the Applications pull-down menu appears. You're given the following function keys to work with:

**[F1] Help**     Opens the Top Line Menus Help screen.

**[F2] Index**     Opens the help index for PC Shell.

**[F3] Exit**     Closes the Applications pull-down menu.

**[F4] Add**     Adds a new program to an entry on the Applications menu list.

**[F5] Edit**     Allows editing of an existing entry on the Applications menu list.

**[F6] Delete**     Deletes an entry on the Applications menu list.

**[F7] Move**      Moves an existing entry on the Applications menu list.

The last four of these keys let you customize the Applications menu for your own use. If PCSETUP didn't recognize a program you like to use, or if you install another program after installing PC Tools Deluxe, you must install the program yourself on the Applications pull-down menu.

## CUSTOMIZING THE APPLICATIONS MENU

To open the Applications menu, first ensure the PC Shell is loaded and displayed on your screen:

   **Press:** [Alt]-[A]

Your Applications pull-down menu should now resemble figure 4.2. At least you should see the PC Tools Deluxe programs, the three activities for MCI Mail, and CPS LOGON.

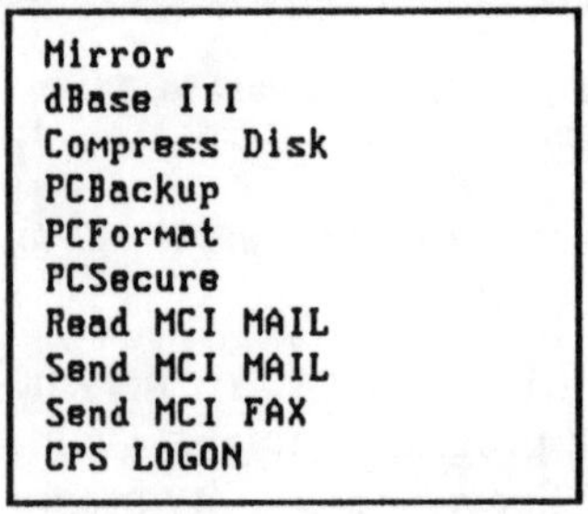

```
Mirror
dBase III
Compress Disk
PCBackup
PCFormat
PCSecure
Read MCI MAIL
Send MCI MAIL
Send MCI FAX
CPS LOGON
```

*Figure 4.2. The Applications menu*

You can launch applications from this menu three ways:

1. Press the highlighted letter assigned to the menu entry.

2. Highlight the menu entry and press [Enter].

3. Highlight the menu entry and double-click your mouse.

The easiest method is to hotkey into the program. For example, to run the Mirror program:

**Press:** [M]

The PC Shell screen disappears and tells you its freeing memory for the program. In a moment your DOS command line appears with the command to load the Mirror program after it:

```
C:\>MIRROR.COM
```

When Mirror is finished running, press any key to return to the PC Shell.

> When you run a program from PC Shell and then bail out of the program temporarily to access DOS, the PC Shell screen will not reappear. You will be left with the raw DOS prompt.

Running programs installed in the Applications menu is very easy. The trick is to design the menu so it serves you.

## Adding New Applications

You can install any DOS application program on the Applications pull-down menu. First, open the menu:

**Press:** [Alt]-[A]

To add an entry:

**Press:** [F4]

This inserts the marker <location of new entry> on the bottom of the menu. You'll be guided by instructions on the bottom line of the screen. Notice also how the assignments for function keys [F4] through [F7] disappear, and [F4] changes to *Accept*. You'll press [F4] to accept all the information you insert for this first entry.

To accept the new location:

**Press:** [Enter]

This opens the *Application Editor* window, which looks like figure 4.3.

```
                         ┌Application Editor┐
      Application.......[                          ]
      Initial Directory..[                             ]
      Execute Path......[                        ]
      Run File Name.....[        ]
      Run File Extension.[    ]
      Run Parameters......[                       ]
      User Prompt........[                    ]
      Keystrokes........[                  ]
      File Specs.......[                   ]

      Quick Run this Application......(Y/N)      [N]
      Run With Selected File.......(Y/N)     [N]
      Wait on Last Application Screen_(Y/N)      [N]
      Exit to DOS when Application ends.(Y/N)      [N]
```

*Figure 4.3. The Application Editor window*

There are 13 settings on this screen that you can use, but you probably won't need to enter information into most of them.

The cursor should be blinking in the first position of the Application field.

For the first example, I will load the Sprint word processing program. If you prefer to load another program, just substitute the program name, executable file, path, and default extension for the values in this example. (The executable file is most likely the file that contains the name or acronym of the program plus the extension .EXE, such as WP.EXE for WordPerfect and 123.EXE for Lotus 1-2-3). Popular programs, such as WordPerfect and 1-2-3, however, will be installed automatically by PCSET-UP, unless you installed them after you installed PC Tools Deluxe.

The Sprint program is run by the file SP.COM that resides in my directory SPRINT off the root directory (C:\SPRINT). I keep my Sprint documents in a directory off the SPRINT directory called DOCS (C:\SPRINT\DOCS). The Sprint programs create files using the default extension .SPR.

**Type:** S^print

To type the caret (^), press [Shift]-[6]. The caret character turns the letter following it into the hotkey for that application. The hotkeyed letter will appear highlighted or in a different color. Make sure you don't use the same letter for two different programs, otherwise only the first program name on the list will respond when you press the hotkey. I chose the *p* as the hotkey for Sprint because the letter *S* is already used by the PCSecure program.

**Press:** [Enter]

**Type:** C:\SPRINT\DOCS

This is called *Initial Directory.* It assigns the disk and directory you enter here as the current directory.

**Press:** [Enter]

**Type:** C:\SPRINT

This is called the *Execute Path,* which means the drive and directory that's current when the program starts up.

**Press:** [Enter] twice

**Type:** SP

**Press:** [Enter]

**Type:** COM

Your *Application Editor* window should now look like figure 4.4.

```
┌─────────────────Application Editor──────────────────┐
│                                                      │
│ Application......[^Sprint              ]             │
│ Initial Directory..[C:SPRINT\DOCS           ]        │
│ Execute Path....[C:SPRINT              ]             │
│ Run File Name....[SP      ]                          │
│ Run File Extension.[COM]                             │
│ Run Parameters....[                   ]              │
│ User Prompt....[                 ]                   │
│ Keystrokes....[                ]                     │
│ File Specs....[                ]                     │
│                                                      │
│ Quick Run this Application.....(Y/N)    [N]          │
│ Run With Selected File......(Y/N)    [N]             │
│ Wait on Last Application Screen..(Y/N)  [N]          │
│ Exit to DOS when Application ends.(Y/N)  [N]         │
└──────────────────────────────────────────────────────┘
```

*Figure 4.4. The Application Editor window adding Sprint*

It's easy to insert characters into fields in this window. Some fields have a fixed length marked by the right bracket. Others allow you to insert more characters than shown by the field length. You can use the arrow keys to edit your entries.

To save this first entry:

> **Press:** [F4]

This removes the *Application Editor* window from your screen and returns you to the PC Shell screen.

To open the new entry, make sure that the PC Shell is open:

> **Press:** [Alt]-[A]

> **Press:** [P]

You should see the message saying PC Shell is freeing up memory, then the PC Shell screen will disappear to be replaced by your DOS screen. You'll see the command appear that loads Sprint and then you'll see the Sprint screen (or whatever program you've just inserted in your first entry).

Now see what happens when you exit the program:

> **Press:** [Alt]-[Q]

The Sprint screen will disappear and you'll return to the PC Shell screen.

At this point, take a closer look at all 13 fields and then use more of them to fine tune the Sprint entry. To view them in the Application Editor:

> **Press:** [Alt]-[A]

> **Press:** [F4]

> **Press:** [Enter]

**Application.** The name you want to give the program that will appear on the Applications menu. You can use up to 23 characters for a program name. The only difficulty here is figuring out which letter you want to serve as the hotkey.

**Initial Directory.** The drive and directory that become current when the program starts up. If you keep your data files separate from your program files—in this case, your document files separate from the Sprint program files—you should enter the name of the data directory. If you don't enter a specific directory, PC Shell looks in the current directory for the files. If the program you want to load is on your path, then the program will be loaded and the current directory remains current. You can insert a maximum of 64 characters in this field.

**Execute Path.** The drive and directory that contain the file for the program you want to load. There's no need to enter this information if the program you want to load resides in the current directory or is in your DOS path statement. You can insert a maximum of 64 characters in this field.

**Run File Name.** The program file name that runs the program. This is the part that comes before the extension, for example SP for SP.COM, WP for WP.EXE and 123 for 123.EXE.

**Run File Extension.** The extension of the file you want to run, or the last three characters after the period. For example, COM for SP.COM and EXE for WP.EXE.

**Run Parameters**. Any command-line switches you like to use when you run the program. For example, you can run the Compress program on drive D with the D parameter. You can insert a maximum of 128 characters in this field.

**User Prompt.** A prompt message you design for special purposes. You may wish to be prompted to insert backup disks if you're going to run PC Backup, or to insert a program disk in drive A if the program is copy protected. A prompt message will appear before the program is loaded. You can insert up to 128 characters in this field.

**Keystrokes.** A key or series of keystrokes you want to pass to the program as keyboard input. For example, upon loading Sprint, I always prefer to start working with a file formatted as a daily log. You can insert up to 128 characters in this field. You'll find out more about using keystrokes in the section Editing Entries.

**File Specs.** Lets you launch a program associated with a file containing the specification from the File List window. For example, if you enter *.SPR in this field, you're specifying files with the .SPR file extension. Whenever you highlight or select a file in the File List ending in .SPR and press [Ctrl]-[Enter], you'll load the program associated with the file, in this case Sprint.

**Quick Run this Application**. Quick-running an application runs the program without freeing up any memory. This takes less time than conventional running. With small programs, you might want to quick-run them just for a single task. You probably can't quick-run a large program because it needs all the memory you can provide. The default answer in this field is no, which means that the program will not be quick-run.

**Run With Selected File.** Loads the selected file in the *File List* window. If no file name is selected, it loads the currently highlighted file. This feature depends upon the ability of the program to accept a file name at the DOS command line after the program name. Most word processors allow this. Some programs, such as dBASE and Lotus 1-2-3, don't.

**Wait on Last Application Screen.** Pauses the program on its last screen and provides a message telling you to press any key or double-click your mouse to return to PC Shell.

**Exit to DOS when Application ends.** Returns to DOS after the application has finished running. The default answer is no, which returns you to your PC Shell screen.

These various fields might not make complete sense to you; they're the sort of settings you have to experiment with to understand how they really work. Fortunately, you can't do any damage to data by this type of experimentation.

Once you've inserted an entry, you can use it, edit it, move it to another location on the Applications menu, or delete it.

Before you proceed with this chapter to learn how to perform these operations, first make sure the Applications Editor or Applications pull-down menu is not showing on your screen.

Press [Esc] once if viewing the Applications pull-down menu, twice if viewing the Applications Editor screen:

**Press:** [Esc]

## Editing Entries

You can edit entries as easily as you created them. This example will edit Sprint; however, the principles behind this example are the same with any applications program.

To edit an entry, first open the Applications menu:

**Press:** [Alt]-[A]

Then start the edit process:

**Press:** [F5]

Now select the entry you want to edit:

**Highlight:** Sprint

**Press:** [Enter]

This opens the *Applications Editor* window and displays the information for the Sprint entry.

To change the hotkey from *P* to *T*, place your cursor on the caret (^):

**Press:** [Del]

Now move your cursor to the letter *T*.

**Press:** [Shift]-[6]

This should make the application name look like this: `Sprin^t`.

If you want to launch Sprint by highlighting or selecting a Sprint file, move your cursor to the File Specs field:

**Type:** *.SPR

**Press:** [Enter]

When you've made these changes, the *Application Editor* box should look like figure 4.5

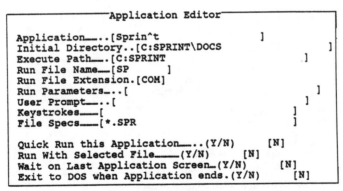

*Figure 4.5. The Applications Editor box after editing*

To save these changes:

**Press:** [F4]

This returns you to the PC Shell menu. Now try the change out. First, open the Applications pull-down menu:

**Press:** [Alt]-[A]

Notice that the Sprint program name is hotkeyed by the letter *T* and not *P*.

## Using Keystrokes

The Keystrokes field, located in the Applications Editor, refers to the key or keys you want to press immediately upon entering a program. For example, when I load Sprint I almost always insert formatting commands that apply to all of my documents. I can insert these keystrokes in my Applications menu entry for Sprint, and my documents will automatically be formatted.

The best way to learn how to use Keystrokes is to see how PCSETUP recorded them for the default entries it inserted automatically into your Applications menu.

Open the menu and edit the entry for CPS LOGON (this program is used to automatically log on to the Central Point Software bulletin board).

**Press:** [F5]

**Highlight:** CPS LOGON

**Press:** [Enter]

This opens the *Application Editor* window for the CPS LOGON entry as shown in figure 4.6.

```
┌──────────────Application Editor───────────────┐
│                                                │
│ Application......[CPS LOGO^N            ]       │
│ Initial Directory..[C:\PCTOOLS              ]  │
│ Execute Path.....[C:\PCTOOLS            ]      │
│ Run File Name.....[DESKTOP ]                   │
│ Run File Extension.[EXE]                       │
│ Run Parameters....[/mm·····················]   │
│ User Prompt.....[                        ]     │
│ Keystrokes.......[tm4<Enter>           ]       │
│ File Specs......[                     ]        │
│                                                │
│ Quick Run this Application......(Y/N)    [N]   │
│ Run With Selected File........(Y/N)    [N]     │
│ Wait on Last Application Screen..(Y/N)   [N]   │
│ Exit to DOS when Application ends.(Y/N)    [N] │
└────────────────────────────────────────────────┘
```

*Figure 4.6. The Applications Editor window*

The keystrokes inserted for this entry are fairly simple: tm4<Enter>. If you haven't used Modem Telecommunications in the Telecommunications module (described in chapters 12 and 13), then these keystrokes may not make much sense to you. To understand them, it's necessary to realize what happens when you call this entry from the Applications menu.

First, the Desktop Manager program file DESKTOP.EXE is loaded from the C:\PCTOOLS directory. The /MM switch is used to override whatever modules were already popped up the last time you exited from the Desktop Manager. This means that the Desktop main menu appears regardless of your previous work.

Once the Desktop Manager program has been loaded, the keystrokes go into effect:

1. The two letters, tm, open the Telecommunications screen. The T is the hotkey for *Telecommunications* on the Desktop main menu, and the M is the hotkey for *Modem Telecommunications*.

2. The number 4 highlights the fourth entry in the Telecommunications screen, which in the default configuration is the number for calling the Central Point Software bulletin board.

3. The command <Enter> does the same thing as pressing [Enter]: It dials the highlighted entry.

At this point, the script file assigned to the Central Point Software phone book entry (CPS.SCR) takes over and logs you onto the bulletin board. (You can learn more about script files in chapter 15).

Keystrokes are played back individually and in order, just as if you had pressed them yourself after the program loaded. Which keys you can use, what order you use them in, and their effect depend upon the program in which you use them. For example, the A key opens the Appointment Scheduler module when executed in the Desktop main menu, but the same key opens the Algebraic calculator when the Calculator menu is showing.

There are five key commands that are special to keystrokes in the Application Editor:

**<Delay#>**      Sets a delay of # number of seconds before the next keystroke is executed. <Delay10> sets a delay of 10 seconds.

**<Enter>**      Does the same thing as pressing [Enter].

**<Esc>**      Does the same thing as pressing [Esc].

**<Path>**         Passes the full name of the path and file name you've selected in the File List window to the current program.

**<Typein>**       Lets you type in the name of the file you want to use.

You might want to take a look at another example. Edit the entry for dBASE:

**Press:** [F5]

**Highlight:** dBASE

**Press:** [Enter]

This displays the window shown in figure 4.7.

```
┌──────────────────Application Editor──────────────────┐
│ Application......[^dBase III                ]         │
│ Initial Directory..[C:\DBASE                    ]     │
│ Execute Path....[C:\DBASE                    ]        │
│ Run File Name....[DBASE   ]                           │
│ Run File Extension.[COM]                              │
│ Run Parameters...[                          ]         │
│ User Prompt.....[                         ]           │
│ Keystrokes......[<Enter><Delay3><Esc>USE <Delay]      │
│ File Specs......[*.DBF                    ]           │
│                                                       │
│ Quick Run this Application.....(Y/N)    [N]           │
│ Run With Selected File.......(Y/N)    [N]             │
│ Wait on Last Application Screen.(Y/N)   [N]           │
│ Exit to DOS when Application ends.(Y/N)   [N]         │
└───────────────────────────────────────────────────────┘
```

*Figure 4.7. The Updated Applications Editor Window*

The entry runs the dBASE III PLUS program by loading the file DBASE.COM in the C:\DBASE directory and then runs the keystrokes :

<Enter><Delay3><Esc>USE <Delay1><Path><Enter>

You can't see the last three keystrokes because they run beyond the right margin of the *Application Editor* window.

The keystrokes presume that you have selected a valid database file before you launch the dBASE program. This is what these keystrokes do in sequence:

1.  <Enter> removes the dBASE copyright notice from your screen.

2.  <Delay3> pauses the unfolding of subsequent keystrokes for three seconds. (This gives dBASE time to remove the copyright notice and display the default Assist interface.)

**122**

3. \<Esc\> removes the Assist interface and provides you with the famous dBASE dot prompt.

4. USE issues the dBASE command preparing dBASE to load the program you specify.

5. \<Delay1\> pauses the unfolding of subsequent keystrokes for 1 second. (This gives dBASE time to execute the USE command and respond with a request of which database you want to use.)

6. \<Path\> inserts the path and file name of the selected database file.

7. \<Enter\> inserts the path and file name into dBASE for processing.

You might want to explore the other default entries to see how PCSETUP configured the keystrokes for each one.

## Locating and Moving Entries

You can place entries in specific slots of the Applications pull-down menu before you create them, or you can move entries after you've created them.

To position a new entry halfway down the list on the Applications menu:

> **Press:** [Alt]-[A]

> **Press:** [F4]

> **Press:** [⇓] several times

Position the marker \<location of new entry\> where you want the new entry to appear and:

> **Press:** [Enter]

This fixes the location and opens the *Application Editor* window.

You can also move an entry once it's been inserted. To move our Sprint entry to the top of the list, open the Applications menu:

> **Press:** [Alt]-[A]

Begin the moving process:

> **Press:** [F7]

Now highlight the entry you want to use:

> **Highlight:** Sprint

> **Press:** [Enter]

Move the entry to its new position. As you press [⬆] or [⬇], you'll see the entry move on the list. Once you've positioned it correctly:

> **Press:** [Enter]

Your new menu is ready to use.

## Deleting Entries

You can delete entries on the Applications menu as easily as you inserted or moved them. First open the menu:

> **Press:** [Alt]-[A]

First, begin the deletion procedure:

> **Press:** [F7]

Now select the entry you want to delete. To delete the Sprint entry:

> **Highlight:** Sprint

PC Shell will display a confirmation message. To continue:

> **Press:** [Entcr]

The Sprint entry will then be deleted from the Applications pull-down menu.

# LAUNCHING PROGRAMS

Launching means loading a program directly from the File List window in the PC Shell.

There are two ways you can launch a program. The first way is to launch the program file name. An example of this is launching WordPerfect using the file name WP.EXE in the *File List* window. The second way to launch a program is to an associated file name, for example, launching a document created with WordPerfect.

## Launching a Program with its File Name

To launch a program using its file name, just highlight or select the proper file name and press [Ctrl]-[Enter]. For example, to launch the WordPerfect program using the file name WP.EXE, move to the WORD directory in the Tree List window. Then press [Tab] to move to the *File List* window and highlight WP.EXE. To launch the program:

**Press:** [Ctrl]-[Enter]

> You can also use two alternate methods for launching a program with the program file name. Instead of pressing [Ctrl]-[Enter], you can select the Launch command on the File pull-down menu or you can select the file name and double-clicking with the mouse.

PC Shell will display a window, shown in figure 4.8, that lets you specify and program parameters you wish to run with the file.

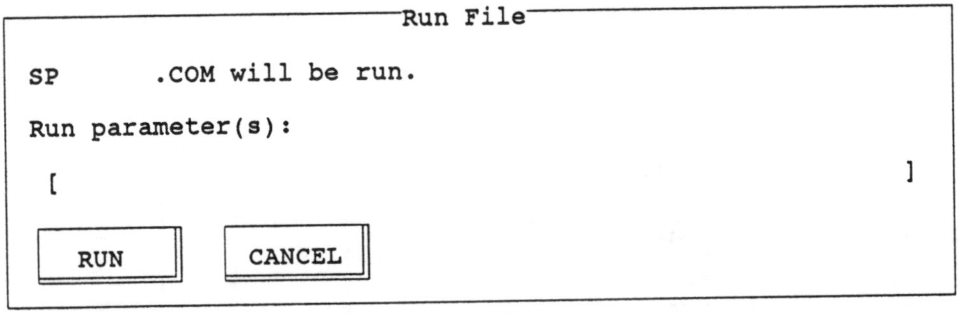

```
┌──────────────────────Run File──────────────────────────┐
│                                                         │
│   SP        .COM will be run.                           │
│                                                         │
│   Run parameter(s):                                     │
│                                                         │
│   [                                                   ] │
│                                                         │
│   ┌─────────┐  ┌───────────┐                            │
│   │  RUN    │  │  CANCEL   │                            │
│   └─────────┘  └───────────┘                            │
└─────────────────────────────────────────────────────────┘
```

*Figure 4.8. The Run File box*

You'll find your cursor in the first position of the Run parameter(s) field. You can type a file name or any switches that configure the program the way you want to use it.

Once you've typed the parameters, or if you want to skip over the parameters entirely:

**Press:** [Enter] twice

This highlights and accepts the *RUN* command. The PC Shell screen disappears and you'll see the selected drive and pathway appear after the DOS prompt, followed by the program path name. After a few moments, the WordPerfect screen will appear.

The beauty of launching programs from the PC Shell screen is that when you exit the program, the PC Shell screen returns to your display. This lets you launch another program or perform some DOS housekeeping chores without having to pop the shell up again.

> If you've loaded the PC Shell as a resident program and you pop it open at the DOS prompt to launch various programs, you can still pop the PC Shell open while you're working in any one of the programs. This gives you the full use of PC Shell. Just don't launch another program when PC Shell has been popped over another program that has already loaded.

## Launching a Program with an Associated File

You can also launch programs using file names associated with the program. To do this, you first have to insert the program as an entry in the Applications pull-down menu.

For this example, I'll assume you have inserted an entry for WordPerfect that looks like figure 4.9.

```
                         Application Editor
  Application.......[^WordPerfect                ]
  Initial Directory..[C:WP\DOCS                                ]
  Execute Path....[C:WP                               ]
  Run File Name....[WP    ]
  Run File Extension.[EXE]
  Run Parameters....[                                ]
  User Prompt.....[                               ]
  Keystrokes....[                          ]
  File Specs....[                          ]

  Quick Run this Application.....(Y/N)      [N]
  Run With Selected File.......(Y/N)    [N]
  Wait on Last Application Screen.(Y/N)     [N]
  Exit to DOS when Application ends.(Y/N)     [N]
```

*Figure 4.9.  The Application Editor for WordPerfect*

To launch this program using associated files, you should edit the *File Specs* field. For this example, move your cursor to this field and:

**Type:** *.DOC

This is the default extension created by WordPerfect if you don't declare another extension. Now, whenever you highlight or select a file name ending in .DOC and then launch that file, WordPerfect will load automatically.

**126**

You should watch out when using the .DOC extension. Other word processing programs also use this extension by default, including MultiMate Advantage and Microsoft Word. This means that every file name ending in .DOC, regardless of whether it was created in WordPerfect or another program, will launch the WordPerfect program.

Once you've configured the WordPerfect entry this way, exit the PC Shell and see if it works. For this example, I'll use a file named CHAP02.DOC, but you can use any text file ending in .DOC.

> **Highlight:** CHAP02.DOC

> **Press:** [Ctrl]-[Enter]

You won't be given the option for entering any parameters. The PC Shell screen will disappear, the command for loading WordPerfect will be passed to your DOS command line, and the WordPerfect screen will appear. The file you used to launch WordPerfect will *not* appear in your WordPerfect screen. You'll have to load that yourself, specify the file in the *Run with Selected File* field for the WordPerfect Applications menu entry, or launch the WordPerfect program file WP.EXE and enter the file as a parameter.

Whenever you exit a program launched from the PC Shell, you'll return to the PC Shell when you exit the program. You can always access PC Shell from within a program if it has been installed resident.

## Using a Viewer

You can also launch a program while viewing the program file or an associated file in any one of the viewers provided as part of PC Shell. As with launching programs in general:

- You don't need to install the program on the Applications menu if you're viewing a program file (.BAT, .COM, or .EXE) in the Binary Viewer.

- You do have to install the program and associate file specifications if you want to launch the program while viewing an associated file in a viewer.

For example, take a quick view of the WordPerfect program WP.EXE in the Binary Viewer:

> **Highlight:** WP.EXE

> **Press:** [F2]

This opens the highlighted file. Because it is a binary file it is displayed in the Binary Viewer. To launch this program file, notice that the [F4] function key at the bottom of your screen will Launch the file.

**Press:** [F4]

You'll be shown the *Run File* window, which lets you specify any parameters.

**Press:** [Enter] twice

WordPerfect will be loaded and you'll see the WordPerfect editing screen. When you exit WordPerfect, you'll return to the Binary Viewer still displaying the contents of WP.EXE.

You can load WordPerfect while viewing a file ending in .DOC, as long as the *.DOC specific has been entered in the File Specs field for the WordPerfect entry on the Applications menu (as you did earlier).

To launch the example associated file:

**Highlight:** CHAP02.DOC

**Press:** [F4]

You'll move directly into the WordPerfect editing screen.

## USING PC SHELL AS AN APPLICATIONS LAUNCHER ONLY

Launching applications from the PC Shell is such a useful procedure, it's possible to configure your version of PC Shell to only launch applications. This locks out all the other commands and procedures and keeps someone who shouldn't have access to all your files away from working with the full capabilities of PC Shell.

To use the PC Shell as an Applications Launcher, open the Change User Level submenu screen:

**Press:** [Alt]-[O]-[C]-[U]

The submenu looks like figure 4.10.

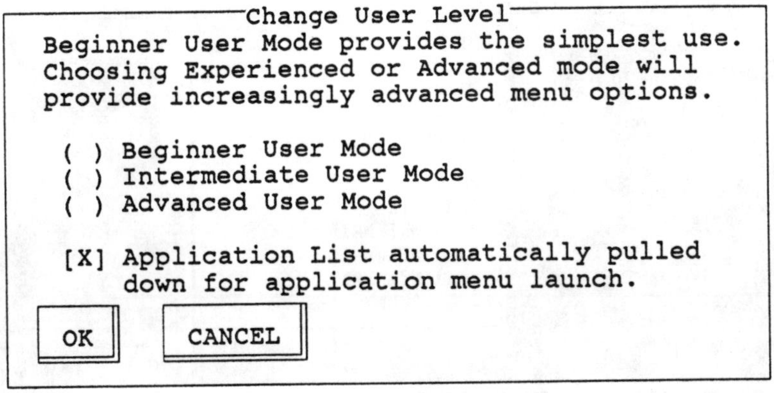

```
┌──────────────────Change User Level──────────────────┐
│ Beginner User Mode provides the simplest use.        │
│ Choosing Experienced or Advanced mode will           │
│ provide increasingly advanced menu options.          │
│                                                      │
│   ( ) Beginner User Mode                             │
│   ( ) Intermediate User Mode                         │
│   ( ) Advanced User Mode                             │
│                                                      │
│   [X] Application List automatically pulled          │
│       down for application menu launch.              │
│  ┌──────┐  ┌──────────┐                              │
│  │  OK  │  │  CANCEL  │                              │
│  └──────┘  └──────────┘                              │
└──────────────────────────────────────────────────────┘
```

*Figure 4.10. The Change User Level window*

To toggle Application List on:

**Press:** [L]

Once an X appears next to that selection:

**Press:** [Enter] twice

This returns you to a highly modified version of the PC Shell screen, which looks like figure 4.11.

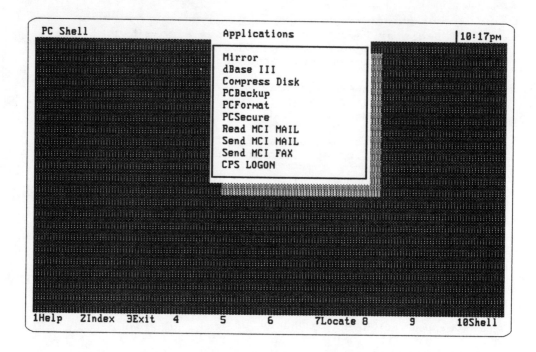

```
PC Shell              Applications                    |10:17PM
                  ┌─────────────────────┐
                  │ Mirror              │
                  │ dBase III           │
                  │ Compress Disk       │
                  │ PCBackup            │
                  │ PCFormat            │
                  │ PCSecure            │
                  │ Read MCI MAIL       │
                  │ Send MCI MAIL       │
                  │ Send MCI FAX        │
                  │ CPS LOGON           │
                  └─────────────────────┘

 1Help    2Index  3Exit   4     5     6     7Locate 8     9     10Shell
```

*Figure 4.11. PC Shell configured to launch applications only*

This limits most of your work in the PC Shell to launching applications. Five function keys are active in this version of PC Shell. The only two important ones are [F7] Locate, which help you locate files throughout your system, and [F10] Menu. You can't activate any menu by pressing [Alt], but you can access your previous version of PC Shell by pressing [F10].

**Press:** [F10]

Your previous version of the PC Shell reappears. You can open up menus in this screen as before, but you can only access commands using hotkeys. You can't access a command by highlighting it and pressing [Enter].

After reconfiguring PC Shell to become an applications launcher and when you exit the PC Shell, you'll be asked to save or discard this change. If you save it, PC Shell will always appear as shown in figure 4.11 after you load it.

To return the full use of PC Shell, reopen the Change User Level submenu and toggle Application List off, then exit PC Shell and save the new configuration.

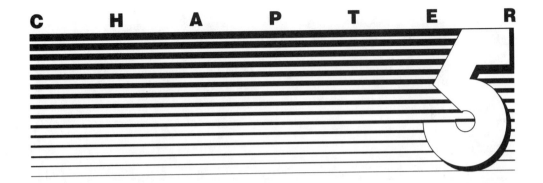

CHAPTER

5

# THE DESKTOP
# MANAGER

In chapter 1 you took a quick tour of some of the Desktop Manager features. This chapter provides a more thorough explanation of the ways you can load the Desktop Manager and use its features.

## OPENING THE DESKTOP MANAGER

As explained in chapter 1, you can load the Desktop Manager two ways: as a standard program and as a resident program. To load it as a standard program:

**Type:** DESKTOP

**Press:** [Enter]

This presumes that either your PC Tools directory is part of your path or you're logged in to your PC Tools directory.

To run the Desktop Manager as a resident program, you must first load it into memory:

**Type:** DESKTOP/R

**Press:** [Enter]

Use the hotkeys to pop up the program:

**Press:** [Ctrl]-[Spacebar]

When the Desktop main menu appears, your screen should look like figure 5.1.

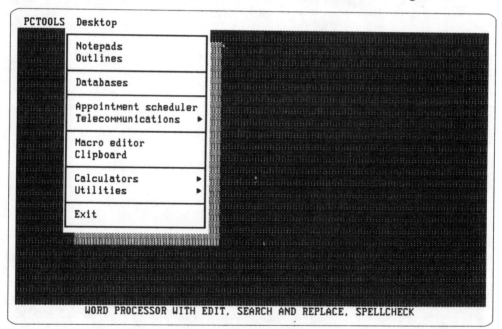

*Figure 5.1. The Desktop main menu*

The top line shows you're working in the Desktop Manager. If you loaded the PC Shell resident before loading the Desktop Manager, you should see 11 commands on the Desktop menu, as shown in figure 5.1. If you didn't load the PC Shell as resident, you'll see only 10: the command *PC Shell* will not appear.

Loading the PC Shell resident first lets you access PC Shell from the Desktop main menu, but I find this superfluous. When I want to open the PC Shell over any screen in the Desktop Manager, I just press [Ctrl]-[Esc], and as long as PC Shell has been loaded resident, it will pop up, regardless of whether I loaded it before or after the Desktop Manager.

## Submenus

There are three submenus under the Desktop main menu, as shown in figure 5.2.

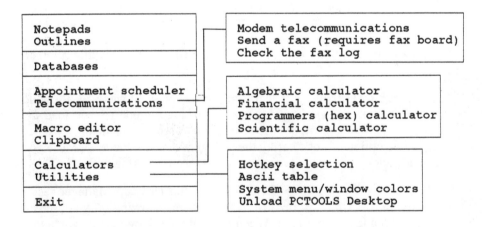

*Figure 5.2. Three submenus under the Desktop main menu*

Three function keys have assignments in this screen that aren't shown:

**[F1] Help**    Opens context-sensitive interactive help for the highlighted menu selection or the current module you're working in.

**[F2] Index**     Opens the general help index.

**[F3] Exit**     Quits the Desktop Manager and returns you to your previous work.

When you load the Desktop Manager as a standard program, the various module files will be called into play as you select them from the Desktop menu. This keeps your memory usage to a minimum.

## Switches

When you load the Desktop Manager, particularly as a resident program, you can use various switches that change its appearance and behavior.

The following is a list of the 16 acceptable switches you can use when loading the Desktop Manager.

**/350**     The *VGA switch*. Displays features in the program in 350 lines if you have VGA display screen. This means you can see more things on your screen, such as more text files in the Notepads window, however, the tradeoff is that everything appears smaller and often harder to see.

**/C#**     The *communications port switch,* also called *base port address switch*. You use this switch followed, by the number 3 or 4 to specify COM3 or COM4 for IBM PCs with serial ports installed. These two serial ports are standard on PS/2 computers but not on IBM PCs, including XTs and ATs.

**/CS**     The *clear screen switch*. Clears the screen of whatever was showing before loading the Desktop Manager in resident mode (if you load the program in standard mode, the screen is cleared automatically). You're given the option of not clearing the screen in resident mode, because you might want to keep your eyes on what you were working with.

**/DQ**     The *Desktop quick switch*. Lets you load the Desktop Manager faster from your DOS prompt because whatever was showing on your screen before it loaded is not saved. When using the Desktop quick switch, you will *not* be able to pop the Desktop Manager back down again to resume your previous work.

**/IN**     The *Hercules InColor card switch*. Lets you run the program in color if you're using a Hercules InColor card. If you don't use this switch, the program will be displayed in black and white because resident programs can cause some conflict with Hercules InColor card displays.

/IM      The *disabling mouse switch*. Disables any mouse you have installed. This prevents input conflicts if you use an older mouse.

/LE      The *exchange left for right mouse switch*. Swaps control behavior of the left and right buttons on a mouse.

/LCD      The *liquid crystal display switch*. Configures your screen display for a laptop LCD screen.

/MM      The *minus modules switch*. Lets you run the Desktop Manager without using any of the modules that were in the stack the last time you used the Desktop Manager in resident mode. If you don't use this switch, the modules that were saved in currently active windows will be made active again.

/Odrive      The *Other drive switch*. Lets you swap data to a drive other than the default drive by specifying the drive letter after the switch (for example, /OD swaps data to the D drive). The default drive is the drive that's current when you load the program in standard mode or pop up the program in resident mode.

         Periodically, the Desktop Manager moves data to the DESKTOP.OVL, DESKTOP.IMG, and DESKTOP.THM files. The program needs to know where these files are, or else it won't work. You can use the /O switch to place these files on a RAM drive or in extended memory for more rapid performance. Since these can grow in size as you use the program, you must make sure enough space is available on the drive you specify, or the default drive will be used regardless of your instructions.

/R      The *resident switch*. Loads the program in TSR mode. Without this switch, the Desktop Manager is loaded as a standard program.

/RA      The *resident appointment switch*. Loads the program in resident mode and automatically pops open the Appointment Scheduler module. This way, you can see what is on your to-do list before you begin any other work.

/RL      The *large memory switch*. Loads Desktop Manager resident in the large mode, occupying 241 kilobytes of memory. This is the default setting.

/RM      The *medium memory switch*. Loads Desktop Manager resident in the medium mode, occupying 158 kilobytes of memory.

/RS      The *small memory switch*. Loads Desktop Manager resident in the small mode, occupying 119 kilobytes of memory.

**/RT**      The *tiny memory switch*. Loads Desktop Manager resident in the tiny mode, occupying 11 kilobytes of RAM.

You can use several switches at the same time, as long as they don't contradict each other. If your switches are contradictory, only the rightmost switch will have an effect because parsing is done from right to left. For example, the first switch read in the command DESKTOP/R/T/M is /M which allocates memory usage. The /T switch, which also allocates memory usage, will be disregarded.

When setting memory size with a memory-usage switch, you do not have to separate the resident switch and the memory-usage switch with a slash. For example, you can load the program as resident and specify that it occupies the medium resident mode by typing either /R/M or /RM.

You can place switches adjacent to each other or separate them with one or more spaces. I prefer a single space between each switch; it helps to keep track of them. For example, I sometimes load the Desktop Manager using DESKTOP /R /S. The characters for each switch must always appear together; however, / R is not a valid switch.

## Examples For Using Switches

If you want to become adept at using the Desktop Manager, you should experiment with a few of the examples that follow. They demonstrate the effects of loading the Desktop Manager using the most common switches. Begin at your DOS prompt:

**Type:** DESKTOP /DQ

**Press:** [Enter]

This loads the program more quickly that usual, because the previous screen display is not saved.

Before you try another switch, you must first unload the Desktop Manager program from memory. A switch won't have an effect on the program unless it's loaded along with the program.

**Type:** KILL

**Press:** [Enter]

This runs a small PC Tools batch file program, called KILL.BAT, that removes the resident-loaded Desktop Manager from memory. It will also remove the PC Shell if that's been loaded as resident.

The KILL.BAT program works only from your root directory if you placed your PCTOOLS directory on your path. Otherwise, you'll have to enter that directory first (CD PCTOOLS) and run the command.

If you have a VGA monitor, load the Desktop Manager in VGA mode:

**Type:** DESKTOP /350

**Press:** [Enter]

If your screen is not configured for VGA, this command will have no effect or it will blank out your screen, in which case you'll probably have to reboot your computer.

If you want to see how the clear screen switch works, first load the Desktop Manager in resident mode using the /CS switch:

**Type:** DESKTOP /R /CS

**Press:** [Enter]

Now load a standard program, such as a word processor, database, or spreadsheet program that fills your screen. Next, pop up the Desktop Manager:

**Press:** [Ctrl]-[Spacebar]

You'll notice that only the main menu and top menu bar appear. Most of what you were looking at before remains on your screen. This is helpful when you want to use the Notepads editor to copy information to or from the program you were working with before you popped up the Notepads.

## USING THE UTILITIES COMMAND

The *Utilities* command does not lead you into a module like the other commands on the Desktop menu. Instead, you're given a menu of four additional commands that let you twiddle with features in the program, including unloading the Desktop Manager from memory.

Before exploring the *Utilities* command, kill the Desktop Manager if you've loaded it as resident.

When the Desktop menu is showing:

**Press:** [U]

This opens the Utilities submenu, which lets you select one of the following items:

**Hotkey selection**      Opens a menu with four features of the Desktop Manager that have been assigned to unique hotkeys.

**Ascii table**      Opens a representation of the ASCII character table including the 256 characters and their equivalents in decimal and hexadecimal notation.

**System menu/window colors**      Opens the *color selection* box and works with the *Change colors* command.

**Unload PCTOOLS Desktop**      Unloads the PC Tools Desktop Manager program when installed as a TSR program. You'll be given a warning message reminding you of the conditions under which you can unload the programs.

## Resetting Hotkeys

The Desktop Manager comes loaded with four features that can be accessed by pressing hotkeys.

Four features in the Desktop Manager program have been assigned hotkeys, and you can see these by opening the PCTOOLS *Desktop Hotkey selection* box, shown in figure 5.3. From the Desktop menu:

    **Press:** [U]-[H]

```
┌──────═ PCTOOLS Desktop Hotkey Selection ═──────┐
│                                                │
│  DESKTOP HOTKEY: <CTRL><SPACE>                 │
│                                                │
│ CLIPBOARD PASTE: <CTRL><INS>                   │
│                                                │
│  CLIPBOARD COPY: <CTRL><DEL>                   │
│                                                │
│ SCREEN AUTODIAL: <CTRL><O>                     │
│                                                │
└────────────────────────────────────────────────┘
```

*Figure 5.3. The PCTOOLS Desktop Hotkey selection box*

There are four hotkey assignments:

**Desktop Hotkey**  Pops the Desktop main menu up or down.

**Clipboard Paste**  Pastes whatever is in the Clipboard to your current screen. This can be a PC Tools module screen or an outside application screen, such as WordPerfect or Lotus 1-2-3.

**Clipboard Copy**  Prepares to copy whatever is showing on your screen to the Clipboard, within the limits of the Clipboard.

**Screen Autodial**  Automatically dials the first number the program finds on your screen. A modem must be connected and turned on.

To change any of these hotkey assignments, highlight the feature whose keys you want to change, then press the new hotkeys you want to use. For example, if you use WordStar, you might want to change autodial from [Ctrl]-[O] to [Ctrl]-[Z]. This is a more sensible selection because WordStar (and programs that emulate it) use [Ctrl]-[O] to adjust the margins. If you do not change the autodial hotkey, you might not be able to use autodial.

To reset the autodial hotkey:

**Highlight:** SCREEN AUTODIAL

**Press:** [Ctrl]-[Z]

The bottom hotkeys selection should now look like this:

SCREEN AUTODIAL: <CTRL><Z>

The new keys work as soon as you assign them, and they are saved when you close the window.

If you reassign the hotkeys that pop open the Desktop main menu, you may find you can't pop the program open or closed. If this happens, exit to DOS (reboot if you have to), kill all PC Tools programs, then load the Desktop as a standard program and reset the hotkeys to their original settings.

Be cautious when want to open the Desktop or Window pull-down menus while working in this screen. One of the four hotkey selections remains highlighted at all times. Pressing the two keys [Alt]-[D] or [Alt]-[W] assigns the two keys as hotkeys to whatever hotkey is currently highlighted.

To open either pull-down menu available in the *Hotkeys selection* box, first press [Alt] (or [F10]) and then press [D] (for the Desktop pull-down menu) or [W] (for the Window pull-down menu). The top menu bar will remain highlighted.

If you inadvertently change a hotkey assignment while trying to pull down a menu, reset the hotkeys immediately, or the change will become permanent.

### Using Hotkeys to Pop the Program Up and Down

If the Desktop Manager program is loaded into your computer's memory as a TSR program, you can pop up the Desktop main menu at any time by pressing [Ctrl]-[Spacebar]. You can also use this hotkey combination to pop down the Desktop Manager.

If you've already worked with the Desktop Manager program and popped it down using the hotkeys, pressing those keys again to pop it back up, returns you to the screen you were looking at when you popped it down. This lets you move into and out of a specific feature quickly and easily.

### Using Hotkeys for Autodialing

You can use hotkeys to dial phone numbers from the Desktop Manager. Dialing numbers automatically can be helpful if you frequently make calls and work with a computer. Although the Telecommunications module lets you dial numbers in a phone book, there may be times when you want to make a quick call and remain looking at your current screen.

To do this, just type the number you want to dial (anywhere on your screen) and press [Ctrl]-[O]. The Desktop Manager will load its overlay programs and display a box with the number you've just typed in it. It will then ask whether you want to proceed with the call, search for another number, or cancel the autodial.

For example, type in an innocuous phone number, such as the time or weather.

**Press:** [Ctrl]-[O]

When the *Autodial* box appears:

**Press:** [Enter]

This accepts the default answer *Dial,* and dials the displayed number.

When you autodial a number, the program begins searching for numbers in the top-left corner of the screen and proceeds to scan each line until it either finds a number or scans the entire screen without finding a number. It displays the first number it runs across. If you want to dial a number that appears further down the screen:

**Press:** [N]

You can try to dial any number. PC Tools will display whatever number it runs across in its *Autodial* box; it won't filter for valid or invalid numbers.

## Viewing the ASCII Table

The ASCII character set is used by IBM and compatible personal computers for screen display. There are 256 characters in each set, and there are various sets. The first 128 characters are usually the same in all sets, the second 128 characters are graphic characters that can vary from set to set. Just because you see ASCII characters on screen doesn't mean you can print them; that depends on which ASCII sets have been installed in the printer.

You can open an ASCII Table from the Utilities submenu by selecting Ascii table on that menu. When you do this, the table appears as shown in figure 5.4.

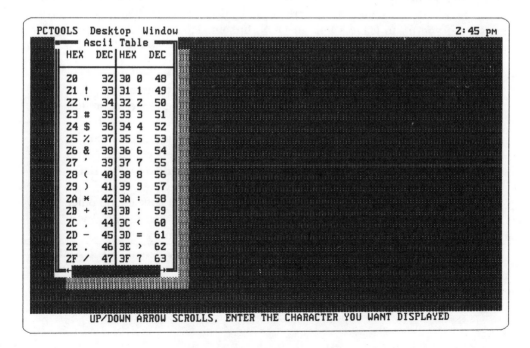

*Figure 5.4. The Ascii table window*

The hexadecimal and decimal values for each character are displayed on either side of the ASCII graphic symbol for the character. You can move down one screen by pressing [⇓] or [PgDn], and you can move back up by pressing [⇑] or [PgUp]. Your relative position in the numerical sequence of characters is shown on the horizontal scroll bar below the window. You can keep on cycling through the table as long as you want to. If you resize the window, the distance of your movements in screens and on the scroll bar will change.

## Unloading the Desktop Manager Safely

You shouldn't try to unload the Desktop Manager when it's loaded in resident mode under either of the following two conditions:

1.  You've loaded another TSR program into memory.

2.  You've popped up the Desktop Manager while working in another application; that is, you popped up the Desktop Manager from a screen other than your DOS screen.

DOS will go crazy if you leave a hole in its memory. You have to unload programs in the *reverse* order in which they were loaded. In most cases, you'll get a warning message if you try to leave a hole in DOS. In some cases, though, no message will appear and you'll have to reboot the computer.

> When I began using PC Tools, I found that the program-management setup caused lockups in my system and forced me to reboot too often. Each time I rebooted, the operation took awhile for all the PC Tools programs to load themselves. To correct this, I removed the commands inserted into my AUTOEXEC.BAT file by the PC Setup program and placed them in a separate batch file called LOAD.BAT.
>
> With LOAD.BAT, I can wait until my DOS prompt appears, do other work, then type LOAD and press [Enter]. That's when the PC Tools programs load themselves into my computer's memory.

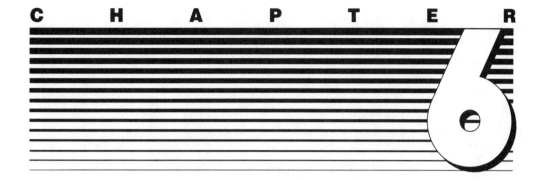

# WORKING WITH NOTEPADS

The Notepads module is an abbreviated form of word processor that lets you create text files, edit text in a variety of ways, and print files. You can also insert headers or footers, as well as change the margins and line spacing to customize the printed format. You can open up to 15 different text files at the same time and move between them.

The Notepads editor has two limitations. First, it is not a full-featured word processor, although you can create more complex formats than most other editors allow. Second, you can work only with files containing 60,000 or fewer bytes.

Most of the time you spend in Notepads will probably be for creating simple text files, such as notes, brief descriptions, and letters.

# OPENING THE EDITOR SCREEN

To access the Notepads module from the main menu:

**Press:** [N]

If you're working in another module:

**Press:** [Alt]-[D]-[N]

This opens the *NOTEPADS* dialog box, which looks like figure 6.1.

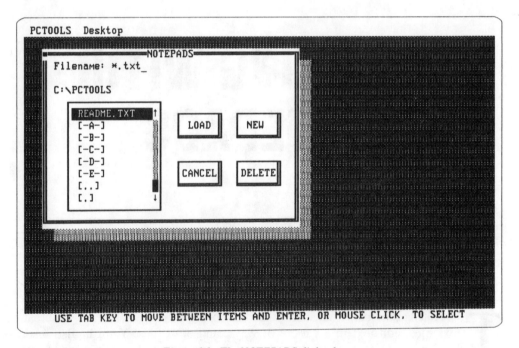

*Figure 6.1. The NOTEPADS dialog box*

Your current directory appears beneath the file name line. Beneath the directory name is the file-name window, which shows all files ending in .TXT, as well as a list of other drive letters you might want to access. The program scans for all drives. I don't use any drive letters below C, yet they show in my dialog box.

Four command buttons show on the right side of the dialog box:

**Load**        Loads the specified file name into the Notepads editor screen.

**Cancel**      Cancels your work in Notepads and returns you to the main menu or the module you were working in previously.

**New**         Creates a new file. You can also create a new file by typing in a new file name, pressing [Enter], and then selecting the command Create.

**Delete**      Deletes the file highlighted in the list window.

You can use any of these four commands by pointing at them with your mouse cursor and pressing a key. Another way is to press [Tab] as many times as necessary to highlight the desired command, then press [Enter].

Take a look at the README.TXT file provided as part of the PC Tools program files:

    **Press:** [Enter]

This moves your cursor down to the first item at the top of the list window, which most likely is README.TXT. If it's not, press [⇓] to highlight the file name, then press [Enter]. If you get a message asking how you want to format the file, press [A] for ASCII.

The contents of README.TXT are fully loaded into the Notepad editor screen. It should look like figure 6.2.

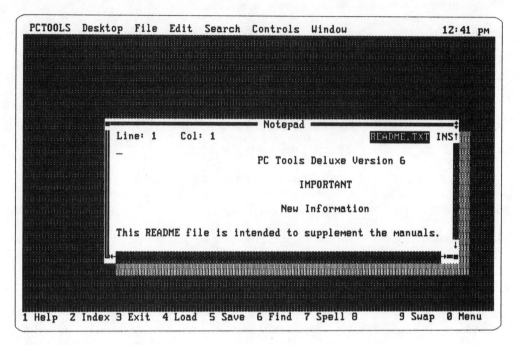

*Figure 6.2. The Notepad editor screen*

To view the next screen:

    **Press:** [PgDn]

You might notice that some text lines are cut short. The editor does this to squeeze all characters into the screen so you can see them, even if they look a bit awkward. To correct this, you can expand the screen:

    **Press:** [Alt]-[W]-[Z]

This selects *Zoom* on the Window menu and expands the editor screen to fill your display screen, as shown in figure 6.3.

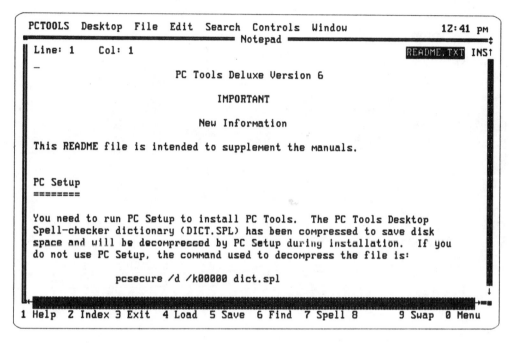

```
  PCTOOLS  Desktop  File  Edit  Search  Controls  Window              12:41 PM
  ═══════════════════════════════════ Notepad ═══════════════════════════════
  Line: 1     Col: 1                                        README.TXT  INS↑
    ─
                          PC Tools Deluxe Version 6

                               IMPORTANT

                            New Information

  This README file is intended to supplement the manuals.


  PC Setup
  ========

  You need to run PC Setup to install PC Tools.  The PC Tools Desktop
  Spell-checker dictionary (DICT.SPL) has been compressed to save disk
  space and will be decompressed by PC Setup during installation.  If you
  do not use PC Setup, the command used to decompress the file is:

           pcsecure /d /k00000 dict.spl

  1 Help  2 Index 3 Exit  4 Load  5 Save  6 Find  7 Spell 8      9 Swap  0 Menu
```

*Figure 6.3. The Notepad editor screen zoomed to fill your screen*

## Key Activities

The standard cursor control keys, including [PgDn] and [PgUp], control cursor movement.

There are two markers above the cursor, *Line: 1* and *Column: 1*. These show your cursor's current location. Press [Spacebar] to see the column count increase and then press [Enter] to see the line count increase. To return your cursor to Line 1 Column 1:

**Press:** [PgUp]

The name of the file, README.TXT, appears in the upper-right corner. You'll find the current time in the lower-left corner of the screen. To see more of the text in README.TXT:

**Press:** [PgDn]

The keys you can use in the Notepad editor screen are shown in table 6.1.

*Table 6.1. Key activities in the Notepad screen*

| Function | Keys |
|---|---|
| Right one character | [⇒] |
| Right one word | [Ctrl]-[⇒] |
| End of line | [End] |
| Down one line | [⇓] |
| Down one line fixing cursor | [Ctrl]-[PgDn] |
| End of screen | [End]-[End] |
| Down one screenful | [PgDn] |
| End of file | [Ctrl]-[End] |
| | |
| Left one character | [⇐] |
| Left one word | [Ctrl]-[⇐] |
| Beginning of line | [Home] |
| Up one line | [⇑] |
| Up one line fixing cursor | [Ctrl]-[PgUp] |
| Beginning of screen | [Home]-[Home] |
| Up one screenful | [PgUp] |
| Begining of file | [Ctrl]-[Home] |
| | |
| Insert character | Press character key |
| Insert space | [Spacebar] |
| Insert control character | [Ctrl]-character key |
| Insert tab stop | [Tab] |
| Insert hard carriage return | [Enter] |
| Delete current character | [Del] |
| Delete character to right | [Backspace] |

Experiment with these keys now so you can get the feel of how they behave. While you're doing this, read the text file.

## Document Control

The format of a text file is crucial if you want to view the contents in a recognizable form on your screen. It's important, therefore, that you understand a few things about how text characters appear on screen, and the various ways different programs display text characters.

There are three general types of formats you can use when working in the Notepad editor screen:

**WordStar**     Displays the file in WordStar document mode with a variety of control codes in effect.

**ASCII**    This is the simplest format. It displays and saves file characters in pure ASCII form, with only a hard carriage return after each line. This is equivalent to the WordStar nondocument mode.

**PC Tools**    Saves the file and includes the page layout features as defined in the Page layout menu.

Most of the time, you'll view files in ASCII format and save them in PC Tools format. These are the default settings. If you try to read a text file into the Notepad screen that contains formatting commands PC Tools doesn't recognize, it will ask whether you want to load the file using the WordStar format or the ASCII format.

When you save a file, you'll be given the choice of saving it in PC Tools format or ASCII format. ASCII doesn't include even the minimal format controls provided on the Page layout menu. You can't save a WordStar-formatted file in the editor.

## NOTEPADS MENUS

There are six pull-down menus available in the Notepads module. You should already be familiar with two of the them, Desktop and Window, which were described in chapter 5. The remaining four pull-down menus are shown in figure 6.4.

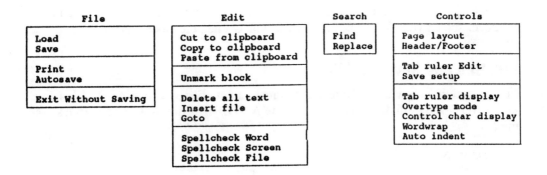

*Figure 6.4. Menu map of the Notepads module*

**File**    Loads, saves, and prints files. Also, you can set an autosave time period and quit a file without saving it.

| | |
|---|---|
| **Edit** | Cuts, pastes, and copies text using the clipboard. This menu also lets you work with blocks of text, delete all text and insert text from another file, go to specific lines, and check spelling in the current file. |
| **Search** | Finds and replaces characters. |
| **Control** | Controls the appearance of a text file both on screen and when it's printed. This is where you work with page layout. |

To open the Edit menu:

> **Press:** [Alt]-[E]

You can scroll through all six pull-down menus by pressing [⇐] or [⇒].

# A NOTEPADS TUTORIAL

For the rest of this chapter, you'll work with the primary commands on these menus in a tutorial that leads you through creating, editing, and then printing a new file.

To exit the Notepads module:

> **Press:** [Esc]

This should close the editor screen and return you to the Desktop main menu, or whatever screen you were working in when you opened the Notepads module.

## Creating and Saving a File

In this section, you will use Notepads to create a new file by declaring the file name in the *NOTEPADS* dialog box. To open the *NOTEPADS* dialog box at the Desktop menu:

> **Press:** [N]
>
> **Type:** TEST

The default characters *.TXT disappear from the file name field and are replaced by the characters you type. Don't worry. The default extension will be added to this file name. Now, to actually create the file:

> **Press:** [Enter]

This sends the program looking for the file. When it doesn't find the file, the program asks whether you want to create the file or cancel the creation.

**Press:** [Enter]

This tells the program to create the file. You could also press [O] for OK. If you want to cancel, press either [C] or [Esc].

> If you want to declare a different default extension, such as .ASC, you should:
>
> **Type:** *.ASC
> **Press:** [Enter]
>
> This is the extension considered most appropriate for ASCII files. You can declare any three-letter extension you want, but I don't recommend the use of .EXE, .COM, .SYS, or .OVL. Files with these extensions could get confused with DOS program files. You should use .BAT when you create DOS batch files.

When the Notepad screen appears, expand it to full size.

**Press:** [Alt]-[W]-[Z]

## Insert and Overtype

You can find the label INS on the right end of the top line. This means *insert* mode is active. When you type a character inside existing text, it will move characters to the right of your cursor farther to the right. To switch off the insert mode:

**Press:** [Ins]

This switches you to *overtype* mode, shown by the absence of the INS indicator. This means anything you type will write over existing characters.

You can also switch between insert and overtype modes using the Controls pull-down menu:

**Press:** [Alt]-[C]-[T]

## The Tab Line

A tab line appears as the second line in the Notepad editor window, marking every fifth tab stop with a triangle. To switch the tab line off:

> **Press:** [Alt]-[C]-[T]

This switch acts as a toggle. Just repeat it to turn the tab line back on.

You can change the tab stops easily:

> **Press:** [Alt]-[C]-[E]

To delete a tab stop, first move to the one you want to delete:

> **Press:** [Tab]

> **Press:** [Del]

To insert a new stop, move to the location where you want a tab stop; use the cursor control keys to position your cursor:

> **Press:** [Ins]

A triangular tab-stop marker should appear in your cursor position. when you are finished editing the tab line:

> **Press:** [Esc]

This returns the cursor to where to was when you started to edit the tab line. Sometimes, you'll find you can't delete tab stops you've just inserted. If this happens, press [Esc] to exit the tab line and start the edit again.

## Mouse Controls

You can use your mouse to close the Notepad editor window by pointing to the small box in the upper-left corner and clicking the left or right button. You can adjust the size of the editor screen by pointing to the box in the lower-left corner, clicking either button, and then dragging the mouse.

## Function Key Assignments

On the bottom line, you can see nine function-key assignments:

**[F1] Help**            Opens the general help screen for the Notepads module.

**[F2] Index**       Opens the help list index.

**[F3] Exit**        Closes the current Notepad screen and returns to your previous work.

**[F4] Load**        Opens the *NOTEPADS* dialog box and lets you load a new or existing file into the editor screen.

**[F5] Save**        Saves the current file to disk. If you haven't set autosave, it's wise to press this key periodically while working in the editor.

**[F6] Find**        Opens the *Find and Replace* box, letting you specify search and replacement conditions.

**[F7] Spell**       Begins to spell check the current file. There are no options with this procedure.

**[F9] Swap**        Swaps you to another active window. If more than two windows are open, it displays the *SWITCH ACTIVE WINDOW* box and lets you pick which window to work with. If only two windows are open, swaps you directly to the other window.

**[F10] Menu**       Activates the pull-down menu bar.

There are three other features that can appear as options in the editor window: Control char display, Wordwrap, and Auto indent. To observe the effects of these features, you first need to insert some text.

## Inserting Text

You can write any text you want to for the sample file in this chapter.

First, you must check three settings:

   **Press:** [Alt]-[C]

Make sure that musical notes appear to the left of the bottom two settings on this menu, *Wordwrap* and *Auto indent*. And make sure that a musical note doesn't appear next to the command *Control char display*. These are the default settings for these three commands.

Now begin your work in the Notepad editor window. First, press [Tab] to move the cursor right five spaces. Type in words just as if you were using a typewriter.

Notice that when you pass column 75 on a line the text drops down to the next line. This is called *Wordwrap*. Notepads automatically wraps text lines in column 75. Also notice that the next line begins directly beneath the first character of the first line. This is called *Auto indent*, and it lets you keep on typing without worrying about the position of the right margin.

Type several lines of text so you can see how these features continue to control the text.

Pressing [Enter] inserts a *hard carriage return*. This moves your cursor down to the left margin of the next line. If Auto indent is on, the cursor will move to the left margin as defined by the previous line. If Auto indent is off, you'll move to the left edge of the screen.

To turn Wordwrap off:

> **Press:** [Alt]-[C]-[W]

Notice how several lines of text disappear from your screen, and only the beginning of paragraphs remain on screen. Turning Wordwrap off places all text on the same line until a hard carriage return is encountered. The single lines of text scroll off the right side of your screen. Toggle Wordwrap back on:

> **Press:** [Alt]-[C]-[W]

If your screen looks a bit different when you toggle Wordwrap back on, press [PgUp] or [Home] to reposition your view of the text.

To turn auto indent off:

> **Press:** [Alt]-[C]-[A]

Notice how the second and subsequent text lines move over to the left edge of the editor window. Toggle Auto indent back on:

**Press:** [Alt]-[C]-[A]

## Control Codes

Control codes control the way text appears on the screen and when printed. You insert control characters into text when you press [Tab] and [Enter]. The first inserts a tab control symbol, the second a hard carriage return control symbol.

You can see these two characters displayed graphically by turning on the display of control characters:

**Press:** [Alt]-[C]-[C]

Notice how a small arrow appears before the first line. This is a tab control code symbol. Notice the arrows at the end of each line where you pressed [Enter]. These are hard carriage return control codes.

As a general rule, you don't need to worry about control codes. If you start viewing text files created in other editors or word processors, switching on the display of control characters is a good way to search for unwanted control codes: you'll end up with some problems if you try to print text files that contain strange control codes or to send files through electronic mail.

If you want to use the Notepads editor to create files you want to put in another program, you can insert control codes specific to that program.. Simply hold down [Ctrl] and press the letter key that matches the control code you want to insert.

For example, ^I is the letter code for a tab stop (the caret symbol ^ stands for control). You might want to insert this code as an experiment. Place your cursor before some characters.

**Press:** [Ctrl]-[I]

Notice how the characters following your cursor move to the right five spaces, the same thing pressing [Tab] does. You can do the same thing with the hard carriage return control code, which is ^J.

**Press:** [Ctrl]-[J]

This moves all characters after your cursor down to the next line, the same thing that pressing [Enter] does.

If you try to insert a control code that has no effect in the Notepad editor, you'll see the ASCII character instead. For example, you can see standard and reverse video funny faces, if you press [Ctrl]-[A] and [Ctrl]-[B]. You can see the complete list of control codes at the top of the ASCII table.

**Press:** [Alt]-[D]-[U]-[A]

This pops open the ASCII table over the Notepad editor screen as shown in figure 6.5.

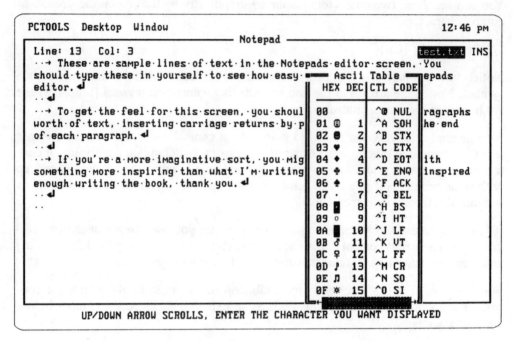

Figure 6.5. The ASCII Table overlaying the Notepad editor screen

> You can create fancier formats for files you print in the Notepads module, as long as you know what effects the control codes will have in the printer you're using. You can customize the printing of Notepads files to your printer by creating and loading specific printer macro files. You can find sample printer macro files in SAMPLE.PRO, which is provided as a file in the PC Tools Deluxe program. You can find out more about this file in chapter 15.

## Saving Files

Now that you've entered text into TEST.TXT, save your work before going any further. You can save the current file in two ways: Either press [F5] or press [Alt]-[F] and then [S].

When told to save a file, Notepads will open the *Save file to disk* box, shown in figure 6.6

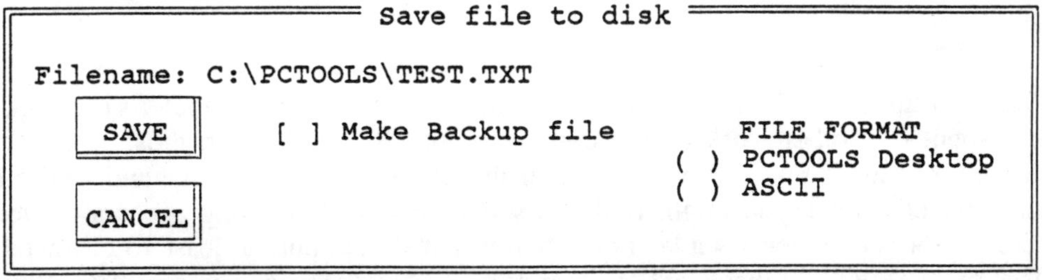

```
╔══════════════════ Save file to disk ══════════════════╗
║                                                        ║
║  Filename: C:\PCTOOLS\TEST.TXT                         ║
║                                                        ║
║    ┌──────────┐                              FILE FORMAT   ║
║    │  SAVE    │    [ ] Make Backup file      ( ) PCTOOLS Desktop ║
║    └──────────┘                              ( ) ASCII      ║
║    ┌──────────┐                                        ║
║    │ CANCEL   │                                        ║
║    └──────────┘                                        ║
╚════════════════════════════════════════════════════════╝
```

*Figure 6.6. The Save file to disk box*

This box lets you specify three save conditions:

1. The name of the file being saved. The current file name will appear as the default, but you can change the name to any other file name acceptable to DOS.

2. Whether or not you want to create a backup file. This lets you protect your work by creating two identical files, but it also uses up twice as much disk space.

3. The file-save format. You can save the file in pure ASCII, which is the default, or in PC TOOLS Desktop format; the settings are defined in your current Page layout submenu, under the Controls menu.

### Autosave

Your work in the Notepad editor screen is saved automatically every five minutes by a feature called *autosave*. However, I never feel very comfortable with a five-minute interval. If the power to my computer fails before five minutes is up, I'll lose quite a bit of work.

To change the interval to one minute:

**Press:** [Alt]-[F]

**Press:** [A]

This opens the *Automatic file save* box displaying your cursor under the time setting.

You specify the new time interval in minutes simply by typing in the new number:

**Type:** 1

To make this the new setting:

> **Press:** [O]

There's a trade-off when you shorten the interval. When your computer saves a file, it suspends all other work on the computer until its finished. In most cases, this doesn't amount to much of a delay, but if the file is particularly large and you're in an impatient mood, you might find yourself typing while nothing appears on your screen. Your computer has a keyboard buffer that should hold at least 15 characters. This memory will be displayed on your screen when the saving is complete. But if you exceed your keyboard buffer memory before the save is complete, the extra key strokes will be lost.

### Saving Your Setup

Now that you've learned how to control the way the Notepads editor screen appears and behaves, you might want to save the settings you'd like to use most frequently.

> **Press:** [Alt]-[C]-[S]

This selects the Save setup command on the Controls menu and records the settings to a file called NOTEPADS.CFG. You can change the settings any time you want to and then save that configuration.

For my work, I turn the tab line and Auto indent off, but leave Wordwrap on.

## EDITING A FILE

Once you've inserted text into a Notepads file, you can edit and change the text using a variety of editing tools. These involve simple text inserting and deleting, deleting all text in the file, inserting text from another file, handling text in blocks, copying to and from the clipboard, and spell-checking your work.

The first thing to do is view the scroll bars tracking your cursor position in the file. Place your cursor on any text line. Notice how the marker on the right side scroll bar matches the line your cursor is on. Move your cursor down one line:

> **Press:** [⇓]

Notice how the marker also moves down one line.

Look at the bottom scroll bar. Move your cursor to the beginning of the current line:

**Press:** [Home]

Notice how the bottom scroll bar marker moves to the left end of the bar. Next, move your cursor to the right end of the text line:

**Press:** [End]

Now back the cursor up a word at a time:

**Press:** [Ctrl]-[⇐]

Press these two keys a few more times to move your cursor back several words. Notice how the marker moves back with your cursor. Now move your cursor back one letter at a time:

**Press:** [⇐]

Experiment with the cursor and scroll-bar marker movements on several different text lines. The interesting effect is that the scroll bar adjusts to each text line. If there are only a few words on a line, the marker will move in bigger jumps since there are fewer letters to fill out the line. When a text line is full of characters, the marker movements are smaller.

## Working With Blocks

You work with blocks of text when you want to copy or move text from one location to another. You can copy or move text within a single file or between two or more files. Use the Clipboard to hold the text while you move to the new location.

There are four steps for copying or moving text:

1. Highlight the block of text.

2. Copy or cut it to the Clipboard.

3. Move to the new location where you want the block of text to appear.

4. Paste the block into the new location.

Whenever you want to work with a section of text, you must first select the text you want to work with by highlighting it. To select text, position your cursor before the first character of the block you want to highlight:

**Press:** [Alt]-[E]-[M]

Now move your cursor to the last character in the block. Highlighting will follow the progress of your cursor. Once you've highlighted all the text you want to work with, select the operation you want to use.

### Copying

To copy the block you've highlighted:

**Press:** [Alt]-[E]-[C]

The highlighting will disappear. The block has now been copied into the Clipboard. If you want to see the contents of your Clipboard:

**Press:** [Alt]-[D]-[B]

This opens the Desktop main menu, selects Clipboard, and opens the Clipboard screen over the Notepad editor screen, as shown in figure 6.7.

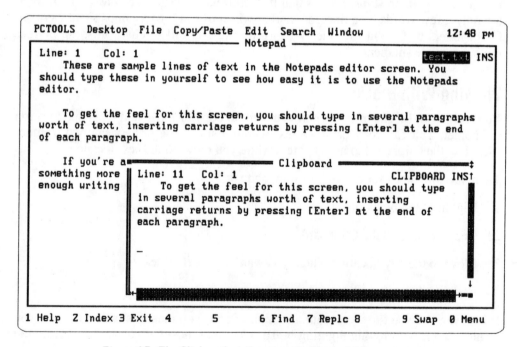

*Figure 6.7. The Clipboard window over the Notepad editor screen*

The Clipboard can only hold 2 kilobytes worth of characters, which is about 60 lines of text. If the block you've selected exceeds that amount, you'll get an error message, in which case you should reduce the size of the block you're copying. If you need to copy more than 2 kilobytes of text, you should complete the copy by repeating these steps for each block of about 60 lines.

### Pasting

Next, move your cursor to the location where you want the text to appear and paste it in:

**Press:** [Alt]-[E]-[P]

The text you copied into the Clipboard (see figure 6.7) should appear at your cursor position. It might take a few moments for all the text to appear because the editor window has to format the text for its new location.

### Cutting

To move the block, first highlight the text. Then:

**Press:** [Alt]-[E]-[T]

This cuts the text from the file and into the Clipboard. The letter *T* is used to make you think twice about what you are doing. When you cut text, you may lose it if you forget to paste it back out from the Clipboard or if the power to your computer fails before you paste it back out.

Once you've cut the block, move your cursor to the location where you want the text to appear, then paste it back in:

**Press:** [Alt]-[E]-[P]

### Highlighting Text

An alternative way for highlighting text that you might find handier is to use the [Shift] key in conjunction with the cursor control keys. For example, to extend highlighting to the right one character at a time, press [Shift]-[⇒]. Hold down both keys until you've highlighted all the text you want. To extend highlighting to the end of the current line, press [Shift]-[End]. To highlight an entire line beginning at the cursor position and extending to the same position one line down, press [Shift]-[⇓].

This is an excellent way to delete passages of text that you don't want to keep. Once you've highlighted the text, just press [Alt]-[E]-[T].

You can extend highlighting in jumps by holding down [Shift] while pressing [Ctrl]-[⇓] to move the cursor. It can be difficult to hold down three keys at the same time, but if you do a lot of cutting and pasting, then you'll soon find this a matter of habit.

While highlighting a block, if you decide you don't want to copy or cut the text, press [Esc] to turn the highlighting off, or press [Alt]-[E]-[U].

## The DIG Commands

Three commands on the Edit pull-down menus let you delete all the text in the file you're viewing, insert all the text from another file, and go to a specific line in the current file. These three appear in the same group of commands and are activated respectively by the letter keys [D], [I], and [G].

### Delete

To delete all text in the current file:

**Press:** [Alt]-[E]-[D]

You'll be given a warning, just in case you don't want to delete all the text. To continue:

**Press:** [Enter]

All characters will disappear from the current file.

> You can resurrect the file text that you have deleted by reloading the disk file into the Notepads editor screen, but you can only do this as long as you or autosave hasn't yet saved the new file to disk.

### Insert

To insert all text from another file into the current file, first place your cursor where you want the text to begin appearing:

**Press:** [Alt]-[E]-[I]

**Type:** name of file to insert

**Press:** [Enter]

As long as you've specified the file name correctly, and the path if necessary, the text from the other file will appear.

### Go to

To go to a specific line in the file:

**Press:** [Alt]-[E]-[G]

**Type:** line number

**Press:** [Enter]

The line you've specified will become the top line in the current window.

## Checking Spelling

The Notepads module comes with a dictionary containing approximately 70,000 words that can be used to check for incorrectly spelled words in a text file.

For spell checking to work correctly, the dictionary file DICT.SPL must be in your PC Tools directory, and it must be decompressed. You can check both of these conditions easily. The dictionary file will measure over 150 kilobytes when not compressed and about 75 kilobytes that when compressed.

You can use three commands on the Edit menu to check the spelling of a single word, all the text displayed on your screen, or the entire file. Since checking the spelling of an entire file is the most usual method, it has been assigned to the [F7] key.

To spell check an entire file, you can begin anywhere in the file:

**Press:** [F7]

The editor will start the spell check at the first word in the file and compare every word against entries in the PC Tools dictionary. While it does this, a message near the top of the editor window tells you that spell checking is in progress. As long as a match is found for each word in sequence, the check progresses smoothly. This procedure is a bit slow if you're used to working in a sophisticated word processor, but it's a pleasure to have a spell checker at all in a TSR editor.

When the program finds a word that isn't in its dictionary, the word will be highlighted and the *WORD MISSPELLED* box appears. For example, when I spell check a file that contains the word "Tols," my screen looks like figure 6.8.

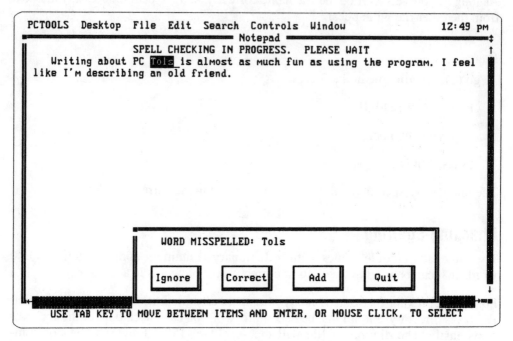

*Figure 6.8. The WORD MISSPELLED box*

This box displays the flagged word and gives you four options:

**Ignore**           Ignores the word for the rest of the spell check and continues the spell check. Pressing [Esc] also ignores the flagged word, closes the box, and continues the spell check.

**Correct**         Opens a list of possible substitutes for the flagged word.

**Add**              Adds the flagged word to your dictionary so it won't be flagged again in the future.

**Quit**             Closes the window, ends the spell check, and returns to your work in the file.

If you press [C] to select Correct, the editor will try to find a list of words that come closest to what it thinks you want to use. The possible substitutes for "Tols" is shown in figure 6.9.

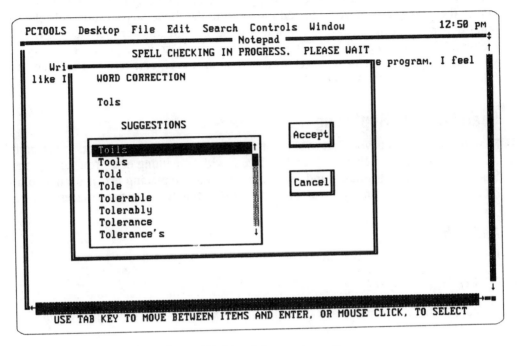

*Figure 6.9. List of alternate suggestions*

The closest match to the misspelled word appears at the top of the list and is highlighted. If this is the correct spelling of the word you want:

**Press:** [Enter]

If the highlighted word is not the one you want, but there's another on the list that might be more suitable, use the arrow keys to highlight the correct word and then press [Enter].

You can cancel the spell checking any time while it's running by pressing [Esc]. You can cancel the spell check when the *WORD MISSPELLED* box appears by pressing [C], or highlighting *Cancel* and pressing [Enter].

A word is flagged when a match is not found in the dictionary, but this doesn't necessarily mean the word is misspelled. Because of the 70,000-word limit in the PC Tools dictionary and certain limitations in the checking spelling procedure, a word might be flagged when it is not really misspelled.

When a word that is not misspelled is flagged, you can either ignore the word for the rest of the spell check or you can add the word to the dictionary so future checks in other documents will not flag the word. Adding a word to your dictionary ensures the word won't be flagged in the future, but the word becomes a permanent entry in your dictionary. You can't remove words. You can't even edit DICT.SPL using the FileEdit command in the PC Shell.

## Searching and Replacing

Searching for text lets you find a string of text quickly. Replacing text lets you search for a specific string of characters and replace it with something else. You can use the Search menu for both finding and replacing text. Since replacing text is such a common procedure in writing, you can also use the [F6] function key for replacement.

### Finding Text

If all you want to do is find text:

   **Press:** [Alt]-[S]-[F]

This opens the Search menu and then the *Find* box, which look like figure 6.10.

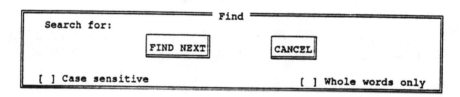

Figure 6.10. The Find box

You can find your cursor blinking in the *Search for:* field, which is where you type the text you want to search for. For example, if you want to search for *I love you dearly*:

   **Type:** I love you dearly

   **Press:** [Enter] twice

This highlights and then executes the *Find* command. The program will move you to the first occurrence of this string of text, place your blinking cursor under the first letter of the string, and reopen the *Find* box. If you want to find the next occurrence of the text:

**Press:** [Enter]

You can keep on searching for more occurrences of the same text by continuing to press [Enter] after each find. When the editor can't find another occurrence, it will beep. Searching always begins in the current cursor position and proceeds towards the end of the file.

You can narrow down the search criteria by turning on one or the other of two conditions at the bottom of the *Find* box.

**Case sensitive**     When on, the editor will search for text exactly as you specify it. For example, if you don't turn case sensitivity on and specify "me" as the text to search for, the editor will flag all occurrences of *ME, Me, mE,* and *me*. If you turn case sensitivity on, the editor will only flag *me*.

**Whole words only**     When on, the editor will search for text that corresponds to the words you've specified. The editor assumes that you're entering whole words. For example, if *Whole words only* isn't turned on and you specify "men" as the text to search for, the editor will flag all occurrences of men, including *mentor, amen,* and any other words that contain the three letters men. If you turn *Whole words only* on, the editor will flag only those words composed of the three letters, *men,* with a space on both sides.

The default settings for both of these conditions is off. To toggle either on or off, press [Tab], which highlights the condition, and then press [Enter]. The letter X will appear next to a condition when it is turned on.

## Replacing Text

If you want to search for text and replace it, you must tell the editor a few more things:

**Press:** [F6]

This opens the *Find and Replace* box, which looks like figure 6.11.

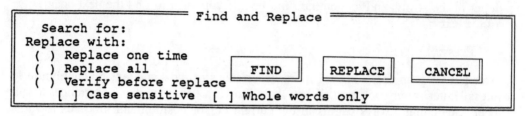

*Figure 6.11. The Find and Replace box*

As before, you'll find your cursor in the *Search for:* field. Type the text you want to search for and press [Enter]. This moves you to the *Replace with:* field. Type the text you want to serve as a replacement and press [Enter]. You can now change the way replacement takes places by turning on the method, or you can replace one-at-a-time by pressing [Enter] repeatedly.

When the first occurrence is found, the *Find and Replace* box reappears. Pressing [Enter] finds the next occurrence.

You can specify text to search for, case sensitivity, and whole words in this window just as you did in the *Find* box. You also specify the text you want substitute as a replacement.

You can refine the replacement process with three additional commands:

**Replace one time**    Substitutes the second string for the first and proceeds to the next occurrence.

**Replace all**    Substitutes the second string for the first in all occurrences in the current file.

**Verify before replace**    Finds the next occurrence of the first string and displays this text on the bottom line of you screen:

ENTER:make change ESC:abort SPACE:skip

If you want to replace the string, press [Enter]. If you want to cancel the replacement procedure, press [Esc]. If you want to skip this occurrence and proceed to the next one, press [Spacebar].

Searching and replacing text is one of the more powerful editing features you can use in the Notepads module.

# CHANGING THE FORMAT

Even though the Notepads module is just an editor, you're given a basic amount of format control within the program with the Page layout and Header/Footer selections and printer macros.

## Working with Page Layout

You can work with seven format settings using the *Page layout* selection under the Controls pull-down menu.

**Press:** [Alt]-[C]-[P]

When the *Page layout* box appears, it should look figure 6.12.

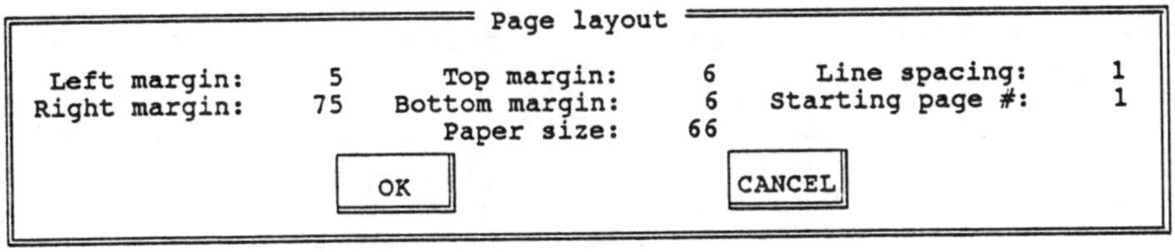

```
======================= Page layout =======================

  Left margin:     5    Top margin:      6    Line spacing:    1
  Right margin:   75    Bottom margin:   6    Starting page #: 1
                        Paper size:     66

           ┌────────┐              ┌────────┐
           │   OK   │              │ CANCEL │
           └────────┘              └────────┘
```

*Figure 6.12. The Page layout box*

The default settings that show the printed left margin will be in column 5 and the right margin appears in column 75. The top margin is six lines down from the top edge of the page, while the bottom margin is 6 lines up from the bottom edge. The paper size setting shows 66 lines to a page. So if you subtract the 12 lines not used at the bottom and top, this leave 54 lines for printed text using the default *Line spacing* setting of 1. If you set line spacing to 2 (double-spaced text), you'll end up with only 27 printed lines per page (2 x 27 = 54).

You might want to experiment with different values for these settings to see which appeals to you most.

You can move among the seven settings by pressing [Tab] or [Enter] and typing in new values. If you change a value and then issue the OK command (highlight OK and press [Enter]), the values will remain in effect until you change them again.

I use the default six lines for my top and bottom margins, but I prefer a left margin in column 0 and a right margin in column 65. The *Starting page* number is 1, which you'll want to use most of the time. If you want to print part of a longer document, you should adjust the starting page number to the number of the page where your printing begins. Page numbers will be printed by default in a blank footer. To display page numbers, you must use a header or footer.

## Headers and Footers

A header is text that appears at the top of every printed page, and a footer is text that appears at the bottom. Some word processors let you select odd or even pages of headers and footers, but you can't do this in the Notepads module.

To declare headers and footers:

**Press:** [Alt]-[C]-[H]

This opens the *Page header & footer* box, shown in figure 6.13.

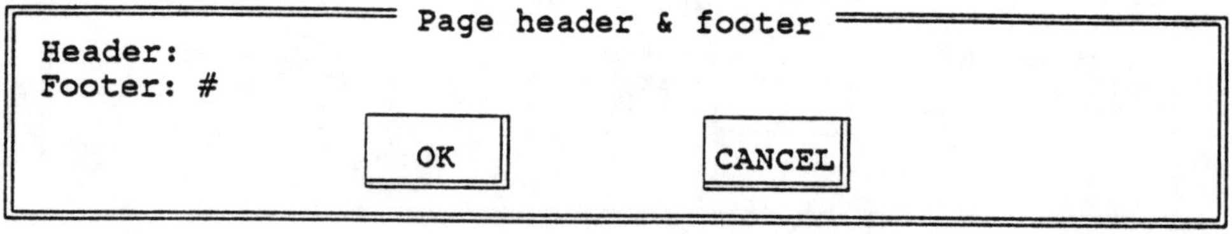

```
┌══════════════════ Page header & footer ═══════════════════┐
│ Header:                                                     │
│ Footer: #                                                   │
│              ┌─────────┐          ┌─────────┐               │
│              │   OK    │          │ CANCEL  │               │
│              └─────────┘          └─────────┘               │
└─────────────────────────────────────────────────────────────┘
```

*Figure 6.13. Page header & footer box*

You can find your cursor in the first position of the header field. You're given space for 50 characters maximum in the header and footer. This limits you to one line of text even if you've set your margins to create a text line of less than 50 characters. Headers and footers appear in the top and bottom margins and remain unaffected by your margin settings.

Notice the number character (#) in the footer field. This is the symbol you use to declare where the page number should appear. If you insert the same symbol in the header field, you'll get page numbers in both the header and footer of every page.

If you want the page number to appear in the header only:

**Type:** #

**Press:** [Enter]

**Press:** [Backspace]

**Press:** [Enter] twice

This changes the field entries, issues the OK command, and closes the *Page header & footer* box. These settings will remain in effect for the next printing, or until you exit the Notepads module.

You can see header and footer text only when you print the file. You can use headers and footers not only to print page numbers, but also to print the name of the file, the time and date of printing, and other information that helps you organize your works.

## Printer Control Macros

You can insert fancier formats for several types of printers using macro commands supplied in SAMPLE.PRO. These files contain a variety of commands that let you enter special format commands—such as near letter quality, boldface, and italics—into a Notepads file that will yield the formatting features when printed.

To make these commands work, you have to make active the printer control macro file for your printer active by using the Macros module and its associated commands to achieve the desired effects.

For example, to make the EPSON.PRO file active:

**Press:** [Alt]-[D]-[M]

**Type:** EPSON

**Press:** [Enter]

When the contents for the file appear on screen:

**Press:** [F8]

**Press:** [⇓]

This should highlight *Active* when in PC Tools Desktop.

**Press:** [Enter] twice

Now exit the Macros module (macros are fully explained in chapter 15).

When you work in the Notepad editor screen and you want to print some text in bold typeface:

**Press:** [Ctrl]-[B]

**Type:** this appears in boldface

**Press:** [Ctrl]-[H]

On screen, the commands and text look like figure 6.14

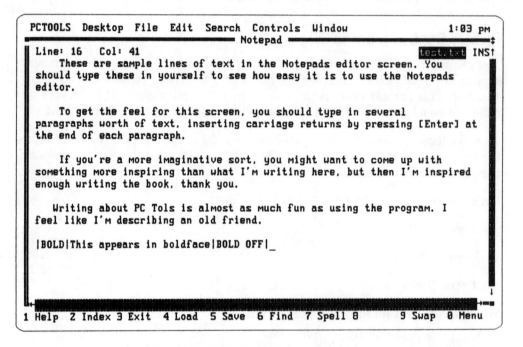

```
 PCTOOLS  Desktop  File  Edit  Search  Controls  Window          1:03 PM
 ══════════════════════════════ Notepad ══════════════════════════════
 Line: 16   Col: 41                                       test.txt INS↑
     These are sample lines of text in the Notepads editor screen. You
 should type these in yourself to see how easy it is to use the Notepads
 editor.

     To get the feel for this screen, you should type in several
 paragraphs worth of text, inserting carriage returns by pressing [Enter] at
 the end of each paragraph.

     If you're a more imaginative sort, you might want to come up with
 something more inspiring than what I'm writing here, but then I'm inspired
 enough writing the book, thank you.

     Writing about PC Tols is almost as much fun as using the program. I
 feel like I'm describing an old friend.

 |BOLD|This appears in boldface|BOLD OFF|_


 1 Help  2 Index 3 Exit  4 Load  5 Save  6 Find  7 Spell 8      9 Swap  0 Menu
```

*Figure 6.14. Bold commands inserted into text*

The command before the text turns on bold, and the command after the text off turns bold. It does this by inserting the command assigned to the macro you've made active.

The four printer-control files are HPLJF.PRO for the HP Laserjet, EPSON.PRO for most Epson printers, PROPTR.PRO for IBM Proprinters, and PANA.PRO for most Panasonic printers. The commands for each format feature for a specific printer are defined within each macro file, and are shown in the following four tables.

| Format | Press | Format | Press |
|---|---|---|---|
| Setup | [Alt]-[Z] | Underline on | [Ctrl]-[U] |
| Times 10 pitch | [Ctrl]-[N] | Underline off | [Ctrl]-[Y] |
| Bold on | [Ctrl]-[B] | Superscript on | [Ctrl]-[S] |
| Bold off | [Ctrl]-[H] | Superscript off | [Ctrl]-[A] |
| Times 8 pitch | [Ctrl]-[C] | Subscript on | [Ctrl]-[T] |
| Italics on | [Ctrl]-[I] | Subscript on | [Ctrl]-[R] |
| Italics off | [Ctrl]-[J] | Helvetica 14.4 points | [Ctrl]-[O] |

*Table 6.2. Format macros in HPLJF.PRO*

| Format | Press | Format | Press |
|---|---|---|---|
| Setup | [Alt]-[Z] | Superscript on | [Ctrl]-[S] |
| Near letter quality on | [Ctrl]-[N] | Superscript off | [Ctrl]-[A] |
| Near letter quality off | [Ctrl]-[O] | Subscript on | [Ctrl]-[T] |
| Comp on | [Ctrl]-[C] | Subscript off | [Ctrl]-[R] |
| Comp off | [Ctrl]-[V] | Underline on | [Ctrl]-[U] |
| Exponent on | [Ctrl]-[X] | Underline off | [Ctrl]-[Y] |
| Exponent off | [Ctrl]-[Z] | Italics on | [Ctrl]-[I] |
| 12 draft on | [Ctrl]-[E] | Italics off | [Ctrl]-[J] |
| 10 draft on | [Ctrl]-[P] | Pro on | [Ctrl]-[F] |
| Bold on | [Ctrl]-[B] | Pro off | [Ctrl]-[G] |
| Bold off | [Ctrl]-[H] | | |

*Table 6.3. Format macros in EPSON.PRO*

| Format | Press | Format | Press |
|---|---|---|---|
| Setup | [Alt]-[Z] | Superscript on | [Ctrl]-[S] |
| Near letter quality on | [Ctrl]-[N] | Superscript off | [Ctrl]-[A] |
| Near letter quality off | [Ctrl]-[O] | Subscript on | [Ctrl]-[T] |
| Comp on | [Ctrl]-[C] | Subscript off | [Ctrl]-[R] |
| Comp off | [Ctrl]-[V] | Underline on | [Ctrl]-[U] |
| 12 pitch draft | [Ctrl]-[E] | Underline off | [Ctrl]-[Y] |
| 10 pitch draft | [Ctrl]-[P] | Draft ft | [Ctrl]-[D] |
| Bold on | [Ctrl]-[B] | Exp on | [Ctrl]-[X] |
| Bold off | [Ctrl]-[H] | Exp off | [Ctrl]-[Z] |

*Figure 6.4. Format macros in PROPTR.PRO*

| Format | Press | Format | Press |
|---|---|---|---|
| Setup | [Alt]-[Z] | Double underline on | [Ctrl]-[L] |
| NLQ 10 pitch | [Ctrl]-[N] | Double underline off | [Ctrl]-[K] |
| NLQ 12 pitch | [Ctrl]-[O] | Superscript on | [Ctrl]-[S] |
| Comp on | [Ctrl]-[C] | Superscript off | [Ctrl]-[A] |
| Comp off | [Ctrl]-[V] | Subscript on | [Ctrl]-[T] |
| Exp on | [Ctrl]-[X] | Subscript off | [Ctrl]-[R] |
| Exp off | [Ctrl]-[Z] | Underline on | [Ctrl]-[U] |
| 12 pitch draft | [Ctrl]-[E] | Underline off | [Ctrl]-[Y] |
| 10 pitch draft | [Ctrl]-[P] | Italics on | [Ctrl]-[I] |
| Bold on | [Ctrl]-[B] | Italics off | [Ctrl]-[J] |
| Bold off | [Ctrl]-[H] | Pro on | [Ctrl]-[F] |
| | | Pro off | [Ctrl]-[G] |

*Table 6.5. Format macros in PANA.PRO*

## PRINTING A FILE

To print a file, you must be viewing it.

**Press:** [Alt]-[F]-[P]

This opens the *Print* box, which looks like figure 6.15.

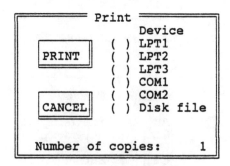

*Figure 6.15. The Print box*

Before you begin printing something, make sure your *Number of copies* and *Device* settings are correct. With the Print window open, press [Tab] to highlight the six choices you have under *Device*.

When you've highlighted the current device setting, press [⇓] or [⇑] to highlight the device you want to use. LPT ports are parallel ports, and COM ports are serial ports. The sixth setting, *Disk file,* lets you print a text file to disk.

For example, print the file README.TXT using a header that identifies the file.

First, load the README.TXT file into the Notepad editor.

**Press:** [Alt]-[F]-[L]

**Type:** README

**Press:** [Enter]

When the text appears, insert the header text:

**Press:** [Alt]-[C]-[H]

**Type:** Contents of PC Tools README.TXT

**Press:** [Enter] three times

Now open the *Page layout* box:

**Press:** [Alt]-[C]-[P]

Make the left margin begin in column 5, the right margin in column 65, and leave the top and bottom margins at 6.

Now begin the printing. Make sure your printer is turned on, has enough paper, and is connected to your computer. When you're all set:

**Press:** [Alt]-[F]-[P]

**Press:** [Enter]

In a few moments, your printer should start to give you the printed output.

# PRINTING TO A DISK FILE

One of the options you're given as a device is Disk file. This means you print the file to disk. This includes all the printing characteristics of the Page layout and Header/Footer settings. When you print a file to disk, the disk file is given the same name as the file, but the extension is changed to .PRT.

There are three reasons why you might want to print a file to disk:

1. You can view the results of printing in the Notepad editor to see if they're what you want.

2. You can send the printed file by electronic mail, changing it to a format that might be more acceptable to your e-mail service.

3. You can print the file using the DOS redirection command: TYPE FILENAME >PRN.

To print the README.TXT to a disk file, begin by viewing the file:

**Press:** [Alt]-[F]-P]

**Press** [Tab] to select Disk file

**Press:** [Enter] twice

When the printing is finished, you can view the results:

**Press:** [Alt]-[D]-[N]

**Type:** README.PRT

**Press:** [Enter]

Your screen will look like figure 6.16.

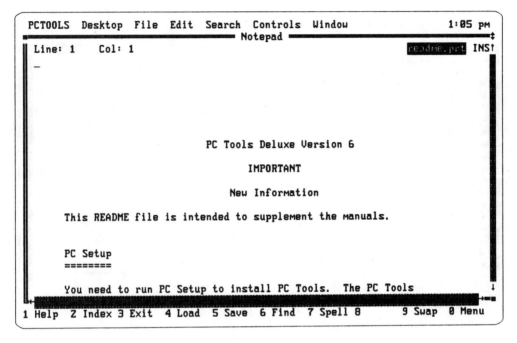

```
 PCTOOLS  Desktop  File  Edit  Search  Controls  Window          1:05 PM
 ═════════════════════════════════ Notepad ══════════════════════════════╪
║ Line: 1    Col: 1                                        readme.prt  INS↑ ║
║ ─                                                                         ║
║                                                                           ║
║                                                                           ║
║                                                                           ║
║                     PC Tools Deluxe Version 6                             ║
║                                                                           ║
║                           IMPORTANT                                       ║
║                                                                           ║
║                         New Information                                   ║
║                                                                           ║
║      This README file is intended to supplement the manuals.             ║
║                                                                           ║
║                                                                           ║
║      PC Setup                                                             ║
║      ========                                                             ║
║                                                                           ║
║      You need to run PC Setup to install PC Tools.  The PC Tools        ↓ ║
 ════════════════════════════════════════════════════════════════════════
 1 Help  2 Index 3 Exit  4 Load  5 Save  6 Find  7 Spell 8     9 Swap  0 Menu
```

*Figure 6.16. Viewing README.PRT*

Notice how the header and page layout margin settings appear. These can be crucial when you send text messages via MCI Mail. MCI Mail occasionally gives a line length format error when lines exceed 65 characters in length. Setting the right margin to column 65—or even 55 to be safe—and printing the file before you send it makes sure you won't get that error.

If you send disk files via e-mail, you should watch out for one more item. When you print a text file to disk, the program inserts a lot of useless hard-carriage-return symbols at the end of the file. As an example, figure 6.17 shows the end of a file I printed to disk and plan to send by MCI Mail.

```
 PCTOOLS  Desktop  File  Edit  Search  Controls  Window          1:06 PM
 ══════════════════════════════ Notepad ═══════════════════════════════
 Line: 456  Col: 1                                      readme.prt  INS↑
 ·····Department·at↵
 ·····(503)·690-8080.··We·hope·you·enjoy·using·the·product!↵
 ↵
 ↵
 ·····························································7↵
 ↵
 ↵
 ↵
 ↵
 ↵
 ↵
 ↵
 ↵
 ↵
 ↵
 ↵
 ↵
 ↵
 ↵
 ↵
 ↵
 1 Help  2 Index  3 Exit  4 Load  5 Save  6 Find  7 Spell  8    9 Swap  0 Menu
```

*Figure 6.17.  The end of a file printed to disk*

Notice all those hard carriage returns after the slash mark. The slash mark tells MCI Mail it has come to the end of my text. When it runs across this symbol, MCI Mail asks how it should handle the file and whether I want to send the file. The first hard carriage return after the slash steps through the first command, but you can't tell MCI Mail how you want to send the message simply by entering a hard carriage return. Instead, MCI Mail keeps on asking for a legitimate answer. It will keep on asking for the answer until all the hard-carriage-return symbols play out one-by-one. This doesn't prevent you from finally telling MCI Mail to send the message, but it does waste your time.

If you plan to send a disk file over e-mail and after printing the file, view it in the Notepad editor, turn on control-character display, move to the end of the file, and delete all the hard-carriage-return symbols after the slash. Then save the file. Now you're ready to send it.

C H A P T E R 7

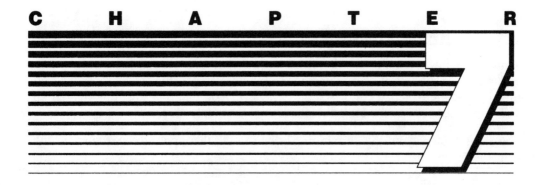

# WORKING WITH THE CLIPBOARD

The Clipboard is a specialized form of the Notepad editor screen that lets you store, edit, and transfer character text from one application to another, either inside or outside the Desktop Manager.

## USING THE CLIPBOARD

While working in the Clipboard, you're limited to 2 kilobytes of characters, which amounts to about half of a page of text printed with single-line spacing, or about 60 text lines of the Notepad editor screen. Whenever you bump against this limitation, you should cut or copy the group of characters in several moves.

You should understand the definition of three terms that apply to operations in the Clipboard.

**Copy**   Leaves the original text in place and duplicates it in a new location.

**Cut**   Removes text from one location and inserts it in another.

**Paste**   Places text from the Clipboard into another application or file.

You'll use the Clipboard to perform all three of these procedures.

You should view the Clipboard only as a temporary storage area. While you can edit text there, you cannot save text in the Clipboard except by printing it to disk or paper. Whenever you cut or copy text to the Clipboard, any text it previously held is replaced.

## THE CLIPBOARD SCREEN

To open the Clipboard screen from the Desktop menu:

> **Press:** [B]

If you're working in another Desktop application:

> **Press:** [Alt]-[D]-[B]

The Clipboard screen appears immediately.

Your screen should now look like figure 7.1.

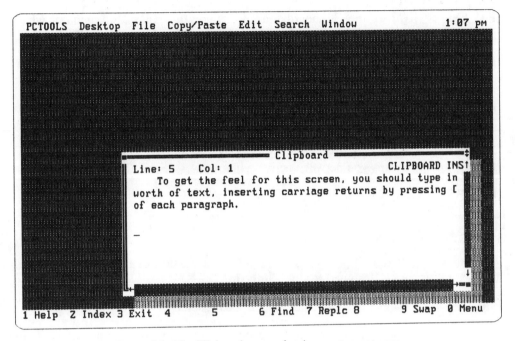

*Figure 7.1. The Clipboard screen showing most recent copy*

When the Clipboard screen appears, expand it to full-screen size:

**Press:** [Alt]-[W]-[Z]

In this case, you're looking at the text you copied from a Notepads editor screen in the previous chapter. The Clipboard will display the text you've most recently cut or copied. If you've not yet cut or copied anything into it, nothing will be displayed.

The top of the screen shows you're working in the Clipboard. The Line and Column markers are the same as the Notepads, as is the INS reminder. Notice how no file name appears in the upper-right corner—only the label CLIPBOARD.

The Clipboard is an abbreviated implementation of the Notepad editor screen. Only six function keys have assignments in the Clipboard editor screen:

**[F1] Help**   Displays general information about the Clipboard and lets you move to the index.

**[F2] Index**  Displays help index items.

**[F3] Exit**  Closes the Clipboard and returns you to the Desktop menu or whatever you were working in previously. Same as pressing [Esc].

**[F6] Find**  Opens the *Find* box, which lets you search for specific text the same way you search in the Notepads.

**[F7] Replc**  Opens the *Find and Replace* box, which lets you find text and optionally replace it with something else the same way you can in the Notepads.

**[F9] Swap**  Swaps you between active windows.

**[F10] Menu**  Activates the top menu bar.

## Pull-down Menus

The menu map of the Clipboard is an abbreviated version of the Notepad screen. There are four menus designed for the Clipboard:

**File**  Prints the contents of the Clipboard screen.

**Copy/Paste**  Copies or pastes the Clipboard screen contents to another application, and sets the rate of playback.

**Edit**  Erases text and marks or removes the mark from a text block to paste or copy. Also deletes all the text showing in the Clipboard screen, inserts text from another file (up to the 2 kilobyte limit), and goes to a specific line number in the Clipboard.

**Search**  Finds text or searches and replaces text the same way as in the Notepad editor screen. Use [F6] and [F7] respectively for quicker response.

Most of these menus are similar to the menus in the Notepad editor screen. However, the Clipboard has no Controls menu and the Clipboard Copy/Paste and Edit menus contain subsets of the Notepads Edit menu. Figure 7.2 is the complete Clipboard menu map.

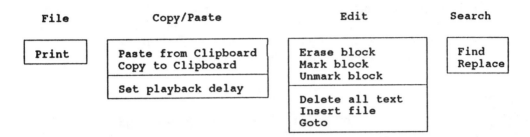

*Figure 7.2. The Clipboard menu map*

These controls all behave as described for the Notepads. You can enter characters in either insert or overtype mode.

## Saving and Printing the Clipboard Contents

There are two ways to save the contents of the Clipboard screen:

1.  Print them to paper or a disk file.

2.  Paste them into another file and save that file

To print the contents to paper or a disk file:

> **Press:** [Alt]-[F]-[P]

This opens the *Print* box, which lets you select the output device and number of copies to print. All Clipboard files, when printed to disk, are saved as CLIPBOAR.PRT. If you intend to copy more than one Clipboard file to disk, you should change the name of each file after it's been printed. If you don't, the newer file will overlay the older file. You'll be given a warning if this is about to happen.

How to save the contents of the Clipboard by pasting into another file will be explained in the following sections.

## COPYING AND PASTING

In chapter 6, you used specific Clipboard commands in Notepads. You can also use commands on the Clipboard Copy/Paste pull-down menu with other Desktop modules, outside applications, and even your DOS screen.

You can copy and paste between other Desktop modules when the program is both resident and run in standard mode, but you can only use the Clipboard with outside applications (including your DOS screen) in resident mode. You must first pop open the Clipboard screen over the outside application or hotkey.

## Copy and Paste Hotkeys

Two commands on the Copy/Paste pull-down menu, Paste from Clipboard and Copy to Clipboard, can be activated by hotkeys. This lets you Copy and Paste any time you're working with your computer, not just when you're working in the Clipboard screen or even in the Desktop Manager. You can use the menu commands, but the hotkeys work more quickly.

The hotkey assignments are:

**[Ctrl]-[Del]**     Begins the copy procedure. You then have to highlight the block you want to copy and then press [Enter] to copy it to the clipboard.

**[Ctrl]-[Ins]**     Executes the paste.

You can view these two hotkey assignments and change the keys assigned to them on the *PCTOOLS Desktop Hotkey Selection* box, shown in figure 7.3:

 **Press:** [Alt]-[D]-[U]-[H]

```
┌════ PCTOOLS Desktop Hotkey Selection ════┐
│                                          │
│  DESKTOP HOTKEY: <CTRL><DEL>             │
│                                          │
│ CLIPBOARD PASTE: <CTRL><INS>             │
│                                          │
│  CLIPBOARD COPY: <CTRL><DEL>             │
│                                          │
│ SCREEN AUTODIAL: <CTRL><O>               │
│                                          │
└──────────────────────────────────────────┘
```

*Figure 7.3. The PC TOOLS Desktop Hotkey Selection box*

If you want to change any of these assignments, highlight its command and press the two new keys you want to assign it. However, the [Ctrl]-[Ins] and [Ctrl]-[Del] key combinations are practically universal for cut and paste routines in DOS utility programs.

The third command on the Copy/Paste menu, Set playback delay, is described at the end of this chapter.

## Copying and Pasting Within the Desktop Manager

You can copy characters from any Desktop Module and paste them into the editing portion of any other module within the Desktop Manager. The term *editing portion* refers to the fact that some modules only allow you a small area to enter characters. For example, in the Telecommunications screen, you can only insert text into individual phone-book entries; and in Calculators screens, you can only insert characters into the display registers. You probably won't want to paste any characters into these modules anyway.

Here are the basic steps for copying

1. Open the screen you want to copy from

2. Press [Ctrl]-[Del]

3. Highlight the first character you want to copy

4. Press [Enter]

5. Press the arrow keys to extend the block to cover the last character you want to copy

6. Press [Enter]

That's all there is to it. The text is now in the Clipboard.

Example:

Copy the entire Algebraic calculator and save this image as a file. To open the Algebraic calculator:

**Press:** [Alt]-[C]-[A]

This should open the Algebraic calculator. Now initiate copying to the Clipboard.

**Press:** [Ctrl]-[Del]

You should see a block-shaped cursor in the middle of your screen, as shown in figure 7.4.

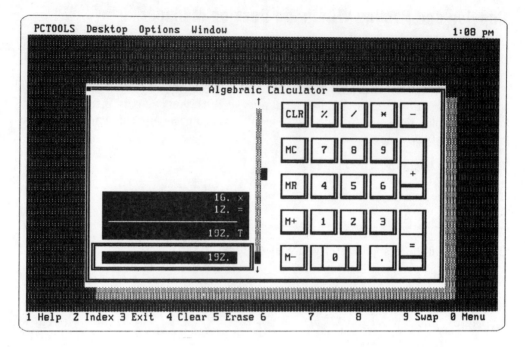

*Figure 7.4. The copy cursor over the Algebraic calculator*

Move the cursor over the first character that you want to copy, in this case the upper-left corner of the Algebraic clipboard. You can only use the arrow keys to move the cursor; the other cursor-control keys, such as [Home] and [PgUp], have no effect. Once your cursor is in position:

**Press:** [Enter]

Now move the cursor over the last character you want to copy, again using the arrow keys. This would be the lower-right corner of the calculator. As your cursor moves, you'll notice that the highlighted area expands. This is the area that will be copied to the clipboard. As you expand the highlighting, notice that you have free control over what part of the screen you want to highlight. You can even highlight the border area. Unfortunately, you can only copy characters in the current screen—you can't scroll the screen up or down to copy more characters that aren't showing. Figure 7.5 shows a substantial part of the Algebraic calculator highlighted.

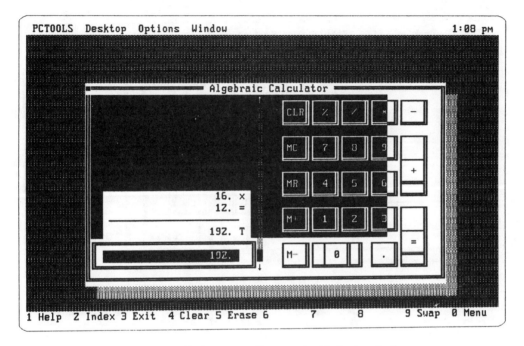

PCTOOLS  Desktop  Options  Window                         1:08 PM

============= Algebraic Calculator =============

| CLR | % | / | × | – |

| MC | 7 | 8 | 9 |
| MR | 4 | 5 | 6 | + |

16. ×
12. =
_____
192. T

192.

| M+ | 1 | 2 | 3 |
| M– | 0 | . | = |

1 Help  2 Index  3 Exit  4 Clear  5 Erase  6      7      8      9 Swap  0 Menu

*Figure 7.5. Highlighting extending over the Algebraic calculator*

You can highlight any shape of box on your screen. All you're doing is marking a section of the screen to copy. This lets you select whatever characters are showing, including data in a spreadsheet and text in a word processor. Once all the characters you want to copy have been highlighted:

**Press:** [Enter]

The highlighting will disappear. Check the Clipboard to see how successful you were:

**Press:** [Alt]-[D]-[B]

Figure 7.6 shows the result.

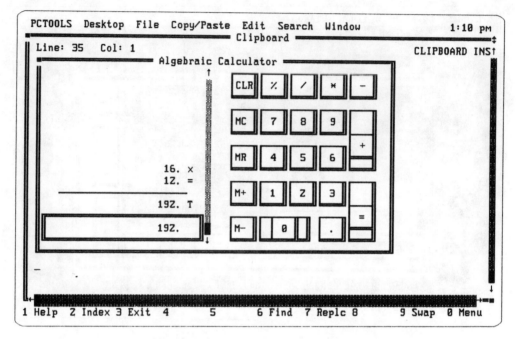

*Figure 7.6. The Algebraic calculator image copied into the Clipboard*

Now save this as a separate file that will be needed for a later chapter in this book:

**Press:** [Alt]-[F]-[P]

**Select:** Disk file

**Press:** [Enter] twice

Check the current directory and make sure a file called CLIPBOAR.PRT has been created recently. Use the PC Shell for this:

**Press:** [Ctrl]-[Esc]

When the PC Shell screen appears:

**Press:** [F7]

**Press:** [Enter]

**Type:** CLIPBOAR.*

**Press:** [Enter] twice

In a moment, your screen should change to look something like figure 7.7.

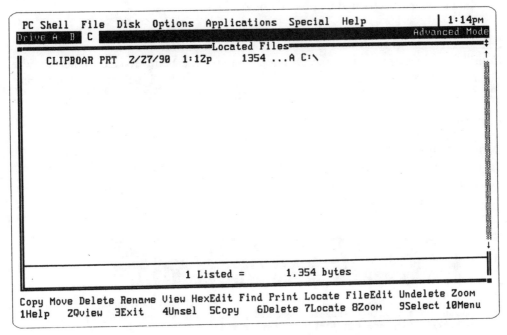

*Figure 7.7. PC Shell finding CLIPBOAR.PRT*

You can double check the contents of this file by making sure CLIPBOAR.PRT is highlighted, and then press [V] to view the file contents.

If you intend to make files like this again, you should change the name of CLIP-BOAR.PRT to something else, such as ALGE.CAL.

## Copying and Pasting Outside the Desktop Manager

When you use the Clipboard with an outside application—such as WordPerfect, dBASE, or Lotus 1-2-3—you can copy characters from the application screen to the Clipboard, as well as copy the clipboard contents to the application. To copy characters from an outside application, the Desktop must be loaded as a resident program. The steps are substantially the same as copying within the Desktop.

Work through an example of copying text from a WordPerfect word processing screen. First, move to the screen that contains the text you want to copy. Make sure all the text you want to copy appears on your screen, since you can't scroll up or down once you've activated Clipboard copy.

**Press:** [Ctrl]-[Del]

You'll see the message that the Desktop overlays are being loaded. When they're loaded, no menu or module screen will appear. Instead, the block cursor will appear. Place the cursor on the first character you want to copy:

**Press:** [Enter]

Move the cursor to the last character and make sure the highlighted box includes all the text you want to copy. Do not press [Enter] again yet. My screen looks like figure 7.8.

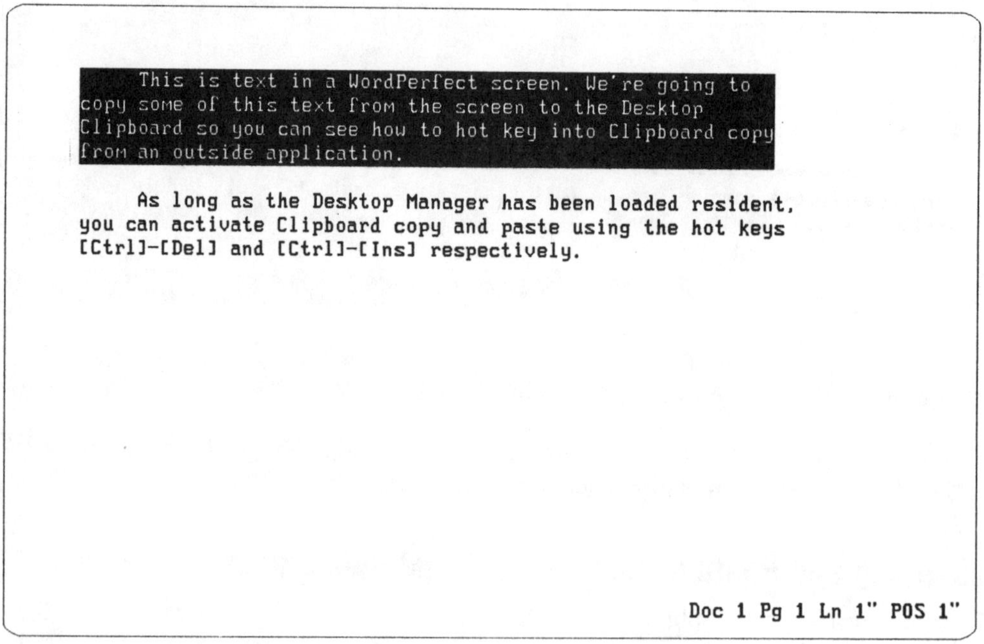

```
        This is text in a WordPerfect screen. We're going to
copy some of this text from the screen to the Desktop
Clipboard so you can see how to hot key into Clipboard copy
from an outside application.

        As long as the Desktop Manager has been loaded resident,
you can activate Clipboard copy and paste using the hot keys
[Ctrl]-[Del] and [Ctrl]-[Ins] respectively.




                                              Doc 1 Pg 1 Ln 1" POS 1"
```

*Figure 7.8. A WordPerfect screen with Clipboard copy active*

Once you're sure the block is complete:

    **Press:** [Enter]

Highlighting will disappear, and you'll see a message that the system is being restored. This means that the text is being pasted into the Clipboard, and the Desktop program is being popped down. The application screen will remain, and you can continue to work in it.

Now, paste the example you've just cut into another part of the WordPerfect file. Then paste the same characters into a Notepads file. First, open the Desktop menu and look at the current contents of the Clipboard:

    **Press:** [Ctrl]-[Spacebar]

Open the Clipboard:

    **Press:** [B]

My Clipboard looks like figure 7.9.

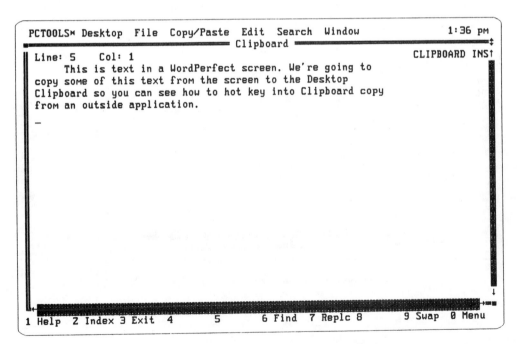

*Figure 7.9. My Clipboard after copying WordPerfect text*

Now, move this text to a Notepads file:

> **Press:** [Alt]-[D]-[N]

> **Type:** CLIP

> **Press:** [Enter]

> **Press:** [Enter]

This creates a text file called CLIP.TXT and moves you into the file.

> **Press:** [Ctrl]-[Ins]

This pastes the current contents of the Clipboard into the Notepads screen. After doing this, my screen looks like figure 7.10.

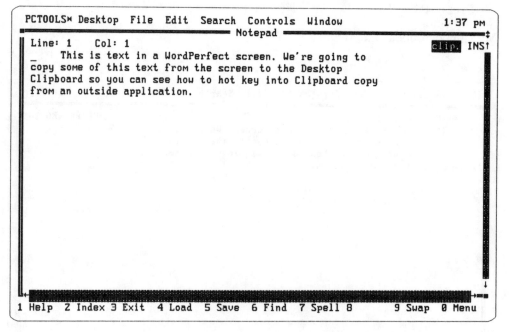

*Figure 7.10. A Notepads file containing application text*

## Copying from the Clipboard to an Application

You can work in the reverse direction and copy current Clipboard characters to an outside application. If you're working directly from the previous example, you can just exit the Notepad editor screen:

>**Press:** [Esc]

This returns you to the Clipboard screen shown in figure 7.1. To copy this text to the outside and underlying application:

>**Press:** [Alt]-[C]-[P]

This exits the Clipboard, restores the system, and returns you to the application screen, where the characters will begin to appear at the cursor location. When the characters have been pasted, in the application remains.

If you're working in the application when you want to paste the current Clipboard characters, and you already know what characters are in the Clipboard, position your cursor to where you want the characters to appear:

>**Press:** [Ctrl]-[Ins]

Again, the characters will appear, starting at the cursor position.

## Adjusting Playback Delay

You can adjust the amount time delay between the pasting of each character using a menu selection in the Clipboard. In most cases, you will not need to adjust this factor.

Whether characters should be delayed depends upon what applications you're working with. Most word processors don't need a delay; however, it's wise to delay the pasting in spreadsheets and databases a few clock ticks.

To increase the delay, begin in the Clipboard screen and:

>**Press:** [Alt]-[C]-[P]

This opens the *Macro/Clipboard playback delay* box, which looks like figure 7.11.

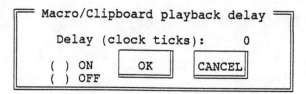

*Figure 7.18. The Macro/Clipboard playback delay*

There are 18 clock ticks per second. To set a delay of 1/3rd of a second:

**Type:** 6

**Press:** [Enter]

Notice that the OFF button is highlighted.

To highlight the ON button:

**Press:** [⇑]

**Press:** [Enter]

With ON highlighted, select OK and then accept it:

**Press:** [Enter] twice

What you've done is insert a 1/3-second delay between the pasting of each character. You can adjust this figure if it's too slow or too fast.

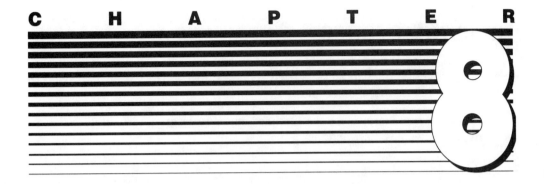

# WORKING WITH
# OUTLINES

O utlines are lists of individual text lines organized according to a specific structure. They are ideal for organizing the contents of a text file. For example, a *to-do* list is a simple outline which gets more complicated when you organize—in a hierarchy—the things you have to do, such as putting the most important items first, or putting the things you have to do first at the top.

Pseudocode for software programs is a more complex example of an outline. Although most computer users don't write computer programs, they do write text. The text can have various effects on a reader, depending upon the way its contents are organized.

# THE OUTLINES EDITOR

The Outlines editor is a specialized form of text editor. It lets you work with lines of text and arrange the lines in an organized sequence that reflects your perception of how each line relates to the other lines.

For example, if you were to use the Outlines editor to create a structured to-do list, you might include these instructions:

Pack lunch

Take daughter to school

    make sure she has breakfast

    make sure she washes her face

Pick up newspaper on the way back

The lines that are flush against the left margin are your primary to-do activities. The second activity, taking your daughter to school, is dependent upon the fact that she should eat her breakfast first and then wash her face. If you want her to wash her face before she eats, you might structure the outline this way:

Pack lunch

Take daughter to school

    make sure she washes her face

    make sure she has breakfast

Pick up newspaper on the way back

While this is a superficial example, it illustrates how lines relate to each other and how the flow of your activities can be deduced from the physical arrangement of each line.

It's been my experience that not many people use outliners because they feel little urgency to be so organized. For them, the Appointment Scheduler will be sufficient. You can create a to-do list in the Appointment Scheduler and not worry about such arcane terms as headlines, collapsing and expanding, and promoting and demoting.

Still, there is a solid core of users whose specific activities are well-served by outlining. These are the programmers, project planners, and individuals who need to keep track of a variety of activities, relating each one to the others. For them, an outline is a godsend, and it's these users who will benefit the most from this chapter.

The Outline editor screen is an expanded version of the Notepad editor screen, described in chapter 6. All the commands in the Notepad screen are available in the Outline screen except for two on the Controls pull-down menu: Wordwrap and Auto indent. In the Outline editor, these two features are set in specific ways and can't be changed: Wordwrap is always off, and Auto indent is always on. You'll see what effects these have when you begin working with an outline.

There's one additional pull-down menu in the Outline screen that you can't find in Notepad; it's called Headlines. You can find this menu between the Controls and the Window pull-down menus. To see it:

**Press:** [Alt]-[H]

It should look like figure 8.1.

```
Expand Current
Expand All

Show level

Collapse Current
Main headline only

Promote
Demote
```

*Figure 8.1. The Headlines menu*

## What Are Headlines?

Headlines are the distinctive feature of outlines. They're the thing that makes outlines different from text files created in the Notepad editor. Once you understand the concept of headlines, you'll have no trouble creating outlines.

A headline is a single line of text. It extends from the left margin to the end of the line, which is always marked by a hard carriage return. Since wordwrap doesn't work in the Outline editor screen, a line of text containing more than 80 characters will continue beyond the right edge of your screen.

Understanding headlines may seem difficult at first because a line of text can serve as both a headline and a heading. Although it's easy to confuse these two terms, it's not so easy to clarify them without looking at an outline. The distinction should become clearer as you read the section "Working With Headlines" in this chapter.

# OPENING THE OUTLINES MODULE

To open the Outlines module from the Desktop menu:

**Press:** [O]

To open it from any other Desktop module:

**Press:** [Alt]-[D]-[O]

Both of these move you to the *Outline* dialog box, which looks like figure 8.2.

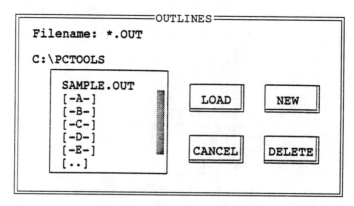

*Figure 8.2. The Outlines dialog box*

This box behaves identically to the *Notepads* dialog box, with one exception. In the default configuration, the *Outlines* dialog box displays only file names that end in .OUT, which stands for outline. You can view a complete list of files in the current directory this way:

**Type:** \*.\*

**Press:** [Enter]

You can filter for any other arrangement of file names using the DOS wild-card characters ? and \*.

If no other outline files have been created, only one file should show in the default display of the *Outlines* box: SAMPLE.OUT. This is a sample outline file provided as part of the PC Tools program

> If for any reason the file SAMPLE.OUT is not available to you, its contents are provided in the section Creating an Outline at the end of this chapter. This file makes understanding outlines easier, since it lets you see one. Many readers will have access to SAMPLE.OUT.

To open SAMPLE.OUT:

**Press:** [Enter] twice

This highlights and then selects the top file. When your Outline screen first appears, it might be in the small size. If it is, you should expand it to full-screen:

**Press:** [Alt]-[W]-[Z]

Your screen should look like figure 8.3.

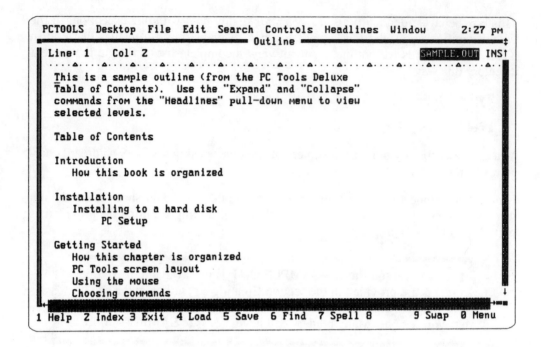

*Figure 8.3. The Outlines editor screen full size*

The features on this screen, excluding the text and file name, are identical to those on the Notepad screen, except for two items. The word *Outline* replaces *Notepads* in the top center of the screen, and the additional pull-down menu name, Headlines, appears on the right side of the top menu bar.

The line and column markers, tab line, the INS label, scroll bars, and time in the upper-right corner are the same features that appear in the Notepad editor screen.

There are eight function-key assignments:

[F1] **Help**   Opens the general help screen.

[F2] **Index**   Opens the help index.

[F3] **Exit**   Closes the Outline editor screen and returns you either to the Desktop menu or to your previous work.

[F4 ] **Load**   Opens the *Outlines* dialog box so you can load another outline.

**[F5] Save**    Opens the Save file to disk screen, which lets you determine how you want to save the file.

**[F6] Find**    Opens the *Find* box, which lets you specify text to find.

**[F7] Replc**    Opens the *Find and Replace* box, which lets you replace text.

**[F9] Swap**    Swaps between currently open windows.

**[F10] Menu**    Activates the top menu bar. Same as pressing [Alt] and holding it down.

The complete menu map for the Outline editor screen is shown in figure 8.4.

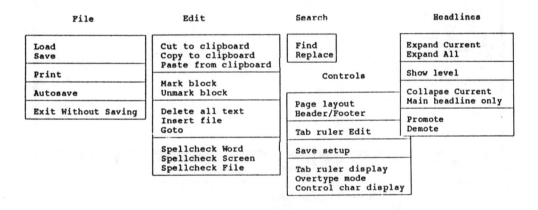

*Figure 8.4. Menu map for the Outline editor screen*

Take a closer look at the text as shown in figure 8.3. The first four lines describe the file and how you expand and collapse headlines. Each text line, beginning with the line *Table of Contents* and ending with the line *Choosing Commands*, is a headline. To see more of the file:

**Press:** [PgDn]

# WORKING WITH HEADLINES

The best way to start working with headlines is to follow the instructions at the top of the SAMPLE.OUT file. In its default appearance, all headlines are expanded in the file, so you should collapse them first. The meanings of these terms will become clearer as you work through the following example.

**Press:** [Alt]-[H]-[M]

Notice how the outline shrinks to show just four headlines, as shown in figure 8.5.

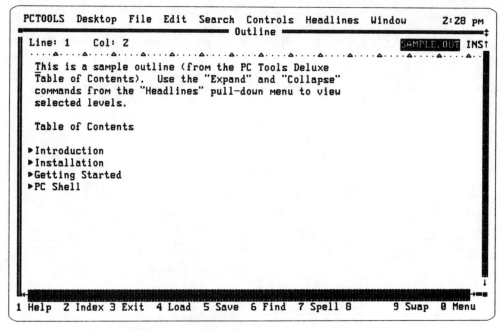

*Figure 8.5. All headlines below main collapsed*

What you did when you selected the command *Main headline only* was to collapse all headlines so only the main ones remained.

Commands on the Headlines menu are defined as follows:

**Expand Current**    Expands and displays the current level of headlines. The current level is the one below your current cursor position.

**Expand All**        Expands and displays all levels of headlines.

**Show level**        Displays first level headlines only.

**Collapse Current**  Collapses and hides all headlines at the current level.

**Main headline only**    Collapses the outline so only the main headlines show. Main headlines are the text lines that begin at the left margin.

**Promote**    Moves the current headline up one level. The level of a headline is determined by its level of indentation.

**Demote**    Moves the current headline down one level.

The question of current level is an important one, so expand the outline back to its original appearance.

    **Press:** [Alt]-[H]-[A]

This expands all levels of the current outline, regardless of what's been collapsed before. Notice there are two levels of indentation on your screen when you're looking at the top of the SAMPLE.OUT file  (figure 8.3). This means there are three levels of headlines. The main level always begins at the left margin. Pressing [Tab] once moves your cursor to the second level. Pressing [Tab] a second time moves your cursor to the third level.

> Don't worry about making changes to the SAMPLE.OUT file. As long as you don't save the changes, they won't become permanent. If for any reason you can't back out of a change you're making, such as hiding headlines or promoting or demoting them, just exit from the Outlines editor, return to the main menu, and reload SAMPLE.OUT. The contents and structure of the original disk file will appear.

You can change the column position of each tab stop using the Tab ruler edit command on the Controls pull-down menu. Changing the position of tab stops doesn't change the levels of headlines.

## Collapsing and Expanding Headlines

One advantage of working with outlines is that you can hide and then display selected headlines. The term "collapse" means the same thing as "hide displayed headlines," and the term "expand" means the same as "display hidden headlines."

Collapsing or redisplaying headlines lets you view an abbreviated or expanded version of an outline to obtain different visual readings of the outline's organization. This might not be appropriate when working with a small outline; but as soon as an outline grows and exceeds the viewing capacity of your computer screen, you'll find that collapsing part of the outline to see major features can be very helpful.

The *current headline* is the one at the level below your current cursor position. In the next example, you will identify a current headline in the SAMPLE.OUT file. You will first move the cursor down the file contents and reposition the text. To do this:

**Press:** [PgDn]

**Press:** [⇑] three times

You're correctly positioned when the screen resembles figure 8.6.

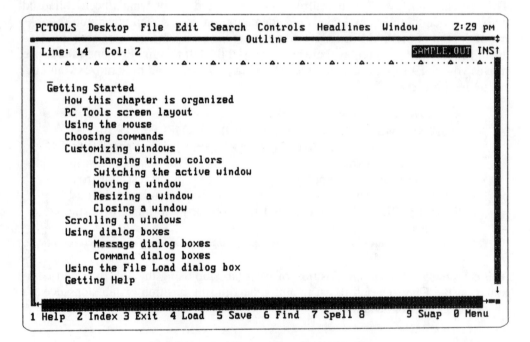

*Figure 8.6. Viewing a section of SAMPLE.OUT*

Now place the cursor anywhere on the line *Customizing windows*. This makes the five text lines directly beneath your cursor the current level. Close this level and watch what happens.

**Press:** [Alt]-[H]-[C]

**204**

The effects are shown in figure 8.7.

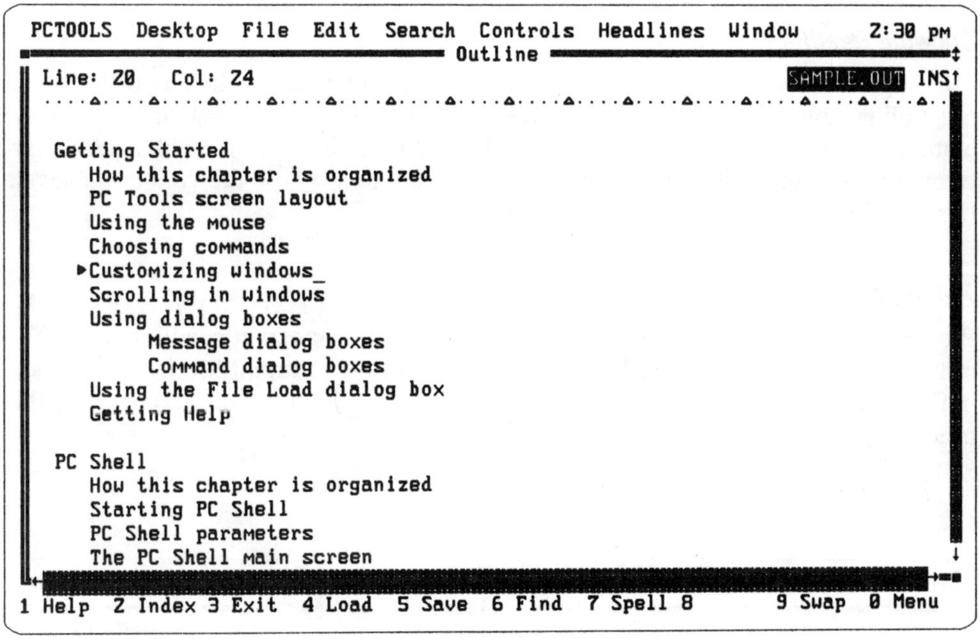

```
 PCTOOLS  Desktop  File  Edit  Search  Controls  Headlines  Window      2:30 pm
══════════════════════════════════ Outline ══════════════════════════════════‡
║ Line: 20    Col: 24                                              SAMPLE.OUT INS↑
║···▲····▲····▲····▲····▲····▲····▲····▲····▲····▲····▲····▲··
║
║    Getting Started
║       How this chapter is organized
║       PC Tools screen layout
║       Using the mouse
║       Choosing commands
║      ►Customizing windows_
║       Scrolling in windows
║       Using dialog boxes
║             Message dialog boxes
║             Command dialog boxes
║       Using the File Load dialog box
║       Getting Help
║
║    PC Shell
║       How this chapter is organized
║       Starting PC Shell
║       PC Shell parameters
║       The PC Shell main screen                                              ↓
║◄━━━━━━━━━━━━━━━━━━━━━━━━━━━━━━━━━━━━━━━━━━━━━━━━━━━━━━━━━━━━━━━━━━━━━━━▶═■
 1 Help  2 Index 3 Exit  4 Load  5 Save  6 Find  7 Spell 8    9 Swap  0 Menu
```

*Figure 8.7. Collapsing current headlines*

Notice how all five subordinate lines disappear. Notice also how the next headline, on the same level as the current headline, moves up to fill the gap. And a right-facing arrow appears next to the headline marked by the current cursor. This symbol indicates that there are headlines beneath the line and that those headlines are hidden.

To redisplay the hidden (or collapsed) headlines:

**Press:** [Alt]-[H]-[E]

This expands the current headlines.

Collapsing headlines can be somewhat tricky until you learn how to select the appropriate level. Now move your cursor around the SAMPLE.OUT file and practice collapsing other current levels. You'll soon get a feel for how this works. You can always expand hidden levels this way:

Set the cursor at a headline marked with a right-facing arrow

**Press:** [Alt]-[H]-[A]

### Showing Headlines

The single command, *Show headlines,* displays all headlines at the cursor level and hides all headlines below the cursor level. This lets you pick a level that serves as the bottom level of an outline. This can be useful when you're working with a particularly intricate outline with many levels, and you want to see how the various sublevels line up with one another.

### Promoting and Demoting Headlines

Promoting and demoting headlines means changing the apparent headline level. You can only promote and demote headlines at and below the current level. For instance, in figure 8.6, place your cursor on the line *Changing window colors.* To promote this headline one level, as shown in figure 8.8:

**Press:** [Alt]-[H]-[P]

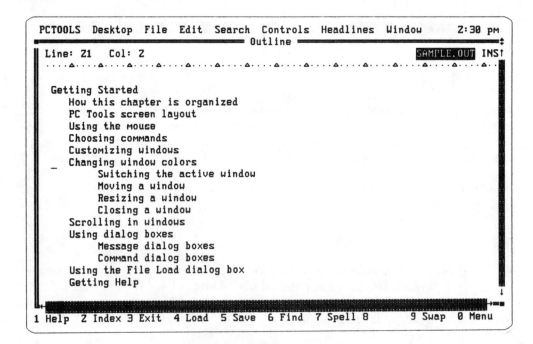

*Figure 8.8. A headline promoted*

To demote the same headline, leave your cursor where it is:

**Press:** [Alt]-[H]-[D]

Notice the changes in figure 8.9; they're quite dramatic.

```
┌─────────────────────────────────────────────────────────────────┐
│  PCTOOLS  Desktop  File  Edit  Search  Controls  Headlines  Window      2:30 PM
│ ═══════════════════════════════ Outline ═══════════════════════════
│  Line: 21    Col: 5                                    SAMPLE.OUT INS↑
│ ···▲···▲···▲···▲···▲···▲···▲···▲···▲···▲···▲···▲···
│
│  Getting Started
│     How this chapter is organized
│     PC Tools screen layout
│     Using the mouse
│     Choosing commands
│     Customizing windows
│   _    Changing window colors
│            Switching the active window
│            Moving a window
│            Resizing a window
│            Closing a window
│     Scrolling in windows
│     Using dialog boxes
│         Message dialog boxes
│         Command dialog boxes
│     Using the File Load dialog box
│     Getting Help
│                                                                 ↓
│ ◀██████████████████████████████████████████████████████████████▶─■
│ 1 Help  2 Index 3 Exit  4 Load  5 Save  6 Find  7 Spell 8    9 Swap 0 Menu
└─────────────────────────────────────────────────────────────────┘
```

*Figure 8.9. Headlines demoted*

Notice how you demoted more than the one headline you previously promoted. This shows the different effects of promoting and demoting. When you promote a headline, only the current headline is effected. When you demote a headline, you also demote all the levels beneath it.

To promote the five lower-level headlines that were "inadvertently" demoted, place your cursor on each one in turn and:

**Press:** [Alt]-[H]-[P]

# CREATING AN OUTLINE

Once you've become familiar with the concept of headlines, you should experiment with the various commands to reinforce your understanding. In this section you will re-create the example provided in the SAMPLE.OUT file. Thus, if you don't already have a copy of the file, this re-creation will help you learn to use the Outlines module. Headlines for the SAMPLE.OUT file are displayed in figure 8.10.

```
            Table of Contents

            Introduction
                Installing to a hard disk
                PC Setup

            Getting Started
                How this chapter is organized
                PC Tools screen layout
                Using the mouse
                Choosing commands
                Customizing windows
                    Changing window colors
                    Switchng the active window
                    Moving a window
                    Resizing a window
                    Closing a window
                Scrolling in windows
                Using dialog boxes
                    Message dialog boxes
                    Command dialog boxes
                Using the File Load dialog box
                Getting Help

            PC Shell
                How this chapter is organized
                Starting PC Shell
                PC Shell parameters
                The PC Shell main menu screen
                Selecting and moving around in windows
                    Two list display
                    One list display
                Help
```

*Figure 8.10. The text for SAMPLE.OUT*

The text for SAMPLE.OUT contains 32 individual headlines arranged in three levels under eight headings. The four additional lines of text that appear at the top of the file are not part of the outline.

To create this outline, begin at the Desktop main menu:

**Press:** [O]

**Type:** SAMPLE

**Press:** [Enter] twice

Expand the screen to full size, if it's not already that way:

**Press:** [Alt]-[W]-[Z]

**Type:** Table of Contents

**Press:** [Enter]

**Type:** Introduction

**Press:** [Enter]

**Press:** [Tab]

**Press:** [Enter]

**Type:** How this book is organized

Notice that when you pressed [Enter], the cursor moved to the indented starting point for the headline below the letter *H* in How. (Auto indent is always on in the Outline editor screen.)

**Press:** [Enter] again

This moves the cursor down one more line and places it flush against the left margin. This happens when there is no text on the previous line or when text on the previous line is already flush left.

**Type:** Installation

**Press:** [Enter]

**Press:** [Tab]

**Type:** Installing to a hard disk

**Press:** [Enter]

**Press:** [Tab]

**Type:** PC Setup

**Press:** [Enter] twice

This moves the cursor down two lines and sets it flush against the left margin. You can now continue with the rest of the headlines, (or text lines), shown in figure 8.10.

You've indented the line PC Setup to the third level, which is the deepest you need to go in this outline.

When you're finished entering all the text, and the structure is identical to figure 8.3, save the file:

**Press:** [F5]

**Press:** [Enter] twice

After creating this outline, experiment on your own by collapsing and expanding headlines, as well as promoting and demoting them.

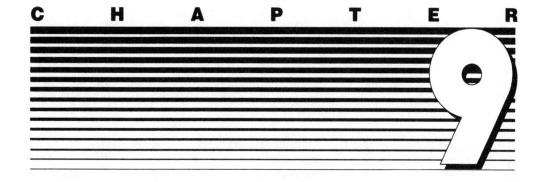

C H A P T E R

9

# THE DATABASES MODULE

A database is nothing more than a collection of information that you want to keep together. Encyclopedias, cookbooks, and telephone directories are examples of databases you've used before.

Your own personal address book also is an example of a database. It includes special information that's of particular interest to you. Perhaps you keep track not only of the home and work telephone numbers of your friends and family, but also of their birthdays. This is a database of personally important information.

The microcomputer has finally made computer power available to you for creating a database to maintain you own personal information. PC Tools utilities provide quick and easy ways for creating, viewing, and editing this information.

# dBASE PROGRAMS AND THE DATABASES MODULE

Although there are many different types of database programs for microcomputers, the dBASE implementation has become the most popular. This includes the family of dBASE programs produced by Ashton-Tate: dBASE II, dBASE III PLUS, and dBASE IV.

The main element of interest regarding the dBASE programs is called file structure. The PC Tools Deluxe Databases module lets you work with databases that subscribe to the dBASE standard file structure or format. Not only is the dBASE family of products immensely popular, but also other database programs subscribe to it. These include FoxBase, Works, Clipper, and dBXL. You can also import and export dBASE data directly while working in Paradox.

While this covers a lot of programs, you should realize that the Databases module in PC Tools doesn't offer you the full functionality of the dBASE programs. There are several important limitations:

- The Databases module is a flat-file database program; it is not relational.

- All activities are run from menu commands. This isn't a limitation if you're a new or infrequent user, but it does limit how far you can go with the program.

- You're limited to 10,000 records in a single database, 128 fields in a record and 4000 characters in each field. This is a lot of information capacity for most individual users, but it can fall short for some businesses.

- You can't use memo fields; nor can you use catalogs, filters, reports or any of the other more technical features available in dBASE programs.

- You can't run dBASE programs, but you can use the Notepads editor to write dBASE source code. Source code must be compiled in a separate program and will run only in full-fledged dBASE-type programs.

- You can't create your own indexes. The PC Tools program creates a record file for each database that determines how record fields will appear on your screen.

- Once you've created a database structure, your ability to modify it is limited. You can add and delete records, you can edit field entries, and you can change field names. But you can't add or delete fields. You'll have to do this sort of work in a dBASE-type program.

This might sound like you're not getting very much in the Databases module, but that's not the case. You can probably accomplish 85% of your routine data work using the PC Tools Databases module. It has several distinct advantages over any dBASE program. The PC Tools program lets you:

- Pop up the Databases module over whatever else you're working with, work with the data, and then pop the module back down to continue your previous task. This alone offers a considerable advantage.
- Create database files more easily and quickly.
- Pop the program up and down more quickly, even when you are running in a standard mode.
- Design your screen display of information more easily.
- Print notes and letters, including information merged from a database, more conveniently.

While these aren't significant advantages for a professional database programmer, they're advantageous enough to make even the many stalwart dBASE programmers prefer to use the PC Tools Databases module for some of their routine chores.

There are ten ways that the Databases module lets you work with data files that subscribe to the dBASE standard. You can:

1. Create new database files.

2. View and edit records in existing database files (except for memo fields) in the browse and edit modes.

3. Delete records and pack database files.

4. Select and hide records for special handling.

5. Print database record information according to customized formats.

6. Change existing database field names.

7. Transfer selected records from one database to another.

8. Sort data files on a variety of fields.

9. Search selected records for text.

10. Autodial phone numbers in database records using the Telecommunications module. The dBASE programs cannot do this unless you use a separate communications program that pops up over the dBASE screen.

The rest of this chapter helps you learn about databases by working with real files.

## OPENING THE DATABASES MODULE

You can open the Databases screen the same two ways you can open the PC Tool's other module screens—by viewing an existing file or by creating a new one first and then viewing it. First, you will view an existing file.

With the Desktop main menu showing:

**Press:** [D]

This opens the *DATABASES* dialog box, as shown in figure 9.1.

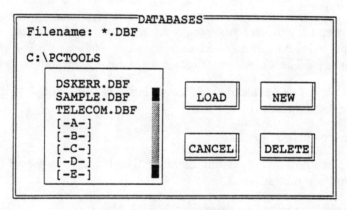

*Figure 9.1. The DATABASES dialog box*

If you're still logged onto the default PC Tools directory, three database file names should be displayed in the *DATABASES* dialog box: DSKERR.DBF, SAMPLE.DBF, and TELECOM.DBF. The first is a database of disk error messages the PC Tools program uses to tell you when you've done something wrong. The second is a sample database you can use for practice. The third is a database you can use for telecommunications.

> You should be aware that .DBF is the default dBASE database file-name extension, which stands for database file. The Databases module looks for and displays all files ending with this extension in the selected directory. As with all DOS file names, you can add any extension to any file name, however, the Databases module will only load files that subscribe to the dBASE file format.

I prefer working with DSKERR.DBF. To see the contents of that file:

   **Press:** [Enter] twice

This moves the cursor to the file name at the top of the list and selects the file for viewing.

You can also open the file this way:

   **Type:** DSKERR

   **Press:** [Enter]

Remember, you don't need to type the default file extension appropriate for the module you're using (in this case is .DBF) as long as it hasn't been changed.

## The Browse Screen

The browse screen lets you look at a series of records in a database file. Field information is lined up in vertical columns. When the DSKERR.DBF file is loaded, you should see the data displayed in the browse screen, which looks like figure 9.2.

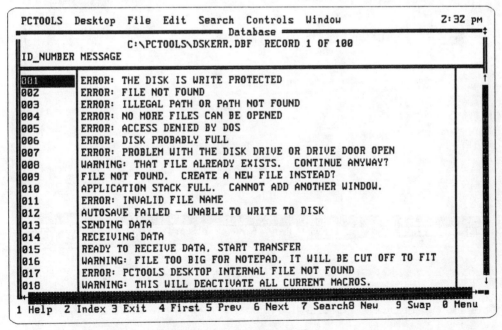

```
 PCTOOLS  Desktop  File  Edit  Search  Controls  Window           2:32 PM
========================================= Database =============================↕
                    C:\PCTOOLS\DSKERR.DBF   RECORD 1 OF 100
 ID_NUMBER MESSAGE

 001       ERROR: THE DISK IS WRITE PROTECTED                                  ↑
 002       ERROR: FILE NOT FOUND
 003       ERROR: ILLEGAL PATH OR PATH NOT FOUND
 004       ERROR: NO MORE FILES CAN BE OPENED
 005       ERROR: ACCESS DENIED BY DOS
 006       ERROR: DISK PROBABLY FULL
 007       ERROR: PROBLEM WITH THE DISK DRIVE OR DRIVE DOOR OPEN
 008       WARNING: THAT FILE ALREADY EXISTS.   CONTINUE ANYWAY?
 009       FILE NOT FOUND.   CREATE A NEW FILE INSTEAD?
 010       APPLICATION STACK FULL.   CANNOT ADD ANOTHER WINDOW.
 011       ERROR: INVALID FILE NAME
 012       AUTOSAVE FAILED - UNABLE TO WRITE TO DISK
 013       SENDING DATA
 014       RECEIVING DATA
 015       READY TO RECEIVE DATA, START TRANSFER
 016       WARNING: FILE TOO BIG FOR NOTEPAD, IT WILL BE CUT OFF TO FIT
 017       ERROR: PCTOOLS DESKTOP INTERNAL FILE NOT FOUND
 018       WARNING: THIS WILL DEACTIVATE ALL CURRENT MACROS.               ↓
 1 Help  2 Index 3 Exit  4 First 5 Prev  6 Next  7 Search8 New   9 Swap  0 Menu
```

*Figure 9.2. The Database browse screen*

In this screen, a single record occupies one horizontal line. A field occupies a single column. Several fields can usually be displayed on a screen, but this may vary, depending on field sizes. In larger databases you can display other fields by moving right or left, but for DSKERR.DBF this is not necessary.

In figure 9.2, there are 18 records displayed, each composed of two fields. The fields are titled ID_NUMBER and MESSAGE. The former field contains the reference number of each error message, and the latter contains the text of the error message itself. Whenever an identifiable error occurs while you work in PC Tools Deluxe, the program calls a specific error message ID number. This in turn displays the message attached to the ID number. For example, whenever disk error 1 is called by the program, it will flash the message: DISK IS WRITE PROTECTED. If your screen doesn't look like this, you're probably operating in what's called the *edit* mode. The Database edit mode screen looks like figure 9.3.

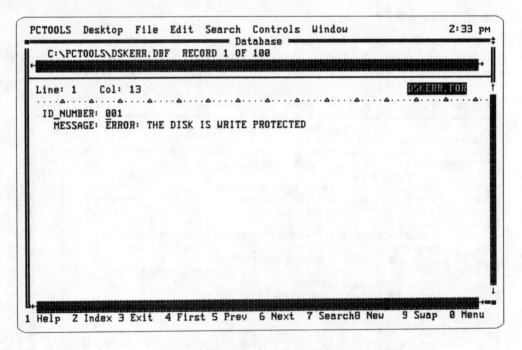

*Figure 9.3. DSKERR.DBF viewed in edit mode*

If you are viewing in edit mode, switch to browse mode:

**Press:** [Alt]-[F]-[B]

Next, expand the browse screen to full size:

**Press:** [Alt]-[W]-[Z]

Also, you might want to change the colors. If you do:

**Press:** [Alt]-[W]-[C]

Once you've zoomed the browse screen and selected the colors you want to use, save the configuration:

**Press:** [Alt]-[C]-[S]

Now you're ready to a look at the details of the browse screen. It's called browse because you can skim through the database and glance at several records at the same time. The number of fields that show in a single screen depends on field size and the number of fields in the database. For the DSKERR.DBF database, you don't notice this limitation because each record in the file contains only two fields.

The top line of the browse screen shows the six pull-down menus. The menu map specific to the Databases module is shown in figure 9.4.

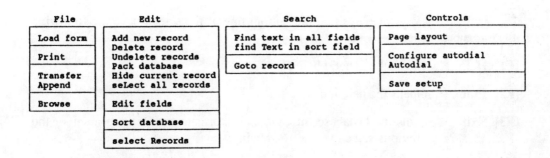

*Figure 9.4. Menu map for the Databases module*

**File**        Lets you load different form files, print database information, transfer and append new records, and switch between browse and edit modes.

**Edit**          Lets you work with records and fields, as well as sort the database.

**Search**        Searches for text in all fields or just the sort field, as well as go to a specific record number.

**Controls**      Lets you set a default page layout dimensions for printing, configure and use the autodial feature, and save the current configuration.

The current time is also displayed on the right side of the menu bar in the browse and edit screen. The next line down shows that this is a Database file, and the third line shows the path and the file name, the record number, and the total number of records in the database file. A vertical scroll bar is on the right side of the screen. These features are identical in both the browse and edit screens.

The fourth line down is where features on the browse screen become unique. There are only two fields in the DSKERR.DBF file, ID_NUMBER and MESSAGE. The cursor should be blinking under the ID_NUMBER field name.

> Although it's possible to change characters in a highlighted field in the browse screen, don't change this database. If you do make a change inadvertently, either change the characters back to their original values or press [Esc]. Either of these actions restores the characters that were originally read into the screen.

The ten function keys displayed on the bottom line of the screen have the following assignments attached:

**[F1] Help**     Opens the general help screen.

**[F2] Index**    Opens the help index.

**[F3] Exit**     Quits the Databases module and returns to the Desktop menu or the previous screen you were viewing.

**[F4] First**    Toggles the cursor between record number 1 and the last record in the current database.

**[F5] Prev.**    Moves the cursor to the next lowest record number until record number 1 is reached.

**[F6] Next**     Moves the cursor to the next highest record number until the last record in the database is reached.

**[F7] Search**    Opens the *Search sort field* dialog box, which lets you designate a specific record that contains the text you specify in a sorted field. You can find more information in chapter 10 under the heading "Organizing Records and Searching for Records."

**[F8] New**    Inserts a blank record at the top of the database, where you can enter new record information in the appropriate fields. After information is entered, the insertion point is determined by how you've sorted the database.

**[F9] Swap**    Switches between active windows.

**[F10] Menu**    Activates the top menu bar. It has the same effect as pressing [Alt].

When working with a database file, you'll probably perform the following procedures most frequently. You might want to experiment with some of these keys now to test their effects. Just make sure you don't add a new record. If you accidentally insert a blank record, leave it empty (do not enter data) and delete it this way:

**Highlight:** the blank record

**Press:** [Alt]-[E]-[D]

Do not delete any of the legitimate records in the DSKERR.DBF file.

All the keys you can use to move around the browse screen are shown in table 9.1.

*Table 9.1. Keys for moving around the browse screen*

| | |
|---|---|
| **Moving Among Records** | |
| Move right one field | [Tab] |
| Move left one field | [Shift]-[Tab] |
| Move down one field | [⇓] |
| Move down on record | [F6] |
| Scroll down one line | [Ctrl]-[PgDn] |
| Move down one screen | [PgDn] |
| Move to the last record | [Ctrl]-[End] |
| Move up one field | [⇑] |
| Move up one record | [F5] |
| Scroll up one field | [Ctrl]-[PgUp] |
| Move up one screen | [PgUp] |
| Move to first record | [Ctrl]-[Home] |
| Go to a specific record # | [Alt]-[S]-[G]-# |
| Toggle between 1st/last record | [F4] |
| | |
| **Moving Within a Screen** | |
| Move to beginning of window | [Home] twice |
| Move to end of window | [End] twice |
| | |
| **Moving Within a Record** | |
| Move right on field | [Enter]-[Tab] |
| Move left one field | [Shift]-[Tab] |
| | |
| **Moving Within a Field** | |
| Move right on character | [⇒] |
| Move right one word | [Ctrl]-[⇒] |
| Move to end of field | [End] once |
| Move left one character | [⇐] |
| Move left one word | [Ctrl]-[⇐] |
| Move to beginning of field | [Home] once |

Besides the menu commands that let you go to a particular record, you can move the cursor to the last record in the database by pressing [Ctrl]-[End]. You can move the cursor back to the first record by pressing [Ctrl]-[Home]. If you're at the beginning of the database, you can go to the end by pressing [F4]. Pressing [F4] a second time takes you back to the first record.

Use a menu command to go to a specific record. For example, to go to record number 50:

**Press:** [Alt]-[S]-[G]

**Type:** 50

**Press:** [Enter] twice

In this example, it's only coincidental that record numbers and ID_NUMBER numbers are identical; in other files, they may differ. The current record number only shows at the top of the browse screen after the path and file name; for example: RECORD 50 OF 100.

Using the browse screen, you can also add, edit, and delete records, as well as select and hide records and re-sort the entire database. Because altering DSKERR.DBF in any way will corrupt the file, do not make any changes to it. Instead, begin to tackle real work by creating a database file of our own.

First, switch to the edit screen:

**Press:** [Alt]-[F]-[B]

## The Edit Mode Screen

The edit mode screen, as shown in figure 9.3, displays information for a single record, or at least all the information that can fit into a single screen. It's called the edit mode screen because you can use it to edit and insert information into a record.

The top three lines are similar to the browse screen. The menu bar at the top and the function key assignments at the bottom are identical. The fourth line contains a horizontal scroll bar, and the next line down displays the Line and Column indicators; the name of the current form appears on the right side, in this case DSKERR.FOR. The fifth line down is the tab line.

These changes make the Database edit screen seem more like the Notepad editor screen. In fact, the it is a version of the Notepad editor screen. You're viewing the representation of data for a single field in DSKERR.DBF in a text file called DSKERR.FOR.

At the top of the screen you see the path and file name you're working with, C:\PCTOOLS\DSKERR.DBF, along with the currently displayed record number and total number of records in the file. You can move the cursor around this screen similar to the way you move it around the Notepads editor screen. Additional movement controls are shown in table 9.2.

*Table 9.2. Cursor movement keys for the edit screen*

| | |
|---|---|
| **Moving Within a Record** | |
| Move right one character | [⇒] |
| Move right one word | [Ctrl]-[⇒] |
| Move to end of current line | [End] |
| Move to end of record | [End] twice |
| Move left one character | [⇐] |
| Move left one word | [Ctrl]-[⇐] |
| Move to start of current line | [Home] |
| Move to start of record | [Home] twice |
| Move to start of field date | [Tab] |
| | |
| **Moving Among Records** | |
| Move to next record number | [F6] |
| Move to previous record number | [F5] |
| Move to last/first record | [F4] |

You can't move sequentially between database records by pressing [PgDn] or [PgUp]. The only difference between moving around in the Notepad editor and the Database edit screen is that pressing [Tab] in the Database edit screen doesn't move the cursor to the next tab stop. Tab stops have no effect in the Database edit screen, even though there's a tab line. You can't edit the tab line the way you can in the Notepads editor screen, nor can you turn it off.

Pressing [Tab] in the Database edit screen only moves you to the next word or to the next character after a space.

> Because overtype mode is on by default after you load a file into the Databases module, do not immediately begin typing in data. The program presumes that you want to edit data when you enter a database file. If you start pressing keys immediately, you might type over some data in the file. Instead, switch to the insert mode, by pressing [Ins].

The best way to understand the fundamental structure of all databases is to create one. After that, you can work with it.

# CREATING A DATABASE FILE

A database file in its simplest terms consists of individual fields that are repeated for every record. In this section, you will learn about the elements of a database file, by creating one yourself.

When you create a database file, you give it a name and then design its structure. You design the structure by deciding what types of fields you want to use and how large you want to make each field type.

Fields are the basic building blocks of a database. Each field is designed to hold individual pieces of information; the type and size of field you use depend upon the information you want to enter. Once you've created a field structure, you should save it to disk. During the save operation the PC Tools program will add the extension .DBF to the name you've given the file.

> In the Databases module, you must use the default extension .DBF. In other modules, you can change the extension; in the Databases module. All database files must end with the extension .DBF.

The process isn't completed yet. When PC Tools saves the .DBF file, it also creates two other files automatically. These assist the Databases module to present data correctly on screen. Each file is given the same name as the database file. One file is assigned the extension .REC, which serves as the record file. This is a type of index file that determines how fields are organized and records displayed on screen.

The second file is assigned the extension .FOR and serves as the default form file. This controls the way data from a database file appears on your screen and is printed out. The default form file serves as the basic template for displaying and printing data until you design and load another form.

For example, you're going to create a personal telephone book database called ABLE.DBF and save it to disk. The PC Tools program will then create two additional files, ABLE.REC and ABLE.FOR.

To create your first file, start at the Desktop main menu:

**Press:** [D]

**Type:** ABLE

The extension .DBF is added automatically by the program.

Although you can use any file name you want, keep in mind that the *DATABASES* dialog box lists file names in alphabetical order. Therefore, you'll find it handy to use a file name that most often appears at the top of the list. Then all you have to do is press [Enter] twice when the *DATABASES* dialog box appears, and you'll move directly into your most frequently used database file. (Not much can come before ABLE.DBF, except perhaps AABLE.DBF.)

## Entering Fields

To build a database correctly, you must know beforehand what fields you want to use. For example, in a personal telephone book, the minimum information you probably want is the name of the person and the home and work phone numbers. You might or might not include the mailing address. Just this information requires five fields: the person's name, home phone number, home address, work phone, and work address—one field to hold each piece of information.

Actually, you will need more than five fields. Two people may have the same first name, so you have to distinguish between them. This means you'll need two fields for names: first name and last name. Also, you may even need another field for a second work address, such as a post office box.

After typing the file name correctly:

    **Press:** [Enter]

This moves you directly into the *Field Editor* dialog box, which looks like figure 9.5:

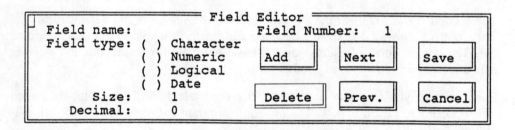

*Figure 9.5. Field Editor dialog box*

Use this box to define each type of field you want to create. You can move forward through the various selections by pressing [Tab]; move backwards by pressing [Shift]-[Tab].

You'll find the cursor blinking in the field after *Field name:*. This is where you type the name of the field you want to use. Create the first field to hold a first name. To title this field:

**Type:** FIRSTNAME

You could as well have typed NAMEFIRST or FIRST_NAME. (You must use the underline character to separate field-name information, because dBASE field names cannot contain a dash character.). Use whatever suits you, as long as you stay within the dBASE field-name allowances. You can use all letters and numbers on your keyboard, but you're limited to 11 characters. You can't use dashes or spaces, and you can't begin a field name with a number.

When the field name is as you want it:

**Press:** [Enter]

This moves the highlight bar to *Field type:*. You can use four different types of fields:

**Character** Contains simple text characters. You'll use this field type most often; it's appropriate for all names, addresses, and any other textual information.

**Numeric** Contains numbers on which you want to perform calculations when working in a dBASE-type program. Although you can't perform calculations in the PC Tools Databases module, you might want to create files using PC Tools that you'll later use in a dBASE or compatible program.

**Logic** Contains one logical character, either **T** for true or **F** for false. Use this field to specify one of two possible conditions, such as gender (T=female, F=male) or an update for developments (T=sent, F=not sent). The default entry is F.

**Date** Contains date information in an eight-place field. This lets you enter a date using the mm/dd/yy (month/day/year) format, as in 12/25/90.

Experienced dBASE users will recognize that the Databases module does not provide a memo field. In dBASE and compatible programs, memo fields are created and stored in separate files, which require more work than the Databases module can perform. However, you can enter up to 70 characters in a character field, which should be enough for most routine text entries.

Be careful when loading a database file created in a dBASE or compatible program into the PC Tools Databases module. Because of the PC Tools field size limitations, character fields containing more than 70 characters will be truncated—the excess will not be displayed in the Databases screen.

As long as you don't make any changes to the database file, such as saving it or modifying its structure, you can view truncated information in the Databases module screen and then exit the file. The original data will remain intact. If you change or save a database file that contains fields with more characters than can be handled by the PC Tools Databases module, you might lose the excess data.

Since you'll use the *Character* field most often, it's highlighted by default.

**Press:** [Enter]

This moves you to the Size field in the *Field Editor* box, where you declare the maximum number of characters you want to enter into the FIRSTNAME field. Since, most first names won't go beyond 15 characters:

**Type:** 15

**Press:** [Enter]

This moves you to the *Decimal* field. Use this field only when you've selected the numeric field type.

**Press:** [Enter]

This highlights the *Add* box. Accepting this box adds the field you've just created into the new database file.

**Press:** [Enter]

This moves you back to the top of a fresh *Field Editor* dialog box. The only thing different is that it shows you're creating *Field Number 2*. You can see this more clearly by moving back to the previous field.

**Press:** [Shift]-[Tab] three times

This should highlight the *Prev.* box.

> **Press:** [Enter]

This moves you back to your first field. Notice that it is *Field Number 1*. To move back to field number 2:

> **Press:** [Tab] six times

This should highlight the *Next* box.

> **Press:** [Enter]

This moves you on to the next field, which is number 2.

The following explains the six box commands:

**Add**       Adds the field displayed in the *Field Editor* box to the current database file.

**Del**       Deletes the field displayed in the *Field Editor* box from the current database file.

**Next**      Displays information for the next field in the current database file.

**Prev.**     Displays information for the previous field in the current database file.

**Save**      Saves all field information for the current database file, completes the building process, and moves you into the Database display screen showing the current file structure.

**Cancel**    Cancels building the current database and returns you to the Desktop main menu or to the module you were working in previously.

Finish building the first database structure. When the *Field Editor* box for record number 2 is showing:

> **Type:** LASTNAME
>
> **Press:** [Enter] twice
>
> **Type:** 15
>
> **Press:** [Enter] three times
>
> **Type:** ADDRESS

**Press:** [Enter] twice

**Type:** 35

Addresses usually require more field space than names.

**Press:** [Enter] three times

**Type:** CITY

**Press:** [Enter] twice

**Type:** 20

Although there are city names with more than 20 characters, your chances of using them are slim.

**Press:** [Enter] three times

**Type:** STATE

**Press:** [Enter] twice

**Type:** 2

**Press:** [Enter] three times

**Type:** ZIP

**Press:** [Enter] twice

You might think that the zip-code field should be numeric because it contains numbers, but numeric fields are only for numbers that will be used for calculations, such as prices and quantities. Since zip codes are not used in calculations—even in full-fledged database programs—use the *Character* field type.

**Type:** 10

**Press:** [Enter] three times

**Type:** PHONE

**Press:** [Enter] twice

**Type:** 15

This gives you enough room to enter a phone number, area code, out-of-building codes, and out-of-area prefixes. If you intend to call people with extensions in their offices, add a few more digits for the extension number and defining characters; for example three more characters for x73 or six more characters for ext.73.

**Press:** [Enter] three times

Now create another field type.

**Type:** MONEY

**Press:** [Enter] once

When *Field type: Character* is highlighted:

**Press:** [⇓]

This should highlight *Numeric*.

**Press:** [Enter] once

**Type:** 4

**Press:** [Enter]

**Type:** 2

This allocates four characters to the left of the decimal point and two characters after the decimal point in the *MONEY* field, which facilitates entering dollar amounts up to $9999.99.

**Press:** [Enter] twice

**Type:** MAILED

**Press:** [Enter] once

**Press:** [⇓]

This should highlight *Logical*.

**Press:** [Enter] four times

When you create a logical field, need to specify the number of characters or decimal points because you can enter only a True or False reply.

**Type:** DATE

**Press:** [Enter]

**Press:** [⇓]

This should highlight *Date*.

**Press:** [Enter]

**Press:** [Enter] four times

When you create a date field, there's also no need to specify the number of characters or decimal points because the program automatically creates the mm/dd/yy format.

**Press:** [Tab] eight times

This creates the seven fields and saves the structure you've just built. The new structure can be displayed on your screen. To see what this structure looks like, switch to the edit mode:

**Press:** [Alt]-[F]-[B]

Your screen should look like figure 9.6.

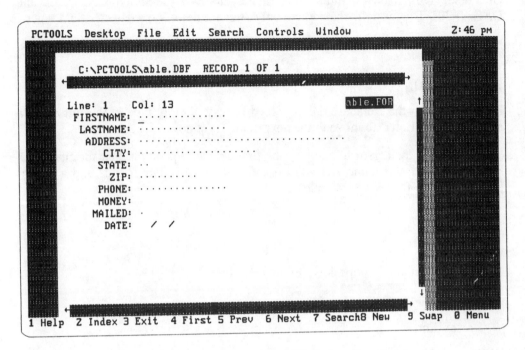

```
PCTOOLS  Desktop  File  Edit  Search  Controls  Window                2:46 PM

      C:\PCTOOLS\able.DBF   RECORD 1 OF 1



      Line: 1     Col: 13                                    able.FOR
       FIRSTNAME: ..............
        LASTNAME: ..............
         ADDRESS: .............................
            CITY: ................
           STATE: ..
             ZIP: .........
           PHONE: ..............
           MONEY:
          MAILED: .
            DATE:   /  /



 1 Help  2 Index 3 Exit  4 First 5 Prev  6 Next  7 Search8 New   9 Swap  0 Menu
```

*Figure 9.6.  The structure for ABLE.DBF displayed in edit mode*

This is the template you'll use for every record in ABLE.DBF. You can see the ten fields just created; their names are on the left, and the format of the field is to the right. For each character field, the format shows dots, which indicate the maximum number of characters you can insert in that field. Creating this template yourself gives you a clearer idea of its structure than using a sample database created by someone else.

The three noncharacter fields—MONEY, MAILED, and DATE—show no dots; instead, they display a form of their own:

- For numeric fields, such as money, the number 0 shows in the first digit position.
- For logic fields, such as MAILED, the default character, F (for false), shows in the first position.
- For date fields, such as DATE, the slashes in mm/dd/yy show, although no month, day, or year numerals appear.

Of course, your personal mail list database may not have the MONEY, MAILED and DATE fields. They were included here only as examples of noncharacter field types.

Now use the structure you created to enter data.

## Entering Data

Entering data in the Database editor screen is easy. Simply type in the information and then press [Enter] to move to the next field. Try it now.

You should see the cursor blinking in the first character position after the first field, FIRSTNAME. Enter name and address information for your friends and acquaintances using the following example.

**Type:** Milan

**Press:** [Enter]

Notice how your cursor pops down to the next line.

**Type:** Moncilovich

**Press:** [Enter]

**Type:** 2 Holly Lane

**Press:** [Enter]

**Type:** Beaverton

**Press:** [Enter]

**Type:** OR

**Press:** [Enter]

**Type:** 97000

**Press:** [Enter]

**Type:** 1-503-555-0000

**Press:** [Enter]

Your screen should look like figure 9.7.

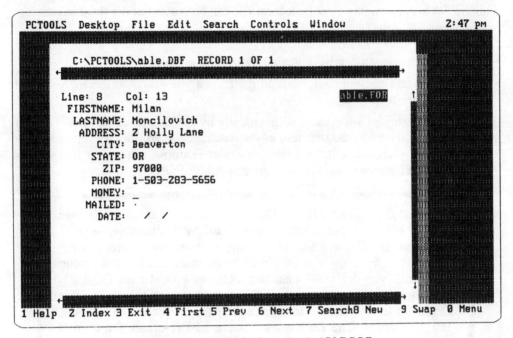

*Figure 9.7. First field information in ABLE.DBF*

You've now inserted the preliminary information for a single record, which contains a name, home address, and phone number.

On your own, enter several more records to get the feel of logging in data. In the rest of this chapter and in the next chapter, you will work with the multirecord database file that you just created.

# WORKING WITH FORM FILES

Form files display selected database information in your edit screen (when the browse screen is switched off). They also print information to paper or disk. As its name implies, a form file is one that contains the format in which the database information will appear.

The best way to understand form files is find out how they are created and then examine various examples. A default form file can be created under three situations:

- When you first create a database.
- When you first view a database created by another program.
- When you create one yourself, designing a format you prefer to use for your own customized needs.

The first two examples are created automatically by the Databases module. The program automatically reads the structure of the database file you're creating or want to view and quickly creates a default form file. For example, when you first created ABLE.DBF, the Databases module also created ABLE.FOR.

> A second file, called ABLE.REC is also created automatically (see chapter 10). You need three files to work with databases—.DBF, .FOR, and .REC. Each file has the same name, but different extensions. Extensions are how PC Tools keeps track of files that belong together. If you delete the matching .REC and .FOR files, PC Tools will re-create new default files. If you ever change the names of a database file, you'll have to change the name of the matching .FOR and .REC files. The Databases module will re-create the correct matching .FOR and .REC files the next time you view the renamed database.

Take a look at the structure of the default file ABLE.FOR that was created automatically.

**Press:** [Alt]-[D]-[N]

**Type:** ABLE.FOR

**Press:** [Enter]

> This series of commands works as long as the Notepads and Databases modules are both logged on to the same directory. Otherwise, you'll have to specify the Databases directory when you look for a form file.

When ABLE.FOR appears on your screen, it will look like figure 9.8.

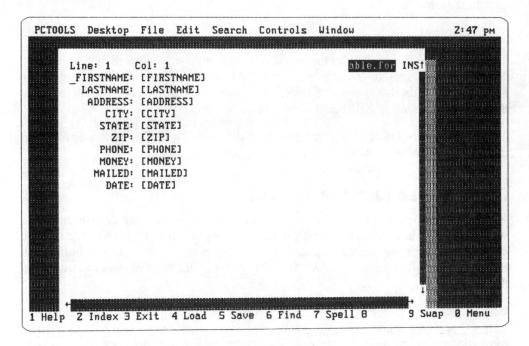

```
 PCTOOLS  Desktop  File  Edit  Search  Controls  Window              2:47 PM

     Line: 1     Col: 1                              able.for  INS↑
    _FIRSTNAME: [FIRSTNAME]
     LASTNAME: [LASTNAME]
      ADDRESS: [ADDRESS]
         CITY: [CITY]
        STATE: [STATE]
          ZIP: [ZIP]
        PHONE: [PHONE]
        MONEY: [MONEY]
       MAILED: [MAILED]
         DATE: [DATE]



                                                               ↓
   ←
 1 Help  2 Index 3 Exit  4 Load  5 Save  6 Find  7 Spell 8       9 Swap  0 Menu
```

*Figure 9.8. ABLE.FOR displayed in the Notepads editor screen*

Notice how each field has been placed on a line of its own, flush against the left margin, and how the name of every field is duplicated on the same line; the first is followed by a colon, the second is surrounded by brackets. The first field name appears on the view-mode screen is the title of the field. The second field name (in brackets) is a variable: it displays the contents of the matching field name in the selected record of the database you're using.

Remember that this format is similar to what appears when you view the contents of ABLE.DBF in the Databases module screen. You can check this out by opening the matching database file and switching back and forth between it and the form file.

**Press:** [Alt]-[D]-[D]

**Type:** ABLE

**Press:** [Enter]

Make sure you're looking at a record in the edit-mode screen, which means that information for just one record appears on your screen. Now switch back to the matching form file:

> **Press:** [F9]

Notice how the fields line up the same way in both the Databases screen and the Notepad editor screen. Switch back and forth until you realize how similar the screens look. This shows you the effect of a form file. The ABLE.FOR file controls the way information in ABLE.DBF appears in the edit view.

You can see this better when you create a different form file and redisplay the database information, which is what you'll do next.

## Creating a New Form File for Viewing

If you want to view field information in a different format than the default, or if you want to print it in a custom format (either on paper or on a disk file), you need to create a new form file that corresponds to your appearance specifications. In this section, you'll use form files to view data. Using form files to print data is covered in the next chapter.

Use the Notepads editor screen to create a form file. Just type in the field names you want to view or print and specify exactly where you want to view or print them. The form file you create will display only the names and phone numbers of the people you listed in ABLE.DBF. You can use this form as a phone-number locator.

Before creating a form file, you need to know the exact structure of the database file you're working with. You can either write down the structure of the database you're using or open two Notepads screens: one containing the default form file, which displays all the fields, and the other containing your customized form file.

> **Press:** [Esc]

Now return to ABLE.DBF in the Databases editor screen. Pop open the Notepad editor screen over the Databases edit mode screen.

To create the new form file:

> **Press:** [Alt]-[D]-[N]
>
> **Type:** NAMENUM.FOR
>
> **Press:** [Enter] twice

Be sure to include the extension .FOR.  If you don't, you'll create a text file with the default extension, most likely .TXT.

You can create and use a form file with an extension other than .FOR, but you'll have to type the extension each time you want to load the form file.

Consider a shorter name if you use this form often, because you'll have to call it up each time you want to use it. When the second Notepads editor screen appears, the file name NAMENUM.FOR should appear in the upper-right corner. Next, resize the Notepads editor screen to let you view the Databases screen underneath:

**Press:** [Alt]-[W]-[R]

**Press:** [⇒] approximately 30 times

**Press:** [⇐] approximately eight times

To fix this new shape:

**Press:** [Enter]

Now move the smaller current window to the lower-right corner of the screen.

**Press:** [Alt]-[W]-[M]

**Press:** [⇒] approximately 30 times

**Press:** [⇓] approximately five times

Fix this new location:

**Press:** [Enter]

Your screen should now look like figure 9.9.

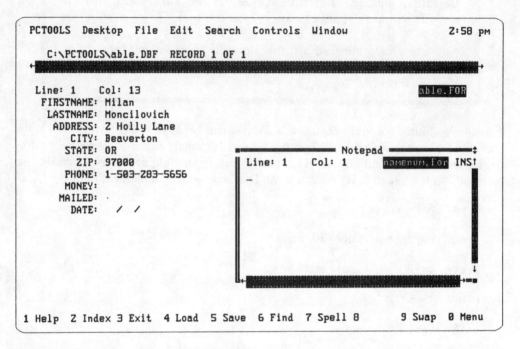

*Figure 9.9. A resized and repositioned Notepad editor screen overlaying the Databases editor screen*

Position the cursor in Line 1 Column 1 and type the first field you want to view:

**Type:** NAME: [FIRSTNAME] [LASTNAME]

The line might wrap due to the small window size. Don't worry about that.

**Press:** [Enter]

This is identical to the first line in the default ABLE.FOR. It's not necessary to use the field name for the first of the two field names, but you will for this example.

The second field name of the pair has to match a valid field name in the database you're using. It can be uppercase or lowercase characters, or a mixture of the two, but it has to match the field name, letter for letter of the data you want to view.

Now prepare to insert the second field, PHONE:

**Type:** PHONE: [PHONE]

Your screen should now look like figure 9.10.

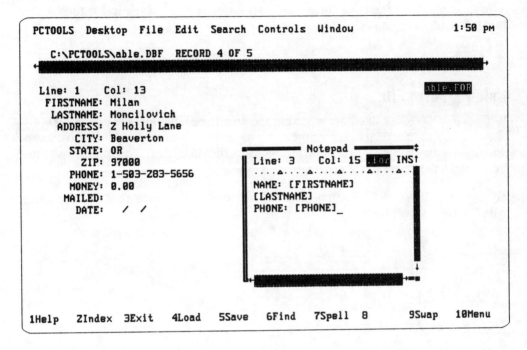

*Figure 9.10. The new form NAMENUM.FOR*

If the form file is as you want it, save it:

**Press:** [F5]

**Press:** [Enter] twice

You can save forms in either PC Tools or ASCII format.

You can change the form if necessary. The first field name in the pair is what appears on screen. You can type anything you want to designate the field. Some users prefer to view a first-caps mix of uppercase and lowercase letters (for example, Name:). For this, you would either:

**Type:** Name: [NAME]

Or you could:

**Type:** Person> [NAME]

This would display Person> on the screen in place of NAME: (or Name:).

Now that you've created a form file, you can put it to use. First return to the Databases editor window:

**Press:** [Esc]

## Using a Form File

Whenever you view a database record in the edit screen, the information will be displayed in a form file that contains the same name as the database file. In most cases, this will be the default form file. To use a form file other than the default, you must load it from the Databases edit screen.

To load NAMENUM.FOR, first switch back to the Databases module displaying ABLE.DBF.

**Press:** [F9]

To load the new form:

**Press:** [Alt]-[F]-[L]

This opens the *Form* dialog box.

**Type:** NAMENUM

As long as you're using the current default extension, you only need to type the form file name.

**Press:** [Enter]

Whenever you use a new form or record file (for example, if you've deleted the previous record file), the Databases editor screen will appear in its original default mode. The size and colors you've picked before, even if you saved the configuration, won't have an effect.

In a moment, your Databases editor screen should change to reflect the new form, as shown in figure 9.11.

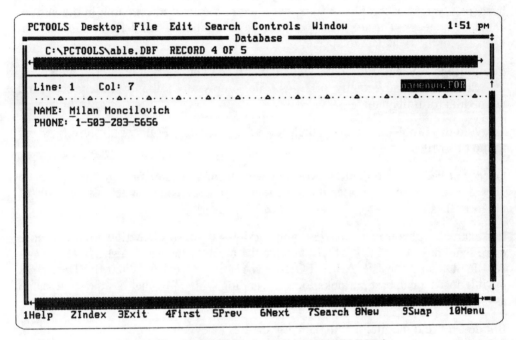

```
PCTOOLS  Desktop  File  Edit  Search  Controls  Window          1:51 PM
═════════════════════════ Database ═════════════════════════════╪
│   C:\PCTOOLS\able.DBF   RECORD 4 OF 5                           │
┼────────────────────────────────────────────────────────────────┤
│                                                                  │
│ Line: 1    Col: 7                                 namenum.FOR  ↑ │
│ ....▲....▲....▲....▲....▲....▲....▲....▲....▲....▲....▲...      │
│ NAME: Milan Moncilovich                                          │
│ PHONE: 1-503-283-5656                                            │
│                                                                  │
│                                                                  │
│                                                                  │
│                                                                  │
│                                                                  │
│                                                                  │
│                                                                  │
│                                                                  │
│                                                                  │
│                                                                ↓ │
┼────────────────────────────────────────────────────────────■─╪
 1Help   2Index  3Exit   4First  5Prev   6Next   7Search 8New   9Swap   10Menu
```

*Figure 9.11. ABLE.DBF displayed in NAMENUM.FOR form*

Notice how the label NAMENUM.FOR appears in the upper-right corner of your screen; this lets you keep track of which form you're using. Using the custom form NAMENUM, you can move through records in the database and view only the names and phone numbers in your address book.

As long as the form you've just created remains the form in use, you can switch back to the Notepad editor screen to make changes to the form, save the changes, and then switch back to the Databases editor screen to view the new effects. This is a great way to build more complex forms and to make sure the information is displayed the way you want it.

To return your display to the default form:

> **Press:** [Alt]-[F]-[L]
>
> **Type:** ABLE
>
> **Press:** [Enter]

Be careful when you load form files. You can load any text file as a form file. A text file doesn't have to end with the extension .FOR to appear in the edit screen of the Databases module as long as you specify the full file name and extension. When this happens, the text of the file appears, but none of the field information in the current database appears. The text file would have to contain a valid field name within brackets for the field data to appear.

You'll use this type of file in the next chapter when you learn how to print merge letters. Should you inadvertently load a text file, simply repeat the form file process and use a valid form file name.

To avoid this problem, use the default form file extension .FOR for all form files and for no other files.

Once you become experienced working with form files and find that you want to view a certain form more often than the default form, consider switching the name of the form files.

For example, if you want to view your address book in NAMENUM form more often than the default ABLE.FOR, change the name of the file NAMENUM.FOR to ABLE.FOR and the file ABLE.FOR to NAMENUM.FOR. When the Databases module loads a database, it looks for a file ending with .FOR that has the same name as the database and then displays the database information according to that form.

If it doesn't find the file, it automatically creates a new one, inserting all the fields in the database. Whenever you view a database for the first time, whose structure has been changed, you should delete the current default form file for the database and let PC Tools build a new one for you.

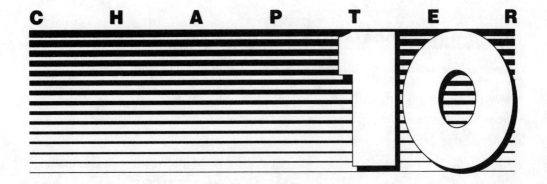

C H A P T E R

# 10

# WORKING WITH DATABASES

A good database remains in flux; its information is continuously changing. The value of existing information also changes, with some things becoming more important and others less so. New things appear and old things disappear. All this requires that you keep updating your database or it will soon be outmoded.

# CHANGING INFORMATION IN A DATABASE

There are four basic ways you can change information in a database:

• Reorganize the records to display them in a different order.

• Select some records and hide others to get a range of records.

• Add, edit, and delete records.

• Change the field names to reflect changes in the type of information you maintain.

For example, if you want to write letters to everyone in ABLE.DBF, you would want to sort the database by name to verify that everyone's listed. If you want to write letters to only those people in California, you would select all records with a California address. As you gain and lose friends, or they get married and change their names, you can add and delete records or edit the record contents. Finally, if you want to add names of people living abroad, you can change the name of the ZIP field to MAIL-CODE, since foreign countries don't use the zip system.

These are just a few of the many reasons why you would want to make changes to a database. In this chapter, you'll learn how to make these changes. You'll also discover the various ways can you print database information, so you can maintain paper copies of your database files. The last topic of this chapter will describe ways you can automatically dial phone numbers from a database record.

# MODIFYING DATABASE RECORDS

Most of your time changing a database will be spent adding new records and editing or deleting existing records. Editing and deleting records are the simplest tasks. You can add new records in several ways: insert them one-by-one in an existing database, append an entire database to another database, or transfer selected records from one database to another.

## Editing Records

You can edit information in records just by typing over the original information. You can also delete the old information first by pressing [Del] or [Backspace], but typing over and deleting unneeded information is the best method. Whenever you enter a browse or edit Databases screen, the overtype mode is the default condition. It's a good idea, therefore, to press [Ins] each time you enter a Databases screen so you don't accidentally type over information you want to keep.

> As long as you don't press [Enter], information you type into a field will not be saved. If you accidentally type information you don't want to keep, press [Esc] to exit the Databases screen, then load the file a second time.

If you make changes to a database often, you should create a backup version of the database file to protect against inadvertent changes or to refer back to the original data.

# Adding New Records

Once you create a database, you'll be surprised how fast it grows. Inserting new data is so easy using computers, you'll soon find yourself logging in information you didn't expect to save when you first created the database.

Adding new records is a basic operation to all database management. You can add new records to a database three ways:

- Add them one at a time.
- Transfer them in a block from another database.
- Attach one database to another.

### Adding Records One-by-One

To add a new record, you need to first view the database using either the browse or the edit screen. The edit screen is more appropriate, since it shows all the fields for a single record when you use the form file created by the program.

To add a record to the current database, use either the *Add new record* command on the Edit pull-down menu or the [F8] function key. The easiest way is to:

**Press:** [F8]

This opens a blank record screen you saw earlier in figure 9.6. This is the screen you used to enter the first records in ABLE.DBF. When adding a record to a database that already has one or more records, you work in the first record screen, but the total count of existing records will show at the top. If you're working in the browse screen, an empty record slot will appear at the top of the file.

In either screen, just type the record information. Figure 10.1 shows ABLE.DBF containing four additional records that were added in this way.

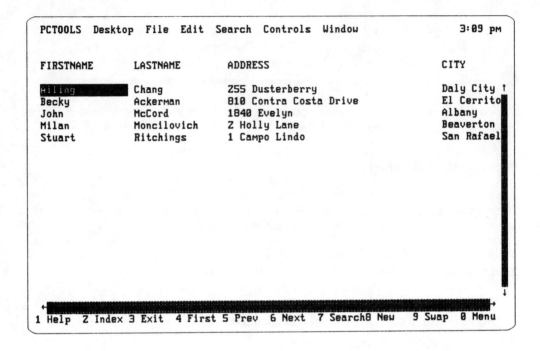

```
 PCTOOLS  Desktop  File  Edit  Search  Controls  Window              3:09 PM

 FIRSTNAME       LASTNAME        ADDRESS                          CITY

 Hiling          Chang           255 Dusterberry                  Daly City ↑
 Becky           Ackerman        810 Contra Costa Drive           El Cerrito
 John            McCord          1840 Evelyn                      Albany
 Milan           Moncilovich     2 Holly Lane                     Beaverton
 Stuart          Ritchings       1 Campo Lindo                    San Rafael



                                                                          ↓
 ◄━━━━━━━━━━━━━━━━━━━━━━━━━━━━━━━━━━━━━━━━━━━━━━━━━━━━━━━━━━━━━━━━━━━━━━►
 1 Help  2 Index 3 Exit  4 First 5 Prev  6 Next  7 Search8 New   9 Swap  0 Menu
```

*Figure 10.1. Four additional records added to ABLE.DBF*

You'll use these records to demonstrate other ways of adding records to a database. For these demonstrations, you'll be adding records of your own. The only requirements for using the examples in this chapter are that you retain the same first and last names in the records shown in figure 10.1 and you place only two of these records in California (using CA in the STATE field). You can then enter as many of your own records as you want, up to the PC Tools Deluxe limit of 10,000 (in version 6).

### Appending Databases

You can add records to a database by appending another database to it. This procedure requires that you have two databases: the active one that receives the appended records and the source that supplies the records.

> If you only have one database at this point, for example ABLE.DBF, you can create a new database either from scratch or by making a copy of the existing database. To make a copy, use the PC Shell, then give the database different names, for example, BAKER.DBF.

To transfer the contents of BAKER.DBF into ABLE.DBF, make sure you're in the browse screen of the active database, ABLE.DBF, so you can view the results of appending. Although you can append a database using either the browse or the edit screen, you can see the results immediately when you're viewing the browse screen.

Begin the appending process:

**Press:** [Alt]-[F]-[A]

This opens a version of the *Databases* dialog box called *Append*.

**Type:** BAKER

**Press:** [Enter]

In a moment, the records in BAKER.DBF (which is a copy of ABLE.DBF) appear in ABLE.DBF, as shown in figure 10.2. The BAKER.DBF database remains as a separate file on your disk.

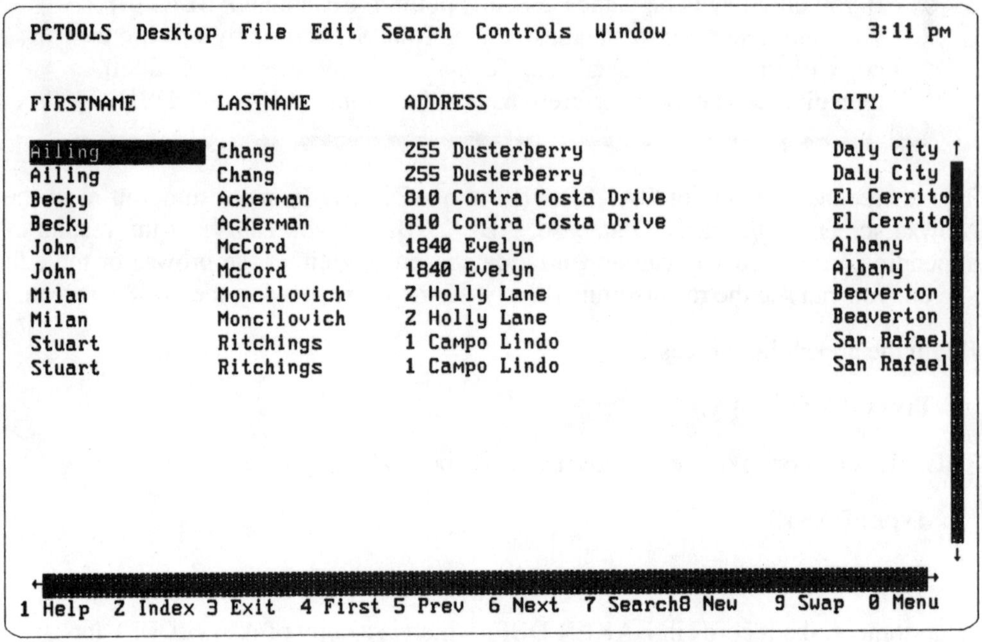

```
 PCTOOLS  Desktop  File  Edit  Search  Controls  Window              3:11 pm

 FIRSTNAME        LASTNAME        ADDRESS                       CITY

 Ailing           Chang           255 Dusterberry               Daly City ↑
 Ailing           Chang           255 Dusterberry               Daly City
 Becky            Ackerman        810 Contra Costa Drive        El Cerrito
 Becky            Ackerman        810 Contra Costa Drive        El Cerrito
 John             McCord          1840 Evelyn                   Albany
 John             McCord          1840 Evelyn                   Albany
 Milan            Moncilovich     2 Holly Lane                  Beaverton
 Milan            Moncilovich     2 Holly Lane                  Beaverton
 Stuart           Ritchings       1 Campo Lindo                 San Rafael
 Stuart           Ritchings       1 Campo Lindo                 San Rafael



                                                                          ↓
 ◄                                                                        ►
 1 Help  2 Index 3 Exit  4 First 5 Prev  6 Next  7 Search8 New  9 Swap  0 Menu
```

*Figure 10.2. Records in BAKER.DBF appended to ABLE.DBF*

The records you just appended from BAKER.DBF were added sequentially to the end of ABLE.DBF, but this isn't apparent from the screen display because of the default sort order. The first field you create in a database is designated the primary field. PC Tools automatically sorts the database according to information in this field. Since the first field you created is FIRSTNAME, all the records in ABLE.DBF are organized alphabetically according to the first name of each person in a record. When you appended BAKER.DBF to ABLE.DBF, all the appended records were re-sorted automatically by first name. You'll find out more about sorting and ways you can re-sort later in this chapter.

> Everything works smoothly when you append records from a database with an identical field structure. But when you append records from a database with different fields, only matching fields will be transferred. Fields that don't exist in the active database ( the one receiving the records) will be ignored. You'll be prompted for default entries for fields that don't exist in the appended records but do exist in the active database.

If you want to add some, but not all, of the records from another database, you should use the transfer process, which is described next.

### *Transferring Selected Records*

You can selectively append records from one database to another, which is called transferring records. To do this, select the records you want to transfer in the source database and then transfer them to the destination database. Here are the steps you should follow:

1. Open the source database.

2. Select the records you want to transfer in the source database.

3. Execute the transfer command by specifying the destination database.

4. View the destination database to make sure the records were transferred to it correctly.

Transfer two records from BAKER.DBF, the source, to ABLE.DBF, the destination. First open (load) the source database, BAKER.DBF.

**Press:** [Alt]-[D]-[D]

**Type:** BAKER

**Press:** [Enter]

Now select the records you want to transfer. For this example, transfer the four records having addresses in California (STATE = CA).

**Press:** [Alt]-[E]-[R]

This opens the *Select Records* box.

**Type:** STATE

**Press:** [Enter]

**Type:** CA

**Press:** [Enter]

Now press either [Tab] or [Enter] as many times as it takes to move the highlight bar to the *SELECT* box (about 15 key presses). Don't press [S] to execute the *Select* command or else you'll insert the letter *s* in a field name or data field.)

You should now be viewing two records on your screen, as shown in figure 10.3.

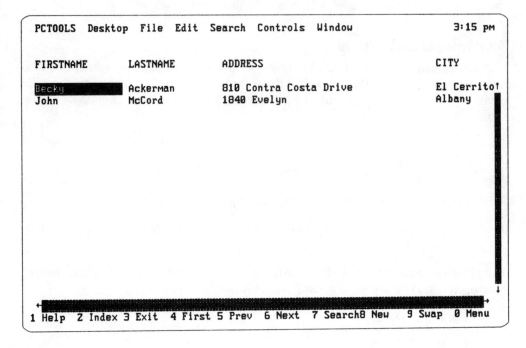

```
 PCTOOLS  Desktop  File  Edit  Search  Controls  Window                3:15 PM

 FIRSTNAME        LASTNAME        ADDRESS                        CITY

 Becky            Ackerman        810 Contra Costa Drive         El Cerrito↑
 John             McCord          1840 Evelyn                    Albany

                                                                             ↓

 1 Help  2 Index 3 Exit  4 First 5 Prev  6 Next  7 Search8 New   9 Swap  0 Menu
```

*Figure 10.3. Two records selected in BAKER.DBF*

These are the records you're going to transfer to ABLE.DBF.

Next, begin the transfer process:

**Press:** [Alt]-[F]-[T]

This opens a version of the *Databases* dialog box called *Transfer,* in which you specify ABLE.DBF as the destination database.

**Type:** ABLE

**Press:** [Enter]

That's all there is to it. If you want to double-check the success of the transfer, load ABLE.DBF into a Databases screen. If everything went according to plan, your screen should look like figure 10.4.

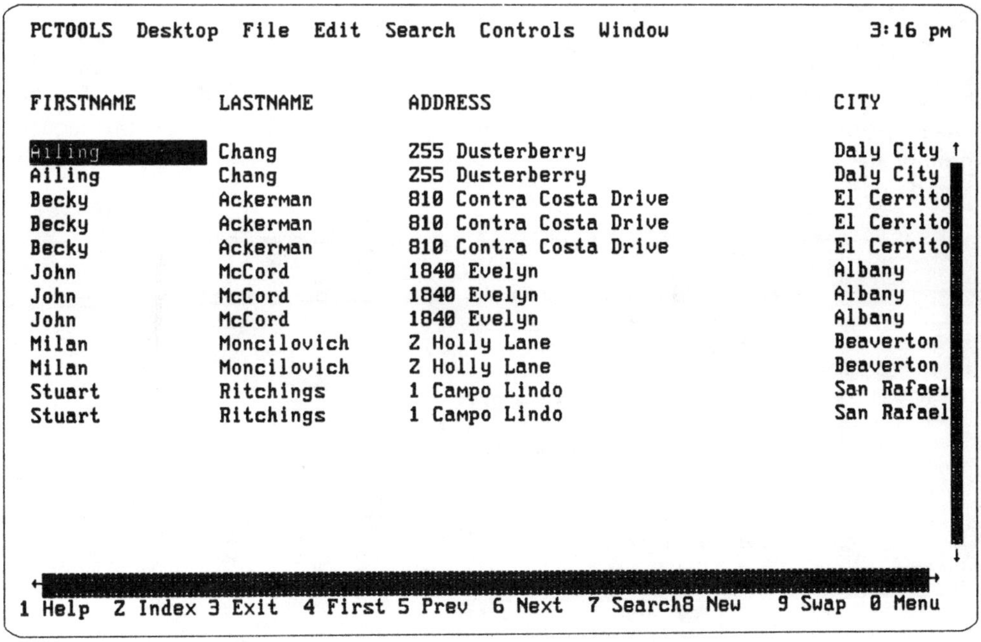

```
 PCTOOLS  Desktop  File  Edit  Search  Controls  Window              3:16 PM


 FIRSTNAME        LASTNAME        ADDRESS                         CITY

 Ailing           Chang           255 Dusterberry                 Daly City ↑
 Ailing           Chang           255 Dusterberry                 Daly City
 Becky            Ackerman        810 Contra Costa Drive          El Cerrito
 Becky            Ackerman        810 Contra Costa Drive          El Cerrito
 Becky            Ackerman        810 Contra Costa Drive          El Cerrito
 John             McCord          1840 Evelyn                     Albany
 John             McCord          1840 Evelyn                     Albany
 John             McCord          1840 Evelyn                     Albany
 Milan            Moncilovich     2 Holly Lane                    Beaverton
 Milan            Moncilovich     2 Holly Lane                    Beaverton
 Stuart           Ritchings       1 Campo Lindo                   San Rafael
 Stuart           Ritchings       1 Campo Lindo                   San Rafael




                                                                            ↓

 1 Help  2 Index  3 Exit  4 First 5 Prev  6 Next  7 Search8 New   9 Swap  0 Menu
```

*Figure 10.4. Two additional records in ABLE.DBF*

If ABLE.DBF was previously loaded into a Databases editor screen, it doesn't contain the new transferred records. In this case, you'll have to reload the file before you can view the updated information

## Deleting Old Records

You'll find you need to delete existing records as their information goes out of date. Deleting records is a two-step process designed to let you recover any records you've deleted accidentally. The first step marks the record for deletion. The second step actually deletes the record.

For example, suppose you wish to remove the record for Milan from the database. First, view the record in the edit screen or highlight it in the browse screen.

**Press:** [Alt]-[E]-[D]

The record will disappear from your screen, and the next record will appear in its place. You can only delete records one-by-one. At this point, you can continue deleting other records or you can delete just the one record. If you delete all but one record from a database and then try to delete the last record, you'll get the security prompt shown in figure 10.5.

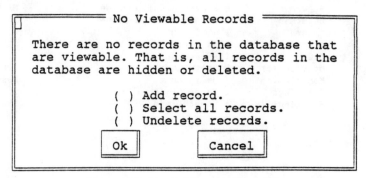

*Figure 10.5. The No Viewable Records box*

This gives you several options for continuing your work in the current database. After all, if you delete the last record, the database will no longer exist.

You should be aware that the record for Milan you just deleted is not yet gone from the database. Deleting a record only marks it for deletion and hides it from view. The record won't actually be removed until you pack the database.

### Undeleting Records

To protect against accidentally marking a record for deletion and losing a valuable record, PC Tools requires that you confirm a record marked for deletion. Confirmation to delete or a decision to retain a record is made when you initiate the packing operation. If you've marked a record but haven't yet started to pack the database, you can recover the marked record:

**Press:** [Alt]-[E]-[U]

All the records marked for deletion will pop back into view. Although you delete records one-by-one, you undelete all records that were previously marked for deletion.

### *Packing the Database*

Once you've decided that you indeed want to delete all the records you've marked, you should pack the database. Packing is a dBASE term that describes the process of removing the marked records and storing the remaining records so no empty space remains in the database. Obviously, when you remove records, you make the database smaller.

To pack a database containing records marked for deletion:

> **Press:** [Alt]-[E]-[P]

The program will display a security prompt warning you that it's about to pack the database. If you change your mind and decide you don't want to delete certain marked records, you should back out of the pack now.

> **Press:** [C]

This lets you undelete all marked records and begin the deletion process again. If you want to continue the packing process:

> **Press:** [O]

It might take a few moments for the program to complete the packing, depending upon how many records you've marked.

## Hiding Records

Hiding a record prevents it from being viewed on screen. This is the best way to protect the record from being changed. You can't mark a hidden record for deletion nor can you edit information in a record you can't see.

To hide a record, view it first in the edit screen or highlight it in the browse screen. Then:

> **Press:** [Alt]-[E]-[H]

When you hide a record, the next record appears in its place. Hiding a record doesn't remove it from the database; the record is only hidden from view until you reveal it again.

To bring the hidden record back to your display:

> **Press:** [Alt]-[E]-[L]

Selecting all records reveals all hidden records at once. You can't reveal hidden records selectively. In fact, because it's possible to hide records and then forget about them, you might want to periodically select all records just to make sure you're aware of all the records in the current database.

# ORGANIZING RECORDS

You can organize records in a database two ways: by selecting them within a database or by reorganizing the entire database in a special sorted order. Before you learn how to use these two procedures, you should know a little background about how PC Tools remembers what order you specified for displaying records.

## About .REC Files

When you first worked with form files in chapter 9, you learned that the Databases module creates two additional files automatically when you create a database. These are the form file (.FOR extension) and the record file (.REC extension). For ABLE.DBF, these files were given the names ABLE.FOR and ABLE.REC.

The record file controls the way records are organized within the matching database. You can't create custom record files the way you can create custom form files. Only one record file can apply to a database, and the Databases module creates the record file automatically. It does this by scanning the database, when you create or change it and stores the field entries for the sorted field.

> When a .REC file becomes corrupted or PC Tools can't create a new version of the .REC file for a modified database, you'll get the error message ERROR: BAD .REC FILE, DELETE AND RELOAD DATA BASE. If this happens, follow the displayed instructions. If you continue to have trouble loading a database file, refer to methods for solving the problem later in this chapter, in the section Backing Up Your Data.

When you create a database, the order in which you enter the records is considered the sorted order. The first field is the one used for sorting until you select another. Each time you open a database to view or identify its contents, the Databases module reads the matching .REC file and organizes the records according to the file's contents. When you re-sort a database according to another field, the information is saved to a corresponding record file in the new sorted order.

In ABLE.DBF, since the database has not yet been sorted, the order of record listing is by NAME, which is the first field. Take a closer look at this record file. First, use the PC Shell to make a backup copy of ABLE.REC. Name the backup copy ABLEREC.TXT. Next, read ABLEREC.TXT into the Notepad editor screen:

**Press:** [Alt]-[D]-[N]

**Type:** ABLEREC.TXT

**Press:** [Enter] twice

If the program asks how you want to display the contents of the file, press [A] for ASCII and move into the file. When the contents are displayed on your screen, turn off the highlighting by unmarking the block.

**Press:** [Alt]-[E]-[U]

You might have to do this twice to remove all the highlighting. (Because there are so many control codes in a .REC file, highlighting is sometimes unpredictable.)

Make sure the Wordwrap and Control character display commands on the Control pull-down menu are turned on (have a mark next to them). Your screen should now resemble figure 10.6.

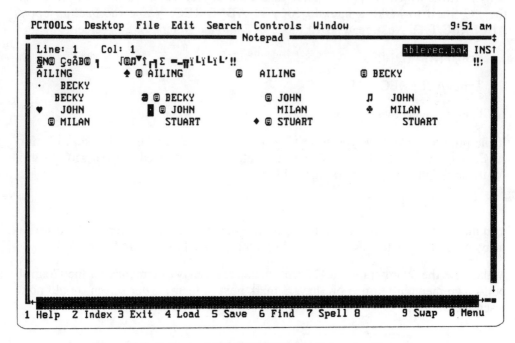

*Figure 10.6. Contents of ABLEREC.TXT in the Notepads editor screen*

Most of the file contents might be gibberish to you, but you can make some sense out of the obvious entries.

The characters in the upper-left corner of the screen are crucial to DOS but do not affect this operation. Instead, look at the first name AILING. This is the FIRST-NAME field entry for the first sorted record of ABLE.DBF. The second name in ABLEREC.TXT corresponds to the second record in ABLE.DBF. Identical field entries, such as these two first records, are identified by control characters that appear after the name. These characters—the light and dark happy faces, the bullet, the box, and the heart sign, and the others—are the control codes that begin the ASCII character set. That's how records with identical sort-field information are organized.

For now, close the Notepads screen without saving the file:

    **Press:** [Alt]-[F]-[X]

You should realize that record files are unique to the PC Tools Databases module. No such files exist for any dBASE program. Record files serve as shortcuts for the PC Tools program, so the program gives you quick control over dBASE database files.

## Selecting Records

The selecting-records technique for organizing database records lets you gather together records having similar characteristics. You select a group of records by specifying a field value. For example, in ABLE.DBF you can select everyone who lives in California by selecting records that share the value CA in the STATE field. Once you've selected a group, you can view the group and print it if you want to.

To select these records, display ABLE.DBF on your screen:

**Press:** [Alt]-[E]-[R]

This opens the *Select Records* box, as shown in figure 10.7.

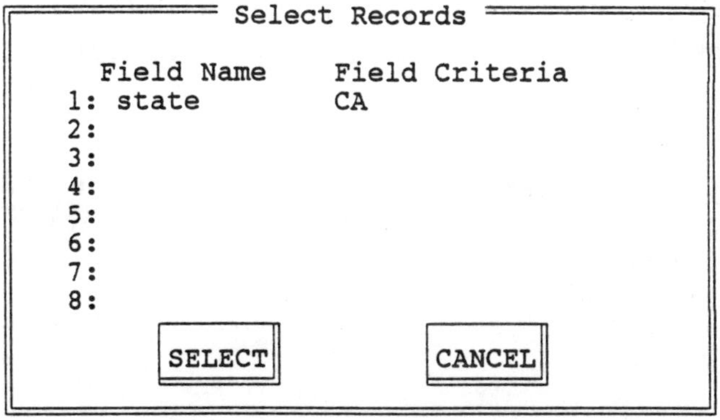

```
╔══════════════ Select Records ══════════════╗
║                                             ║
║      Field Name     Field Criteria          ║
║   1: state          CA                       ║
║   2:                                         ║
║   3:                                         ║
║   4:                                         ║
║   5:                                         ║
║   6:                                         ║
║   7:                                         ║
║   8:                                         ║
║         ┌────────┐        ┌────────┐         ║
║         │ SELECT │        │ CANCEL │         ║
║         └────────┘        └────────┘         ║
╚═════════════════════════════════════════════╝
```

*Figure 10.7. The Select Records box*

When this box first appears, you'll find the cursor in the first field of the *Field Name* box. The two columns, Field Name and Field Criteria, let you specify the record-selection factors.

To select all records in ABLE.DBF that pertain to people living in California:

**Type:** STATE

**Press:** [Enter]

**Type:** CA

**Press:** [Enter]

Field names and criteria are case-insensitive, so you can use either upper- or lower-case for these entries. You have to make sure, however, that the field names and criteria are spelled correctly. If you type ST for the field name or CALIF for the field criteria, no records will be selected because the STATE field name requires five letters and the field criteria allows only two letters.

Now press [Tab] as many times as it takes to move your cursor to the *SELECT* box.

**Press:** [Enter]

The selection process begins, and a message is displayed on the screen. When the entire database has been scanned for all STATE field entries, the records that match will be displayed. This is most obvious in the browse screen.

Once a group of records is selected, you can view, edit, and print it. The selecting records technique limits most of your activities in the database to the selected records.

You can specify up to eight field names in the *Select Records* box. You can also use the DOS wild cards when specifying ranges and values in the search criteria. Table 10.1 shows these refinements.

*Table 10.1. Ranges and wild cards to refine record selection*

? Replaces a single character. For example:

1001? selects the numbers 10010, 10011,..., 10019.

?100 selects the numbers 0100, 2100,..., 9100.

ABLE? selects ABLE plus all five character field entries that begin with ABLE, such as ABLED, ABLEE, and ABLET.

?ABLE selects all five character field entries ending in ABLE, including ABLE, plus such names as CABLE, SABLE, TABLE, 1ABLE, and 2ABLE.

.. This wild card has two uses. The first is similar to its use in DOS, the second to specifying a range.

Same as DOS *. For example:

*100.. selects field entries between 10000 and 10099. Also selects field entries having any characters that appear before the number 100; for example: A100. B100, AB100, or AB9100.

100* selects field entries beginning with 100, including 1000, 1001 and up, 100NAMES, and so on.

*ABLE selects entries such as TABLE, SABLE, STABLE, and DURABLE.

ABLE* selects field entries that begin with ABLE, including ABLE, ABLED, ABLEET, and ABLE10.

Specifying a range of first characters:

1 .. 5 selects field entries that start with the number 1, 2, 3, 4, or 5. You can narrow this down further by specifying something like 35 .. 37, which selects entries beginning with 35, 36, or 37.

A .. C selects field entries that start with the letters A, B, or C. You can narrow this down further by specifying AD .. AF, which selects entries beginning with AD, AE, and AF.

Specifying criteria that no records can match creates an interesting condition for a database—no records show on the screen. When you select this group of records to view, you're really selecting *not* to view the rest of the records. In other words, you're *hiding* the records that were not selected. Thus, if no records match your selection criteria, you hide all records.

To protect against this development, the Databases module asks whether or not you want to hide the last record in the database. Viewing at least one record reminds you that the database contains data and is not an empty structure.

To deselect the group of records and view all records in the database:

**Press:** [Alt]-[E]-[L]

## Sorting a Database

Sorting a database means organizing and displaying all the records according to criteria that you specify. PC Tools will organize a database on one field only. For example, suppose you want to sort the records in ABLE.DBF according to the alphabetical order of entries in the LASTNAME field:

**Press:** [Alt]-[E]-[S]

This opens the *Sort Field Select* box, shown in figure 10.8.

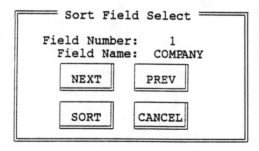

*Figure 10.8. The Sort Field Select box*

When this box appears, it displays the name and number of a field. If this is not the field you want to sort on, press [N] (or highlight Next) and move to the next field. You can continue moving forward through field names this way—or you can move backwards by pressing [P] (or selecting Prev)—until you find the field you want to sort on.

Once you display the correct field name, press [S] (or select, Sort then press [Enter]) to begin the sort. When the sort process ends, records are displayed on screen in the new order. This is most obvious when you're working in the browse screen.

For this example, sort ABLE.DBF on the LASTNAME field. To perform this sort:

**Press:** [Alt]-[E]-[S]

Move to the field you want to sort on, LASTNAME, by pressing [N] or [P]. You've picked the right field when Field Number shows as 2 and Field Name shows as LASTNAME. Then:

**Press:** [S]

In a moment, the contents of ABLE.DBF will return to the screen, displaying records in the newly sorted order, as shown in figure 10.9.

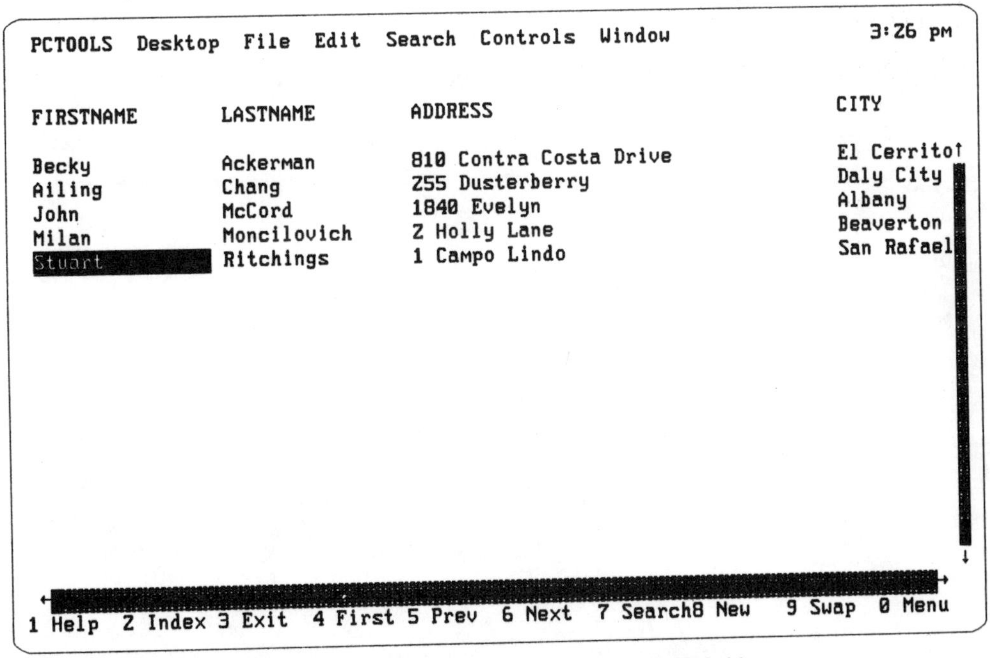

```
 PCTOOLS  Desktop  File  Edit  Search  Controls  Window          3:26 PM

 FIRSTNAME        LASTNAME        ADDRESS                    CITY

 Becky            Ackerman        818 Contra Costa Drive     El Cerrito
 Ailing           Chang           255 Dusterberry            Daly City
 John             McCord          1840 Evelyn                Albany
 Milan            Moncilovich     2 Holly Lane               Beaverton
 Stuart           Ritchings       1 Campo Lindo              San Rafael


                                                                      ↓
 ◄──────────────────────────────────────────────────────────────────►
  1 Help  2 Index 3 Exit  4 First 5 Prev  6 Next  7 Search8 New   9 Swap  8 Menu
```

*Figure 10.9. ABLE.DBF sorted on LASTNAME field*

Notice that the last names are listed in alphabetical order.

> The sort order is always ascending. When you specify a sort field that contains alphabetic characters, the sort will be in alphabetical order. When you specify a field that contains numbers, the sort will start with the lowest number and proceed to the highest.

Earlier in this chapter you learned about .REC files, which are unique to the PC Tools Databases module. They keep a record of the current organization for the matching database. Now that you've re-sorted ABLE.DBF, look at what happened to the ABLE.REC file. First, make a copy of ABLE.REC to ABLEREC.TXT using the PC Shell. When you return to the Desktop Manager, presuming you're still viewing the newly sorted contents of ABLE.DBF:

**Press:** [Alt]-[D]-[N]

**Type:** ABLEREC.TXT

If you're asked to specify the format:

**Press:** [A]

When the contents for ABLEREC.TXT appear on your screen, they should look like figure 10.10.

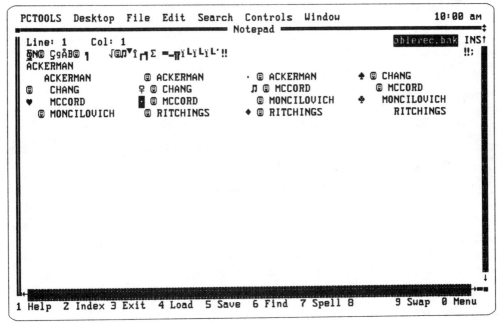

*Figure 10.10. New contents of ABLEREC.TXT (actually ABLE.REC)*

You can see how the last names have been arranged in the record file matching the database you just sorted. (Overlook the fact that each field entry is repeated three times.) This is how PC Tools remembers how to display individual records. When you sort on a field that contains the same data for two or more records, entries in the .REC file will be organized by an internal code, which consists of specific ASCII characters placed before each identical field to determine its order among other identical fields.

## SEARCHING FOR RECORDS

In the Databases module, you can search for specific records three ways. To see your choices:

**Press:** [Alt]-[S]

This opens the Search pull-down menu and shows that you can search for text in all fields, for text in the sort field only, and by moving to a specific record. Moving to a specific record explained in chapter 9, is not the same as searching.

The two top search methods both help you find records when you don't know the record number, but you know something about the data in the record. The more specific method, searching for data in the sort fields, is quicker, but it narrows your search options. The more general method, searching for data in all fields is slower, but it lets you use anything you can remember about a record.

To remove the Search menu from your screen:

**Press:** [Esc]

## Searching on the Primary Field

You'll use the more specific method, searching on the sort field, most frequently, because you usually will want to remember the primary field data in a record. In this example, assume that the NAME field of ABLE.DBF is the sorted field. (Re-sort ABLE.DBF if you have to.) To find the record of someone you know, all you need to do is search for the name. Because searching is a common procedure in database management, it has been assigned to the function key [F7]. To begin a search on the primary or sort field:

**Press:** [F7]

This opens the *Search Sort Field* box, shown in figure 10.11.

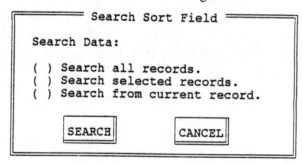

*Figure 10.11. The Search Sort Field box*

You can also open this box using menu commands:

**Press:** [Alt]-[S]-[T]

You'll find the cursor blinking in the empty field after *Search Data:* heading. This is where you type the data you want to search for. It doesn't have to be all of the data in the field; it can be only a few consecutive characters. For instance, if you want to search for the name Milan Moncilovich, you could type the whole name, just Milan, or just Monc and probably come up with the same record. Searching is not case specific; both upper- and lowercase characters are searched for. For example:

**Type:** mil

Naturally, the fewer characters you specify, the broader the search, which means that sometimes you'll locate intermediate records that match the data, but aren't the record you're looking for. The more specific you can make the search data, the more quickly you'll move to the right record.

Once you've specified the string to search for, you're given three record-search options:

1.  Searching through all records.

2.  Searching through the currently selected records.

3.  Searching from the current record to the end of the database.

The default setting is Search selected records, which searches through the selected group, if you have one, or all the records if you haven't selected any. For example:

**Press:** [Enter] twice

This selects the method and begins the search. When the first record that contains mil in the NAME field is found, the record will be displayed on your screen in edit mode or highlighted in browse mode. Then the *Search Sort Field* box will reappear. This lets you move quickly to the next occurrence if you want to.

At this point, look at the first record found. It's for Michael Milken. Since this is not the record you want, just press [Enter] twice to move on. Pressing [Enter] twice switched the default search method to *Search from current record.* This prevents you from locating the same record over and over again. The characters you typed remain in the *Search Data* field. Eventually, you'll get to the record for Milan Moncilovich. Of course, if you had specified this name completely at the beginning, you would have gone directly to the record.

## Searching Through All Fields

You can also search for a record by scanning for specific data throughout all fields. To do this:

**Press:** [Alt]-[S]-[F]

This opens the *Search All Fields* box, which is identical to the previous box except for the name. Type the data you want to look for, pick one of the three methods for searching, and begin the search.

# CHANGING THE DATABASE STRUCTURE

As you use a database, you'll find you want to change its structure to accommodate more information or save current information in different ways. You can't change the structure very much using PC Tools. The most you can do is change the name of existing field names. You can't insert new field names or delete existing field names, nor can you change the field length.

If you work with dBASE databases a lot, you should keep handy a full-fledged version of dBASE, or compatible program, to do the things you can't do in the PC Tools Databases module.

## Changing Field Names

Changing field names is perhaps the trickiest thing you can do in the Databases module. This is because you're making a fundamental change to the database structure.

> You should be aware that when you change a field name, it will appear in the database without any data. This means that all the data in the field before the name change will be lost. To prevent data loss, create a backup file of the original database file before you change any field names in it.
>
> You can use dBASE or another full-featured compatible database program to swap data from the old field in the backup file into the new field.

To change a field name in a database, start out by viewing the contents of the database. Next, use the *Edit fields* command on the Edit pull-down menu:

**Press:** [Alt]-[E]-[E]

This opens the *Field Editor* box, which looks like figure 10.12.

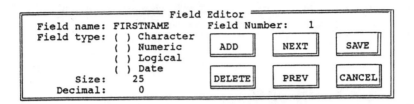

*Figure 10.21. The Field Editor box*

You might recognize this box. It's the same one you used in chapter 9 to create fields for ABLE.DBF. The first field name will be displayed along with the information you declared for the field. To change a field, first display its name in this box. If you don't want to change the first field, move to the field whose name you want to change and type in the new field name. Then accept this name and save it to the file.

For example, to change the *NAME* field in ABLE.DBF to PERSON:

> **Press:** [Alt]-[E]-[E]

Move to the *NAME* field.

> **Type:** PERSON

> **Press:** [Enter]

> **Press:** [A]

> **Press:** [Enter]

> **Press:** [S]

The Databases module will reconfigure the default form file and then display the database information using the new field name. You'll notice that the new field name contains no data. All the data for the field you changed has disappeared.

Notice also how all display features have returned to the default setup. You'll have to reconfigure the colors, screen size, and position you prefer to use.

Once you've changed a field name, you'll have to change any matching form files or else the new field name and information you put into this field will not appear in them.

## BACKING UP YOUR DATA

Once you've created a database, you should protect the data as best you can. This means making backup copies of the database, both on the current disk and on floppies, tape, or some other storage medium that allows you to access the database if your original becomes lost.

Database files in dBASE become corrupted easily. Another complication can arise from the practice of PC Tools using its own .REC file to organize database records. You can tell a file is corrupted when you can't load it into the PC Tools Databases module. A corrupted file doesn't mean the data is lost. It only means something has happened to the file that renders it unreadable by your database management program—in this case PC Tools Databases module.

If PC Tools tells you the .DBF is corrupted or the .REC file is damaged, delete the matching .REC file and try to load the database program a second time. PC Tools will attempt to build a new matching record file, and in many cases this is all that's necessary to read the database file correctly.

If that isn't successful, and you work with databases regularly, try to correct the problem by loading the corrupted database file into a full-fledged dBASE-type database management program. This won't construct a .REC file—only PC Tools can do that. But it might straighten out small problems in the database file.

If that doesn't work, you should copy the corrupted database file to a new and separate file. To make a copy, use either the *Copy* command assigned to [F5] in the PC Shell or the *Copy File* command on the Files pull-down menu. For example, if you can't load ABLE.DBF into the PC Tools Databases module, copy that file to something like ABLE1.DBF. (Remember to use the .DBF extension.) Now try to read the copy into the Databases module.

In most cases, one of these three tricks should solve the problem. If the problem persists, and you use dBASE files often, you should obtain a dBASE salvage program, which works with more precision on dBASE database files.

If all else fails, you can load the faulty database file into a text editor, strip out all the control codes, delimit the data, and reread the data back into a database file. I won't expand on these instructions; if they don't make sense to you, you shouldn't try the procedure. Complete books have been written about salvaging dBASE data.

One of the best ways to back up your data is printing it to a paper or disk file. While it might be tedious to type the data back into a database file, it's a better alternative than losing the data completely.

# PRINTING DATABASE INFORMATION

Database information can be printed to two media: through your printer to paper or to a disk file. The disk file that contains text characters arranged in the printed format you want to use, plus the most common printing control characters, such as line feed and carriage return.

To print database information, follow these four steps:

1. Design the form file you want to use.

2. Adjust the page layout menu settings for the form.

3. Select the way you want to print record information.

4. Select the device you want to print with.

Printing database information is straightforward. You must decide whether to print a default list of all record data or a format of your choice. For a complete list, print from the browse screen. For a custom format using a form file you've designed, print from the edit screen.

The format of printed information remains the same whether you print to paper or disk. You should know a few more details about printing to disk files, however, should you want to use them.

## Printing Database Information to a Disk File

There are three reasons why you might want to print to a disk file first:

1. To send the file via e-mail or on disk to someone else with a computer.

2. To view the printed file first and change the format before you finally print it.

3.  To print the file through a printer not supported by PC Tools, such as a PostScript printer. You must use a word-processing program that supports the printer you want to use.

When you print to a disk file, the file name PC Tools uses depends upon whether you start printing the file while viewing the information in the browse mode or in the edit mode. If you're viewing the database information in browse mode, PC Tools uses the same name for the file as the database file you're viewing. The program always adds the extension .PRT. For example, if you're viewing ABLE.DBF in browse mode and print the file to disk, you'll end up with a disk file called ABLE.PRT.

If you're viewing the database information in edit mode, PC Tools names the disk file after the form file you're currently using and adds the extension .PRT. For example, if you're viewing ABLE.DBF using NAMENUM.FOR and print to a disk file, the disk file name will be NAMENUM.PRT.

For the rest of this section printing refers to printing through your printer.

## Printing a Complete List

The best way to maintain a printed record of all the information in a database is to print the database in tabular format, which is identical to the browse mode screen.

To print a list, begin by viewing the database you want to print in browse mode:

**Press:** [Alt]-[F]-[P]

This opens the *Print* box, which lets you select where you want to print the information. Once you've made the selection:

**Select:** PRINT

This begins the printing process. You'll notice a bar appear near the top of your screen telling you that printing is in progress. It disappears when printing is finished. Should you wish to stop the printing before it is completed, press [Esc]. It might take a moment or two before the printing stops, since printers usually contain a buffer that will empty on its own.

Figure 10.13 shows the result of printing ABLE.DBF using the browse mode screen.

| FIRSTNAME | LASTNAME | ADDRESS | CITY |
|-----------|----------|---------|------|
| Becky | Ackerman | 810 Contra Costa Drive | El Cerrito |
| Ailing | Chang | 255 Dusterberry | Daly City |
| John | McCord | 1840 Evelyn | Albany |
| Milan | Moncilovich | 2 Holly Lane | Beaverton |
| Stuart | Ritchings | 1 Campo Lindo | San Rafael |

*Figure 10.13. Records in ABLE.DBF printed in browse mode*

When you print in browse mode, only information in the fields that show on screen will be printed. You might want to remember this when you design a database and create individual fields of finite length. You should shorten the field length if you want to show more information on the browse mode screen.

To adjust the way field information is printed, you should adjust settings in the *Page layout* box, shown in figure 10.14:

**Press:** [Alt]-[C]-[P]

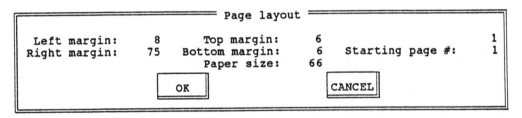

*Figure 10.14. The Page layout box*

The menu is identical to the page layout settings for the Notepad and Outlines editor screens. It lets you set the four margins, paper size, line spacing, and the first page to print. You'll need to adjust the right and left margins to control how much information is printed on a single line. You can't control how much information is printed for each field.

Each time you change these settings, save the new configuration:

**Press:** [Alt]-[C]-[S]

The settings remain current until the next time you change and save them.

## Designing a Form File for Printing

To customize the positions where individual field information appears when printed, you should use the edit mode screen, design a form file for the format you want to use, then readjust the page layout settings to accommodate the form file.

You can use the same form file for both viewing and printing database information. Viewing form information on screen is probably the best way to see how the printed results will look.

For the next example, you'll create a form file that prints the names and addresses of people in ABLE.FOR in label form. To do this, open the Notepad editor screen:

**Press:** [Alt]-[D]-[N]

**Type:** LABELS.FOR

**Press:** [Enter] twice

Type the field names according to the format of a label. With your cursor in position Line 1 Column 1:

**Type:** [FIRSTNAME] [LASTNAME]

**Press:** [Enter]

Notice that you don't have to use a preliminary label such as NAME: or Person>. If you did, the field names would also be printed on your labels.

**Type:** [ADDRESS]

**Press:** [Enter]

**Type:** [CITY], [STATE] [ZIP]

This places the city and state names (separated by a comma) and zip code on the same line. Your screen should now look like figure 10.15.

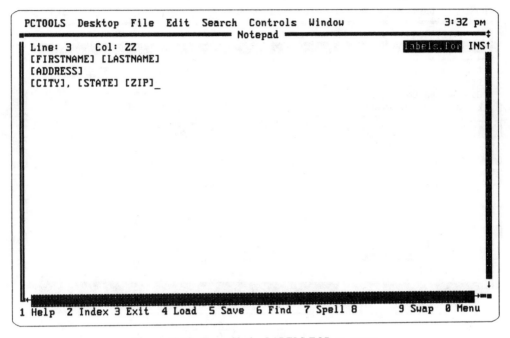

*Figure 10.15. Form file for LABELS.FOR on screen*

Switch back to the Databases editor screen for ABLE.DBF and load this new form file, then look at the results in edit mode. Your screen should look like figure 10.16.

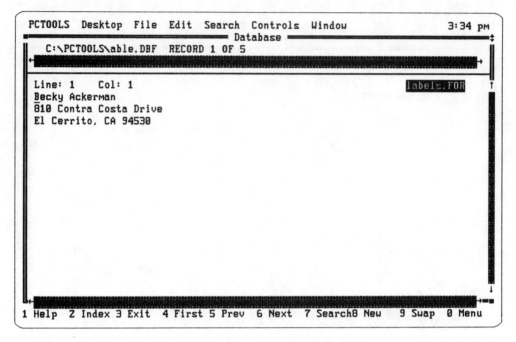

*Figure 10.16. The effect of LABELS.FOR on screen*

## Adjusting Page Layout

When you print a database file, its form file will be controlled by settings in the current page layout configuration. To view the configuration:

**Press:** [Alt]-[C]-[P]

Suppose you're using a long strip of labels measuring one inch high and three inches wide. With these dimensions, you can fit up to six lines of text on each column, and each column can hold about 30 characters. The exact number of characters depends upon your pitch setting.

> To print labels using a laser printer that doesn't accept strip labels or to print master labels that you can duplicate in a copy machine using multicolumn label paper, you should first print the labels to a disk file then read the disk file into a text editor that supports printing of columns.

To make sure you don't print on the left edge of the label (unless the left edge of the label paper is inserted to the left of column 0 on the printer), set the left margin to 5.

To prevent unwanted text wraparound, set the right margin to 40. A setting of 40 is longer than the width of the labels you're using. You can also adjust the right margin to the longest line length you'll use, even if that means losing some characters off the right side of the label.

Set the top margin to 0, the bottom margin to 6, and the paper size to 66. This forces a page break after every sixth line. You should view each label as a single page.

## Selecting Record Information

Now that you've set the form and page layout, prepare to print the labels. Make sure you're viewing the information in ABLE.DBF using the form LABELS.FOR.

> **Press:** [Alt]-[F]-[P]

This opens the *Print Selection* box, which looks like figure 10.17.

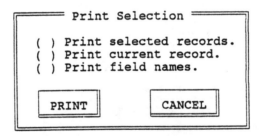

*Figure 10.17. The Print Selection box*

You're given three options for printing record information:

- **Print selected records.** Prints all selected records in the current database according to the current form file and page layout configurations. If you haven't selected a group, this option will print all records.

- **Print current record.** Prints only the currently displayed record according to the current form file.

- **Print field names.** Prints a record of all the field names in the current database.

For your labels, select the first option. This moves you to the *Print* box. Select the device you want to use and the number of copies you want to print, then select PRINT.

The contents of each label will be printed on screen as they are printed to paper. When all your labels are printed, they'll look like figure 10.18.

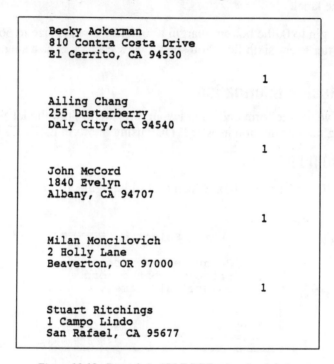

```
Becky Ackerman
810 Contra Costa Drive
El Cerrito, CA 94530
                                         1


Ailing Chang
255 Dusterberry
Daly City, CA 94540
                                         1


John McCord
1840 Evelyn
Albany, CA 94707
                                         1


Milan Moncilovich
2 Holly Lane
Beaverton, OR 97000
                                         1


Stuart Ritchings
1 Campo Lindo
San Rafael, CA 95677
```

*Figure 10.18. Records in ABLE.DBF printed as labels*

You'll have to remove the page numbers using an editor. While printing lists and labels is straightforward, the way you adjust your page layout and customize the form file is a little more complex. You should experiment with these settings and see what happens when you change them.

> If you print database information to a disk file, remember that the name of the file is taken from the form file, not the database. If you printed the example shown in figure 10.18 to disk, you'd end up with a disk file LABELS.PRT.

## Merge Printing

You can also use form files to insert record information into merge letters. Merge letters are documents containing text that is repeated for each letter, but includes personalized information for each person to which a letter is sent. Each letter contains the same text but is addressed individually.

You've already created form files to change the way record information appears on your screen and is printed to labels. Creating a form file for merge letters is almost as easy. All you do is create a form file that contains the text you want to print, then insert field names where you want individual record information to appear.

For example, suppose you wanted to send a copy of this book to your friends listed in ABLE.DBF. You could use the form file shown in figure 10.19 for just such a purpose.

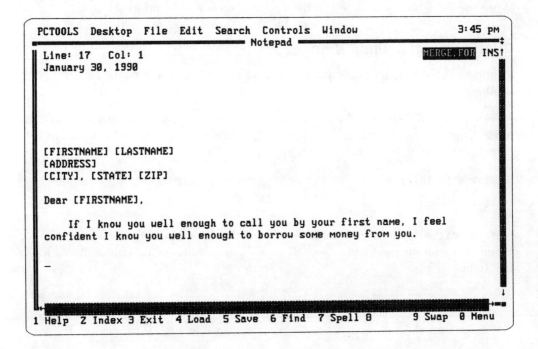

*Figure 10.19. Merge letter form file on screen*

The text of the file appears just like the text in a letter. However, field names (enclosed in brackets) appear at the places you want individual names to be printed.

As usual, double check your page layout settings and make sure they are set to normal page printing; for example, left margin in column 10, right margin in column 65, top and bottom margins on line 6, page length of 66 lines, and so on.

In this case, you might not want to send letters to your friends on your list who are engineers. To do this, you either need to insert a field that displays you friends' occupation of those on your list, or you can hide the records of your engineer friends.

To print the merge letters, return to the Databases screen currently displaying ABLE.DBF. Load the form file MERGE.FOR (the name should appear in the upper-right corner of your Databases editor screen).

> **Press:** [Alt]-[F]-[P]

> **Press:** [Enter] twice

When the *Print* box appears, select the device, then begin the printing.

## Printing a List of Field Names

Printing a list of field names is an excellent way to keep a record of the structure of a database.

To print a list of all field names in a database, begin by viewing the database in edit mode. It makes no difference which form file you're using. All field names in the current database will be printed, regardless of which form you're viewing.

> **Press:** [Alt]-[F]-[P]

> **Select:** Print field names

Next, select the device, then PRINT. You'll see the list appear on your screen briefly. When you print the field names in ABLE.DBF, the results on the screen should look like figure 10.20.

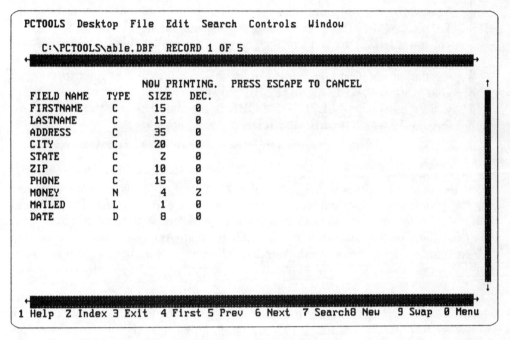

```
   PCTOOLS  Desktop  File  Edit  Search  Controls  Window

      C:\PCTOOLS\able.DBF   RECORD 1 OF 5

                         NOW PRINTING.   PRESS ESCAPE TO CANCEL                    ↑
      FIELD NAME   TYPE   SIZE   DEC.
      FIRSTNAME     C      15     0
      LASTNAME      C      15     0
      ADDRESS       C      35     0
      CITY          C      20     0
      STATE         C       2     0
      ZIP           C      10     0
      PHONE         C      15     0
      MONEY         N       4     2
      MAILED        L       1     0
      DATE          D       8     0




                                                                                  ↓
   1 Help  2 Index 3 Exit  4 First 5 Prev  6 Next  7 Search8 New   9 Swap  0 Menu
```

*Figure 10.20.  Printed list of field names in ABLE.DBF printed on screen (momentarily)*

Printing a list of field names is the one exception to the rule that a form file controls the fields that appear in a printed layout. When you print a list of field names, all the field names for the database will appear, not just those that appear in the current form file.

# USING AUTODIAL

You can use the Autodial feature in the Databases module to make a voice phone call. This feature dials a phone number that appears in a record field. There are two ways you can execute Autodial in the Databases module:

- Use Screen Autodial by pressing the hotkeys [Ctrl]-[O].

- Use Autodial configured for the Databases module by pressing [Alt]-[C]-[A]. You should configure the program for your hardware first. Autodial in the Databases module automatically dials the first valid phone number it runs across in the current record.

You can use a database supplied by PC Tools called TELECOMM.DBF to record and use various phone numbers that you might want to send messages to via e-mail. This database applies only to your work in the Telecommunications module. You'll use the information you learned in this and the previous chapter for your work with TELECOMM.DBF. However, a description of how you actually use TELECOMM.DBF is discussed in chapters 11 through 13,which describe the Telecommunications module.

The *first valid phone number* is a crucial phrase in the Databases Autodial method. It means the first three digits in the series of fields for the displayed record. This lets you dial people on another extension in your company phone system. If an address field comes before the phone field and the address begins with three or more numbers (like some of the addresses in ABLE.DBF), then Autodial will try to dial the address number when you execute Autodial. There is no way to change this procedure.

When you execute Autodial, it scans the series of fields as they exist in the database, which is not necessarily the order that shows on your screen. Suppose you're using a form other than the default form, and you've designed it so the phone field comes before any other field that contains numbers. In this case, executing Autodial will dial the phone number, because Autodial works off the actual structure of the database, not what's displayed on your screen.

When viewing a database, you can also use the standard form of Autodial by pressing [Ctrl]-[O], unless you've changed these hotkeys. The version specific to the Databases module allows you to quickly call a number in a specific field.

Before you can use the version of Autodial specific to the Databases module, you must configure certain hardware settings.

## Configuring Autodial

To configure Autodial in the Databases module:

**Press:** [Alt]-[C]-[C]

This opens the *Configure Autodialer* box, which looks like figure 10.21.

```
╔═══════════════ Configure Autodialer ═══════════════╗
║                                                     ║
║   ( ) Tone dial     ( ) COM1        ( )  300 baud  ║
║   ( ) Pulse dial    ( ) COM2        ( ) 1200 baud  ║
║                     ( ) COM3        ( ) 2400 baud  ║
║                     ( ) COM4        ( ) 9600 baud  ║
║                                                     ║
║         Access code                                 ║
║                                                     ║
║   Long distance code                                ║
║              ┌──────┐          ┌──────────┐         ║
║              │  OK  │          │  CANCEL  │         ║
║              └──────┘          └──────────┘         ║
╚═════════════════════════════════════════════════════╝
```

*Figure 10.21. The Configure Autodialer box*

You'll find the *CANCEL* box is highlighted. Press [Tab] to highlight the settings you need to change. Once you've entered the settings you want to use:

**Select:** OK

## Making a Call

To make a call using Autodial in the Databases module, highlight the record you want to call and:

**Press:** [Alt]-[C]-[A]

This begins Autodial. When the first valid number for the current record is found, you'll see figure 10.22 on your screen:

```
┌─────────────────────────────────────────────┐
│                                               │
│   Once the phone is done dialing and the phone│
│   is ringing, pick up the phone's handset     │
│   for voice communications. Then disconnect the│
│   modem by typing the Escape or Enter key.    │
│                                               │
│            ┌───────────────────┐              │
│            │ Disconnect Modem  │              │
│            └───────────────────┘              │
│                                               │
└─────────────────────────────────────────────┘
```

*Figure 10.22. The Autodial message*

You can cancel the call by pressing [Enter], which disconnects the modem. Otherwise, the call will proceed.

You can always use the program-wide Autodial by pressing [Ctrl]-[O] and selecting appropriate commands.

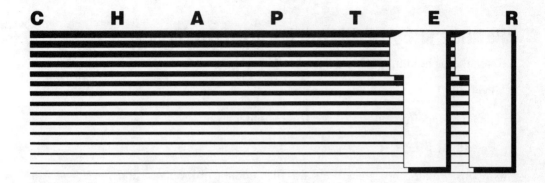

C H A P T E R

11

# WORKING WITH THE APPOINTMENT SCHEDULER

The Appointment Scheduler was designed to let people manage their time efficiently. You can use it just to check the current date, to log in important appointments, and to set a few alarms for your working day, such as when to check your mail or when to go pick up your children.

You can also make the Appointment Scheduler starts other programs or macros at preset times to perform complex functions automatically, such as downloading your mail or routinely compressing files on your hard disk.

## OPENING THE APPOINTMENT SCHEDULER

To open the Appointment Scheduler from the main menu:

> **Press:** [A]

To open the Appointment Scheduler from another module:

> **Press:** [Alt]-[D]-[A]

This opens a dialog box that filters for files ending in the extension .TM. You can remember this as *time manager*. To create an appointment file called A.TM:

> **Press:** [A]

> **Press:** [Enter] twice

You can create several appointment-schedule files, but you'll find that one file is large enough to accommodate most of your appointments. A file with the name A.TM will appear at the top of the Appointment Scheduler dialog box each time you enter this module. From now on, to enter A.TM from the Desktop menu, all you have to do is press [A] and then [Enter]. When the Appointment Scheduler screen appears for a new file, it looks like figure 11.1.

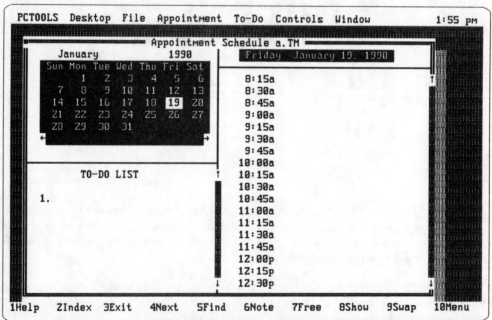

*Figure 11.1. The blank Appointment Scheduler screen*

You'll notice the screen is divided into three sections:

1.  A calendar in the upper-left corner

2.  An hourly schedule on the right side

3.  A *To-Do* list in the lower-left corner

You can move forward through the calendar, the daily schedule, and the To-Do list by pressing [Tab]. You can move backwards by pressing [Shift]-[Tab]. You can tell that a section is active by its highlighted title. You might notice how each section has its own scroll bars (in the calendar these are arrows). This lets you use a mouse to move ahead or backward in the section you're working with.

## Pull-down Menus

The top line on your screen shows four pull-down menus specific to the Appointment Scheduler:

**File**              Duplicates the commands in the Notepads and Outlines File pull-down menus, letting you load and save schedules, customize autosave, print schedules, and exit without saving.

**Appointment** Gives you eight commands for working with appointments in the daily scheduler. Five of these commands are duplicated on function keys active in this screen.

**To-Do**           Gives you three commands for working with items on your To-Do list. One of these commands is duplicated on a function key.

**Controls**       Gives you four customizing commands; three work in the daily schedule, and a fourth toggles the wide display on and off.

The menu map specific for the Appointment Scheduler is shown in figure 11.2.

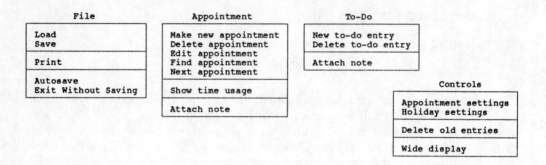

*Figure 11.2. Pull-down menus in the Appointment Scheduler*

You also have access to the Database and Window pull-down menus that are active in each Desktop module. The Window menu in this module, however, doesn't contain the Resize command. The only way you can change the size of the Appointment Scheduler screen is to toggle the Wide display on or off. When Wide display is off, the only thing you can see is the daily scheduler:

   **Press:** [Alt]-[C]-[W]

You can toggle Wide display back on by repeating the command.

You can also set the autosave feature for the current Appointment Schedule this way:

   **Press:** [Alt]-[F]-[A]

Toggle on and type in the time between each automatic save, then select OK.

## Active Function Keys

You can find five function keys defined at the bottom of your screen:

**[F1]  Help**    Opens the general help screen.

**[F2]  Index**    Opens the help index.

**[F3]  Exit**    Exits the Appointment Scheduler screen and returns you to your previous work.

| | | |
|---|---|---|
| **[F4] Next** | | Finds the next appointment. You must have created an appointment in the Scheduler section for this to work. This is described in the section on the Scheduler. |
| **[F5] Find** | | Opens the *Find appointment* box and lets you locate a specified appointment. You must have created an appointment in the Scheduler section for this to work. |
| **[F6] Note** | | Opens the Notepad editor screen and lets you write a note and attach it to a specific appointment. You can do this either while creating an appointment or after an appointment is created. |
| **[F7] Free** | | Opens the *Find free time* box, which lets you find free time in your schedule. |
| **[F8] Show** | | Shows your current weekly schedule on a time-line graph and marks appointments, free time, and possible conflicts. |
| **[F9] Swap** | | Swaps between active screens. |
| **[F10] Menu** | | Activates the top menu bar. |

None of these commands will work until you've inserted appointments in a schedule.

## THE CALENDAR

When you call up the Appointment Scheduler, the calendar displays the current month and highlights the current day. To make the calendar active, press [Tab] until the name of the month and year are highlighted in the upper-right corner. You can move to other days, months, and even years in the calendar using the cursor keys as described in table 11.1.

*Table 11.1. How to change dates in the calendar*

| Action | Press: | Action | Press: |
|---|---|---|---|
| Ahead one day | [⇒] | Back one day | [⇐] |
| Ahead one week | [⇓] | Back one week | [⇑] |
| Ahead one month | [PgDn] | Back one month | [PgUp] |
| Ahead one year | [Ctrl]-[PgDn] | Back one year | [Ctrl]-[PgUp] |
| Current date | [Home] | | |

As you use these keys to change calendar dates, notice how the date and month at the top of the calendar change. Notice also how the date for the daily schedule changes to match the highlighted calendar date. When you move from one week to the next, the same day of the week will remain highlighted. When you move from one month or year to the next, the same date will remain highlighted. Return to the current date before you begin experimenting with appointments:

**Press:** [Home]

# WORKING IN THE DAILY SCHEDULER

The Daily Scheduler is on the right side of the Appointment Schedule window. It is the core of the Appointment Scheduler.

Once you've selected a date to work with on the calendar, switch to the daily schedule:

**Press:** [Tab]

When first displayed, the daily schedule shows the range of times between 10:30 and 2:45. Each time slot is 15 minutes apart. You can move around the display by pressing [PgUp], [PgDn], [⇑], and [⇓]. If you press [⇐] or [⇒] while working in the daily schedule, you'll switch dates in the Calendar.

## Making an Appointment

The easiest way to make an appointment is highlight the appointment time slot and press [Enter]. For example, suppose you want to check your mail at 11:30 every morning:

**Highlight:** 11:30a

**Press:** [Enter]

This opens the *Make appointment* window, which looks figure 11.3.

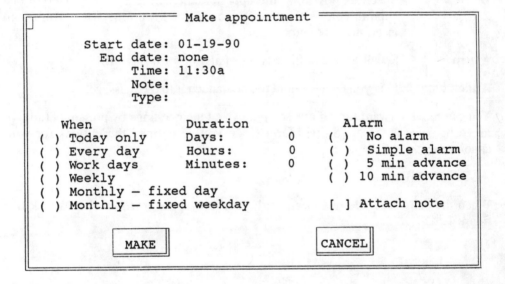

```
╔════════════════ Make appointment ════════════════╗
║┌─                                                ─║
║                                                   ║
║       Start date: 01-19-90                        ║
║         End date: none                            ║
║             Time: 11:30a                          ║
║             Note:                                 ║
║             Type:                                 ║
║                                                   ║
║    When             Duration            Alarm     ║
║   ( ) Today only    Days:      0     ( )  No alarm       ║
║   ( ) Every day     Hours:     0     ( )  Simple alarm   ║
║   ( ) Work days     Minutes:   0     ( )  5 min advance  ║
║   ( ) Weekly                         ( )  10 min advance ║
║   ( ) Monthly — fixed day                         ║
║   ( ) Monthly — fixed weekday        [ ] Attach note     ║
║                                                   ║
║       ┌───────┐              ┌────────┐           ║
║       │ MAKE  │              │ CANCEL │           ║
║       └───────┘              └────────┘           ║
╚═══════════════════════════════════════════════════╝
```

*Figure 11.3. The Make appointment window*

You can also open this menu using the *Make appointment* command on the Appointment menu by pressing [Alt]-[A]-[M].

The selected date and time are displayed at the top of the window. You can find your cursor in the *Note:* field. This is where the text that shows in the Daily Scheduler time slot is typed. For this example:

**Type:** check mail

**Press:** [Enter]

This moves you to the *Type:* field, where you specify what type of appointment you're creating. You're given room for one letter, so you might want to classify types of appointments as *P* for personal and *B* for business. Make this first one personal:

**Type:** P

**Press:** [Enter]

This moves you into the first of four options you can use to fine tune your appointments:

**When**          Specifies when the appointment will be effective.

**Duration**      Specifies how long the appointment will last. If you overlap one appointment with another, you'll get a warning when you try to insert the appointment.

**Alarm**         Specifies one of three types of alarms, or no alarm.

**Attach note**   Lets you create a note file and attach it to the message.

You can move forward through these options and their settings by pressing [Tab]. To move backwards, press [Shift]-[Tab]. Once you've defined the options for your appointment:

**Press:** [M]

When the daily scheduler reappears with your new appointment, it should look like figure 11.4.

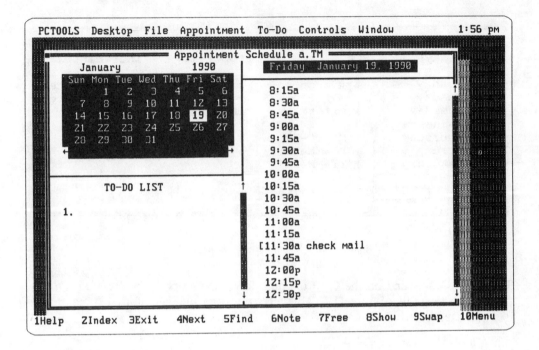

*Figure 11.4. Your new appointment inserted*

The musical note denotes that an alarm has been set.

When the appointment time arrives, the message "check mail" appears on your screen along with two options: Snooze and OK. Pressing [Enter] accepts OK and removes the message from your screen for good. Selecting Snooze also removes the message from your screen, but it will return in five minutes, much like a snooze alarm on a clock. The message will keep on reappearing every five minutes until you select OK.

## Global Settings

You can use two settings on the Controls pull-down menu to change the appearance of features on the Appointment Scheduler. The first is the *Appointment settings* box, which looks like figure 11.5. This screen lets you change which days, starting and stopping times, time slots, and time.date formats will be displayed.

```
╔══════════════════ Appointment settings ══════════════════╗
║ ┌                                                         ║
║                                                           ║
║   Work days          Start time       Stop time       Increment   ║
║                                                           ║
║   [ ] Sunday           8:00a            5:00p         ( ) 15 minutes ║
║   [X] Monday                                          ( ) 30 minutes ║
║   [X] Tuesday        Date format       Time format    ║
║   [X] Wednesday                                       ║
║   [X] Thursday       ( ) MM-DD-YY      ( ) am/pm      ║
║   [X] Friday         ( ) DD-MM-YY      ( ) 24 hour    ║
║   [ ] Saturday       ( ) YY-MM-DD                     ║
║                    ┌────────┐       ┌──────────┐      ║
║                    │   OK   │       │  CANCEL  │      ║
║                    └────────┘       └──────────┘      ║
╚═══════════════════════════════════════════════════════════╝
```

*Figure 11.5. The Appointment settings box*

The second command on the Controls pull-down menu opens the *Holiday settings* box, which looks like figure 11.6. This lets you insert the dates for each major holiday in the current year.

```
╔═══════════════════ Holiday settings ═══════════════════╗
║                                                         ║
║        U.S. Federal                    User-defined     ║
║                                                         ║
║    [X] New Years Day                   Date:            ║
║    [X] Martin Luther King Day          Date:            ║
║    [X] President's Day                 Date:            ║
║    [X] Memorial Day                    Date:            ║
║    [X] Independence Day                Date:            ║
║    [X] Labor Day                       Date:            ║
║    [X] Columbus Day                    Date:            ║
║    [X] Veterans Day                    Date:            ║
║    [X] Thanksgiving Day                Date:            ║
║    [X] Christmas Day                   Date:            ║
║                                                         ║
║             ┌────────┐        ┌──────────┐             ║
║             │   OK   │        │  CANCEL  │             ║
║             └────────┘        └──────────┘             ║
╚═════════════════════════════════════════════════════════╝
```

*Figure 11.6. The Holiday settings box*

## Using Alarms

Alarms alert you to pending appointments as well as to other activities you've logged into your schedule. A simple alarm displays the appointment message on your screen at the starting time of the appointment. You can set an alarm to give you advance warnings of five or ten minutes.

## Attaching a Note

You can attach a longer note to an appointment if you need additional information. For example, this could be a list of people attending a meeting and what their role will be, the notes of the meeting you'd like to present, or an agenda. When the appointment time arrives, the Notepad editor screen appears and displays the text of the note.

You can create a note for an appointment in two ways:

1. When you create an appointment in the *Make appointment* screen, toggle on the Attach note option.

2. When you've already created an appointment, highlight the time slot and then press [F6].

Both of these move you directly to the *NOTEPADS* dialog box. You should not try to type anything in this box; the program will create the note file for you. You'll see the note file name unfold as the program inserts the path and file name. First, the program inserts the default directory name, PCTOOLS, followed by the name of the file. This file name will be the same name as the Appointment Schedule you're using. Next, the program assigns a three-digit number as the extension. The first note for the current appointment schedule will be given the extension .001, the second note .002, and so on, up to 999 notes for each appointment schedule.

When PC Tools has inserted the complete file name, you'll move into the Notepad editor screen. PC Tools then inserts the date and time information of the appointment at the beginning of the note. The note for the check-mail appointment is shown in figure 11.7.

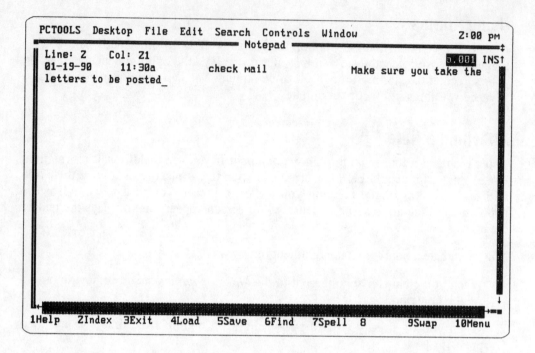

```
PCTOOLS  Desktop  File  Edit  Search  Controls  Window          2:00 pm
════════════════════════════════════ Notepad ═══════════════════════════╪
 ‖ Line: 2     Col: 21                                      a.001  INS↑
 ‖ 01-19-90      11:30a          check mail          Make sure you take the ▮
 ‖ letters to be posted_                                                 ▮
 ‖
 ‖
 ‖
 ‖
 ‖
 ‖
 ‖
 ‖
 ‖
 ‖
 ‖
 ‖                                                                       ↓
 ◄▬▬▬▬▬▬▬▬▬▬▬▬▬▬▬▬▬▬▬▬▬▬▬▬▬▬▬▬▬▬▬▬▬▬▬▬▬▬▬▬▬▬▬▬▬▬▬▬▬▬▬▬▬▬▬▬▬▬▬▬▬►▬▬■
 1Help   2Index  3Exit   4Load   5Save   6Find   7Spell  8       9Swap  10Menu
```

*Figure 11.7. A sample note attached to an appointment*

Since you're using an Appointment Schedule called A.TM, its first note is called A.001, as you can see in the upper-right corner. To write the note, press [Enter] and start typing. You can edit and print note text like you can any other Notepad text file. When you're finished creating the note, save the file as usual:

**Press:** [F5]

Notice how the Notepad defaults to an ASCII format save. When the note file is saved, you'll return to the Appointment Schedule screen, not the Desktop. Notice that the letter *N* has been inserted to the left of the appointment time slot. This means a note has been attached to the appointment.

The second way you can create a note is to attach it to an already existing appointment. The easiest way to do this is to highlight the appointment in the daily Schedule and press [F6]. You can also press [Enter] and select Alter Note or use the menu commands [Alt]-[A]-[A] (Attach note on the Appointment pull-down menu). This begins the process whereby the program creates the note file and leaves you in the Notepad editor screen.

# Finding Appointment Information

There are several ways to find an appointment or find more information about an appointment.

| | |
|---|---|
| **Move to the next appointment** | Press [F4] to move to the next appointment. |
| **Find an appointment** | Press [F5] to open the *Find appointment* box and specify as much about the appointment as you can remember. |
| **Find free time** | Press [F7] to view free time in the current day's schedule. |
| **View all your time** | Press [F8] to view the next five days' appointments, which will be arrayed on daily time lines. |

### *Searching for an Appointment*

To find a specific appointment:

    **Press:** [F5]

This opens the *Find appointment* box, which looks like figure 11.8.

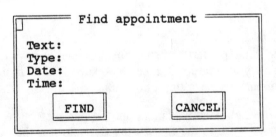

*Figure 11.8. The Find appointment box*

You can also use the menu commands [Alt]-[A]-[F] to open up this box.

The *Find appointment* box lets you find an appointment by specifying some information about the appointment. You can search for text in the name of the appointment, for the type of appointment (P or B), for the suspected date of the appointment, or for the suspected time of the appointment.

You can also use combinations of search criteria, such as appointment text and date. The more specific you are about an appointment, the sooner you'll find the one you're looking for.

### Searching for Free Time

You can find what free time you have in a day by searching for free time.

    **Press:** [F7]

This opens the *Find free time* box, which looks like figure 11.9.

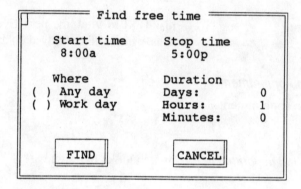

*Figure 11.9. The Find free time box*

You can specify the range of start and stop times as well as days of the week that you want to use to narrow your search. You can also specify the amount of free time you want to search for using fields for days, hours, and minutes.

You should move through each selection, set the parameters you want to use, then select FIND. This takes you to the first empty time slot for the current day. You can continue searching for free time until you find a slot you want to use.

### Viewing Your Time

You can view your schedule for the next five days. To do, first move to any day within the week you want to check.

    **Press:** [F8]

This opens a window that shows the current day's appointments at the top followed by the next four days' appointments below, as shown in figure 11.10.

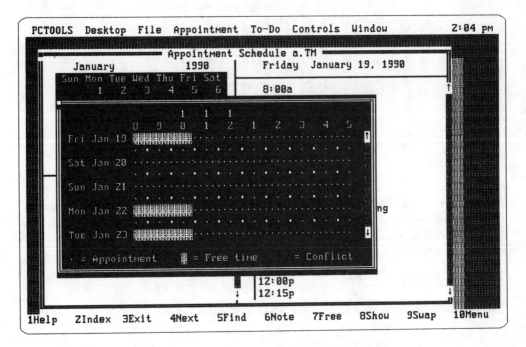

*Figure 11.10. A view of a week's worth of daily schedules*

You'll find all your appointments, free time, and any conflicts marked on these time lines.

## Printing a Schedule

To print a copy of the current appointment schedule to your printer or a disk file:

**Press:** [Alt]-[F]-[P]

This opens the *Schedule printout* box, which looks like figure 11.11.

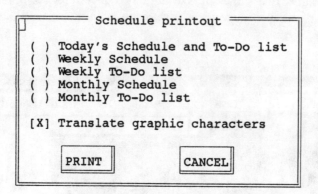

```
┌─────────────────── Schedule printout ───────────────────┐
│                                                          │
│  ( ) Today's Schedule and To-Do list                     │
│  ( ) Weekly Schedule                                     │
│  ( ) Weekly To-Do list                                   │
│  ( ) Monthly Schedule                                    │
│  ( ) Monthly To-Do list                                  │
│                                                          │
│  [X] Translate graphic characters                        │
│                                                          │
│      ┌─────────┐          ┌─────────┐                    │
│      │  PRINT  │          │ CANCEL  │                    │
│      └─────────┘          └─────────┘                    │
└──────────────────────────────────────────────────────────┘
```

*Figure 11.11. The Schedule printout box*

You're given five ways to print your schedule. You're also given the option of whether you want to print the graphic characters that form the outline of the Appointment Schedule window and markers next to certain appointments. Once you set the parameters:

   **Select:** PRINT

This opens the *Print* box, where you select the printing output device.

## USING THE TO-DO LIST

The third feature on the full version of the Appointment Schedule screen is the To-Do list. This displays a list of reminders. You can display this list when you first load the Desktop Manager using the /RA switch.

### Inserting Items

To insert an item in the To-Do list, first make the list active by pressing [Tab] until TO-DO LIST is highlighted. If you're inserting the first item, press [Enter]. This opens the *New to-do entry* box, which looks like figure 11.12.

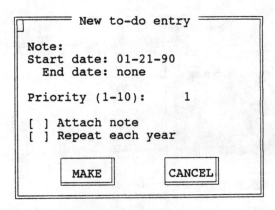

*Figure 11.12. The New to-do entry box*

You'll find the cursor in the *Note:* field. The current date appears as the *Start date,* A priority of 1 will be assigned automatically, since this is the first item you've inserted into the list. When you have entered more than one item into the list you can display them according to priority.

You can attach a note to any item on the list, just as you can attach a note to any appointment. When you attach a note to an item on the To-Do list, the letter *N* will precede the item on the list.

You can also repeat an item each year; for example, to remind you of birthdays and anniversaries.

For this example, create several items to do:

**Type:** Call MIS Press

**Press:** [Enter]

**Press:** [Tab] five times

This skips over the fields that are not to be changed and moves you to *MAKE:*

**Press:** [Enter]

The box will disappear, and your screen should look something like figure 11.13.

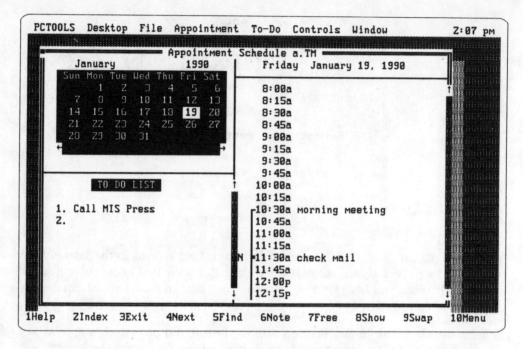

*Figure 11.13. First item in To-Do list*

To insert a second item:

**Press:** [Enter]

**Type:** Write IRS

**Press:** [Enter]

**Press:** [Tab] five times

**Press:** [Enter]

Repeat these steps and type another message to insert a third item of your own choosing. When you're finished, you should have three items on your screen as shown in figure 11.14.

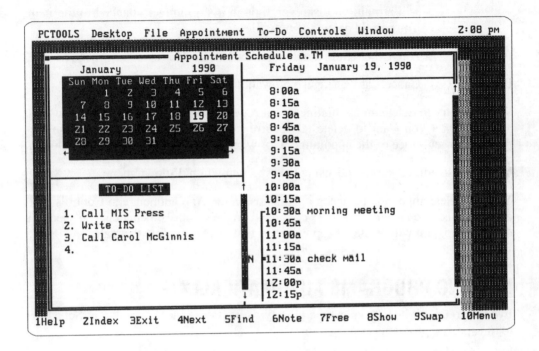

PCTOOLS  Desktop  File  Appointment  To-Do  Controls  Window          2:08 pm
════════════════ Appointment Schedule a.TM ════════════════
     January    1990                   Friday   January 19, 1990
   Sun Mon Tue Wed Thu Fri Sat
         1   2   3   4   5   6        8:00a                                    ↑
     7   8   9  10  11  12  13        8:15a
    14  15  16  17  18  19  20        8:30a
    21  22  23  24  25  26  27        8:45a
    28  29  30  31                    9:00a
   ←                         →        9:15a
                                      9:30a
                                      9:45a
           TO-DO LIST          ↑      10:00a
                                      10:15a
    1. Call MIS Press               ┌10:30a morning meeting
    2. Write IRS                     10:45a
    3. Call Carol McGinnis           11:00a
    4.                               11:15a
                               N    ►11:30a check mail
                                      11:45a
                               ↓      12:00p
                                      12:15p                                   ↓

1Help   2Index  3Exit   4Next   5Find   6Note   7Free   8Show   9Swap   10Menu

*Figure 11.14. Three items on the To-Do list*

You can enter more than eight items on a list, but the To-Do List window can only display eight items at a time.

You can only sort the first 10 items by priority.

## Editing and Deleting Items

To edit or delete an item on the list, highlight the item:

**Press:** [Enter]

To complete the editing, press one of following four keys:

**Delete**      Deletes the item from the list.

**Edit**        Opens the *New to-do entry* box, displaying settings for the highlight-
                ed item. This lets you change any part of the item. If you attach a
                note and later edit the item and toggle *Attach note* off, the note file

will remain on disk even though it's no longer attached to the item. You should delete the note file.

**Alter Note**    Alters the text in a note attached to a To-Do item.

**Cancel**    Cancels any changes you want to make to an item.

When you try to delete an appointment that repeats over two or more days, you'll be asked whether you want to delete all occurrences of the appointment, only the current day's occurrence of the appointment, or whether you want to cancel the deletion.

You can also edit appointments using the Appointment pull-down menu.

You can delete appointments using commands on the Appointment and Controls pull-down menus. The *Delete old entries* command on the Controls menu lets you specify a date; the program will delete all appointments that were set before that date.

# LOADING PROGRAMS AUTOMATICALLY

Even if you don't budget your time closely, you can use the Appointment Scheduler to run specific programs at preset times.

## Opening Notepads Automatically

To schedule a time to open the Notepad screen and display a file, first make the daily schedule active. Note that you can't create a new file this way, you can only work with a file that's already been created.

Highlight the time you want the Notepad editor to open, and press a bar symbol (|), then enter the name of the file you want to appear in the editor screen. On most keyboards, you can insert the bar symbol by pressing [Shift]-[\].

Next, specify the path of the file if it's not in the default path as shown in the *NOTEPADS* dialog box.

For example, to open the file DOWOP.TXT in the PCTOOLS directory at 10 A.M., begin in the daily schedule:

**Highlight:** 10:00a

**Type:** | DOWOP.TXT (the space between the bar and text is optional)

**Press:** [Enter]

This opens the *Make appointment* box. Here you can set other parameters such as a five-minute warning that Notepads is about to appear.

Once you set the time a program is to appear, it will appear in the daily schedule like any other appointment, but it will be indicated with a bar symbol.

If you want to display a warning message that the Notepad editor screen is about to appear, place the message before the bar:

**Type:** Here comes DOWOP | DOWOP.TXT

When the warning time arrives, you'll see the message: Here comes DOWOP

## Loading an Outside Application

You can load an outside application the same way you opened the Notepad editor screen. If you want to spend an hour a day putting data into a database, you can schedule the time of day when the Appointment Scheduler will load your database management program and the specific file you want to work with.

To load dBASE at 2 P.M. every day, open the Appointment Scheduler and move to the daily schedule.

**Highlight:** 2:00p

**Type:** load data! | <cmd>1:00 dbase

You should recognize most of this appointment. The message text comes first, then the bar, and finally the name of the file that loads the program you want to use. The program file name must end with the extension .BAT, .COM, or .EXE. The file must be in your path, or you must specify its path as part of the file name.

The syntax of this appointment also borrows from the PC Tools macro language. The new command, *<cmd>1:00,* gives PC Tools one minute to bail out and call the dBASE file name from DOS. You need this amount of time at the very minimum, or the command will not work.

When 2:00 P.M. rolls around each day, the Appointment Scheduler passes the file name to DOS and loads the program, if you've specified a valid file name. If you don't specify a file name to load, the program will automatically default to the Notepad editor screen and load the program in that module.

You're given room for only 24 characters of text in an appointment slot, which isn't very much. If you don't have enough room to type in all the information—the warning message, the file name, the current path—you can write the text in a batch file in your root directory and then call the batch file as the program to run in your appointment.

## Using a Batch File to Run Programs

You can run a batch program as well as .COM and .EXE programs in appointments. This is a great help when you want to run a program that's not on your path, or a program that can parse the DOS command line for switches or a specific file name.

You can use the Notepad editor to create the batch file; just make sure you don't insert any control characters and that you save the file in ASCII mode. For example, suppose you want to load the dBASE program at 2:00 P.M. every day and enter data in the database file MYDATA.DBF. Assume your dBASE program file is called DBASE.COM and that it's not on your path, but in a first-level directory called C:\DBASE. The database file MYDATA.DBF is in the path C:\DBASE\DATA. To open the program and the file, you insert this line into a simple ASCII text file:

**Type:** | <cmd>1:00 C:\DBASE\DBASE C:\DBASE\DATA MYDATA.DBF

The macro command *<cmd>1:00>* delays the call for one minute, as required by the PC Tools program. The first group of commands tells the Appointment Scheduler to search the DBASE directory off the root for the executable file DBASE. The second group of commands is interpreted solely by the dBASE program, which searches for a file MYDATA.DBF in the path DBASE\DATA off the root directory.

You can precede this appointment with a message by placing the message text before the bar.

## USING MACROS WITH THE APPOINTMENT SCHEDULER

When used in conjunction with macros, the Appointment Scheduler can also be used as a timer to do other things you want done on your computer at specific times.

This is such a useful technique, PC Tools provides a sample macro you'll probably want to use often if you have an MCI Mail box. You can find the sample macro as the last example in SAMPLE.PRO. It looks like this:

```
Read MCI mail:
<begdef><ctrlf9><desk>T<enter><cmd>d20:0<enter><esc><esc><enddef>
```

There are 11 commands in this macro. Go through them one-by-one.

**<begdef>**      Begins the string of commands.

**<ctrlf9>**      Attaches this macro to the keys [Ctrl]-[F9], so that when you press them together, the macro executes.

**<desk>**      Opens the Desktop Manager if it's been installed in resident mode.

**T**      Opens the Telecommunications module on the Desktop menu (same as pressing T).

**<enter>**      Selects the first entry in PHONE.TEL and begins the phone call (same as pressing [Enter]).

**<cmd>d20:0**      Pauses all activity from your computer for 20 seconds. This lets the script MCI.SCR run long enough to log your computer on to MCI Mail and check your mail box. If it finds any mail, it downloads the messages and saves them to disk regardless of how long it takes. Each command must play out before the next one is called. Once you start downloading mail, you don't have to worry about inserting any more delays.

**<enter>**      Inserts a carriage return.

**<esc>**      This appears twice and is designed to unload the Desktop Manager from your screen if you aren't using background communications. The first time it returns you to the Desktop menu. The second time it unloads the Desktop Manager from your screen.

**<enddef>**      Ends the string of commands.

This macro is helpful when running your communications in background. It loads the Desktop Manager, opens the Telecommunications screen, makes a call to MCI Mail using the MCI.SCR, reads your mail box and downloads the messages, saves them to disk, then exits MCI Mail, Telecommunications, and the Desktop Manager—all in the background.

Once you've activated this macro, all you need to do is press [Ctrl]-[F9] to download your MCI Mail box, while you continue working in other things.

Read chapter 15 describing the Macro editor for more information about how you can view, edit, activate, and deactivate this and other macros.

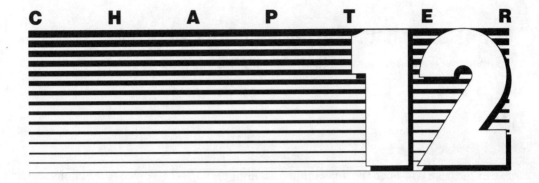

C H A P T E R

**12**

# THE TELECOMMUNICATIONS MODULE

The information for working in the Telecommunications module has been divided into three chapters. This chapter describes basic aspects of computer communications and basic features of the Telecommunications module. Chapter 13 provides working examples about the Telecommunications module. Chapter 14 describes telecommunications using the PC Tools script programming language.

Telecommunications is the ability to communicate electronically over wire and broadcast transmissions. With telecommunications you can communicate with a computer halfway around the world or a computer on the desk next to yours. To telecommunicate you need a communications software program, a modem, and an active telephone line.

The Telecommunications module is a communications program. It facilitates your telecommunications ability by keeping track of all the activities going on during a call.

## THE TELECOMMUNICATIONS MODULE SCREEN

To open the Telecommunication menu from the Desktop menu:

**Press:** [T]

If you're working in another module:

**Press:** [Alt]-[D]-[T]

Either of these will open the Telecommunications menu and give you three choices:

| | |
|---|---|
| **Modem telecommunications** | Opens the default phone book PHONE.TEL or another phone book, if it was showing the last time you used the telecommunications module. |
| **Send a fax** | Loads the Intel communications program CONNECT (requires an Intel fax board). |
| **Check the fax log** | Displays entries in your fax log directory. |

## MODEM TELECOMMUNICATIONS

To open Modem telecommunications:

**Press:** [Enter]

This moves you directly into the default phone book called PHONE.TEL.

> If someone else has already created another phone book with the .TEL extension, you'll see the Telecommunications dialog box first, which lets you select which phone book file you want to work with. This dialog box filters for files ending with .TEL.

When the Telecommunications screen appears for the first time, it resembles figure 12.1.

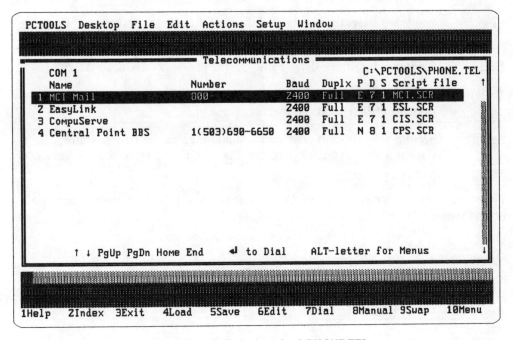

```
  PCTOOLS  Desktop  File  Edit  Actions  Setup  Window

  ┌══════════════════════ Telecommunications ══════════════════════┐
  │  COM 1                                        C:\PCTOOLS\PHONE.TEL │
  │   Name                    Number         Baud  Duplx P D S Script file   ↑ │
  │  1 MCI Mail              800-            2400  Full  E 7 1 MCI.SCR          │
  │  2 EasyLink                             2400  Full  E 7 1 ESL.SCR          │
  │  3 CompuServe                           2400  Full  E 7 1 CIS.SCR          │
  │  4 Central Point BBS     1(503)690-6650 2400  Full  N 8 1 CPS.SCR          │
  │                                                                           │
  │                                                                           │
  │                                                                           │
  │                                                                           │
  │        ↑ ↓ PgUp PgDn Home End     ↵ to Dial     ALT-letter for Menus     ↓ │
  └───────────────────────────────────────────────────────────────────────────┘

  1Help   2Index  3Exit   4Load   5Save   6Edit   7Dial   8Manual 9Swap  10Menu
```

*Figure 12.1. Default phone book PHONE.TEL*

The label COM1 on the top-left side shows you're connected to the COM1 serial port. PHONE.TEL on the right side shows the phone book you're viewing.

When you view this screen for the first time, four default phone book entries will appear: MCI Mail, EasyLink (CompuServe's mail program), CompuServe, and the Central Point Software bulletin board.

The bottom line of the screen tells you how you select phone book entries, how to make a call, and how to access menus.

The light bar highlights the entry to be selected for a call. To move down and up one entry at a time, press the arrow keys. When you add several entries you can move around the phone book with [PgUp], [PgDn], [End], and [Home]. You can also type the number displayed to the left of the entry you want to use.

To make a call, highlight the entry to be called and press [Enter].

As in other Desktop modules, to activate the top menu bar, you press [Alt] or [F10].

The four pull-down menus unique to the Telecommunications module are:

**File**      Loads a different phone book and saves the current phone book if you've made any changes.

**Edit**      Creates, edits, and deletes entries in the phone book you're viewing.

**Actions**      Dials a phone number either automatically, and manually or hangs up from a finished phone connection.

**Setup**      Sets up your modem configuration and toggles the size of your On-Line screen. You only see this screen once you've established a connection with another computer.

Figure 12.2 shows a menu map of all selections on the Telecommunications pull-down menus.

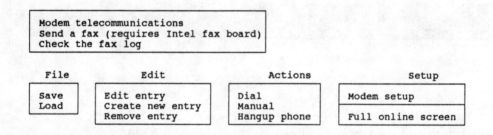

*Figure 12.2. Menu map for the Telecommunications module*

All ten function keys have assignments in the Telecommunications screen:

**[F1] Help**      Opens the general help screen.

**[F2] Index**      Opens the help index.

**[F3] Exit**      Exits the Telecommunications screen and returns you to your previous work.

**[F4] Load**      Opens the *Telecommunications* dialog box and lets you load another phone book.

**[F5] Save**      Saves the current phone book to the disk file of the same name or a different name.

**[F6] Edit**    Opens the *Edit Phone Directory* window, and lets you create a new entry and edit an existing entry.

**[F7] Dial**    Dials the highlighted entry number automatically.

**[F8] Manual**    Opens the On-Line screen, which lets you communicate with another computer connected to yours via a hard-wire link (minimum three-wire cable containing a null modem).

**[F9] Swap**    Switches you between active windows.

**[F10] Menu**    Activates the top menu bar.

Function keys [F4] through [F8] contain unique communications commands, explained in detail in the next chapter.

## SETTING UP YOUR MODEM

You should have no trouble making modem settings, the program does most of the work for you.

    **Press:** [Alt]-[S]-[M]

This opens the *Modem setup* window, which for my modem looks like figure 12.3.

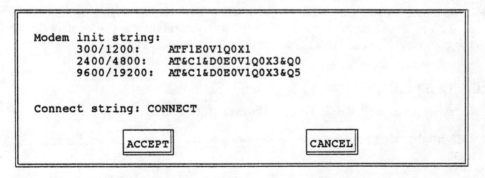

*Figure 12.3. The Modem setup window*

This screen lets you tell PC Tools the speed of your modem. So that it will assign the proper modem-initialization string to communicate through your modem. To set the speed of your modem, highlight the proper baud-rate category and press [Enter]. You can move forward through fields by pressing [Tab] and move backward by pressing [Shift]-[Tab].

Once you've selected an entry, to ACCEPT it:

**Press:** [Tab]

**Press:** [Enter]

If you're not using Hayes-compatible modem, you should highlight the CONNECT field and type the string of characters specific to your modem. You should be able to find this string of characters printed in the modem's documentation. If you can't, call the modem manufacturer customer support number.

Once you've typed in the string:

**Highlight:** ACCEPT

**Press:** [Enter]

Once you enter a string, the *Modem setup* window will close, and you'll be returned to the *Telecommunications* window.

# WORKING WITH PHONE BOOK ENTRIES

A phone book entry *must* contain the number you want to call and the communications parameters you've selected for the number. You can add additional information later, such as whose number it is and other ways you might want to contact the person or company. You can create new entries, change or edit them, and delete them.

## Editing an Entry

Edit the first entry in PHONE.TEL, as shown in figure 12.1. To begin the edit:

**Highlight:** MCI Mail

**Press:** [F6]

This opens the *Edit Phone Directory* window, as shown in figure 12.4.

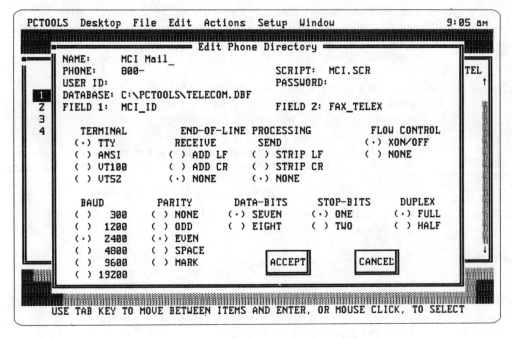

```
PCTOOLS  Desktop  File  Edit  Actions  Setup  Window              9:05 am
╔════════════════════════ Edit Phone Directory ═══════════════════════╗
║  NAME:      MCI Mail_                                                  ║
║  PHONE:     800-                      SCRIPT:  MCI.SCR            TEL   ║
║  USER ID:                             PASSWORD:                    ↑   ║
║  DATABASE: C:\PCTOOLS\TELECOM.DBF                                      ║
║  FIELD 1:  MCI_ID                     FIELD Z: FAX_TELEX               ║
║                                                                        ║
║    TERMINAL         END-OF-LINE PROCESSING         FLOW CONTROL        ║
║   (·) TTY          RECEIVE        SEND            (·) XON/OFF          ║
║   ( ) ANSI       ( ) ADD LF    ( ) STRIP LF       ( ) NONE            ║
║   ( ) VT100      ( ) ADD CR    ( ) STRIP CR                           ║
║   ( ) VT52       (·) NONE      (·) NONE                               ║
║                                                                        ║
║    BAUD        PARITY      DATA-BITS    STOP-BITS    DUPLEX            ║
║   ( )   300  ( ) NONE     (·) SEVEN    (·) ONE      (·) FULL          ║
║   ( )  1200  ( ) ODD      ( ) EIGHT    ( ) TWO      ( ) HALF          ║
║   (·)  Z400  (·) EVEN                                                  ║
║   ( )  4800  ( ) SPACE                                                 ║
║   ( )  9600  ( ) MARK        ┌────────┐     ┌────────┐               ║
║   ( ) 19Z00                  │ ACCEPT │     │ CANCEL │               ║
║                              └────────┘     └────────┘               ║
╚════════════════════════════════════════════════════════════════════╝
  USE TAB KEY TO MOVE BETWEEN ITEMS AND ENTER, OR MOUSE CLICK, TO SELECT
```

*Figure 12.4. The Edit Phone Directory window*

There are two groups of settings in this window. The top group lets you insert characters and define the entry. The bottom group contains eleven communications parameters that control the way communications are sent and received by your computer. Some of these are crucial, such as the modem and port settings; others have a less dramatic effect, such as end-of-line and parity settings. The default settings for the four default entries are recommended, although you might have to adjust the modem and communication port settings.

### *Defining an Entry*

The five lines at the top of this window let you define an entry:

**Name**       The name of the person or company. You can enter up to 54 characters here. The name will be displayed on the telecommunications screen.

**Phone**      The phone number. This is the only required entry, and it also shows on the telecommunications screen. If you try to call an entry that doesn't have a phone number, PC Tools will prompt you to enter the number manually. You can enter up to 25 characters here. When dialing this number, the program will ignore any spaces, dashes, and parentheses that appear between numbers. For example, 1-555-528-1040 will do the same thing as 15555281040.

**Script**    The script file assigned to this entry. This shows on the far right of each phone book entry line. A script file is a text file containing commands specific to the PC Tools communication program that automate many of the routine tasks of communicating. You can enter up to twelve characters here, the limit of a file name. You'll learn more about script files in chapter 14.

**User ID**    A user name you select for a mail box on with MCI Mail. You need to log in both your MCI Mail user ID and password whenever you try to connect to MCI Mail.

**Password**    A password assigned to your MCI Mail account. For secrecy, when you type it into this field, the characters will not appear.

**Database**    The path and database file name of fax and other phone numbers you might want to access using the menu-driven script supplied by a PC Tools program called MCI.SCR.

**Field 1**    The first field to be used with an optional database. The default entry is MCI_ID, a field in TELECOM.DBF.

**Field 2**    The second field to be used with an optional database. The default entry is FAX_TELEX in the TELECOM.DBF.

### Communications Parameters

There are eleven communications parameters that control the way data is sent and received by your computer. Five of the most important parameters are displayed in the modem Telecommunications screen. These are Baud, Duplex (Duplx), Parity (P), Data-bits (D), and Stop-bits (S).

**Terminal**    You can use one of four terminal displays:

1. TTY (for TeleTYpe), the original and simplest screen, displays characters and numbers only.

2. ANSI displays the full range of ASCII characters.

3. VT100 emulates the Digital Equipment Corp. (DEC) VT100 terminal.

4. VT52 emulates the DEC VT52 terminal.

**Receive**   *Receive* is an *End-of-Line parameter.* It determines how line feed (LF) and carriage-return (CR) characters are received by your computer. How you set it depends on the computer you're communicating with. In most cases, you should set Receive to *None.*

**Send**   *Send* is an *End-of-Line parameter.* It determines how line feed (LF) and carriage-return (CR) characters are received by your computer. If you intend to send messages created in the Notepads editor through MCI Mail, you should set Send to *Strip LF.* This strips line feed characters from your messages. If you do not select *Strip LF,* single-spaced messages will be sent double-spaced.

**Port**   Lets you set the communications port on your computer On XT and AT computers, these are COM1 and COM2. PS/2s have two additional ports, COM3 and COM4. The COM setting shows in the upper-left corner of the Telecommunications screen.

**Duplex**   Controls the transmission of data. Full-duplex instructs the computer you're connected with to send back all the characters you send it.; half-duplex does not send back the characters. If you see two characters on your screen for every one character you type, you should switch to half-duplex. If you don't see any characters on your screen when you type a character, you should switch to full-duplex.

**Dialing**   The dialing method of your phone system: tone or pulse.

**Baud**   The speed rate of data transmission: one baud equals one bit per second. A 1200 baud rate means 1200 bits per second can be transmitted.

**Parity**   Sets the parity bit, used to verify correct communications. The most popular setting is *Even.* It is displayed on the Telecommunications screen under *P.*

**Data-Bits**   Sets a byte to hold either seven or eight bits of data. If you're using any sort of parity, one bit is reserved for checking parity, so you should switch data bits to seven. If you're not using any parity, then switch to eight data bits. When you're using seven data bits, you can only transmit and receive the lower 128 characters of the ASCII character set. The number of data-bits is displayed on the Telecommunications screen under *D*.

**Stop-Bits**   Determines the end-of-character bit. Most computers use 1, but a few use 2.

**Flow Control**   Also called *handshaking,* the receiving computer determines when it can receive data and how much data it wants. If you switch XON/XOFF on, the computer receiving data controls the flow of data by sending an XON signal when it wants to receive data, and an XOFF signal when it wants a computer to stop sending data. In this way, the receiving computer digests information without becoming overloaded. On is the most popular setting.

When you communicate with an electronic mail service (MCI Mail) or a bulletin board service (CompuServe and CPS), the ideal PDS settings are E71 for even parity, seven data bits, and one stop bit. When you're communicating with another computer over a hardware connection using a null modem, you'll probably find the ideal PDS setting to be N81 for no parity, eight data bits, and one stop bit.

Most of your communications with specific entries won't change until you buy new equipment.

### Changing an Entry

For an example of changing a phone book entry, customize the entry for MCI Mail. If you're a subscriber of MCI, you should use your own local MCI phone number. If you're not an MCI subscriber, you should call the Central Point BBS or a local BBS number.

If the *Edit Phone Directory* box is not showing:

> **Press:** [F6]
>
> **Type:** MCI Mail
>
> **Press:** [Enter]
>
> **Type:** 1-800-234-6245 (or a local bulletin board number instead)
>
> **Press:** [Enter] seven times

This moves you over the various character field entries and onto the first parameter, TERMINAL. For most of your purposes on a personal computer, ANSI or TTY will serve. I prefer ANSI.

To accept ANSI:

**Press:** [⇓]

**Press:** [Enter]

This moves you to the second parameter, RECEIVE:

**Select:** NONE

**Press:** [Enter]

**Select:** STRIP LF

For PORT, you should probably accept COM1, but this depends on your computer setup.

For DUPLEX, accept FULL.

For DIALING, select TONE or PULSE depending on your phone system.

For BAUD, pick the rate the suits your modem.

For PARITY, pick EVEN.

For DATA-BITS, pick 7.

For STOP-BITS, pick 1.

For FLOW CONTROL, set XON/XOFF to on.

When you've picked the last setting, highlight ACCEPT:

**Press:** [Enter]

To accept all the changes you've made, insert them in the current phone book, and close the *Edit Phone Directory* box:

**Press:** [Enter]

If you want to go back and change any of the settings, you can open the box, press [Tab] to go to the setting you want to change, make the change, and then press [A] to select Accept. Don't press [A] unless you're on a communications parameter setting, otherwise you'll enter the letter *A* in one of the character fields. If you exit the screen by pressing [Esc] or [C] for Cancel without selecting ACCEPT, none of your changes will be accepted.

As soon as the *Edit Phone Directory* box closes, the new entry should be first one on the Telecommunications screen. Its PDS settings should be E71.

### Making a Call

To make a call, turn on your modem, highlight the entry you want to call, and press [Enter]. You can also press [F7] to make the call.

For example, to call your new entry, highlight entry 1:

**Press:** [1]

**Press:** [Enter]

You should notice the bottom line of the Telecommunications screen change to show the message: Dialing - Press ESC to Cancel

If your call goes through, your screen will change to show the *On-Line screen,* showing that you have connected with another computer. This screen is not titled, but you can identify it when different pull-down menu titles appear on the top line and different commands appear on the bottom two lines of your screen. The middle section will be blank.

Disconnect from the BBS you have signed onto to save subscription and telephone service charges:

**Press:** [F8]

The message Disconnecting will appear at the bottom of the screen for a few seconds, and then you'll return to the Telecommunications screen.

# THE ON-LINE SCREEN

The best way to study the On-Line screen is to view it using manual calling. This will allow you to view all the features on the On-Line screen without connecting to another computer, saving you long-distance and subscription charges.

To move onto the On-Line screen, shown in figure 12.5:

    **Press:** [F8]

```
┌─────────────────────────────────────────────────────────────────┐
│ PCTOOLS  Desktop  Actions  Receive  Send  Window      ALT-ESC Off   8:50 AM │
│ _                                                                 │
│                                                                   │
│                                                                   │
│                                                                   │
│                                                                   │
│                                                                   │
│                                                                   │
│                                                                   │
│                                                                   │
│                                                                   │
│                                                                   │
│                                                                   │
│      Not Connected     |    Send     |    Receive    | 2400 E71 | FDX |  TTY │
│ 1Help   2Index  3Exit  4ASCII  5XModem 6ASCII  7XModem 8Hangup 9Swap  10Menu │
└─────────────────────────────────────────────────────────────────┘
```

*Figure 12.5. The On-Line screen*

Regardless of which type of terminal you've set as a parameter, the On-Line screen will always look the same when it first appears.

The top menu bar gives you three unique pull-down menus:

**Actions**        Hangs up the phone and ends a file transfer.

**Receive**        Allows you to select ASCII or XMODEM protocols to receive files (you can also press [F6] or [F7] respectively). Use ASCII for simple text files and XMODEM for binary or program files.

**Send**          Allows you to select either  ASCII or XMODEM protocols to send files (for which you can also press [F4] and [F5] respectively).

Notice that only the overtype mode is functional in this screen and that [Del] does not delete characters. To delete characters, place your cursor before the character you want to delete and press [End].

The current time is displayed on the right end of the top line. Just to the left of the time display is the ALT-ESC Off label which indicates that special control of the [Esc] key is turned off. This means when you press [Esc], it will exit the On-Line screen:

**Press:** [Esc]

You'll return to the Telecommunications screen. However, when you press [Esc] to exit the On-Line screen, you're still logged on to the On-Line screen. You can switch to another phone book, work in another Desktop module, or switch to the PC Shell, but technically the On-Line screen is still your primary screen.

To return to the On-Line screen from the Telecommunications screen:

**Press:** [Enter]

You can see how you're still tied to the On-Line screen by exiting the Desktop Manager and then returning to it:

**Press:** [Esc] three times

This should return you to your DOS prompt:

**Press:** [Ctrl]-[Spacebar]

**Press:** [T]

This should return you directly to the On-Line screen, bypassing the Telecommunications screen.

You can change the effect of the [Esc] key so it inserts an *escape character*, instead of exiting from the On-Line screen. This can be of value when you communicate with another computer directly and want to send an escape character to the other computer. To make this change, start by viewing the On-Line screen:

**Press:** [Alt]-[Esc]

Notice how the label on the right end of the top line changes the ALT-ESC setting on. It also removes your access to help. To find out how this change effects the program:

**Press:** [Esc]

The On-Line screen didn't close. You did, however, insert an escape character (although you can't see it). If you were connected to another computer, you would have sent that character to the other computer.

This works for all keys, not only [Esc]. When ALT-ESC is on, you're operating in what can be called *raw mode*. When you press a key or keys, the scan code assigned by IBM to that key is inserted on your screen and sent to the other computer.

To see what has happened to help:

    **Press:** [F1]

This inserts the letter P. Normally, pressing [F1] opens the help screen, but when you're operating in raw mode all keys have been assigned scan codes.

When the ALT-ESC is on, the new key assignment for Exit is [Shift]-[Esc] to exit the On-Line screen, as shown on the second-to-bottom line.

The bottom two lines contain status messages and function key assignments. There are six items on the second-to-bottom line:

| | |
|---|---|
| **Connected** | Shows you're connected to another computer. |
| **Send** | Controls the way you send files (applies to the two function key assignments in this group, [F4] and [F5]). |
| **Receive** | Controls the way you receive files and applies to the two function key assignments in this group, [F6] and [F7]. |
| **1200 E71** | Shows current settings: baud of 1200, even parity, 7 data bits, and 1 stop bit. |
| **FDX** | Shows duplex setting: full. |
| **ANSI** | Shows type of terminal: ANSI. |

All ten function keys have assignments in the On-Line window:

| | |
|---|---|
| **[F1] Help** | Opens the general help screen. |
| **[F2] Index** | Opens the help index. |
| **[F3] Exit** | Exits the On-Line screen and returns you to the Telecommunications screen. You are still will still be logged on to the On-Line screen (until you hang up by pressing [F8]). |

**[F4] ASCII**    Opens the *Send ASCII* dialog box, which lets you select the file you want to send according to the ASCII protocol. This should be reserved for simple text messages only.

**[F5] XMODEM**    Opens the *Send XMODEM* dialog box, which lets you select the file you want to send according to the XMODEM protocol. This should be reserved for binary files, or text files containing special control codes.

**[F6] ASCII**    Opens the *Save file to disk* box where you specify the name of the file you're about to receive. This receives the file according to the ASCII protocol, which is designed for simple ASCII text files. You don't have to be as careful receiving text files as you do binary files. If stray characters are also received, you'll probably notice them immediately. You can later go back into the file you've saved and clean up these characters.

**[F7] XMODEM**    Opens the *Save file to disk* box where you specify the name of the file you're about to receive. This receives the file according to the XMODEM protocol, which is designed for binary files and heavily formatted text files. Since files received according to the XMODEM protocol must be received precisely, a second box which shows the progress of the transmission and error checking appears after you've specified the file name to save.

**[F8] Hangup**    Hangs up your connection and returns you to the Telecommunications screen. This is the only way to log off of the On-Line screen.

**[F9] Swap**    Switches you between active windows.

**[F10] Menu**    Activates the top menu bar.

Once you become familiar with communicating in PC Tools, you can do most of your work with the function keys [F4] through [F7].

## Disconnecting

To disconnect form the On-Line screen and return to the Telecommunications screen:

    **Press:** [F8]

You must press [F8] every time you want to disconnect from the On-Line screen in either the manual or automatic modes or every time you call up the Telecommunications module, the On-Line screen will appear.

# CREATING OTHER PHONE BOOKS

You can create, edit, and delete new phone books because they exist as separate disk files. The Telecommunications screen will always display the contents of the phone book that you were viewing when you last exited the Telecommunications module.

## Creating a New Phone Book

To create a new phone book called MY.TEL. To do this, view the Telecommunications screen and:

>    **Press:** [F4]

When the *Communication* dialog box opens:

>    **Type:** MY

>    **Press:** [Enter] twice

This designates the phone-book file name and tells the program to create it as a new file. The .TEL extension is added automatically. If you specify another extension, you must use it each time you want to open that phone book.

You cannot open more than one phone book at the same time. A new phone book will replace the old phone book in the Telecommunications screen.

When MY.TEL first appears on your screen, it will contain no entries, as shown in figure 12.6.

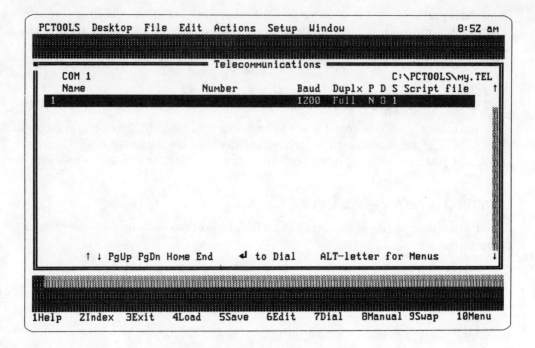

*Figure 12.6. A new phone book without entries*

Notice how the necessary communication parameters from the previous phone book are automatically inserted into the first entry fields. You can now insert new entries and edit them as you did for PHONE.TEL.

If you want to make a call right away:

**Press:** [Enter]

This opens a box that lets you enter number you want to call, shown in figure 12.7.

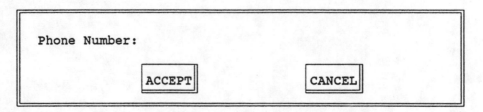

*Figure 12.7. The phone number entry box*

To dial the phone number, type the number into the *phone number entry* box and select ACCEPT. The number will not be inserted in the current phone book. You need to insert a new entry or edit an existing entry to record a number into an entry.

## Deleting a Phone Book

If you want to delete the phone book MY.TEL, you can use the PC Shell and delete the phone book as a file. You can also open the *Communications* dialog box, highlight MY.TEL, Tab over to accept DELETE, and press [Enter].

# USING TELECOM.DBF

Earlier in this chapter, you edited the first entry in PHONE.TEL using the *Edit Phone Directory* box to make the changes. You may have noticed the three character fields at the top of this screen: DATABASE, FIELD 1, and FIELD 2. These three fields are filled with information from a database program called TELECOM.DBF, supplied as with PC Tools Deluxe.

You can use this database to make optional calls to other phone numbers, especially fax numbers, using the menu-driven interface that appears as part of the MCI.SCR and CIS.SCR script files. You can also design your own script files that make calls to this database, or another database of your own design. The best way to understand how you do this is to take a look at the contents of TELECOM.DBF and see how it coordinates with the Telecommunications screen.

Use the Databases module to open TELECOM.DBF:

> **Press:** [Alt]-[D]-[D]
>
> **Type:** TELECOM
>
> **Press:** [Enter]

When the contents of TELECOM.DBF first appear, your screen should look something like figure 12.8.

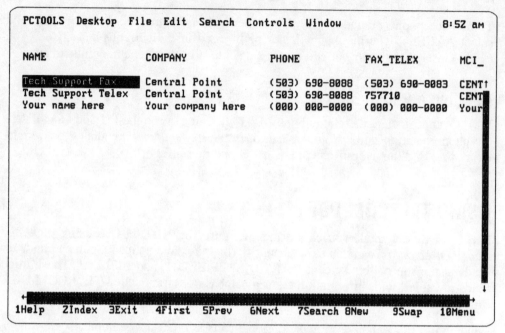

*Figure 12.8. Contents of TELECOM.DBF in browse mode*

Highlight the entry for Tech Support Fax/Central Point and switch to edit mode:

**Press:** [Alt]-[F]-[B]

Your screen should now look like figure 12.9.

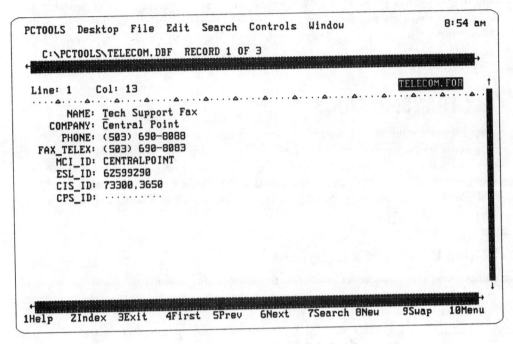

```
PCTOOLS  Desktop  File  Edit  Search  Controls  Window            8:54 am

   C:\PCTOOLS\TELECOM.DBF   RECORD 1 OF 3


  Line: 1    Col: 13                                      TELECOM.FOR    ↑
  ....△....△....△....△....△....△....△....△....△....△....△....△....△...
         NAME: Tech Support Fax
      COMPANY: Central Point
        PHONE: (503) 690-8088
    FAX_TELEX: (503) 690-8083
       MCI_ID: CENTRALPOINT
       ESL_ID: 62599290
       CIS_ID: 73300,3650
       CPS_ID: ..........




                                                                       ↓

  1Help   2Index   3Exit   4First  5Prev   6Next   7Search 8New   9Swap  10Menu
```

*Figure 12.9. A CPS record in TELECOM.DBF in edit mode*

The database contains eight fields: one for the name of the department, another for the name of the company, two for voice and fax phone numbers, and four more fields for the three most popular electronic connection services and the Central Point Software bulletin board. Only the CPS_ID field is empty, to be filled in after you log onto the Central Point bulletin board, described in chapter 13.

To learn how to use this information in phone-book entries, refer back to figure 12.3, the entry for MCI Mail that you edited. In this figure, the DATABASE filed contains the path and file name C:\PCTOOLS\TELECOM.DBF, which designates the TELE-COM.DBF as an alternate source for numbers. The FIELD 1 field is filled with MCI_ID, and the FIELD 2 field is filled with FAX_TELEX. When you call MCI Mail using the MCI.SCR script file, you're given a menu of selections for things to do while logged on to MCI Mail. One of these is to send a message to another MCI Mail box. When you pick this selection, MCI asks who you want to send the message to and automatically opens TELECOM.DBF. You can now highlight the entry you want to use in TELECOM.DBF. The MCI.SCR script file then prepares the message for the MCI Mail account number located in the MCI_ID field.

Another selection on the MCI Mail menu choices is to send an electronic fax message. When you choose this selection, TELECOM.DBF again appears. You pick the record entry you want and then the number in the FAX_TELEX field is called, and your fax is sent.

# FAX TRANSMISSIONS

The Telecommunications module is used to send and receive fax transmissions, if you've installed an acceptable fax board. The two types of boards that have been that can be used with PC Tools are Intel's Connection CoProcessor board and the board from SpectraFax. If you have a fax board from another manufacturer, it might very well work. If the board is incompatible, you'll receive a Non CCP status message when you try to send a fax.

## Setting Up Your Fax Equipment

Before you can send or receive fax transmissions over a fax board, you need to install the board in your computer, make the necessary connection to your phone line, and install the software that runs the fax board. How you install the equipment depends upon the type of computer and board you're using. You should refer to the instructions that came with your equipment.

## Preparing For Fax Transmissions

When you select Telecommunications on the Desktop main menu, You're given three choices:

1. *Modem telecommunications* opens the Telecommunications window, which was described in the previous section of this chapter.

2. *Send a fax (requires a fax board)* opens the *Send FAX Directory* screen.

3. *Check the fax log* opens the *FAX Directory* screen.

Before you can send a fax, you need to configure your FAX Directory the same way you configured your phone book for standard e-mail communications.

To open the *Fax Directory* window from the Desktop main menu:

> **Press:** [Alt]-[T]-[S]

Your screen will change to look like figure 12.10.

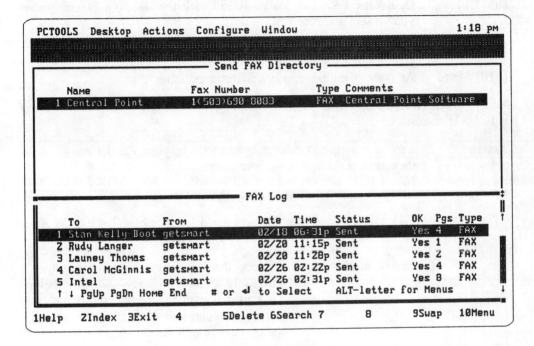

*Figure 12.10. The Fax Directory window*

If you receive an error message that no fax driver has been installed in your fax directory, you can still enter the *Fax Directory* screen by pressing [Enter].

The ten assignments to the function keys are:

**[F1] Help**      Opens context sensitive help for fax transmissions.

**[F2] Index**      Opens the help index for fax transmissions.

**[F3] Exit**      Closes the *Fax Directory* window and returns you to your previous work.

**[F4] Add**      Adds an entry to the *Fax Directory* window.

**[F5] Edit**      Edits the highlighted entry.

**[F6] Delete**      Deletes the highlighted entry.

**[F7] Send**      Makes a call and sends a fax message to the number highlighted in the *Fax Directory* box.

**[F8] Chklog**     Opens the FAX Log so you can check the status of fax messages you've sent and received.

**[F9] Swap**      Switches between active windows.

**[F10] Menu**     Activates the top menu bar. Same as pressing [Alt].

You're given two pull-down menus, shown in figure 12.11, to use while working with fax transmission:

**Actions**       Lets you add, edit, and delete entries in your Fax Directory, send messages, and check your FAX Log.

**Configure**      Lets you enter or set the following parameters:

        **FAX Drive**          Selects the drive that contains the fax messages you want to send.

        **Page Length**         Selects the page length for a fax message. If it's only a short message and the receiver has a fax machine that prints out paper messages, you can save them paper by setting a short page length.

        **Cover Page**         Toggles the cover page on or off. If the receiver is picking up your message at a fax bureau, toggling this to NO saves the receiver some money. On the other hand, if the receiver is working in a large company, toggling this to YES makes sure the message gets routed correctly.

        **Time Format**         Toggles between 12-hour (A.M./P.M.) and 24 hour formats.

        **Sent From**          Enters the name of who's sending the fax. This can be your personal name or your company name.

```
          Actions                          Configure
┌──────────────────────────────┐  ┌─────────────────────────────────┐
│ Add a new Entry              │  │ FAX Drive                       │
│ Edit the current Entry       │  │ Page Length:     11             │
│ Delete the current Entry     │  │ Cover Page:      YES            │
│ Send files to the selected Entry │ Time Format:    24 hr          │
│ Check FAX Log                │  │ Sent From                       │
└──────────────────────────────┘  └─────────────────────────────────┘
```

*Figure 12.11. The pull-down menus in the Fax Directory window*

When the *Fax Directory* window, as shown in figure 12.10, appears for the first time, the Central Point Software fax number is inserted by default. You can use this number to experiment with, or you can insert another valid fax phone number.

### Working With Fax Number Entries

With the function keys you can add [F4], edit [F5], and delete [F6] entries in the Fax Directory.

To insert a new fax number:

**Press:** [F4]

This opens the *FAX Details* window, which looks like figure 12.12.

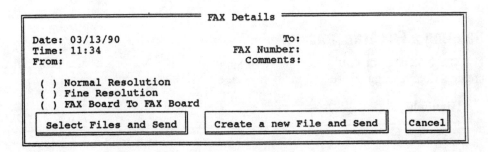

*Figure 12.12. The FAX Details window*

You'll find your cursor in the *To:* field. This where you insert the name of the person or company you'll send faxes to. You insert the fax phone number in the *FAX*

*Number:* field. The *Comments:* field lets you designate the type of faxes you send this entry and is only for your own reference.

You're given three methods for sending fax messages:

| | |
|---|---|
| **Normal Resolution** | Selected by default, this is the standard method for sending text files that contain no graphics. |
| **Fine Resolution** | Use this setting for files containing graphic features that should be transmitted in unusually clear detail. Transmission is considerably slower than Normal Resolution, which means that sending a fine -resolution fax long-distance will result in higher telephone connection charges. |
| **FAX Board to FAX Board** | This lets you send binary files from one fax board to another. Use this setting only when you want to send program files that need to run on a computer. |

Once you've inserted an entry, you can edit it by highlighting the entry and pressing [F5]. This opens the *FAX Details* window for the highlighted entry.

You can move around a screenful of Fax Directory entries the same way you move around a Telecommunications phone book: press [PgDn] or [PgUp] to move by screenfuls and highlight specific fax entries by pressing the number keys that match the entry number.

You can delete an entry by highlighting it in the *Fax Directory* window and pressing [F6].

## Sending a Fax Transmission

Use the Notepads or Outlines or a more sophisticated word processing program to create a fax message. To send this fax message from the *Fax Directory* window:

**Highlight:** the entry

**Press:** [F7]

This opens the *FAX Details* window and highlights the command in the lower-right corner of the window *Select Files and Send*.

**Press:** [Enter]

This opens the *Files To Select* box, shown in figure 12.13.

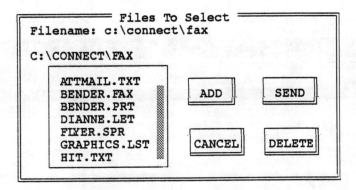

Figure 12.13. *The Files To Select box*

Either type the file name of the message you want to send or highlight it in the file name list. Then:

**Press:** [Enter]

## The Fax Log

When you send a message, you're immediately switched to the *Fax Log* screen, shown in figure 12.14, which monitors the progress of your call and success of transmission.

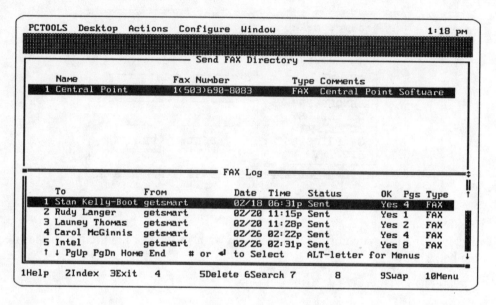

*Figure 12.14. The FAX Log window under the send FAX Directory window*

You can enter this window either directly from the Telecommunications submenu by selecting *Check fax log* or from the *Fax Directory* window by pressing [F8]. This lets you view previous fax activities.

The *FAX Log* window displays eight columns of information about each message you've sent:

**To**          The person or company you sent the message to.

**From**        The name of the person or company who sent the message.

**Date**        The date the message was sent or received.

**Time**        The time the message was sent or received.

**Status**      The current status of the message. You can receive eight specific messages or one of several error messages codes:

**Aborted**    You've canceled the fax message you previously wanted to send.

      **Bad Phone, Drop**    A transmission problem in the telephone lines made successful transmission of the fax you were sending impossible.

      **Dialing**    PC Tools is dialing the number you want to send a fax message to.

      **error message codes**    Hardware problem in your computer or telephone equipment.

      **Non CCP**    The fax board you are using is incompatible with the standard required for PC Tools fax transmissions.

      **Receiving**    Your fax board is presently receiving a fax message.

      **Sending**    Your fax board is sending a fax message.

      **Sent**    The fax message has been sent successfully.

**OK**    If this shows *Yes*, there were no problems encountered in sending or receiving the fax. If this shows *No*, there was a problem which should be defined by the status field.

**Pgs**    The number of pages in the fax according to the page length you've specified and whether or not a cover page was included.

**Type**    The type of fax message sent or received. If was a normal fax message, this will show *FAX*. If it was a binary file, this will show *FILE*.

You can use seven function keys in the *FAX Log* window:

**[F1] Help**    Opens context sensitive help.

**[F2] Index**    Opens the help index.

**[F3] Exit**    Closes the *FAX Log* window and returns you to the *Fax Directory* window.

**[F5] Delete**    Deletes an fax entry in the *FAX Log*.

**[F6] Search**     Searches for a specific item in the fax log by name.

**[F9] Swap**     Switches you between active windows in the Desktop Manager.

**[F10] Menu**     Activates the top menu bar.

The two pull-down menus in the *FAX Log* window share the same names with the pull-down menus in the Fax Directory screen , but they execute different commands:

**Actions**     Deletes or searches for a log entry.

**Configures**     Changes fax drives or changes the auto update setting.

The two menus are shown in figure 12.15.

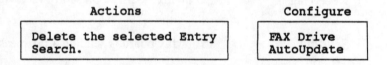

*Figure 12.15. Pull-down menus in the Fax Log screen*

All entries in the Fax Log are made automatically by the PC Tools program. You can delete entries by highlighting them and pressing [F5]. You can search for entries that don't appear in the window by pressing [PgDn] or [PgUp], or by pressing [F6] and specifying some parameters of the file you're looking for.

### Auto Update

The fax transmission section of Telecommunications contains a feature called *auto-update* that updates the fax log on a periodic bases. This accommodates the fact that you can receive fax transmissions at any time of the day or night, even while you're working in the *Fax Directory* or *FAX Log* window. It also lets you send faxes at pre-arranged times using the Appointment Scheduler. The default time setting for auto update is 60 seconds. You'll be given a message when updating occurs.

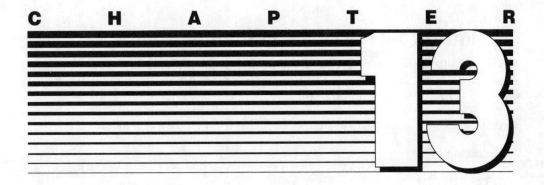

# USING
# TELECOMMUNICATIONS

Thithis chapter shows you how to log onto the Central Point Software help bulletin board. You will learn how to use the Telecommunications module to send and receive messages and download binary files. This chapter also will introduce you how to MCI Mail and CompuServe.

# CALLING THE CPS HELP BULLETIN BOARD

A novel feature provided by Central Point Software, the makers of PC Tools Deluxe, is the ability to obtain information and upgraded program files from a bulletin board system supported by Central Point Software.

To call the CPS bulletin board system (CPS BBS) from the Desktop menu:

> **Press:** [T]-[M]

> **Press:** [Enter]

If you're working in any other Desktop module:

> **Press:** [Alt]-[D]-[T]-[M]

> **Press:** [Enter]

The default Telecommunications screen provides an entry for the Central Point Software bulletin board in slot number 4. The script file CPS.SCR is attached to this entry, but I recommend that you deactivate it for your first call. This is because have to register with the bulletin board the first time you call and select two log-on names; once you've declared the log-on names you want to use, you can enter them in CPS.SCR. Then the script file can do all the log on work for you.

## Deactivating the Script File

To deactivate this script file, first highlight the Central Point Software entry:

> **Press:** [4]

Highlight the script field:

> **Press:** [F6]

> **Press:** [Enter] twice

Your cursor should appear after the last letter of the CPS.SCR. To delete the script file name:

> **Press:** [Backspace] seven times

Now to enter the communications parameters, which begin at TERMINAL:

> **Press:** [Tab] until you enter the communications parameters

To accept the change and return to the Telecommunications window:

   **Press:** [A]

If no file name shows for the SCRIPT field for entry 4, you have deactivated the Central Point Software script file. The script file is still on disk; it just won't be activated when you make a call using the CPS BBS entry.

## Making the Call

During your first call to the CPS BBS, you need to establish a unique user name and password so you can enter the bulletin board directly and Central Point can keep track of you. First, connect with the Central Point Software BBS. Make sure entry 4 is highlighted:

   **Press:** [4]

Now, make the call:

   **Press:** [Enter]

You can also press [F7], or the menu command [Alt]-[A]-[D], to make a call, but pressing [Enter] seems the easiest.

As soon as you press [Enter], the following message appears on the bottom line of your screen:

```
Dialing - Press ESC to Cancel
```

If the audible controls of your modem are on, you'll hear the number being dialed, the sound of a connection, and then a hissing noise. This is the sound of the other computer replying that it's ready to connect to yours. This signal automatically opens your On-Line screen. Wait a few moments to see if the two computers can get to communicating by themselves. If they do not, press [Enter] to speed up making the connection.

When connection is made, CPS BBS will ask you the following question:

```
Can you display ANSI graphics?
If you are not sure select "N".
Would you like ANSI? (Y/N)
```

You'll find your cursor just after the (Y/N) question. If your monitor can display ANSI graphics, you can answer yes, but it's not too important. If you answer yes, you get to see a few colors and flashing text. If you select no, you'll just see plain text:

**Press:** [N]

**Press:** [Enter]

This begins a series of questions scrolling through several screenfuls of text. Your screen should look like figure 13.1.

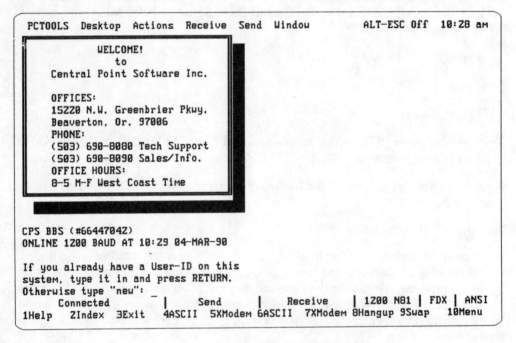

*Figure 13.1. The log-on screen for CPS BBS*

The first screen is a welcome message. The message will stop scrolling when it asks whether you're a new subscriber. You'll find your cursor after the colon. At this point, you might want to start recording the text.

## Recording Text

You can record text characters that appear on your screen by saving the dialog to a simple text file. To do this:

**Press:** [F6]

This opens the *Save file to disk* box. This lets you declare the file name to hold the dialog and looks like figure 13.2.

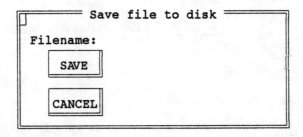

*Figure 13.2. The Save file to disk box*

To begin the recording:

**Type:** RECORD.TXT

**Press:** [Enter] twice

Notice the message that appears at the bottom of your screen:

```
record.txt 0 lines received, ESC end.
```

This will record all text characters that appear on your screen, your dialogue with CPS BBS. As the dialogue progresses, the line count will increase. This is how you *downloaded,* or *received,* a simple text file.

## Continuing the Dialog

To continue with your first communication with CPS BBS:

**Type:** NEW

**Press:** [Enter]

The message will continue:

```
        Welcome
Before you can use the system we need
to get some information. After we get
this information, you will have free
access to the system.

So that we can format output for you
properly, how wide is your screen?
That is, how many columns across can
your display show, left to right?
```

CPS BBS is asking you a second question. Most screens can display a width of 80 columns.

> **Type:** 80

> **Press:** [Enter]

CPS BBS starts asking information about you. I've highlighted my answers, which will necessarily be different from yours. You're allowed to pick your own user name and password, but if you pick a name that's already in use, you'll be asked to select another.

```
Good!  Your answer has been used to control the "word-wrap" feature, as you
can see.  Now if you'll tell us a little about yourself, we'll get underway.

Please enter your first and last name:
Charles Ackerman

Now enter your company name, or just press RETURN if none:
getsmart

Enter the first line of your address (your street address or P. O. Box):
810 Contra Costa Drive

Enter the second line of your address (city, state, and ZIP code):
El Cerrito, CA 94530

Now enter the telephone number where you can be reached during the day:
415-527-1040

We would also like to know what kind of system you are using, so that we can
serve you better.  Do you have...

    1. An IBM PC or compatible
    2. An Apple Macintosh
    3. An Apple other than Macintosh
```

```
     4. A Commodore Amiga
     5. An Atari, any model
     6. A Radio Shack unit, any model
     7. A CP/M system of any sort
     0. None of the above

Select a number from 0 to 7: 1
```

Now you need to choose a "User-ID" for yourself.  Your User-ID will be your "code name" on this system.  You will use it to identify yourself to the system when you log on and other users will know you by this name.  Your User-ID must be 3 to 9 letters long.  There are no digits, spaces or punctuation allowed.  The system will automatically capitalize the first letter of your User-ID and set all of the other letters to lower-case.

Enter the User-ID you want to use to identify yourself: **chas**

Sorry someone else is already using "Chas".  Try a different one...

Enter the User-ID you want to use to identify yourself: **Click**

Here is a simulated message, showing how your User-ID will appear to other users:

     From Click: This BBS is very helpful.

Are you satisfied with your choice of User-ID (Yes/No) ? **y**

Ok Click, that will be your User-ID from now on.  Now you'll also need to select a password so you can keep other people from using your name without your permission.  Make it short and memorable, but not obvious.  The security of your account depends on nobody else knowing what your password is.

Enter the password you plan to use: **clack**

The following account has been created:

```
     User-ID.... Click
     Password... clack
```

WRITE THIS INFORMATION DOWN if you haven't already.  There will be nothing anyone can do for you if you forget either one of these.  We don't give out people's passwords by mail or over the phone, even if they "sound" totally honest.

KEEP YOUR PASSWORD TO YOURSELF.

Press RETURN when you have written down your User-ID and password...

# 13 Using Telecommunications

```
Welcome.
To: CPS BBS

    1 ... Central Point Software Inc.
    2 ... Technical Information
    3 ... Sales Information
    4 ... Download files
    5 ... BBS Information
    6 ... Leave a message
    7 ... Read your messages
    X ... EXIT the system

Select an option, X to EXIT or ? for help: 7
```

This brings you to the Central Point Software bulletin board main menu. You can explore this bulletin board at your leisure.

When you're finished exploring the board, return to the main menu:

**Press and hold:** [X]

Hold down [X] until the main menu reappears. When you press [X] at the main menu, the CPS BBS will tell you:

```
You are about to terminate
this telephone connection!

Are you sure (Y/N, or R to re-logon)?
```

Before logging off, turn off the recording of this dialog:

**Press:** [Esc]

The function key assignments for the On-Line screen should return to your screen. You've saved the dialog to a text file called RECORD.TXT.

You can view the contents of RECORD.TXT in the Notepad editor screen. You can then delete the parts you don't want to keep or delete the entire file if it has no value to you.

Now log off the CPS BBS:

**Type:** Y

**Press:** [Enter]

```
OK, thanks for calling CPS BBS.
Hope to see you back again real soon!!

Have a nice day...

MJQ~
NO CARRIER
```

The NO CARRIER sign shows you're no longer connected to the other computer. It will appear whenever you exit the other computer's program. To disconnect:

**Press:** [F8]

You'll see the message Disconnecting at the bottom of your screen. When the disconnect is complete, the On-Line screen will close and you'll return to the Telecommunications screen.

Once you've declared a user name and password, you can log on to the bulletin board quickly with subsequent calls. You can also insert your user name and password into the script file CPS.SCR, and have that file log you on automatically. This is described in the next chapter.

Now log back on to the CPS BBS to send a message and receive a file.

When the Telecommunications screen is showing, highlight the entry for CPS:

**Press:** [4]

**Press:** [Enter]

When CPS BBS asks you about screen type:

**Press:** Y

**Press:** [Enter]

Enter your user name and password when CPS BBS asks you for them. This moves you directly to the main menu.

## Sending a Message

You can send a message two ways: interactively, if the other computer provides an editor, and *uploading* (or *sending*) a text file you created earlier. If the message is short, no more than a couple of lines, you can use the other computer's editor. If the message is longer than one or two lines, you should create it first and then upload it onto the other computer.

Creating and uploading a message involves the following steps:

1. Compose a message using a text editor of your own, such as the Notepads screen.

2. Save the file to disk.

3. Send the file when the other computer's prepared to receive it.

Uploading is the preferred method of placing messages on other computers, because you don't waste time connected to the other computer while composing the message. Your long-distance charges are minimized, but they will climb quickly when you don't pay attention to them. Using your own editor also allows you time to compose and edit more detailed messages without feeling rushed.

However, if you want to type in an extremely short message, it might be more efficient to type the message directly onto the other computer using the other computer's interactive editor, because it involves fewer steps.

To send a message in this way, first connect with the CPS BBS main menu and select the option that lets you leave messages:

**Press:** [6]

This selects the *Leave a message* option, which opens with the following information:

```
CPS BBS
MESSAGE

Currently, the turnaround time for Tech Support questions is
approximately 4 days. Please select option "I" (Important
Information) before leaving messages. Your cooperation is
appreciated, thank you.
Technical Support

    1 ... Tech Support - PC Tools V6
    2 ... Tech Support - PC Tools V5
    3 ... Tech Support - PC Tools V4
    4 ... Tech Support - Option Board
    5 ... Tech Support - Copy II PC
    6 ... Tech Support - Copy II Mac
    7 ... Tech Support - Copy II Plus
    8 ... Tech Support - Copy II 64/128
    9 ... Tech Support - PC Tools Mac
```

```
    10 ... Product Suggestions
     S ... General Sales Questions
     I ... Important Information

Select an option, X to EXIT or ? for help:
```

For this example:

**Press:** [1]

This logs you on to help for the current version of the PC Tools Deluxe program.

> You should realize that Central Point Software is always updating
> their bulletin board, so the text and menu choices in this book dis-
> play might change when you log on.

You'll now be asked a series of questions, which you answer depending upon the
type of message you want to send. As before, my answers appear in boldface.

```
The message you send can be up to 1920 characters long.   When done,
type OK on a line by itself.  (Or, type /S to save and proceed, without
editing).
```

**Just testing.**
**OK**

```
EDITOR OPTIONS:

    S)ave message      R)e-type a line
    A)ppend message    D)elete line
    L)ist message      I)nsert line(s)
    C)hange text       N)ew message
    H)elp              T)opic change

Select an option from the above list: s

Do you wish to "attach" a file to this message (Y/N)? n

Do you want a "return receipt" when this message is read (Y/N)? n

<<< CONFIRMED: MESSAGE #29840 WRITTEN TO DISK >>>

Do you want to send a copy of this message to anyone (Y/N)? n

The following E-Mail services are available:
```

```
W => Write a message
M => Modify a message
E => Erase a message
X => Exit from E-Mail

Select a letter from the above list, or ? for more info:
```

## Uploading a Message

Suppose you have created a text file called QUESTION.TXT, which contains technical questions you'd like answers to from the CPS BBS tech support group to answer Upload this file, with the preceding E-Mail menu still showing:

**Press:** [W]

When the screen asks you to write the message:

**Press:** [F4]

This opens what's called the *Send ASCII* box. This is the dialog box for sending ASCII text files and looks like figure 13.3.

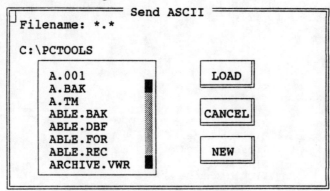

```
══════════════════ Send ASCII ══════════════════
Filename: *.*

C:\PCTOOLS

   A.001                           ┌─────────┐
   A.BAK                           │  LOAD   │
   A.TM                            └─────────┘
   ABLE.BAK
   ABLE.DBF                        ┌─────────┐
   ABLE.FOR                        │ CANCEL  │
   ABLE.REC                        └─────────┘
   ARCHIVE.VWR
                                   ┌─────────┐
                                   │   NEW   │
                                   └─────────┘
```

*Figure 13.3. The Send ASCII box*

This box behaves the same way as the other dialog boxes, but there is no filter for the file names. File names in the selected directory will appear in alphabetical order.

**Type:** QUESTION.TXT

**Press:** [Enter]

This begins the sending of the file. Notice how the bottom line shows the file name and path and how many lines of the file have been sent. Once the message has been sent:

**Type:** OK

**Press:** [Enter]

That's all there is to it.

## Downloading a Binary File

Downloading a file means receiving it from the other computer. You've already downloaded a simple text file when you recorded the dialog of registering on CPS BBS to RECORD.TXT. In this section, you'll download a *binary file,* a file that's written in *machine code.* Machine code is a series of 1s and 0s that signify values. Your computer uses these values to perform software operations.

Binary files are more complex than simple ASCII text files and require special handling to make sure that transmission is correct. You can usually tell when ASCII characters get mixed up in transmission. The transposition of an occasional 1 with a 0 is undetectable, and it will cause lots of trouble.

Download one of the binary files in the CPS BBS user library. To get to this section, begin at the CPS BBS main menu:

**Press:** [4]

**Press:** [Enter]

This moves you through the following text:

```
CPS

CENTRAL POINT SOFTWARE FILES
These files are intended ONLY as upgrades for
registered owners of CPS products. They are not
to be considered freeware or shareware and should
not be uploaded to other Bulletin Board Systems.
Thank you.


    1 ... PC Tools V5.5 files
    2 ... Option Board files
    3 ... PC Tools V1.1 Macintosh files
    4 ... Copy II Plus In-House Parms
```

```
U ... User files

Select an option, X to EXIT or ? for help:
```

To look at the user files:

**Type:** U

**Press:** [Enter]

```
CPS BBS
USERS

The files in this area are provided for your
convenience and in some cases were not written
or tested by Central Point Software.

F ... List of files
D ... Download files
U ... Upload files

Select an option, X to EXIT or ? for help:
```

Look at the list:

**Press:** F

**Press:** [Enter]

> This list changes from time to time, so you if you're an active PC
> Tools user, you should probably check this list occasionally to see if
> there are any new files that can help your work.

For this example, download the file called TELSORT.EXE, a useful utility that sorts
entries in alphabetical order in a PC Tools phone book.

To prepare for downloading the file:

**Press:** [D]

**Press:** [Enter]

The bulletin board asks you which file you want to download:

```
File name(s), keyword, date (MM/DD/YY), or days ago (-DD):
```

**Type:** TELSORT.EXE

**Press:** [Enter]

The bulletin board will first display some facts about the file you want to download. For TELSORT.EXE, the information looks like this:

```
TELSORT.EXE    Sort PC Tools (5.5) dialing directories

Date:  09/02/89    From:  Abrava       Downloads:  751
Time:  21:14:44    Size:  39680 bytes  Download time:  8 minutes

Keywords:  directory  sort  telephone  utility

TELSORT sorts PC Tools version 5.5 dialing directories.  To run the program,
type TELSORT [filename].  [Filename] must include its extension.  TELSORT
will default to PHONE.TEL if no filename is specified.  The program will
create a backup directory before proceeding.  Sorting is alphabetical.

    A —> Download using ASCII text protocol < only on ASCII files >
    C —> Download using XMODEM-CRC
    M —> Download using XMODEM <If using CrossTalk "tm">
    Y —> Download using YMODEM
    Z —> Download using ZMODEM

Please select an option or X to EXIT.
```

Copy this screen to the Clipboard so you can remember the details about TEL-SORT.EXE:

**Press:** [Ctrl]-[Del]

Move your cursor to the upper-left corner of the screen.

**Press:** [Enter]

Now move your cursor to the lower-right corner of the screen to highlight the text that describes the file TELSORT.EXE.

**Press:** [Enter]

This records the screen text to the Clipboard. After you finish with the download, paste the Clipboard text into a Notepads text file and save it to disk.

Note that the estimated time to download the file is eight minutes. Since TEL-SORT.EXE is a binary file, you should use an error-checking mode while download-ing it:

> **Press:** [C]

> **Press:** [Enter]

You're given the message:

```
Ready to begin XMODEM CRC download (CTRL-X to cancel) . . .
```

To prepare PC Tools to receive a binary file:

> **Press:** [F7]

This opens a box that displays the progress of downloading, which looks like figure 13.4.

```
┌────────────────────────────────────────────┐
│  Protocol:              Receive XMODEM      │
│  Filename:              telsort.exe         │
│  Elapsed time:                              │
│                                             │
│  Bytes transferred:                         │
│  Error checking:        CRC                 │
│  Error count:                               │
│  Last message:                              │
└════════ 10:01am ════════════════════════════┘
```

*Figure 13.4. Box showing the progress of the download*

The appearance of this box will trigger the beginning of the download. Numbers will appear in the fields after *Elapsed time:*, *Bytes transferred:*, and *Last message:* as the downloading progresses. You'll hear a beep when the file has been completely downloaded and are shown the message:

```
Transfer Complete - Press any Key to Continue.
```

You will return to the CPS BBS main menu. Exit the bulletin board.

Once you've downloaded a binary file and exited the bulletin board, you should check to ensure that it works. To run the program, first make sure TELSORT.EXE is in your PCTOOLS directory.

**Type:** TELSORT

**Press:** [Enter]

You'll see the following text displayed on screen:

```
ORT - Sort PHONE.TEL dialing directory
Version 1.0 - Victor Abrahamsen / Silicon¯ Memory Systems

SYNTAX: TELSORT [filename.ext], where [filename.ext] corresponds to a
PC Tools
          Deluxe dialing directory's DOS filename.  Default directory:
PHONE.TEL

PHONE.TEL entries: 12

Sorting...

   Writing...

      Complete!

Entries sorted: new PHONE.TEL created; original file is now PHONE.OLD
```

If you look at the contents of PHONE.TEL, or whatever phone book you specified, you'll see that the entries have been reorganized alphabetically.

## USING MCI MAIL

MCI Mail is an electronic subscription service. One of the services is the exchange of messages among MCI Mail subscribers and subscribers to other e-mail services, such as CompuServe, AT&T communications, fax machines, and Internet. MCI Mail charges for each message you send, depending upon the size of the message. However, you are not charged for the time you are connected to the MCI Mail computer.

To send or receive messages using MCI Mail, you must first have joined the service and been given a mail box, a user name, a password, and an MCI Mail account number. Two types of services are available on MCI: Basic and Advanced.

> MCI Mail usually lets you pick your own user name. Most people take the first letter of their first name and add their last name, or the first seven characters of their last name. If I used this technique my user name would be *cackerma*.

Once you have these things, you can look up the local MCI Mail telephone number and log it in to your Telecommunications phone book as described in chapter 12.

> Since I use MCI Mail a lot, I've place my local MCI Mail number as the first entry in PHONE.TEL. This way, when the Telecommunications screen appears, all I have to do is press [Enter] to make the call.

The details for logging on, logging off, and using MCI Mail are explained in the information package you receive when you subscribe to the service. The package includes a description of all MCI Mail services and the commands to access them. A sample log-on screen is shown in figure 13.5.

```
 ┌──────────────────────────────────────────────────────────────────────┐
 │  PCTOOLS  Desktop  Actions  Receive  Send  Window       ALT-ESC Off  10:56 am │
 │                                                                        │
 │  Pad ID: S4 - Port: 12.                                                │
 │  Please enter your user name:  getsmart                                │
 │  Password:                                                             │
 │  Connection initiated. . . Opened.                                     │
 │                                                                        │
 │  Welcome to MCI Mail!                                                  │
 │                                                                        │
 │  Question about the service?  MCI Mail's                               │
 │  on-line helpfiles provide 24 hour customer                            │
 │  support.                                                              │
 │                                                                        │
 │  Type HELP INDEX for listing of helpfiles.                             │
 │                                                                        │
 │                                                                        │
 │  MCI Mail Version V8.0.C                                               │
 │                                                                        │
 │     There are no messages waiting in your INBOX.                       │
 │                                                                        │
 │  Command: _                                                            │
 │                                                                        │
 │                                                                        │
 │       Connected       │    Send    │    Receive   │ 1200 N81 │ FDX │ ANSI │
 │  1Help   2Index  3Exit  4ASCII  5XModem 6ASCII  7XModem 8Hangup 9Swap   10Menu │
 └──────────────────────────────────────────────────────────────────────┘
```

*Figure 13.5. The log on screen for MCI Mail*

## Sending Notepads Disk Files

When using MCI Mail with PC Tools, watch out for one problem. Sending a text file through MCI Mail that's been printed to disk in the Notepad editor sometimes results in receiving a long string of repeated questions from MCI Mail. When you print a Notepads text file to disk, the program often adds a string of hard carriage returns after the slash mark. The hard carriage returns saved to the disk file keep giving the wrong answer to the *Send?* command from MCI Mail.

Figure 13.6 shows what these hard carriage-return symbols look like when you turn control character display on.

You should view the disk file before you send it and delete the hard carriage return symbols. This will save you the trouble of watching a long series of the same question repeat itself on your screen.

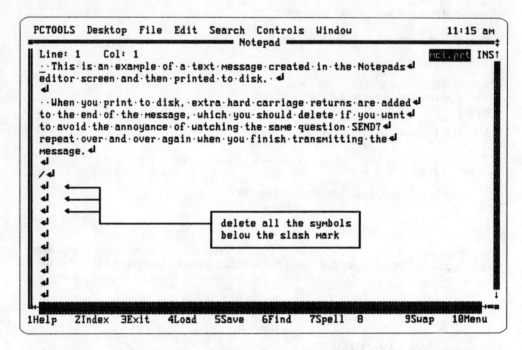

*Figure 13.6. Hard carriage returns in a disk file*

# USING COMPUSERVE

CompuServe is a subscriber electronic database service that connects you to a larger variety of informational bulletin boards. It also provides a mail-exchange service called EasyLink. This service is similar to MCI Mail, but the crucial difference is that you're charged for each minute you're connected to CompuServe. This means that the rapid downloading and uploading of data is more important then when working with MCI Mail.

As with MCI Mail, you have to be a paid subscriber before you can use their services. When you subscribe, you will receive a user name and password, which you can use to log on to the CompuServe main menu.

# USING A DIRECT TELEPHONE LINK

You can also use the Telecommunications module to send and receive messages with another computer to which you're connected a through a modem telephone link with no electronic service to acts as the intermediary.

You do this by dialing manually and typing an initialization string and phone number in the On-Line screen, then pressing [Enter] to process these numbers.

You're using PC Tools Telecommunications on your computer, but the other computer can use either PC Tools or any of a variety of communications programs.

Begin in the Telecommunications screen. Highlight an entry that contains the communications parameters you want to use:

**Press:** [F8]

You can also use the menu commands [Alt]-[A]-[M].

Both of these open the On-Line screen. Now type the proper initialization code. If you're using a Hayes or Hayes-compatible modem, the string will most likely be ATDT.

> If you refer back to the modem setup window in chapter 12, you can see that all three modem initialization strings begin with the letters AT. This wakes up the modem. The letter *D* stands for *Dial*, which is what you'll do next. The letter *T* stands for *tone*, the more common dialing method. If you're using a pulse-type phone, you should use the string *ATDP*. If you're not using a Hayes-compatible modem, you should contact the modem manufacturer for the correct string.

Once you've entered the correct modem initialization string, type the phone number for the computer you want to reach. You can press [Backspace] to delete incorrect characters, but that's about the limit of your editing controls in this screen. When the numbers are correct, press [Enter] to send the numbers through your modem.

When the connection is complete, send a message:

**Type:** HI!

**Press:** [Enter]

You should arrange beforehand with the operator of the other computer to wait for your message, then reply with one of his own. Only one person can type at a time. When you press [Enter], the cursor moves back to the beginning of the current line. Characters from the other computer will replace those you've typed. You both should work out a shorthand message that indicates when you're finished typing.

When your message goes through and you get the reply you're looking for, the connection is secure. You can now send and receive ASCII and binary messages.

To send an ASCII text message, press [F4], type the name of the message you want to send, and press [Enter] twice. The other computer must be set up to receive the message.

To receive an ASCII message, press [F6], type the name of the disk file you want to save the message to, and press [Enter] twice. As long as the operator on the other computer has entered the correct commands for sending the text file, everything should work smoothly. You'll see the text scroll by on your screen. When the message is finished, press [Esc].

To send a binary file, press [F5], type the name of the file, and press [Enter] twice. You can view the progress of sending the file and error checking. The other computer must be set up to receive the message.

To receive a binary file, press [F7], type the name of the disk file you want to save, and press [Enter] twice. If the operator on the other computer has correctly started to send the file, you should receive it on your computer.

Obviously, communicating with a direct telephone link requires close teamwork with the operator of the other computer. You both have to synchronize your activities so that only one is sending and the other is receiving. If you don't coordinate your efforts, communication won't be successful. It might not make sense to communicate this way, if you need to transfer only one or two disk files. But if you want to transfer many files, for example an entire hard disk's worth, a direct telephone link is the best way to do it.

## USING A HARDWIRE CONNECTION

You can also communicate directly with another computer through a *hardwire connection*. This is a cable that contains at least three wires passing through a null modem. In most cases, a hardwire connection begins to fail if its over 50 feet in length, so the computer you communicate with this way must be pretty close to yours.

The procedure is almost identical to communicating with a direct telephone link. Once you've established the hardwire connection, you should turn on both computers and load suitable communication programs. Select an entry that uses communications parameters identical with the parameters used by the other computer.

**Press:** [F8]

This moves you into the On-Line screen. You don't need to type an initialization string or a phone number. You should already be connected via the hardwire. Type a message to make sure you're connected correctly to the other computer. The characters should appear on your screen and on the other computer's screen. When you press [Enter], the cursor will move back to the beginning of the line, but it will not move down a line. You should not try to type something when the operator of the other computer is typing. Use shorthand messages to indicate when you've finished your message.

You can now send and receive messages with the other computer using the instructions explained in the preceding section, "Using a Direct Telephone Link."

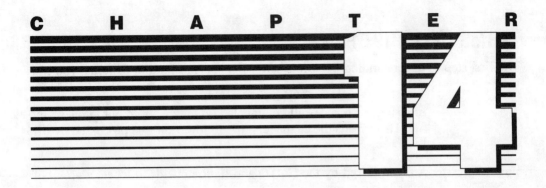

# USING SCRIPT FILES

A script file is a program that controls the behavior of your computer when it communicates with another computer. Script files can automate many of the procedures performed in telecommunications. Even if you've never done any programming before, you'll find the PC Tools script easy to work with.

## TERMS OF SCRIPT FILES

The first step to understanding PC Tools script files is learning the 19 terms you can use.

|  |  |
|---|---|
| * | An asterisk precedes all comments you may want to put into a script file. This means the characters that follow won't be processed by the program. |
| **:label** | A marker used by the GOTO and IF commands to locate a group of related commands. |
| **BACKTALK** | Calls the program file BACKTALK.EXE, if it has been loaded into memory, and tells PC Tools to run the rest of your communications in the background. You can find out more about background communications at the end of this chapter. |
| **DATABASE** | Calls the database declared in the phone book entry you used for the call, and works with variables V1 and V2 to send the entries for two fields in the database. The default database entry is TELECOM.DBF, and the two default fields are MCI_ID and FAX_TELEX. |
| **DOWNLOAD** | Receives a file from the other computer, as long as the receiving protocol has been specified. |
| **ECHO** | Toggles on and off the screen display of characters. This is useful when you try to debug sections of a new script. |
| **GOTO** | Tells the program to go to a group of commands associated with a specific label. (See **:label**.) |
| **HANGUP** | Breaks the connection between your computer and the telephone link or discontinues a file transfer, if one is in progress. |
| **IF** | A conditional command that tells PC Tools to go to a group of commands associated with a specific label, depending upon whether a condition is true or not. |
| **INPUT** | Lets you store up to 80 keyboard characters ending in a carriage return or line-feed character in three different variables: V1, V2, and V3 (or v1, v2, and v3). |
| **PAUSE** | Pauses the execution of the script for the specified number of seconds. If no number is given, the pause lasts for one second. |

**PRINT**        Prints characters on your screen, including the characters defined for variables you might include.

**RECEIVE**      Accepts a string of up to 80 characters ending with a carriage return or line-feed character sent from the other computer and stores them in one or more of the three variables (V1, V2, and V3).

**SEND**         Sends a string of up to 80 characters ending with a carriage return or line-feed character to the other computer. You can store up to three different strings in the three variables (V1, V2, and V3).

**TROFF**        Turns off the effect of the TRON command. Stands for TRace OFF

**TRON**         Displays, at the bottom of your screen, the characters for each line of commands in a script file that's running on your computer. After a line is displayed, the program pauses and waits for you to press [Spacebar] to execute the next line of commands. Pressing [Esc] cancels the script. Stands for TRace ON.

**UPLOAD**       Sends a file from one computer to another, as long as the sending protocol has been specified.

**V1/V2/V3**     Holds character strings for sending and receiving optional character strings.

**WAITFOR**      Precedes a string of characters and tells the program to halt all action until the specified string is received from the other computer.

Some of these commands work with the three variables (V1, V2, and V3).

You can use either uppercase or lowercase letters for script terms. WAITFOR does the same thing as waitfor, as does WaItFOr. An experienced script programmer will realize the PC Tools script glossary (or list of command words) is a lean set. This might prevent you from designing complex script files, but the simplicity makes it easier to learn the language.

# THE DEFAULT SCRIPT FILES

The best way to learn how to use these commands is to understand how they've been used in the several sample script files provided as part of the PC Tools programs.

You get four script files already prepared for your use as part of the PC Tools program:

**CPS.SCR**   Logs you on to the Central Point Software bulletin board.

**CIS.SCR**   Logs you on to your account on the CompuServe bulletin board.

**ESL.SCR**   Logs you on to your account for EasyLink mail.

**MCI.SCR**   Logs you on to your account on MCI Mail and opens a menu for your use.

Your work in the previous two chapters on Telecommunications was spent getting accustomed to the module and logging on manually. In this chapter, you'll automate some of that work.

Script files are all simple ASCII text files. This means you can create, view and edit them in the Notepad editor screen. You might want to print them out so you can study them in closer detail. There's no better way to learn about script files than by studying someone else's files and figuring out how they work.

## The CPS.SCR File

The simplest script file provided is CPS.SCR. This is the file that automatically logs you on to the Central Point Software bulletin board. If you're still viewing the Telecommunications screen:

**Press:** [Alt]-[D]-[N]

**Type:** CPS.SCR

**Press:** [Enter]

You can also select the Notepads module from the main menu.

When your Notepad window is zoomed to full screen size, it should look like figure 14.1.

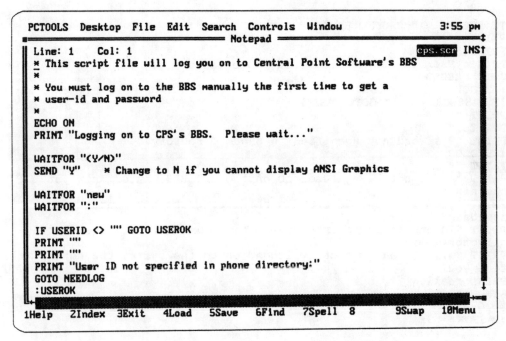

*Figure 14.1. The top of CPS.SCR in the Notepad editor*

You'll have to press [PgDn] three times to view all of the commands. The full contents of CPS.SCR shown in figure 14.2.

```
* This script file will log you on to Central Point Software's
BBS
*
* You must log on to the BBS manually the first time to get a
* user-id and password
*
ECHO ON
PRINT "Logging on to CPS's BBS.  Please wait…"

WAITFOR "(Y/N)"
SEND "Y"    * Change to N if you cannot display ANSI Graphics

WAITFOR "new"
WAITFOR ":"
```

    *continued...*

```
IF USERID <> "" GOTO USEROK
PRINT ""
PRINT ""
PRINT "User ID not specified in phone directory:"
GOTO NEEDLOG
:USEROK
IF PASSWORD <> "" GOTO PASSOK
PRINT ""
PRINT ""
PRINT "Password not specified in phone directory:"
:NEEDLOG
PRINT ""
PRINT "If do not have a User ID on the CPS BBS, enter 'new' at
the next"
PRINT "prompt. When you are finished using the BBS, enter your
new User"
PRINT "ID and Password into your Telecommunications phone
directory. You"
PRINT "will be automatically logged on to the system the next
time you"
PRINT "call."
SEND ""
GOTO BYE
:PASSOK

SEND USERID
WAITFOR "Password"
SEND PASSWORD
:BYE
```

*Figure 14.2. The complete listing of CPS.SCR*

There are eight commands in this file: *, *:label*, *ECHO*, *GOTO*, *IF*, *PRINT*, *SEND*, and *WAITFOR*.

The five asterisks at the top of the file designate those lines as comments, the textual notes that define the file but have no effect upon its execution. You can find a sixth asterisk further down the file, before the line Change to N if . . .. The asterisk turns off any effect the characters in the line after the asterisk might have as commands. As soon as a carriage return or line feed appears, the effects of the asterisk disappear.

The second command is ECHO ON. This turns on the ECHO effect, which will display all the characters received during a WAITFOR command.

The third command is PRINT. This prints the text that follows the command in quotation marks. In this case, it begins with *"Logging on to CPS's . . ."*.

The fourth command is the first WAITFOR command. It waits for the text specified between quotation marks, in this case the exact characters *(Y/N)*. These appear when the CPS bulletin board asks whether you want to view characters on your screen in ANSI form.

The fifth command is another SEND command. It automatically sends the text that follows in quotation marks, in this case a *Y* for yes. The comment after this command tells you to change the character to *N* if you don't want to view characters in ANSI form.

The sixth and seventh commands are both WAITFOR commands. The first waits for the word *new,* which asks if you are a new user. The second waits for the colon that follows *new.* You must specify the colon after new, or else PC Tools will proceed with the script file when it runs across the colon between hours and minutes a few lines below the opening logo screen.

The eighth command begins a new command construction. It begins with the conditional IF and ends by going to the USEROK label (:USEROK). The line looks like this:

```
IF USERID <> "" GOTO USEROK
```

This calls on the entry in the USER ID field of the phone book entry you're using. Referring back to figure 12.3, notice that USER ID is the fourth field from the top. You can enter your CPS BBS user name here, and CPS.SCR will call on it when necessary.

If you use a valid CPS BBS user name, you'll go to the group of commands under :USEROK. If you're not using a valid name, or you haven't specified one, you'll see the message:

```
User ID not specified in phone directory.
```

This moves you to the label NEEDLOG, which walks you through the commands for logging on to the CPS BBS for the first time.

The most important construction in CPS.BBS is the use of labels. The command IF creates a condition which, if met, moves you to a specific group of commands. Otherwise, PC Tools proceeds through the script in linear fashion, from the top to the bottom. Each time PC Tools hops to a new label, it continues its linear progression unless a GOTO command sends it back to an earlier label. Obviously, using labels in a logical fashion is crucial to the success of any script you write and use.

## Using CPS.SCR

To use CPS.SCR, return to the Telecommunications screen and call the CPS bulletin board a second time.

If you popped the Notepad editor screen of the Telecommunications screen:

**Press:** [Esc]

If you started out in the Notepad editor screen:

**Press:** [Alt]-[D]-[T]

Otherwise, enter the Telecommunications screen from the Desktop main menu. When the Telecommunications screen appears:

**Press:** [4]

**Press:** [Enter]

You should notice that the bottom line of your screen shows you which script is active. To cancel a script, press [Esc].

> Pressing [Esc] while a script is running cancels the script. In most cases, you'll revert to manual control of the computer you're communicating with. In rare instances, all communication will stop, and you'll have to hang up and start over again.

This time the revised script file should walk you through all the commands of logging on. When the script is finished executing, you should find yourself at the Central Point Software main menu. This script will repeat itself automatically each time you make a call using an entry that has CPS.SCR in the Script file column of the Telecommunications screen.

## The MCI.SCR Script

The script file MCI.SCR lets you log on to MCI Mail and presents you with a menu, letting you pick four things you might want to do.

Before you use MCI.SCR, you should make sure your phone book entry for MCI Mail contains your MCI user name and password in the appropriate fields. Open your phone book that contains MCI Mail in your Telecommunications screen and:

**Highlight:** the MCI Mail entry

**Press:** [F6]

This opens the window that lets you edit entries.

You should notice two fields in this window: *USER ID* and *PASSWORD*. Insert your user id name in the USER ID field and your password in the PASSWORD field. Close the window and make a call to MCI Mail. When you connect, your screen should look like figure 14.3.

```
 PCTOOLS  Desktop  Actions  Receive  Send  Window        ALT-ESC Off    3:53 pm
 Connecting, please wait
 Supplying logon information
 Logged on to MCI Mail...

              MCI MAIL AUTOMATED SCRIPT

     1 - Read Electronic Mail
     2 - Send Electronic Mail
     3 - Send Electronic FAX
     4 - Exit Script, Enter MCI Command Mode

 ENTER SELECTION ?_




     Connected         |     Send     |    Receive   | 1200 N81 | FDX |  TTY
                             Waiting for User Input
```

*Figure 14.3. The opening screen when using MCI.SCR*

The script file MCI.SCR that just logged you on contains 15 commands. Eight of them you've seen in CPS.SCR. Seven of them are new: BACKTALK, DATABASE, DOWNLOAD, HANGUP, RECEIVE, UPLOAD, and V1. To view this file, you should load it into the Notepad editor screen. When it's loaded, your screen should look like figure 14.4.

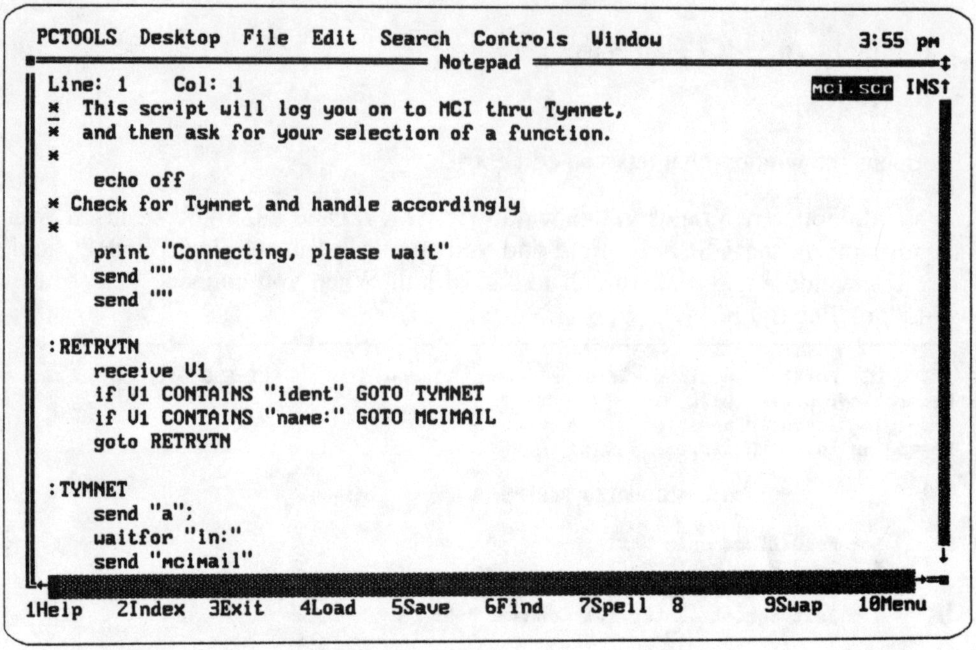

```
PCTOOLS  Desktop  File  Edit  Search  Controls  Window            3:55 pm
========================================= Notepad ==========================
Line: 1     Col: 1                                              MCi.SCr INS↑
  *  This script will log you on to MCI thru Tymnet,
  *  and then ask for your selection of a function.
  *
      echo off
  * Check for Tymnet and handle accordingly
  *
      print "Connecting, please wait"
      send ""
      send ""

  :RETRYTN
      receive V1
      if V1 CONTAINS "ident" GOTO TYMNET
      if V1 CONTAINS "name:" GOTO MCIMAIL
      goto RETRYTN

  :TYMNET
      send "a";
      waitfor "in:"
      send "mcimail"
==============================================================================
 1Help   2Index   3Exit   4Load   5Save   6Find   7Spell   8      9Swap  10Menu
```

*Figure 14.4. The top of MCI.SCR in the Notepad editor screen*

The complete script-file contents are displayed in figure 14.5 for your reference.

```
*   This script will log you on to MCI thru Tymnet,
*   and then ask for your selection of a function.
*
    echo off
* Check for Tymnet and handle accordingly
*
    print "Connecting, please wait"
    send ""
    send ""

:RETRYTN
    receive V1
    if V1 CONTAINS "ident" GOTO TYMNET
    if V1 CONTAINS "name:" GOTO MCIMAIL
    goto RETRYTN

:TYMNET
    send "a";
    waitfor "in:"
    send "mcimail"
    waitfor "name:"

        continued...
```

**370**

```
:MCIMAIL
    print "Supplying logon information"
    send userid
    waitfor "word:"
    send password

    waitfor "MCI"
    print "Logged on to MCI Mail…"
    waitfor "mand:"

:RETRYAS
    print ""
    print "                    MCI MAIL AUTOMATED SCRIPT"
    print ""
    print "        1 — Read Electronic Mail"
    print "        2 — Send Electronic Mail"
    print "        3 — Send Electronic FAX"
    print "        4 — Exit Script, Enter MCI Command Mode"
    print ""
    print "ENTER SELECTION ";
    input V1

    if V1 CONTAINS "1" GOTO READMAIL
    if V1 CONTAINS "2" GOTO SENDMAIL
    if V1 CONTAINS "3" GOTO SENDFAX
    if V1 CONTAINS "4" GOTO LOGON
    goto RETRYAS

:LOGON
    echo on
    print "Type 'exit' to leave MCI"
    send ""
    waitfor "mand:"
    goto BYE

:READMAIL
*
* let's go background if BACKTALK was executed before DESKTOP
*
    backtalk
*
* logged on now check for mail
*
    send ""
    waitfor "mand:"
    print "Capturing mail to 'TODAYS.MCI'"
    send "PRINT INBOX"
    DOWNLOAD ASCII "todays.mci"
    waitfor "mand:"
    print "Mail captured successfully"
    goto EXIT

        continued...
```

```
:SENDMAIL
* Get the needed information entered into variables so this
script
* can go into background mode as soon as possible
*
    print ""
    database V1
    if V1 <> "" goto SMAILOK
    print "Enter MCI User Name to send Mail to:"
    input V1
:SMAILOK
    print "Using MCI User ID ";
    print V1
    print "Enter path and name of file to send:"
    input V3
    send ""
    waitfor "mand:"
    send "create"
* supply name entered from above
    echo on
    waitfor "TO:"
    send V1

:RETRYSM
    receive V2
    if V2 CONTAINS "more than" GOTO NAMEERR
    if V2 CONTAINS "not found" GOTO NAMEERR
    if V2 CONTAINS "not regis" GOTO NAMEERR
    if V2 CONTAINS "TO:" GOTO SMAIL
    goto RETRYSM

* invalid name specified, exit script so user can enter it
manually.
:NAMEERR
    print ""
    print "An exception has occurred, enter MCI commands
    manually..."
    print "At TO: prompt, enter / to exit to command mode"
    goto BYE

:SENDFAX
* Get the needed information entered into variables so this
script
* can go into background mode as soon as possible
*
    database V1 V2
    if V1 <> "" goto NAMEOK
    print "Enter the name you wish to appear on the cover page:"
    input V1
```

*continued...*

```
:NAMEOK
    print "Sending fax to ";
    print V1
    print ""
    if V2 <> "" goto FAXOK
    print "Enter the FAX number you wish to send to:"
    input V2
:FAXOK
    print "Using FAX number ";
    print V2
    print ""
    print "Enter path and name of file to send:"
    input V3
* logged on now, send the FAX
*
    print "Preparing to send FAX…"
    send ""
    waitfor "mand:"
    send "create"
* supply name entered from above
    waitfor "TO:"
    send V1;
* append (EMS) so MCI knows that a message is to be sent
    send " (EMS)"
* now tell MCI that the type of message is a FAX
    waitfor "EMS:"
    send "FAX"
* supply FAX phone number picked from database above
    waitfor "MBX"
    send "PHONE:";
    send V2
* answer rest of questions from MCI about transfer
    waitfor "MBX"
    send ""
    waitfor "No)?"
    send "y"
    waitfor "TO:"
*
* This part of the script is common to SEND MAIL and SEND FAX
*
:SMAIL
*
* a valid name has been entered, continue with script
*
* let's go background if BACKTALK was executed before DESKTOP
*
    backtalk
*
    echo off
    print ""
    print "Now sending ";
    print V3;
    print " to ";
    print V1
            continued...
```

```
    send ""
    waitfor "CC:"
    send ""
    waitfor "Subject:"
    send "Electronic Mail"

* upload text of file specified above
    waitfor "end.)"
    UPLOAD ASCII V3
    send ""
    send "/"
    waitfor "Handling"
    send ""
    waitfor "Send?"
    send "y"
    waitfor "mand:"
    print "File successfully sent."
* request EXIT MCIMAIL
:EXIT
    print "Logging off MCI Mail…"
    send "exit"
    hangup
:BYE
```

*Figure 14.5. The complete listing of MCI.SCR*

The first several lines are introductory comments. You should notice more comments further down the file.

The first command is ECHO OFF, which reduces the amount of text echoed back to your screen. It's nice to see this text when you first start out, but after awhile you won't pay attention to it. However, if you want to follow the progress of MCI.SCR more closely, turn echo on.

After the ECHO OFF command, there's one PRINT and two SEND commands. These tell you PC Tools is logging on.

PC Tools then reads linearly to the *:RETRYTN* label. This group of commands uses the variable V1, which reads the reply from your screen and figures out what to do. Variables require additional explanation.

## Variables

A variable in PC Tools script language is a series of text characters that can vary from one time to the next. You can store up to three variables in PC Tools memory and change them when you want to. You can send and receive variables to and from another computer. These are the crucial elements of a dialogue.

The command RECEIVE V1 takes you to the next text line that appears on your screen (sent by your connection), stores it in memory, and then compares the contents of this line to certain specified IF conditions. For example, PC Tools takes the line and first searches for the characters indent. This is part of a larger message unique to the Tymnet service. If PC Tools finds these characters, it goes to the Tymnet group of commands under the label :TYMNET.

If those characters aren't found, PC Tools checks for the characters name:. This is a unique part of the MCI Mail connection message. If it finds these characters, PC Tools goes to the label :MCIMAIL.

If for some reason neither group of characters is found, the next command GOTO RETRYTN returns it to the top of the current group and walks through the commands all over again. There are times when this causes a message to garble.

If you don't use Tymnet to connect to MCI Mail, you should delete the commands down to and including the label :MCIMAIL. If you do not remove these commands, they will be ignored by the PC Tools programs. However, it's always a good practice not to include more lines of code than you actually need.

You can also use variables to read your own information. Take a look at the commands under the label :RETRYAS. This group of commands begins by printing the menu shown in figure 14.5 on your screen. After selecting one of the four operations, you press the key that matches your selection. This number is put into the variable V1 and then checked against the list of conditions that follow. PC Tools will route itself to either the label or the group of commands that apply to the desired activity.

## Back to MCI.SCR

You can have the program automatically get your mail for reading. The command BACKTALK calls on the program BACKTALK.EXE. For the BACKTALK command to work, BACLTALK.EXE must have been loaded prior to running this script. If it has, you'll exit the On-Line screen. While this is running you can do other things on your computer, since all activity takes place in the *background*. You can find out more about background communications in the section at the end of this chapter.

The following three commands download any awaiting mail the file TODAYS.MCI:

```
print "Capturing mail to 'TODAYS.MCI'"
send "PRINT INBOX"
DOWNLOAD ASCII "todays.mci"
```

When all the mail has been downloaded, the program tells you its finished and proceeds to the :EXIT label, which exits MCI Mail and hangs up for you (HANGUP).

Farther down the file, you can find the following commands:

```
database V1
if V1 <> "" goto SMAILOK
print "Enter MCI User Name to send Mail to:"
input V1
```

This opens the database whose name is in the current phone entry.

You should be able to decipher the meaning of most the remaining commands and groups of commands.

The three commands you haven't used so far are PAUSE, TROFF, and TRON. The PAUSE command lets you pause execution of the script for a certain number of seconds, which you enter after the command. PAUSE 1 means wait one second, and PAUSE 10 means wait 10 seconds.

TROFF and TRON are used to trace problems you might experience when writing script files of your own. They trace the progress of PC Tools through the script file by displaying each line on the bottom of the screen as it is called. The execution is paused until you press [Spacebar], giving you time to check each line. You can insert TROFF ON and TROFF OFF commands through a file to check those parts; you can skip over other sections you know work well.

The INPUT and UPLOAD commands are used to store characters from your keyboard and send a file to the other computer respectively, two activities you'll seldom perform with your computer on an automated basis.

## CREATING A NEW SCRIPT FILE

There are all sorts of script files you can create. The contents depend only upon what you want to do when you communicate with another computer.

The following sections will help you create two script files. The first script file will log you onto CPS BBS and see if you have any messages waiting. If you do, it will download then, send a message you've already created, and then log you off. The second script file will be a refinement of the first. It will send a file only if you downloaded a message from the bulletin board.

## Logging On to CPS BBS and Leaving a Message

The first script you will create will log you on to the Central Point Software bulletin board, leave questions you would like resolved, receive messages waiting for you (presumably replies to previous questions), and then log you off. Suppose that you've already created the list of questions as a message in a file entitled QUESTION.TXT in a subdirectory called MAIL. The file will be referred to as C:\MAIL\QUESTION.TXT. You can give the file any name and put it in any path, as long as you insert the name and path in the script file that sends it.

First, create the script file CPSMAIL.SCR that sends the file. At the Desktop menu:

**Press:** [N]

**Type:** C:\PCTOOLS\CPSMAIL.SCR

**Press:** [Enter] twice

When the empty Notepad editor screen appears:

**Type:** * Script file to send messages to CPS BBS

**Press:** Enter

The entire file should look like figure 14.6.

```
* Script file to send messages to CPS BBS
ECHO ON
WAITFOR "(Y/N)"
SEND "Y"
WAITFOR "new"
WAITFOR ":"
SEND "place your user name here"
WAITFOR "Password"
SEND "place your password here"
WAITFOR "help:"
SEND "6"
WAITFOR "help:"
SEND "1"
WAITFOR "editing)."
PRINT "Path and name of file to send"
INPUT V3
UPLOAD ASCII V3
SEND "/S"
WAITFOR "(Y/N)?"
SEND "N"
WAITFOR "(Y/N)?"
SEND "N"
```

```
WAITFOR "(Y/N)?"
SEND "N"
WAITFOR "info:"
SEND "X"
WAITFOR ">>"
SEND "X"
WAITFOR "help:"
SEND "X"
WAITFOR "re-logon)?"
SEND "Y"
HANGUP
```

*Figure 14.6. The Script file to send messages to CPS BBS*

The first few commands are abbreviated from CPS.SCR, so you can log on correctly. Entering your user name and password directly from entries in the script file saves a few milliseconds. It's not elegant, but you can see how they work. You could make this file considerably shorter by removing all the commands, after saving your file with SEND /S, and replacing them with HANGUP; but it's more elegant to back out of the bulletin board gracefully.

You might need to edit some of the commands in CPSMAIL.SCR, if Central Point changes their bulletin board.

## Checking for Errors

To check for errors in a script file, you should first proofread it for obvious errors and then you should use the script file. It helps to have the command ECHO ON at the top of a file you're using for the first time, so you can see all messages displayed on screen.

The PC Tools Telecommunications program has a learning component built into it. When the program runs across a command that doesn't make sense, it will display the command on screen and show it as an error. You can skip over the command and continue with your call by pressing [Enter]. You can cancel the call by pressing [F8] to hang up, return to the Notepad editor screen, make the necessary change, and try the call again. This can be a tedious process, but it's a foolproof method to make sure your script works correctly.

Try using your script CPSMAIL.SCR now. Return to your Telecommunications screen. If you're working in the Notepad editor screen, switch active windows. Otherwise, you should open the Notepad editor screen:

**Press:** [Alt]-[D]-[T]

Now create a second entry for CPS BBS that looks like figure 14.7.

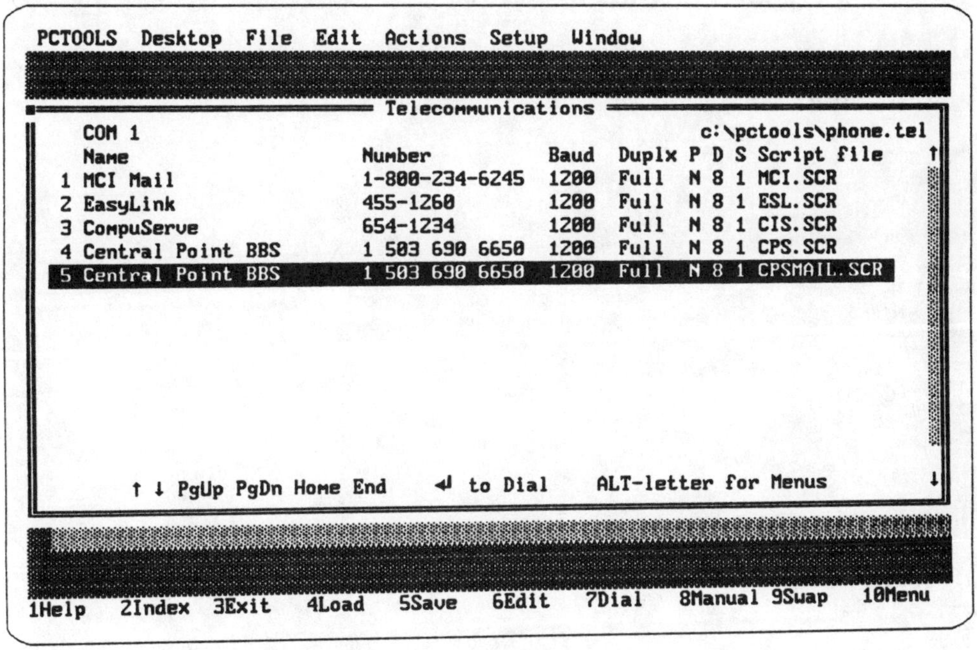

```
 PCTOOLS  Desktop  File  Edit  Actions  Setup  Window

 ▪═══════════════════ Telecommunications ═══════════════════
    COM 1                                        c:\pctools\phone.tel
    Name                 Number        Baud  Duplx P D S  Script file    ↑
  1 MCI Mail             1-800-234-6245 1200  Full  N 8 1  MCI.SCR
  2 EasyLink             455-1260       1200  Full  N 8 1  ESL.SCR
  3 CompuServe           654-1234       1200  Full  N 8 1  CIS.SCR
  4 Central Point BBS    1 503 690 6650 1200  Full  N 8 1  CPS.SCR
  5 Central Point BBS    1 503 690 6650 1200  Full  N 8 1  CPSMAIL.SCR


    ↑ ↓ PgUp PgDn Home End     ↵ to Dial     ALT-letter for Menus       ↓



 1Help   2Index  3Exit   4Load  5Save   6Edit   7Dial   8Manual 9Swap   10Menu
```

*Figure 14.7.  A new CPS BBS entry*

Make sure you type in the CPSMAIL.SCR file name in the third field from the top of the Edit window. Once all parameters are set, accept this entry and make your first call.

If you run across a problem and the program displays an error message, write it down, press [F8] to disconnect, and return to the Notepad editor screen (press [F9]) to make the necessary adjustments. You'll probably run into problems when you start creating script files on your own.

## Revising this Script

You might want to make your own revisions to CPSMAIL.SCR. Of course, you can use several different script files for accessing CPS BBS and create separate phone entries for each one.

For example, you might want to make sending mail conditional upon receiving mail; if Central Point Software Technical Support hasn't yet answered your last questions, there's no point in overloading them with more.

To do this, you would place a few more commands and two new routines into CPS-MAIL.SCR, so it would look like figure 14.8.

```
* Script file to send messages to CPS BBS
ECHO ON
WAITFOR "(Y/N)"
SEND "Y"
WAITFOR "new"
WAITFOR ":"
SEND "place your user name here"
WAITFOR "Password"
SEND "place your password here"
WAITFOR "help:"
SEND "7"
RECEIVE V1
IF V1 CONTAINS "Sorry" GOTO BYE
IF V1 CONTAINS " one ?" GOTO PROCEED
:PROCEED
SEND "6"
WAITFOR "help:"
SEND "1"
WAITFOR "editing)."
PRINT "Path and name of file to send"
INPUT V3
UPLOAD ASCII V3
SEND "/S"
WAITFOR "(Y/N)?"
SEND "N"
WAITFOR "(Y/N)?"
SEND "N"
WAITFOR "(Y/N)?"
SEND "N"
WAITFOR "info:"
SEND "X"
WAITFOR ">>"
SEND "X"
WAITFOR "help:"
SEND "X"
WAITFOR "re-logon)?"
SEND "Y"
:BYE
    HANGUP
```

*Figure 14.8. The revised script file to send messages to CPS BBS*

This file first checks for waiting mail. If there is no mail waiting, you end the call by proceeding to the :BYE command. If there is mail, the script file sends your new message, using the V3 variable.

# BACKGROUND COMMUNICATIONS

You can communicate in the background, if all you want to do is send and receive files. Communicating in the background lets you do other things with your computer, instead of watching the screen go through commands.

Communications takes place in the background in DOS the same way the PC Tools programs can go resident. A TSR program manages your communications out of sight. This means you can be working at something else on your computer while the communications commands are carried out.

Before you can communicate in the background, you must first load the background communications driver file BACKTALK.EXE. This enables background communications, but it doesn't change the way the PC Tools Telecommunications program behaves.

To perform background communications, you also need to automate communications using script files. This is the only way commands can be exchanged in the background with another computer. You have to use a script file that logs you onto the communication service you want to use and passes acceptable commands to the service, which describe what you want to do while communicating.

You can also use the Appointment Scheduler to set certain times when you want calls to be made. This will fully automate your communications: all you would have to do is create the files you want to send, using the same names you've logged into the script file.

This is the handiest way to use background communications, if you're a frequent user of e-mail services. You can arrange for your mail to be downloaded automatically and can read your mail when it's convenient. You can even use commands that tell you when your computer is downloading messages, so you can decide whether you want to read them right away or wait for a more convenient time.

All this requires that you know how to write script files in the Notepad editor screen and create appointments that call Telecommunications in the Appointment Schedule.

## Loading BACKTALK.EXE

The documentation says you have to load BACKTALK.EXE as a command in your AUTOEXEC.BAT file, but that's not strictly true. You can load BACKTALK.EXE any time you want to perform background communications and you can remove it from memory any time you no longer need it by running KILL.EXE. The BACK-TALK.EXE program is a separate TSR program that can be loaded and unloaded on its own.

To enable background communications, begin at the DOS prompt:

**Type:** BACKTALK

**Press:** [Enter]

In a moment, you should see the line:

```
Background communications installed for COM1.
```

The serial port COM1 is the default port, which you can change using a switch with the BACKTALK command. For instance, to install background communications for COM3:

**Type:** BACKTALK /3

**Press:** [Enter]

You must use a serial port for communications, but you can install background communications for serial ports COM1 through COM4.

## Communicating in the Background

You'll communicate automatically in the background once you install BACK-TALK.EXE and make a call using a script file that uses the BACKTALK command. As soon as BACKTALK is called, you'll exit the On-Line screen and return to the Desktop main menu. A blinking capital *B* will appear in the upper-right corner of the screen to remind you that background communications is taking place, as shown in figure 14.9.

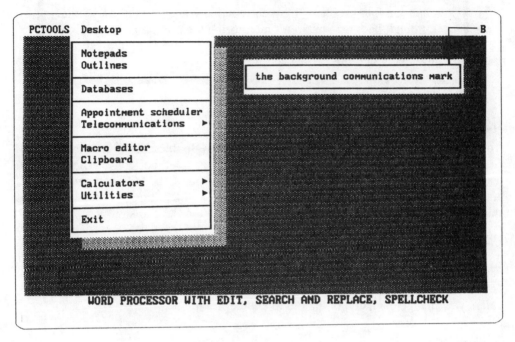

*Figure 14.9. Background communications progressing*

This *B* will appear in all your DOS and applications screens. If the mark stays on longer than you think it should, you can kill background communications by removing BACKTALK.EXE from memory. Just return to your DOS prompt:

**Type:** KILL

**Press:** [Enter]

When you plan to send or receive files while communicating in the background, you need to enter the names of the files you want to send beforehand in the script file. You also need to declare which file name or series of file names will record the files you plan to receive. Since all communication goes on in the background, once you start the call, it proceeds on its own until it's finished, or until the program encounters a problem.

You mark files to send or receive by inserting their names in the script file you're using. If you're not sure how many files you're going to receive, you can copy them all to the same file and then break them out later.

You can run into problems frequently when you communicate in the background, because you aren't monitoring the program and keeping track of its success or failure. Good background communications require that you write perfect script files.

## Using the XMODEM Protocol

You use the XMODEM protocol when you want to double-check the transfer of all files you send and receive to make sure they were handled correctly. Whenever you use this protocol while communicating in the background, the PC Tools program will automatically create a file called TRANSFER.LOG which logs in critical messages relating to each file transferred using XMODEM by the PC Tools program.

Critical messages can consist of all sorts of information. If you want to save this message information, you should change the name of TRANSFER.LOG to another unique file name. Since TRANSFER.LOG is created automatically each time you work in background communications, the new version will always overwrite the old, unless you change the name of the old to another file name.

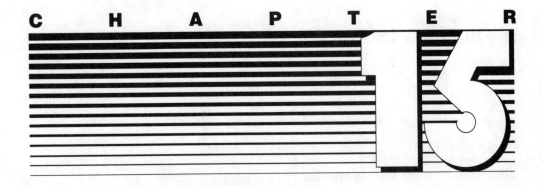

C H A P T E R

15

# WORKING WITH MACROS

A *macro* is sequence of commands that can be replayed whenever you want to execute those commands. Five sample macro files have been provided as part of the PC Tools program. Four of these help you print special formatting in your Notepad text files. The details of these macro printer files are described at the end of chapter 6. The fifth sample macro file provided is called SAMPLE.PRO. This file provides a collection of macros that automate some of the commands frequently performed when working with PC Tools Deluxe.

## OPENING THE MACRO EDITOR

To open the *Macro Editor* dialog box when the Desktop menu is showing:

**Press:** [M]

To open the box from any other Desktop module:

**Press:** [Alt]-[D]-[M]

When the Macros dialog box appears:

**Type:** SAMPLE

**Press:** [Enter]

The following sequence works only if PCTOOLS is your default directory and SAMPLE.PRO has been installed. Otherwise, you'll have to switch directories. If you don't have a copy of SAMPLE.PRO, you can copy all the macro commands in it from table 15.1.

Make sure your Macro Editor screen has been expanded to full size. If it hasn't been:

**Press:** [Alt]-[W]-[Z]

Your screen should now look like figure 15.1.

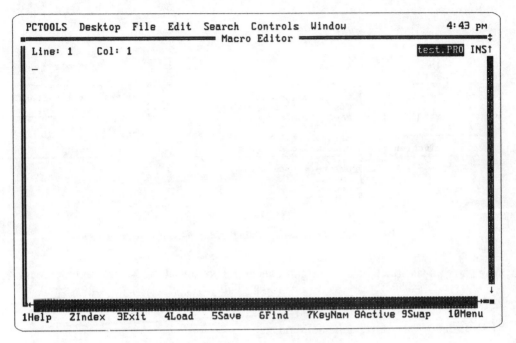

```
 PCTOOLS  Desktop  File  Edit  Search  Controls  Window          4:43 PM
═══════════════════════════════════ Macro Editor ═══════════════════════════╪
║ Line: 1    Col: 1                                              test.PRO INS↑
 ─

                                                                              ↓
 ══════════════════════════════════════════════════════════════════════════■■
 1Help    2Index   3Exit    4Load    5Save    6Find   7KeyNam 8Active 9Swap   10Menu
```

*Figure 15.1. The expanded Macro Editor screen*

This screen is similar in appearance to the Notepad editor screen. The only differences are in the menus and function-key assignments:

- The File pull-down menu has a new command, Macro Activation, in place of the commands *Print* and *Edit Without Saving*. If you want to print a macro file, you must load it into the Notepad editor screen and print it there.

- The Edit pull-down menu doesn't have the three spell-checking commands. If you want to spell check a macro file, do so in the Notepads editor screen.

- The Controls pull-down menu retains only one command from its Notepad equivalent: *Save setup*. Three new commands are specific to macro work: *Erase all macros, Playback delay,* and *Learn mode*.

Figure 15.2 shows the pull-down menus for the Macro Editor.

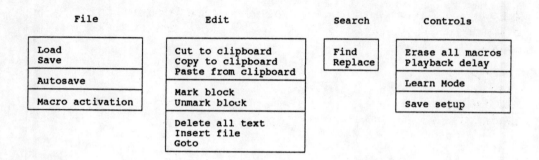

```
        File                     Edit                  Search            Controls

 ┌──────────────────┐  ┌────────────────────────┐  ┌─────────┐  ┌────────────────────┐
 │ Load             │  │ Cut to clipboard       │  │ Find    │  │ Erase all macros   │
 │ Save             │  │ Copy to clipboard      │  │ Replace │  │ Playback delay     │
 ├──────────────────┤  │ Paste from clipboard   │  └─────────┘  ├────────────────────┤
 │ Autosave         │  ├────────────────────────┤             │ Learn Mode         │
 ├──────────────────┤  │ Mark block             │             ├────────────────────┤
 │ Macro activation │  │ Unmark block           │             │ Save setup         │
 └──────────────────┘  ├────────────────────────┤             └────────────────────┘
                       │ Delete all text        │
                       │ Insert file            │
                       │ Goto                   │
                       └────────────────────────┘
```

*Figure 15.2. Pull-down menus in the Macro Editor screen*

You can find six function-key assignments at the bottom of the Macro Editor screen.

**[F1] Help**          Opens the general help screen.

**[F2] Index**          Opens the help index.

**[F3] Exit**          Closes the current Macros Editor screen and returns you to the Desktop menu, or whatever you were working in before opening the Macro Editor.

**[F4] Load**          Opens the dialog box that lets you select or specify another macro file to work with.

**[F5] Save**          Saves the current macro file to disk.

**[F6] Find**          Opens the *Find and Replace* box.

**[F7] Keyname**          Lets you enter a key name directly into the macro file you're building.

**[F8] Active**          Lets you save the current macro file so it can perform in one of four possible ways.

**[F9] Swap**          Swaps you between active windows.

**[F10] Menu**          Activates the top menu bar.

Only the functions of [F7] and [F8] differ from the Notepads. In the Notepad editor screen, pressing [F7] begins spell checking, and [F8] is not assigned.

# WORKING WITH SAMPLE.PRO

Look at the contents of SAMPLE.PRO and activate some the examples in this file as a way of figuring out how the PC Tools macro command language works. To scroll through all the contents of this file:

**Press:** [PgDn] five times

Don't pay much attention to the individual commands. If you don't have a copy of the file, you should make sure you duplicate the commands listed in table 15.1.

*Table 15.1.  Commands in SAMPLE.PRO*

---

Press [Ctrl]-[F8]: Loads the SAMPLE.DBF database file, asks for the client you want to find, then dials the phone number for that entry.

```
<begdef><ctrlf8><desk>DSAMPLE.DBF<enter><alts>T<vfld>
..<vfld><alts><altc><altc><alta><cmd>d15<enter><enddef>
```

Press [Ctrl]-[N]: Creates or loads a daily notepad file.

```
<begdef><ctrln><desk>N<date>.TXT<enter><enter><enddef>
```

Press [Ctrl]-[F9]: Reads your MCI Mail.

```
<begdef><ctrlf9><desk>TM1<enter>1<enter><esc>x<enddef>
```

Press [Ctrl]-[R]: Demonstrates how you use a fixed-length fill-in-the-blanks. This prints DIR on your DOS command line, then waits for you to type the drive letter.

```
<begdef><ctrlr>DIR <ffld>#<ffld>:<enter><enddef>
```

Press [Ctrl]-[F]: Demonstrates how you use a variable fill-in-the-blanks. This prints DIR on your DOS command line, then waits for you to enter a file name.

```
<begdef><ctrlf>DIR <vfld>..<vfld><enter><enddef>
```

*continued...*

Press [Ctrl]-F5]: Runs the PC Tools Compress program.

```
<begdef><ctrlf5>cd\PCTOOLS<enter>Compress C:
/CF<enter><enddef>
```

Press [Ctrl]-[F6]: Pops up the Desktop Manager, loads the file SAMPLE.TXT, then finds the entry for ACME in the SAMPLE.DBF database file.

```
<begdef><ctrlf6><desk>NSAMPLE.TXT<enter><desk>
DSAMPLE.DBF<enter><alts>TACME<alts><altc><enddef>
```

Press [Ctrl]-[F7]: Pops up the Desktop Manager and asks which Notepads file you want to load, then asks which customer you want to find in the SAMPLE.DBF database:

```
<begdef><ctrlf7><desk>N<vfld>..<vfld><enter><desk>
DSAMPLE.DBF<enter><alts>T<vfld>..<vfld><alts><altc><enddef>
```

Press [Ctrl]-[F1]: Loads the Desktop Manager.

```
<begdef><ctrlf1><desk><enddef>
```

Press [Ctrl]-[F2]: Loads the Desktop Manager, then opens the Algebraic Calculator.

```
<begdef><ctrlf2><desk>CA<enddef>
```

Press [Ctrl]-[F3]: Runs the PC Backup program.

```
<begdef><ctrlf3>cd
\PCTOOLS<enter>PCBACKUP<enter><enddef>
```
*continued...*

Press [Shift]-[F3]: Demonstrates how you use linked macros.

```
<begdef><shiftf1>This is a test of one macro<enddef>

<begdef><shiftf2> calling two others<enddef>

<begdef><shiftf3><shiftf1><shiftf2><enddef>
```

Press [Ctrl]-[D]: Demonstrates how you use the date and time

stamps in a macro.

```
<begdef><ctrld><date>, <time><enddef>
```

Press [Ctrl]-[F4]: Demonstrates how you use a delay in a macro.

```
<begdef><ctrlf4>wait 4

seconds...<cmd>d4<enter>Done<enddef>
```

These commands might not make much sense to you now, but you'll learn how they work by activating the file and experimenting with various commands.

First, move back to the top of SAMPLE.PRO:

**Press:** [Ctrl]-[Home]

The first paragraph tells you that the macro file assigns macro commands to sixteen key combinations.

**Ctrl-F1** Opens the Desktop main menu.

**Ctrl-F2** Opens the Algebraic calculator.

**Ctrl-F3** Loads the PC Backup program when run at the DOS prompt.

**Ctrl-F4** Displays the string wait 4 seconds..., waits four seconds, then inserts a hard carriage return and displays Done. This key combination not only specifies a time delay, but also demonstrates how the text character is used in a text editor.

**Ctrl-F5** Loads the PC Compress programs when run at your DOS prompt. You might want to view this play-out in an editor screen.

| | |
|---|---|
| **Ctrl-F6** | Loads the SAMPLE.TXT file in the Notepad editor screen, overlays it with the Databases editor screen, loads SAMPLE.DBF, and goes to the ACME company record. This is a display of menu commands, popping open one module, and then going to another. |
| **Ctrl-F7** | Opens the Notepad dialog box. |
| **Ctrl-F8** | Loads the SAMPLE.DBF in the Databases editor screen and opens the Search Sort Field box, letting you type the text necessary to specify which record you want to go to. |
| **Ctrl-F9** | Opens your Telecommunications screen, calls MCI, reads your mail, and then hangs up. This is a handy way to download your MCI mail. |
| **Ctrl-D** | Automatically types the current date and time at your cursor position (D stands for Date). |
| **Ctrl-F** | Runs the DOS command DIR and lets you fill in the file name you want to list. Start at your DOS prompt. Press [Ctrl]-[F] and after DIR appears, type the name of a file you want to list. This is a demonstration of a *variable fill-in-the-blanks,* a variable that you supply by filling-in the blank (F stands for File). |
| **Ctrl-N** | Creates a Notepad file using the current date for a file name, for example, 12-18-89.TXT (N stands for Notepad). |
| **Ctrl-R** | Runs the DOS command DIR and lets you type the drive you want to check. Start at your DOS prompt. Press [Ctrl]-[R] and after DIR appears, type the drive you want to check. This is a demonstration of a *fixed length fill-in-the-blanks*. |
| **Shift-F1** | Prints the string: `This is a test of one macro.` Make sure you're working in an editor or word processor when you activate this command. |
| **Shift-F2** | Prints the string: `calling two others.` Make sure you're working in an editor or word processor when you activate this command. |
| **Shift-F3** | Prints the string: `This is a test of one macro calling two others.` This macro calls the commands assigned to [Shift]-[F1] and the commands assigned to [Shift]-[F2]. Make sure you're working in an editor or word processor when you activate this command. |

The best way to learn the commands assigned to these macros is to activate this macro file and run on or two of them to see their effects. After you see what they do, you can go back to analyze the command structure and see how they seized control of the program.

## Activating SAMPLE.PRO

You must be viewing the SAMPLE.PRO file to active it. While SAMPLE.PRO is showing in the Macro Editor screen:

**Press:** [F8]

This opens the *macros active* box, which looks like figure 15.3.

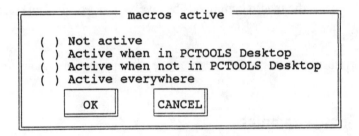

*Figure 15.3. The macros active box*

The four options in this window broaden the discussion of macro performance.

**Not active**

> Deactivates a macro file that's been made active, essentially turning off all the commands. Once *Not active* is initiated, you will have to reactivate the macro file using one of the three following options.

**Active when in PC Tools Desktop**

> Allows the macro to operate only while you're working within PC Tools, either in standard or resident mode.

**Active when not in PC Tools Desktop**

> Allows the macro to operate only when you're working outside of PC Tools—such as in DOS, WordPerfect, or dBASE—when PC Tools has been installed in resident mode.

### Active everywhere

>The macro will work everywhere, both inside and outside of PC Tools, as long as the program has been installed in resident mode.

For example:

>**Press:** [⇓] three times

This should highlight *Active everywhere*.

>**Press:** [Enter] twice

This highlights *OK* and activates the macro. Now all commands within SAMPLE.PRO have been made part of the PC Tools Desktop program.

To see how some of the macro commands behave, bail out of the Desktop:

>**Press:** [Ctrl]-[Spacebar]

This should return you to the DOS prompt or the application you were previously working in.

## Running Some Examples

To test the first key combination:

>**Press:** [Ctrl]-[F1]

This should bring the Desktop menu on screen. You can now access any of the commands on this menu. While pressing [Ctrl]-[F1] is not much different from pressing [Ctrl]-[Spacebar], it does show you how a macro works.

To get rid of the Desktop menu:

>**Press:** [Esc]

Now try another key combination reassigned by SAMPLE.PRO.

>**Press:** [Ctrl]-[F2]

This opens the Algebraic calculator. This macro does save you a step; you do not have to go through the Desktop menu and the Utilities menu.

>**Press:** [Esc] twice

You can try a few more combinations, referring to the list of 16 macro commands earlier in this section.

## Deactivating SAMPLE.PRO

You might find that these new key assignments conflict with commands you want to use in other programs. For example, I use Sprint for much of my word processing, and I save these files by pressing [Ctrl]-[F2]. After I activate SAMPLE.PRO, the PC Tools macro command assigned to those two keys override my Sprint command. Since I use the Algebraic calculator less than I do Sprint, I want to deactivate that command. Unfortunately, to remove the macro [Ctrl]-[F2], I have to deactivate the entire SAMPLE.PRO macro file.

To deactivate SAMPLE.PRO, return to the Macro editor with the file contents for SAMPLE.PRO showing on your screen:

**Press:** [F8]

**Highlight:** Not active

**Press:** [Enter] twice

You can verify that a macro has been deactivated by trying any of the keys it reassigns:

**Press:** [Ctrl]-[F2]

If nothing happens, you successfully deactivated SAMPLE.PRO.

## ALL ABOUT MACROS

Before you can really understand the various macro commands assigned to examples in SAMPLE.PRO, you should learn the features basic to all macro files. Then you'll learn how to use these features to build your own simple macro files.

### Macro File Anatomy

Building macros so they perform successfully require that you follow certain rules. This is similar to other forms of computer programming. The only difference is that building macros is much less difficult than working with computer languages.

A macro command must contain the following four elements in the order shown for it to work:

```
<begdef><key assignment><commands><enddef>
```

Take a closer look at each of these elements:

**\<begdef\>**            BEGins the DEFinition of the macro command.

**\<key assignment\>** Identifies the key combinations you want to assign to the macro command.

**\<commands\>**         Identifies one or more acceptable macro commands strung together that will be acted on in sequence.

**\<enddef\>**            ENDs the DEFinition of the macro command.

The only two elements \<key assignment\> and \<commands\> change from one macro to the next. The first element determines how you execute a macro. The second element determines what the macro does. The \<begdef\> and \<enddef\> elements must always appear at the beginning and the end, respectively, of each macro command.

Before going further, I should clear up the terms *macro, macro command,* and *macro file.*

- A macro is a series of commands.
- A macro command is a single command from the list of valid macro command names in PC Tools.
- A macro file contains at least three valid macro commands and a key assignment. It is usually saved to disk with the .PRO extension; however, you can use another extension if you always want to specify it when you view, deactivate, and reactive the file.

To understand these terms better, create a simple macro that places your name into a text file. To do this, open a new file in the Macro editor. Beginning at the Desktop menu:

   **Press:** [M]

   **Type:** NAME

   **Press:** [Enter] twice

This opens the macro file NAME.PRO. As soon as the blank Macro Editor screen appears:

**Type:** <begdef>

**Press:** [Enter] twice

**Type:** <enddef>

**Press:** [⇑]

This inserts the two mandatory beginning and ending macro commands and a blank line between them. You can find your cursor on the blank line, as shown in figure 15.4.

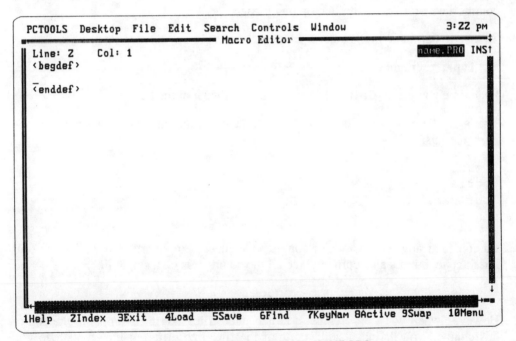

Figure 15.4. The first commands in NAME.PRO

You don't need to insert both beginning and ending macro commands when you start out. I do it from habit.

> You can also use shortcuts for entering the required beginning and ending macro commands. Pressing [Alt]-[+] will insert <begdef> and pressing [Alt]-[-] will insert <enddef>. These keys aren't helpful unless you're working in learn mode, described later in this chapter. I find it easier just to type the commands.

Next, assign keys to activate the macro. To assign [Ctrl]-[X] to the macro:

**Type:** <ctrlx>

You have to make sure you aren't reassigning a key combination you used for something else. You should avoid using [Alt] key combinations, since pressing [Alt] is a common way for activating the top menu bar.

To insert your name in the cursor position:

**Type:** Your name

Each time you press [Ctrl]-[X] your name will appear at the cursor.

That's all there is to it. Four lines of commands should appear on your screen and look like this:

```
<begdef>
<ctrlx>
Your name
<enddef>
```

I prefer to arrange commands or command sequences in a vertical row, like the four lines above, but it's also correct place all the commands on a single line:

```
<begdef><ctrlx>Your name<enddef>
```

However, when you start creating a larger macro file, like the example at the end of this chapter, you'll find placing parts of the file onto different lines will help you make sense of the commands.

> Whether you type the commands in upper- or lowercase makes no difference. The only time that case matters is when you type the text you want the macro command to insert, such as your name.

## Saving and Activating Macro Files

After building a macro file, you need to save it to a disk file, and then activate it. It's not absolutely necessary that you save the file, but it is strongly recommended. You can activate a file that appears on screen and hasn't yet been saved to disk; it will still work, but you will not have a record of it if you want to go back and deactivate it or check it for errors. If you don't save the file before activating it, you might lose the file.

To save the file NAME.PRO:

**Press:** [F5]

This opens the *Save file to disk* box, which is identical in appearance and behavior to the same-named box in the Notepads editor.

**Press:** [Enter] twice

This saves the file to the name you've given it, and accepts all the default options in the box.

If you want to use menus to save a file:

**Press:** [Alt]-[F]-[S]

The file is now saved, but it is not part of the program. You must now activate it. To open the *macros active* box:

**Press:** [F8]

**Highlight:** Active when in PCTOOLS Desktop

**Press:** [Enter] twice

You can also activate a macro file using menus by pressing [Alt]-[F]-[M].

To test this macro in the file you're working in:

**Press:** [Ctrl]-[X]

Your name will appear at your cursor position. Now, any time you want to type your name, just press [Ctrl]-[X]. Your name will appear each time, until you deactivate the macro NAME.PRO.

### Erasing All Macros

To erase all the macros you have previously activated:

**Press:** [Alt]-[C]-[E]

# WORKING WITH MACRO COMMANDS

Now that you've learned about macro anatomy and terminology and created your first macro file, take a look at the complete list of acceptable macro commands you can use to build a macro file.

There are eight commands you can use:

| | |
|---|---|
| **\<begdef\>** | Marks the beginning of a string of macro commands that form a single complete macro. This command must come before all others. |
| **\<cmd\>d#** | Sets a time delay specified by #, or the amount of delay. You use the format *hh:mm:ss:t* to specify hours, minutes, seconds, and tenths of a second. Since most useful delays are only for a few seconds, a number with no specified defaults to seconds. Use \<cmd\>d5 to set a delay of five seconds. To set a five-hour delay, use \<cmd\>d5:0:0. To set a five-minute delay, use \<cmd\>d5:0. And to set a half-second delay (or 5/10ths of a second), use \<cmd\>d.5. You can specify a delay as short as 1/10th of a second (\<cmd\>d.1) or as long as 256 hours (\<cmd\>d256:0:0). |
| **\<date\>** | Inserts the current date at your cursor position, using the mm-dd-yy format. |
| **\<desk\>** | Opens the Desktop main menu. A macro cannot call the currently assigned hotkey combination to pop open this menu. The Desktop Manager must be loaded in resident mode for this command to work. |
| **\<enddef\>** | Marks the end of a string of macro commands that form a single complete macro. This command must come after all others. |
| **\<ffld\>#** | Inserts variable information of a known length at the time you run the macro. For example, if you want to check the directory entries of one of several disks, design the macro so it runs the DOS command DIR, then you type the disk drive letter you want to check. The disk drive can vary from one run of the macro to the next, but the drive |

letter will always be only one character long. This command is often called a fixed-length fill-in-the-blanks variable (ffld for fixed field).

**<time>**          Inserts the current time at your cursor position, using the *hh:mm* format.

**<vfld>**          Inserts variable information of varying length at the time you run the macro. For example, if you want to check a specific range of entries on a disk, design the macro so it runs the DOS command DIR, then type the entry information, or as much of it as you want to, including DOS wild cards. This command is often called a variable-length fill-in-the-blanks variable (vfld for variable field).

The next several examples will help you learn how to use these commands.

## Inserting Time and Date Stamps

You can insert time and date stamps into your files using the <time> and <date> commands. For example, create a macro file called TIMEDATE.PRO. When the empty Macro Editor screen for this file appears, insert these commands:

```
<begdef><ctrlt><time><enddef>
<begdef><ctrld><date><enddef>
<begdef><ctrlb><date><time><enddef>
```

The first line creates a command that inserts the current time when you press [Ctrl]-[T]. The second command inserts the current date when you press [Ctrl]-[D]. The third command inserts both date and time when you press [Ctrl]-[B]. The mnemonic key assignments are T for time, D for date, and B for both.

Activate the macro file:

>   **Press:** [F8]

>   **Press:** [Enter] twice

You're ready to try them out. If for some reason they don't work correctly, deactivate the file so you free up the three key assignments.

# USING THE LEARN MODE

The learn mode is designed to let you build macros by entering commands from the keyboard. These are saved to memory and then recorded to a file that you can subsequently view and edit.

Use the learn mode to build a macro that takes you on a brief tour of the Desktop Manager.

Switch learn mode on:

**Press:** [Alt]-[C]-[L]

Make sure the check mark appears next to the *Learn mode* command. Now exit the Macros editor screen and return to your DOS screen. Do this in steps:

**Press:** [Esc] twice

> Don't hotkey out of the Desktop Manager. Since you're going to take a tour of the Desktop Manager program, you want the Desktop main menu to appear as the first feature. If you hotkey out of the Macro Editor screen and then call the Desktop Manager program, you'll move right back into the Macro Editor screen.
>
> If you were building a macro in an underlying application where you didn't need to access the Desktop main menu, you could hotkey out of the Desktop Manager by pressing [Ctrl]-[Spacebar].

When you see your cursor blinking at the DOS prompt:

**Press:** [Alt]-[+] (Use the [+/=] key on the top row of your typewriter keyboard)

Pressing these two keys begins a macro in learn mode. It's the only way you can insert the <begdef> command in the memory buffer of PC Tools. Notice that your cursor changes to a block shape (unless that's the way you see your cursor normally). The change in cursor shape shows that you're working in learn mode.

Now, walk through the following brief tour of the Desktop Manager. Remember that every keystroke you perform will be stored in memory. Don't worry if you make a mistake, just make your corrections and continue with the tour. Later you can edit your keystrokes.

First, you must declare the keys you want to assign to this macro:

**Press:** [Ctrl]-[T]

Now, begin the tour:

**Press:** [Ctrl]-[Spacebar]

This should open the Desktop main menu.

**Press:** [N]

**Type:** TEST

**Press:** [Enter] twice

**Type:** This is the Notepads screen.

**Press:** [Alt]-[D]

This should open the Desktop menu in the Notepads editor screen.

**Press:** [O]

**Type:** TEST

**Press:** [Enter] twice

**Type:** This is the Outlines screen

**Press:** [Alt]-[D]

This should open the Desktop menu in the Outlines editor screen.

**Press:** [D]

**Type:** TEST

**Press:** [Enter] twice

**Type:** Hi!

**Press:** [Esc] four times

This should return you to your DOS prompt. If it doesn't, keep on pressing [Esc].

Now, check the files you've created.

**Type:** CD PCTOOLS

**Press:** [Enter]

**Type:** DIR TEST*.*

**Press:** [Enter]

As long as all the files that show in the filtered list are file names you created during the tour, delete them.

**Type:** DEL TEST*.*

**Press:** [Enter]

Now sign off:

**Type:** That's all, folks!

Now stop the learn mode:

**Press:** [Alt]-[-] (use the hyphen/underline key)

This should change your cursor back to its original shape.

In some cases, your cursor might take a third shape. Exiting and entering a few applications should change it back to the shape you're familiar with.

Now, re-enter the Macros editor screen and toggle learn mode off:

**Press:** [Alt]-[C]-[L]

The keystrokes you've just placed into memory remain in a file called LEARN.PRO. Take a look at them:

**Press:** [Alt]-[F]-[L]

**Type:** LEARN

**Press:** [Enter]

When the file appears on screen, it looks like figure 15.5.

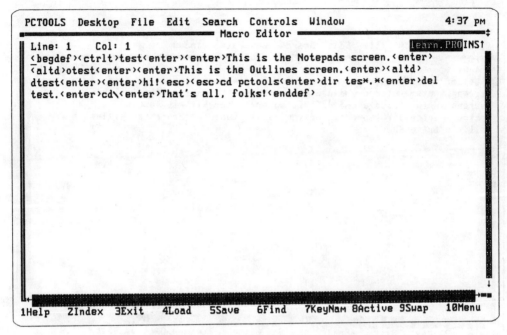

PCTOOLS  Desktop  File  Edit  Search  Controls  Window          4:37 PM
━━━━━━━━━━━━━━━━━━━━━━━━━━━ Macro Editor ━━━━━━━━━━━━━━━━━━━━━━━━‡
Line: 1    Col: 1                                    learn.PROINS↑
<begdef><ctrlt>test<enter><enter>This is the Notepads screen.<enter>
<altd>otest<enter><enter>This is the Outlines screen.<enter><altd>
dtest<enter><enter>hi!<esc><esc>cd pctools<enter>dir tes×.×<enter>del
test.<enter>cd\<enter>That's all, folks!<enddef>

1Help    2Index   3Exit   4Load   5Save    6Find    7KeyNam 8Active 9Swap   10Menu

*Figure 15.5. Commands in LEARN.PRO for the brief tour*

You can now edit these commands. One change you'll have to make is to insert the command <desk> between <ctrlt> and *test*. When you popped open the Desktop main menu to start the tour, you press [Ctrl]-[Spacebar], but the hotkeys do not operate in a macro. You need to use the command <desk> to pop open the Desktop main menu (although you can use [Esc] to exit the Desktop Manager).

Once you start editing LEARN.PRO, you should change its file name, so you can keep a permanent file of the macro commands. Use the PC Shell and change the name to TOUR.PRO. Once you've done this, view TOUR.PRO in the Macro editor, edit it further, and activate it. The changes I made to TOUR.PRO are shown in figure 15.6.

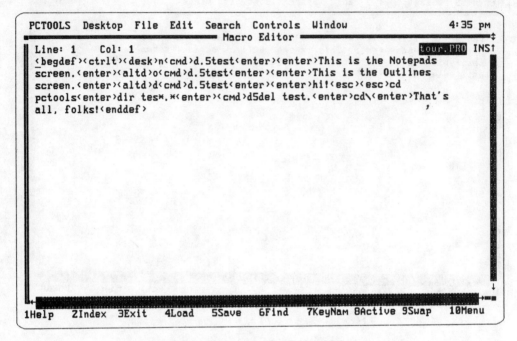

```
 PCTOOLS  Desktop  File  Edit  Search  Controls  Window            4:35 pm
 ═══════════════════════════ Macro Editor ═══════════════════════════╪
 Line: 1    Col: 1                                        tour.PRO  INS↑
 <begdef><ctrlt><desk>n<cmd>d.5test<enter><enter>This is the Notepads
 screen.<enter><altd>o<cmd>d.5test<enter><enter>This is the Outlines
 screen.<enter><altd>d<cmd>d.5test<enter><enter>hi!<esc><esc>cd
 pctools<enter>dir tes*.*<enter><cmd>d5del test.<enter>cd\<enter>That's
 all, folks!<enddef>                                      ,


                                                                     ↓
 ▐▌═════════════════════════════════════════════════════════════▄▄═■
 1Help   2Index  3Exit   4Load   5Save   6Find   7KeyNam 8Active 9Swap   10Menu
```

*Figure 15.6. A modified TOUR.PRO*

The substantial changes are to insert delays of a half-second each between opening the Desktop main menu and selecting the three modules: Notepads, Outlines, and Databases using the command <cmd>d.5.

Save this macro by pressing [F5] and selecting ASCII format. Next, deactivate all macros:

**Press:** [Alt]-[C]-[E]

**Press:** [Enter]

It's a good idea to clear out all macros while you're building one in learn mode.

Now make TOUR.PRO active everywhere.

Once you've gotten TOUR.PRO to work, you should probably deactivate it and then delete it. I don't recommend assigning the keys [Ctrl]-[T] to any macro, because they are used in many word processing programs for deleting the word following your cursor.

# THINGS TO WATCH OUT FOR

There are several constraints you should watch out for when using macros, but they apply at different times to different operations.

- For a macro to call up the Desktop Manager using the <desk> command, the program must be running in resident mode.
- The Desktop manager must be loaded in resident mode to use the learn mode.
- You can call up the PC Shell in either standard or resident mode, but you can't call any of the commands in the shell. Once you enter the PC Shell, you're on your own.
- You can call other utility programs that serve as part of PC Tools Deluxe.
- If you find you can't get a macro to work correctly, try to deactivate it, erase the file and start all over. You might have to erase all macros to start clean (press [Alt]-[C] [E]).

# LOADING PRINTER MACRO FILES

Printer macro files were introduced in chapter 6. They are used to enhance the look of printed text files.

Once you've activated the macro file specific for the printer you want to employ, you can use these commands in your Notepad, Outlines, and Database form files to print your files with special formatting effects.

To load any one of the printer macro files, begin by viewing it in the Macro Editor screen, then:

    **Press:** [F8]

    **Select:** Active when in PC Tools Desktop

    **Press:** [Enter] twice

You can try to design printer macros for other types of printers, but you'll need the printer documentation. Most printers call special escape codes that you'll need to insert as part of the commands you want to use.

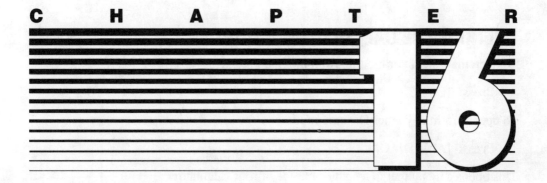

# 16

# WORKING WITH CALCULATORS

I n this chapter you will learn how to work with the four different types of calculators provided in the Calculator module: Algebraic, Financial, Programmers, and Scientific. This chapter is not designed to teach you how to make all the calculations possible within each calculator; entire books have been written about each type. What you will learn are the various commands you can use in each calculator, as well as the basic steps for making all calculations within each calculator.

# OPENING THE CALCULATOR MODULE

To open the Calculator module from the main menu:

**Press:** [C]

To open it from any other Desktop module:

**Press:** [Alt]-[D]-[C]

This opens a menu that gives you a choice of four calculators:

**Algebraic calculator**

Performs routine mathematical and algebraic calculations.

**Financial calculator**

Performs advanced financial calculations emulating a Hewlett-Packard HP-12C hand-held calculator.

**Programmers (hex) calculator**

Converts numbers between hex, octal, binary, decimal, and ASCII equivalents, among other programming calculations. This calculator emulates the HP-16C.

**Scientific calculator**

Lets you perform advanced scientific calculations simulating a Hewlett-Packard HP-11C.

> If you intend to use one of these calculators intensively, I recommend that you supplement your reading with a book describing the equivalent Hewlett-Packard hand-held calculator.

There are general similarities to all four calculators, so you can move among them and use the same basic calculating procedures. There are also crucial differences between the calculators.

# THE ALGEBRAIC CALCULATOR

The Algebraic calculator lets you perform most common algebraic calculations, including addition, division, subtraction, percentage, multiplication , and changing signs.

Since the Algebraic calculator is frequently used, PC Tools designers have provided a handy macro that opens it from any place in your computer, if the Desktop Manager is loaded.

Referring to chapter 15, the macro that comes as part of SAMPLE.PRO looks like this: <begdef><ctrlf2><desk>CA<enddef>.

Once you activate this macro, you'll move into the Algebraic calculator each time you press [Ctrl]-[F2].

To open the Algebraic calculator, shown in figure 6.1, when the Calculators menu is showing:

**Press:** [A]

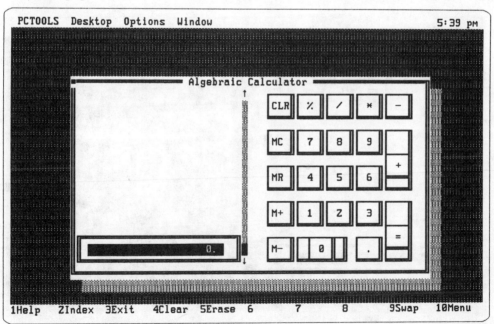

*Figure 16.1. The Algebraic Calculator screen*

This is a fairly simple display. The number keys are on the right, and the display register is on the left, with a window above it which simulates a tape. As you enter numbers and perform calculations on them, your results will appear in the register and the tape window. Each new calculation result replaces the previous number in the display register. New calculations in the tape scroll upwards as you add more numbers. You can edit the tape and move to numbers that have scrolled off the top.

The right half of the calculator screen is intended for use with a mouse. If you're using a mouse, you just point to the key you want to use and press a button.

To enter numbers without a mouse, type the numbers with numeric keypad, usually on the right side of the keyboard.

You can toggle the right side on and off with the wide display. Wide display is on by default. To switch it off:

**Press:** [Alt]-[O]-[W]

When wide display is off, your Algebraic calculator screen should look like figure 16.2.

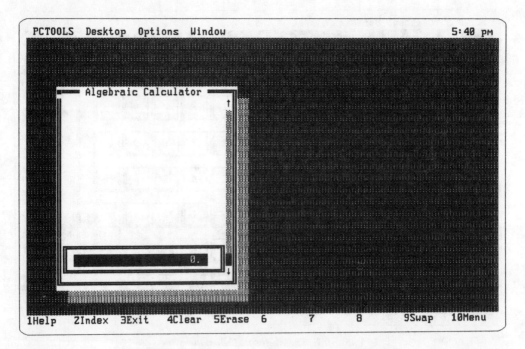

*Figure 16.2. The Algebraic calculator with wide display off*

I recommend that you leave the right side of the Algebraic calculator showing because the key display can remind you of many commands. Switch wide display back on.

Try a simple calculation now. First make sure [Num Lock] is on:

**Press:** [Num Lock]

To multiply 2 X 4:

**Press:** [2]

**Press:** [*] (As an alternative to pressing * for multiplication, you can press [X] on the keyboard)

**Press:** [4]

**Press:** [=]

The result of 8 should appear in the display register. Your tape should now look like figure 16.3

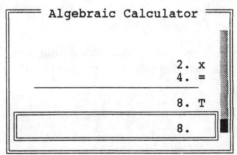

*Figure 16.3. The Algebraic Calculator tape display*

The exact keys you press depend upon what type of keyboard you're using. If you have a separate keypad, then you should use those keys. Most keypads also have a separate asterisk key, however, you can press [Shift]-[8] to get the same effect.

If you get an answer different from 8, clear the display:

**Press:** [F4]

You could also press [C] to clear the display register. This will insert a zero in the tape followed by C, to show that all ongoing calculations up to that point have been cleared.

To clear the tape:

    **Press:** [F5]

Now, look at the menus. The Desktop and Window menus are the same ones you get in the other modules. There's only one new menu, Options, which contains five commands:

**Clear display**          Clears the current display. Same as pressing [F4] or [C].

**Erase tape**              Clears the tape on screen. Same as pressing [F5].

**Copy to Clipboard**      Copies the current tape to the Clipboard. This lets you move your calculations to another document, such as the Notepads screen, or to an outside application, such as a document in WordPerfect or Lotus 1-2-3.

**Print tape**              Opens the *Print* window, which lets you select the print device.

**Wide display**           Toggles the Calculator display between wide, (figure 16.1) and narrow (figure 16.2). You need only the wide display if you're using a mouse.

You need only a few menu commands, because working with the Algebraic calculator is simple and straightforward. Table 16.1 gives you all the commands you can use.

*Table 16.1. List of commands in the Algebraic calculator*

| Function | Keyboard | Mouse |
|---|---|---|
| Add | [+] | [+] |
| Subtract | [-] | [-] |
| Multiply | [*] or [X] | [*] |
| Divide | [/] | [/] |
| Equal | [=] or [Enter] | [=] |
| Total | [=] or [Enter] | [=] |
| Clear | [C] | [CLR] |
| Percentage | [%] | [%] |
| Memory | | |
|   Add | [M]-[+] | [M]-[+] |
|   Subtract | [M]-[-] | [M]-[-] |
|   Recall | [M]-[R] | [MR] |
|   Erase | [M]-[C] | [MC] |
| Edit Tape ([Num Lock] off) | | |
|   Up one line | [Up arrow] | move up |
|   Up one window | [PgUp] | |
|   Down one line | [Down arrow] | |
|   Down one window | [PgDn] | |
| Decimal places set | [D] + decimal places | |
| Toggle comma on and off | [,] | [,] |

To display a number to five decimal places:

    **Press:** [D]-[5]

To turn decimal display off:

    **Press:** [D]-[0]

The bottom line of your screen shows seven function-key assignments:

**[F1] Help**    Opens the definition of the Algebraic calculator, from which you can move into the help index.

**[F2] Index**    Opens the help index list.

**[F3] Exit**    Closes the Algebraic calculator and returns you to the Desktop menu or whatever you were working in previously.

**[F4] Clear**    Clears the display register.

**[F5] Erase**    Erases all contents on the current tape.

**[F9] Swap**      Switches you to other active windows.

**[F10] Menu**    Activates the top menu bar.

## Using the Tape

You can work with the tape in several ways. You can change the figures displayed in the tape and then run a new calculation on the figures. The tape can only show 12 lines of numbers, but it can hold up to 1,000 lines. After that, the oldest calculation is erased to make room for the new. However, you can save the tape to a file periodically by copying the contents of the tape to the Clipboard, where you can paste it into a file in the Notepad editor screen or into an outside application.

### Editing the Tape

The basic procedure for editing the tape is to highlight the number you want to change, make the change, and then perform the calculation again by pressing [End]. The scroll bar down the center of the wide version of the calculator shows the relative position on the current tape.

In the previous calculation, you multiplied 2 x 4 and got 8 as a result. Edit the calculation to change 4 to 8 (that is, multiply 2 x 8).

Turn Num Lock off:

    **Press:** [Num Lock]

    **Press:** [⇑] once

Even though the number 4 is two lines up from the display, you only need to press [⇑] once. You can only edit figures you've entered into the tape, so you skip over the first number, 8, which is the product of the first calculation.

When the number 4 appears on the display register:

    **Press:** [8]

Now recalculate the new numbers:

    **Press:** [End]

You'll get 16 as the result. Your screen should look like figure 16.4.

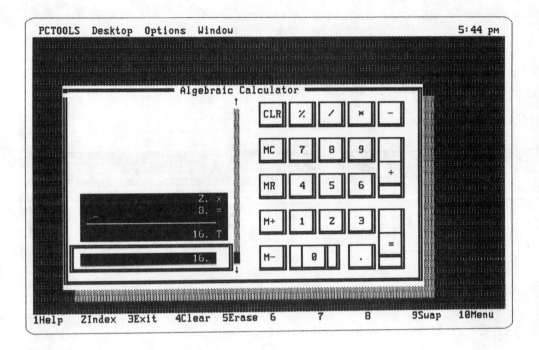

*Figure 16.4. Results of running a recalculation*

Whenever you recalculate numbers, you cannot press [=] to make the recalculation, you must press [End].

### Copying the Tape to the Clipboard

Often you'll want to use one of the calculators to make a quick check on some figures and then return to your work in another application. You can use the calculator, copy the result to the Clipboard, and then paste it from the Clipboard to whatever application you're working with.

For example, copy the calculation you just performed for 2 x 8. (Your screen should look like figure 16.4.)

   **Press:** [Alt]-[O]-[B]

This copies the current contents of the tape to a disk file called CALC.TMP and also to the Clipboard. Verify that this worked:

**Press:** [Alt]-[D]-[B]

Your display screen should look like figure 16.5.

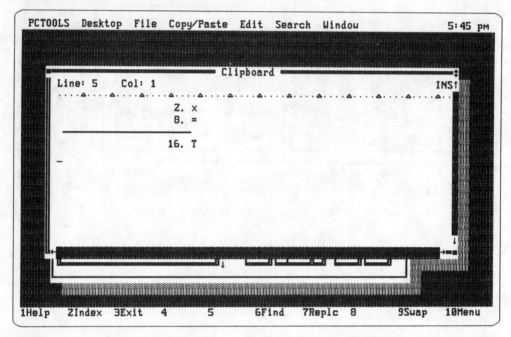

*Figure 16.5. Copying calculator tape into the Clipboard*

To paste the contents of the clipboard into another application, refer to chapter 7.

### *Printing the Tape*

You can print the current contents of the Algebraic calculator tape to your printer or a disk file. You must print the entire contents of the tape, but if you print it to a disk file first, you can edit the file using the Notepad editor and then save and print only the part you want to.

To print a calculator tape:

**Press:** [Alt]-[O]-[P]

This opens the *Print* box, which lets you determine the receiving device for the file to. When you print to disk, the tape contents are saved to a file called CALC.PRT. If you save your tape contents periodically (so you don't bump up against the 1,000 line limit), you'll have to change the name of this file after you print it. You can use the PC Shell File menu command, *Rename*. For example, you could rename the files CALC1.PRT, CALC2.PRT, and so on.

## Using Memory

You can store one number into memory in the Algebraic calculator. The three other calculators can store up to 20 numbers. Storing a number is convenient when you are using it repeatedly, for example, when you are multiplying a series of numbers by a constant.

### Putting a Number into Memory

To place the number 2:

**Press:** [2]

**Press:** [M]-[+]

When you place a number into memory, the letter *M* will show on the left side of the tape, just above the display register.

To recall the contents of memory:

**Press:** [M]-[R]

This stands for memory recall. It places the number in the display register to be used for calculations.

### Changing a Number in Memory

You can change a number in memory by increasing or decreasing its value. To increase the value, type the value you want to increase it by and press [M]-[+]. For example, to increase the number in current memory by 6, or from 2 to 8:

**Press:** [6]-[M]-[+]

You can now check the results by pressing [M]-[R]. Be sure to press [F4] to clear the register so you don't use this new number inadvertently.

To decrease the number in memory, press [M]-[-]. For example, to decrease the number in current memory by 3, or from 8 to 5:

**Press:** [3]-[M]-[-]

Check the results by pressing [M]-[R], then [F4].

### Clearing Memory

Clearing memory is simple:

**Press:** [M]-[C]

You can verify that your memory is cleared when the letter *M* disappears from the left-lower corner of the tape. The current value in memory will be dumped into the display register and on tape. To clear the register:

**Press:** [F4]

## THE FINANCIAL CALCULATOR

Use the Financial calculator to perform calculations for:

- Simple and compound interest rates, including annual percentage rates.
- Financial 5-key problems involved with loans, including for calculations for interest, remaining principal and balance, and periodic payments.
- Mortgage calculations, including discounted rates, prepaid charges, wraparounds, variable rates, and amortization schedules.
- Discounted cash-flow analysis, including net present value, internal rate of return, and yield and rate conversions.
- Computing depreciation and appreciation.
- Statistical analyses, including finding mean averages, linear projections and a weighted mean.

To enter the Financial calculator, when the Calculator menu is showing:

**Press:** [F]

This opens a calculator that fills your entire screen and looks like figure 16.6.

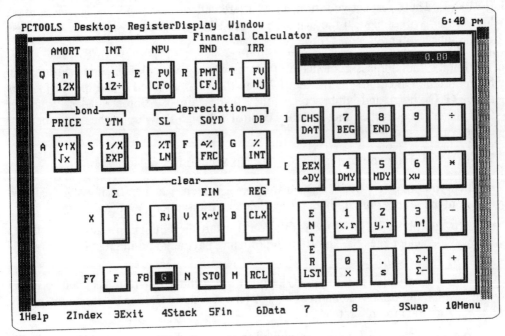

*Figure 16.6. The Financial calculator screen*

You can't toggle the wide display on and off in this or any of the other more sophisticated calculators in PC Tools, because the key display is crucial to your operating these calculators.

Like the lack of a wide-display toggle, many of the rules that apply to the Financial calculator also apply to the Programmers and Scientific calculators, described later in this chapter.

## The F and G Function Keys

Most of the keys in the Financial calculator have several functions displayed in and above each key. Each key is identified by the letter to its left.

For example, the top five keys are assigned to the letters Q, W, E, R, and T. These five keys have three functions each. You execute the one in the middle of the key when you press the letter key itself. You execute the function above the key when you press [F7] and then the key. And you execute the lower function when you press [F8] and then the letter key.

If you look in the lower-left corner of the calculator keypad, you'll see the [F7] and [F8] keys. These respectively turn on what are called *f functions* and *g functions*. A lowercase *f* will appear in the display register after you press [F7], and a lowercase *g* will appear after you press [F8].

The f and g function assignments are features where your color or shade settings can be important. On color screens, the [F7] key shows up as a red F and the [F8] key as a blue G. On black-and-white screens, they'll show up as different shades. Whatever their shade or color, the functions they control will also show up in the same shade or color.

The first key on the top row is the [Q] key. Its functions are:

• When you press [Q] by itself, you'll insert *n,* which is a specific register designed to hold the number of payments for a financial transaction (signified by *n*).

• When you press [F7] and then [Q], you'll insert the f function assigned to the Q key, which calculates the amortization of using payment and interest figures (signified by AMORT).

• When you press [F8] and then [Q], you'll insert the g function assigned to the Q key, which multiplies the number by 12. This is usually used to calculate the yearly total from the monthly rate (12x).

The complete range of functions assigned to the keys displayed in the Financial calculator screen are shown in table 16.2.

*Table 16.2. Key commands in the Financial calculator*

| Key | Performs | [F7] |
|---|---|---|
| Q | number of periods (n) | amortization (AMORT) |
| W | interest rate (i) | interest rate (INT) |
| E | present value (PV) | net present value (NPV) |
| R | payment (PMT) | rounding values (RND) |
| T | future value (FV) | internal rate of return (IRR) |
| A | exponential power $Y^x$ | bond price (PRICE) |
| S | reciprocal or inverse (1/X) | bond yield-to-maturity (YTM) |
| D | percent of total (%T) | straight line depreciation (SL) |
| F | percentage difference (Δ%) | sum-of-the-year's-digits depreciation (SOYD) |
| G | percent (%) | declining balance depreciation (DB) |
| X | | clear (Σ |
| | change sign (CHS) | |
| [ | exponent (EEX) | |
| Enter | Enter key | |
| 0 | insert 0 | no decimal places |
| 1 | insert 1 | one decimal place |
| 2 | insert 2 | two decimal places |
| 3 | insert 3 | three decimal places |
| 4 | insert 4 | four decimal places |
| 5 | insert 5 | five decimal places |
| 6 | insert 6 | six decimal places |
| 7 | insert 7 | seven decimal places |
| 8 | insert 8 | eight decimal places |
| 9 | insert 9 | nine decimal places |
| , | toggles comma on an off | |
| & | calculating statistics (Σ+) | |
| + | addition (+) | |
| − | subtraction (-) | |
| / | division (÷) | |
| * | multiplication (x) | |

| Key | Performs | [F8] |
|---|---|---|
| Q | number of periods (n) | 12 times, such a months in a year (12X) |
| W | interest rate (i) | into 12, such as months in a year (12÷) |
| E | present value (PV) | initial cash flow group (CFo) |
| R | payment (PMT) | next cash flow group (CFj) |
| T | future value (FV) | number of periods for cash flow (Nj) |
| A | exponential power $Y^x$ | square root √x |
| S | reciprocal or inverse (1/X) | exponent (EXP) |
| D | percent of total (%T) | natural log of displayed number (LN) |
| F | percentage difference (Δ%) | digits after decimal point into display (FRC) |
| G | percent (%) | digits before decimal point into display (INT) |
| X | | |
| | change sign (CHS) | Date (DAT) |
| [ | exponent (EEX) | Change (ΔDY) |
| Enter | Enter key | recalls last number displayed into X (LST) |
| 0 | insert 0 | calculates mean average (x) |
| 1 | insert 1 | calculate correlation coefficient (x,r) |
| 2 | insert 2 | calculates linear projection (y,r) |
| 3 | insert 3 | calculates factorial (n!) |
| 4 | insert 4 | day/month/year format in display (DMY) |
| 5 | insert 5 | month/day/year format in display (MDY) |
| 6 | insert 6 | statistical weighted mean (xw) |
| 7 | insert 7 | beginning payment period calculation (BEG) |
| 8 | insert 8 | ending payment period calculation (END) |
| 9 | insert 9 | |
| , | toggles comma on an off | |
| & | calculating statistics (Σ+) | reverse statistical calculation (Σ-) |

You should notice that some keys have been gathered into related groups. The top five keys QWERT perform your most basic financial calculations. The two keys, A and S, work with bond calculations (although you'll use other keys in the process). The keys D, F, and G work with depreciation, and X, C, V, and B clear various registers.

The Financial calculator provides a single menu of its own, RegisterDisplay, which contains three choices:

**Stack Register**        Lets you perform standard math, such as addition, subtraction, multiplication, and division, and stack the intermediate results. You can display this series of registers by pressing [F5] or [Alt]-[R]-[S].

**Financial Register**      Lets you perform financial calculations by storing four values and calculating a fifth value from them. You can display this series of registers by pressing [F6] or [Alt]-[R]-[F].

**Data Register**        Stores 20 numbers for storage and recall at a later time. You can display this series of registers by pressing [F8] or [Alt]-[R]-[D].

## Error Messages

Before we go any further with the Scientific calculator, you should be aware that Financial, Programmer, and Scientific calculators provide error messages in case you make a mistake. When you press a wrong key or try to do something that can't be done, the display register will return an appropriate error message.

There are four possible error messages that can appear in the Financial calculator:

**ERROR**      Incorrect key sequence.

**ERROR 0**    An impossible calculation.

**ERROR 1**    Too many values in registers.

**ERROR 2**    Incorrect statistical calculation.

These error messages do not illuminate the problem as much as a new user would like. An incorrect key sequence can show up as an impossible or incorrect calculation, depending upon what keys you pressed. If you move quickly, the error message can disappear before you have a chance to read it. Pressing any key after an error message removes the message.

Whenever you get an error message, even if you pass over it, check the contents of your registers. It's possible that values were entered accidentally, even though the display register has returned to 0.00. You might want to clear all registers as a matter of habit whenever an error message appears.

**Press:** [F7]-[B]

Other error messages can show up in different calculators.

## Working With Registers

You worked with a single register in the Algebraic calculator. The Financial calculator, along with the Programmer's and Scientific calculators, contain more memory registers. You can see the contents of these registers in all three calculators using the RegisterDisplay pull-down menu:

**Press:** [Alt]-[R]

This opens a menu with three choices of registers to display: Stack Register, Financial Register, and Data Registers. Only the Financial calculator contains the financial register. The stack and data registers are available in all three.

### The Stack Register

The stack registers are designed to hold numbers for standard arithmetic calculations: addition, subtraction, multiplication, and division. To see the stack register display:

**Press:** [F4]

Your screen should resemble figure 16.7.

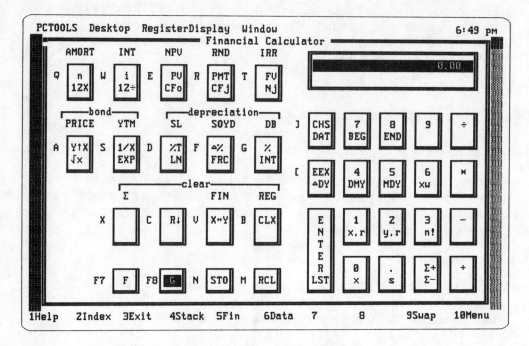

*Figure 16.7. Stack register display in the Financial calculator*

The five stack registers show the position of five values that have been stored in a stack. The T register stands for the top value on the stack. The Z, Y, and X registers refer to values that have been added since, with X the most recent value, at the bottom of the stack. The number in the display register is automatically inserted in the X register.

As you add numbers from the bottom, the numbers above are pushed towards the top. The numbers pushed upwards come down as values are removed from the bottom of the stack. LSTX means the last value that appeared in the X register before the most recent calculation. This lets you refer back one step to a previous value.

To close the stack register display:

**Press:** [Esc]

To multiply 3 x 3, make sure [Num Lock] is turned on:

**Type:** 3

**Press:** [Enter]

**Type:** 3

**Type:** *

The answer, 9, should show in the display register.

Notice that when you performed similar math in the Algebraic calculator, you didn't have to press [Enter]. That's because the Algebraic calculator is designed specifically for standard math. The Financial calculator is designed for more sophisticated calculations, but you can also perform more simple calculations as long as you press [Enter] first.

The figures you used to calculate the simple multiplication have been loaded into the stack registers. To see them:

**Press:** [F4]

Your stack register display should look like figure 16.8.

```
REGISTER
    T                        0.00
    Z                        0.00
    Y                        0.00
    X                        9.00

LSTX                         3.00
```

*Figure 16.8. The Stack register*

The calculated value of 9 has been placed in the X register, where it can be used in other calculations.

The LSTX register shows 3, because that value was inserted in the X register when you first typed 3 and pressed [Enter].

Try a more complex calculation. Close the stack register display:

**Press:** [Esc]

Find the square root of 16:

> **Type:** 16

> **Press:** [F8]-[A]

The answer, 4, appears immediately in the display register. The key that calculates square root is the g function of [A]. Now take a look at how this value has been added to the stack:

> **Press:** [F4]

Your screen should look like figure 16.9.

```
REGISTER
    T                    0.00
    Z                    0.00
    Y                    9.00
    X                    4.00

LSTX                    16.00
```

*Figure 16.9. The Stack register contents*

The result of your most recent calculation, 4, appears in the X register. This bumped up the previous calculated value of 9 to the Y register. The number 16 shows in the LSTX register because this was the most recent value to appear in the X register.

Now switch the values in the X and Y registers. Notice that the V key has been given this assignment (X↔Y):

> **Press:** [V]

The display register changes to 9.00, which is the value that appeared before 4.00 in the Y register. Double check the stack registers:

> **Press:** [F4]

They should look like figure 16.10.

```
┌──────────────────────────────────────────────┐
│                                                │
│  REGISTER                                      │
│      T                       0.00              │
│      Z                       0.00              │
│      Y                       4.00              │
│      X                       9.00              │
│                                                │
│  LSTX                       16.00              │
│                                                │
└──────────────────────────────────────────────┘
```

*Figure 16.10. The Stack register display*

The values in the X and Y registers have changed places, and the previous value inserted in the display register, 16, now appears in LSTX.

### Clearing Registers

You can clear stored values in registers several ways. The established way is to use the f function for the [B] key. This is marked REG and will clear all REGisters:

> **Press:** [F7]-[B]

Now check the stack registers:

> **Press:** [F4]

They should be empty or 0.

You can selectively clear only the X register by just pressing [B] by itself. This is marked CLX, which means CLearing the X register.

You can also clear all values from all registers in any calculator by pressing [Esc] and then re-entering the calculator.

## The Financial Registers

The financial registers are used for specific financial calculations. To see this register display:

> **Press:** [Alt]-[R]-[F]

The five financial registers look like figure 16.11.

```
┌──────────────────────────────────────────────┐
│ ┌────────────────────────────────────────┐   │
│ │ REGISTER                               │   │
│ │    n                           0.00    │   │
│ │    i                           0.00    │   │
│ │   PV                           0.00    │   │
│ │  PMT                           0.00    │   │
│ │   FV                           0.00    │   │
│ │                                        │   │
│ │                                        │   │
│ └────────────────────────────────────────┘   │
└──────────────────────────────────────────────┘
```

*Figure 16.11. The five financial registers*

These five registers have specific properties:

**n**    The number of payments covered by a financial transaction. You enter the number of time periods in the display register using the [Q] key, which transfers the value to this register. When the program calculates the number of payments, it stores it here for future calculations.

**i**    The interest applying to a financial transaction. You enter the interest rate in the display register using the [W] key, which transfers the value to this register. When the program calculates the interest rate, it stores it here for future calculations.

**PV**    The present value of a financial transaction. You enter the present value in the display register using the [E] key, which transfers the value to this register. When the program calculates the present value, it stores it here for future calculations.

**PMT**    The payment amount for a single periodic payment. You enter the payment amount in the display register using the [R] key, which transfers the value to this register. When the program calculates the payment, it stores it here for future calculations.

**FV**    The future value of a financial transaction. You enter the future value in the display register using the [T] key, which stores the value to this register. When the program calculates the present value, it stores it here for future calculations.

You store numbers in these five registers to process them according to various financial calculations. For example, suppose you want to take out a one-year loan for $5,000 at 16.75% interest:

**Type:** 5000

**Press:** [E]

This inserts the present value. Type in the interest rate:

**Type:** 16.75

**Press:** [W]

Make sure you've entered these numbers correctly:

**Press:** [F6]

Your financial registers should now look like figure 16.12.

```
REGISTER
   n                    0.00
   i                   16.75
  PV             5,000.00
 PMT                   0.00
  FV                   0.00
```

*Figure 16.12. An updated financial register display*

To recall any of these stored financial values to the display register, you need to use the STO key, [N]. For example, to recall the interest rate in the previous example:

**Press:** [N]-[W]

The value in the i register will appear in the display register.

To perform a financial calculation, you must place sufficient values into the financial registers and then calculate them. For example, suppose you want to calculate the payment amount for a loan when you know the present value, interest (18%), payment periods (5 years or 60 months), and present value ($5,000).

First, clear all registers:

**Press:** [B]

Now enter the four values you know:

**Press:** [F8]-[8]

This makes sure payments are at month's end.

**Type:** 60

**Press:** [Q]

**Type:** 18

**Press:** [F8]-[W]

**Type:** 5000

**Press:** [T]

**Press:** [R]

The answer is -$126.97, a periodic payment of $126.97. To view the Financial registers, shown in figure 16.13:

**Press:** [F5]

```
n                 60.00
i                  1.50
PV             5,000.00
PMT             -126.97
FV                 0.00
```

*Figure 16.13. The Financial registers*

## The Data Registers

The data registers store up to 20 different figures. The [N] key (called STO) stores numbers in the data registers; the [M] key (called RCL) recalls the stored numbers.

To see the registers:

**Press:** [F6]

The data registers will look like figure 16.14.

```
REGISTER                    REGISTER
R0              0.00        R.0          45450.00
R1           1235.50        R.1            700.00
R2              0.00        R.2              0.00
R3              0.00        R.3              0.00
R4             11.08        R.4               .10
R5              0.00        R.5              0.00
R6              0.00        R.6              0.00
R7              0.00        R.7              0.00
R8              0.00        R.8              0.00
R9              0.00        R.9              0.00
```

*Figure 16.14. The Data registers*

I've inserted some values as examples. The first column of ten data registers are marked R0 through R9, and the second column is marked R.0 to R.9. To insert and recall numbers from these 20 registers, you only need to refer to the number 0, 1, ..., 9 or .0, .1, ..., .9.

To enter a value into any one of these registers, type the value, press [N] (the STO key), and then the number of the register you want to insert the value into. To recall a stored number, press [M] (the RCL key) and then the number of the register containing the number you want to recall.

For example, to insert 16 in R0:

**Type:** 16

**Press:** [N]

**Type:** 0

To view the results so far:

**Press:** [F6]

To store 100 in R1, first close the register display:

**Press:** [Esc]

**Type:** 100

**Press:** [N]

**Type:** 1

Now, to recall the number in the R0 register:

**Press:** [M]-[0]

The number 16 should appear in the display register. To calculate the square root of this number:

**Press:** [F8]-[A]

You can continue to store and recall numbers in the 20 registers this way, and then perform calculations upon the numbers using the various keys.

## THE PROGRAMMER'S CALCULATOR

The Programmer's calculator can perform all sorts of complicated programming calculations. It's been modeled after the HP-16C, but in the PC Tools version you cannot use any of the programming capabilities provided in the HP-16C.

To open the Programmer's Calculator screen (shown in figure 16.15) from the Calculators menu:

**Press:** [P]

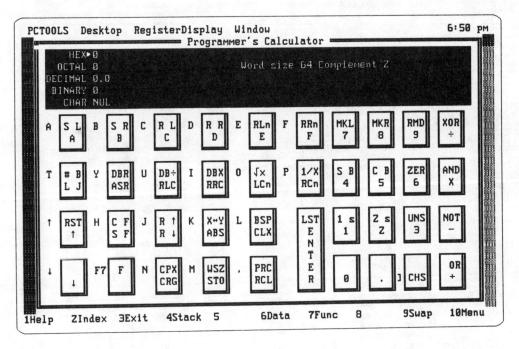

*Figure 16.15. The Programmers calculator screen*

The RegisterDisplay menu is identical to its counterpart in the Scientific calculator, however, the bottom-line function key bar differs, showing only three assignments:

**ESC=CANCEL**          Cancels current calculation.

**F4 STACK REGISTERS**          Displays the stack registers.

**F6 DATA REGISTERS**          Displays the data registers.

The five standard function keys for all four calculators continue to work: [F1]-Help, [F2]-Index, [F3]-Quit, [F9]-Swap, and [F10]-Menu. You can find all key assignments in table 16.3.

Table 16.3. Key commands in the Programmers calculator

| Key | Performs | [F7] |
|---|---|---|
| A | insert A in hex register | shift left (SL) |
| B | insert B in hex register | shift right (SR) |
| C | insert C in hex register | rotate left (RL) |
| D | insert D in hex register | rotate right (RR) |
| E | insert E in hex register | rotate left # (RLn) |
| F | insert F in hex register | rotate right # (RRn) |
| T | left justify (LJ) | number of bits (# B) |
| Y | arithmetic shift right (ASR) | double remainder (DBR) |
| U | rotate left carry through (RLC) | double divide (DBR) |
| I | rotate right carry through (RRC) | double multiply (DBX) |
| O | rotate left through carry # number of bits (LCn) | square root (sym[214]x) |
| P | rotate right through carry # number of bits (RCn) | reciprocal (1/X) |
| ⇑ | up one register | restore start up date (RST) |
| H | set flag (SF) | clear flag (CF) |
| J | roll down (R⇓) | roll up (R⇑) |
| K | absolute value (ABS) | exchange X and Y registers (X↔Y) |
| L | clear X (CLX) | backspace (BSP) |
| ⇓ | down one register | |
| F7 | activate F key (F7) | |
| N | clear register (CRG) | clear prefix (CPX) |
| M | store number (STO) | word size (WSZ) |
| . | recall number (RCL) | precision (PRC) |
| [Enter] | | last X register (LST) |
| 0 | insert 0 all registers | |
| 1 | insert 1 all registers | 1's complement mode (1s) |
| 2 | insert 2 all registers | 2's complement mode (2s) |
| 3 | insert 3 all registers | 3's complement mode (3s) |
| 4 | insert 4 all registers | set bit (SB) |
| 5 | insert 5 all registers | clear bit (CB) |
| 6 | insert 6 all registers | leading zeros (ZER) |
| 7 | insert 7 all registers | mask left (MKL) |
| 8 | insert 8 all registers | mask right (MKR) |
| 9 | insert 9 all registers | remainder after division (RMD) |
| . | insert decimal | |
| ] | change sign (CHS) | |
| → | division | logical or (OR) |
| • | multiplication (x) | logical and (AND) |
| − | subtraction | logical operation (NOT) |
| + | addition | logical sum (OR) |

Notice that only f functions are available in this calculator. Also, you can press [F7] and / (the slash key) for the exclusive OR (XOR).

## The Display Register

The display register in the Programmer's calculator is a bit more complicated than its equivalent in the other calculators. This is because there are several ways to view number values for programming purposes, as well as different ways you can display the results of various computations.

Eight features appear on the default display register of the Programmer's calculator:

**HEX**
The hexadecimal equivalent of a number. The hex system, as it's called for short, is a number system with base 16. This is the most popular system to use for programming because it requires the least number of digits to express a value. The first 10 digits are the same as the decimal system: 0, 1, 2, 3, ..., 9. The remaining six digits are A, B, C, D, E, and F. For example, decimal 16 is equal to hex F.

**OCTAL**
Base 8, this system is not used much any more.

**DECIMAL**
Base 10. The most commonly used notational system, it became popular because most humans have ten fingers.

**BINARY**
Base 2, there are only two digits in this system: 0 and 1. This is the most basic system, and reflects the most fundamental pairing in the solar system: positive and negative.

**CHAR**
The ASCII character equivalent, if any, to the number in question.

**Word size**
The size of a programming word or data bit, which can be from 1 to 64 bits long. 16 bits is the default.

**Complement**
One of three possible complements: 1, 2, or unsigned mode (which shows as U). Complement 2 is the default.

**System flag**
One of four possible flags: C for carry over (the default), Z for leading zero control, G for greater-than-range, and P for pending.

The first five items listed above are just different notational systems that express the same value. You can find an arrow after one of these five names. This shows which system is active or which system you can put a value into. You can move the arrow by pressing [⇑] or [⇓].

## Notational Conversion

The easiest thing you can do in the Programmer's calculator is convert number values between the four commonly used programming notational systems: hex, octal, decimal, and binary. You can see these names on the left side of the display register.

Because this is called the Programmer's calculator, and programmers use the hexadecimal system most often, this calculator is also called the hex calculator.

> If you aren't familiar with these notational systems, this isn't the calculator for you. You need a fundamental grounding in hex and binary notational systems to program correctly, and if you can't program there's little practical use in working with this calculator.
>
> You can, however, use this calculator to get a start on understanding the relationships among all notational systems. By placing a number in the decimal display, which is the notational system people use every day, you can see how its value changes in the other notational displays.

The best way to start out is to enter a decimal number you're familiar with and view its equivalent in the other notational systems.

**Highlight:** DECIMAL

This moves the red arrow next to the DECIMAL name. Now:

**Type:** 1

Your display should now look like this:

```
HEX   1
OCTAL   1 Word Size  16
Complement  2
DECIMAL  1
BINARY  1
CHAR   SOH
```

The first four fields all display the same value, since they all begin with 1. To continue the lesson:

**Press:** [0]

Now things begin to get interesting. Your display should look like this:

```
HEX   A
OCTAL   12                    Word size 16
Complement 2
DECIMAL   10
BINARY  1010
CHAR    LF
```

**438**

You can continue adding to the current decimal number to see how the others change. Or you can check entirely new numbers by clearing the display and entering a new number, using the decimal system or one of the other systems.

### Clearing the Display

You can clear all five notational fields in the display register three ways:

1.  Press [L]. This executes the CLX function, which also clears the five notational fields at the same time and prepares for a new entry in the current field.

2.  Press [⇑] or [⇓] to switch to another notational system and then press [0]. This clears all five notational fields at the same time and lets you enter a new number to convert.

3.  Press [F7]-[L]. This lets you remove digits one-by-one by executing the BSP function (backspace). This erases only the rightmost value in all five fields and is designed to let you remove your most recent entry, although you can repeat this command as often as necessary to clear all fields.

You should realize that numbers you're working with and converting are always being added to the stack register. Press [F4] to see the contents of the stack register and press [F6] to see the contents of the data registers. These registers don't automatically clear when you convert a new number or erase existing digits. To clear the display, stack, and data registers all at the same time:

**Press:** [F7]-[⇑]

This executes the restore function (RST) and removes everything.

### Displaying ASCII Characters

If you want to view specific ASCII characters assigned to keys on your keyboard:

**Highlight:** CHAR

**Type:** A

As long as you don't press [Shift] with this key, you should get decimal 97.0. Now try another key, such as b (lowercase B). Notice how the characters are arranged in sequence; that is, the letter *a* is decimal 97, *b* is decimal 98, and so on. The upper-case equivalents are in a different series.

There are 17 keys that don't bring up an ASCII character: [F1], [F2], [F3], [F4], [F5], [F9], [Alt], [Caps Lock], [Shift], [Ctrl], [PrintScrn], [Scroll Lock], [Num Lock], [Pause], the [5] key on the keypad, and the [⇑] and [⇓] keys. These last two highlight other notational names in the register.

Before moving on to the registers, you might want to double-check the results of the Programmer's calculator with another feature in the Desktop Manager, the ASCII table. To overlay the Programmer's calculator with the ASCII table:

**Press:** [Alt]-[D]-[U]-[A]

This should open the ASCII table from the Utilities menu. If you position the ASCII table window correctly, you can get your screen to look like figure 16.16.

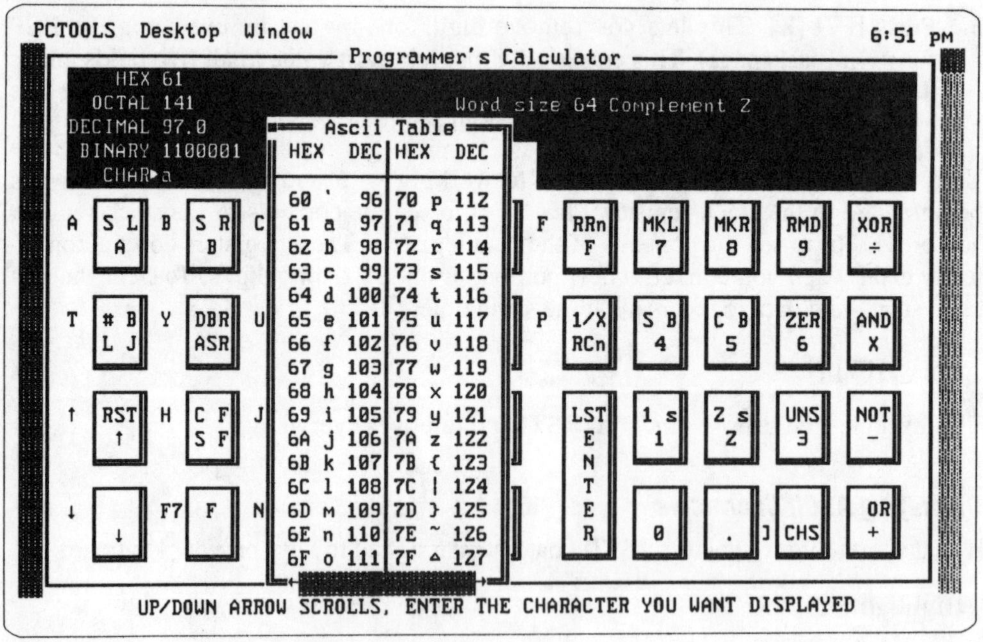

*Figure 16.16. The ASCII Table overlaying the Programmer's calculator*

If you read down the first column in the ASCII table window and come to character 0A (which is the hex number), you can read across the line and see the ASCII character that matches this value, the decimal value 10. You also see the control code assigned to this character, and the ASCII notation. Three of these values appear in the Programmer's Calculator display: the hex and decimal values and the ASCII notation.

### About Word Size

A *programming word* is a group of bits stored in a computer's memory. The size of the programming word you want to use can be crucial for many programming commands.

The size of the word you can use depends upon the capacity of your computer's memory. The phrases, 16-bit computer and 32-bit computer, are defining the maximum decimal word size the specific computer can handle. Word size can range from 1 to 64 decimal bits. The default word size is 16 decimal bits. The size of the current word setting also controls how many digits can appear in the display.

To change the size of the current word, enter the bit size of the number you want to use and press [F7]-[M]. This executes the WSZ, or word size, function. You should realize that the bit-size number you enter will be controlled by whatever notational system is highlighted. For example, to enter the 32-bit-size word:

**Highlight:** DEC

**Type:** 32

**Press:** [F7]-[M]

> The bit-size numbers—16, 32, and 64—are decimal numbers. If another notational system name is selected when you try to change the word bit size, you'll end up with a different decimal value. For example, if the HEX field is selected and you type 32 and then press [F7]-[M], you're going to get a word size of decimal 50 bits. The word size always shows up in a decimal value, although you can control the number using any of the four notational system fields. To get a decimal 32-bit word as a hex number, you must enter 20 in the HEX field.

You can set the maximum word size of 64 by just pressing [F7]-[M]. It doesn't matter which notational field is current.

You can return the word size to the default value of 16 by pressing [F7]-[⇑]. This executes the restore function marked RST on the left side of the keyboard.

Whenever you change the current word size, you will only change future values, not values already stored in the stack or data registers. If you want them switched to the new word size, you need to re-enter those values using the new current word size.

### About the Current Complement

Complements refer to methods for adding and subtracting binary number values and displaying the results. The 1s complement refers to binary addition, and 2s complement refers to binary subtraction. Unsigned complement refers to binary numbers without an additional digit designed to serve as a flag denoting positive or negative status (the sign). The 2s complement is the default setting.

To set 1s complement:

**Press:** [F7]-[1]

You'll see the number 1 appear after the *Complement* field. To set the unsigned complement:

**Press:** [F7]-[3]

To return the default:

**Press:** [F7]-[2]

### About the Four System Flags

There are four system flags, and each one denotes a special condition concerning the most recent calculation. These can be turned on automatically by some calculations or you can turn them on yourself for certain types of control.

Z    Denotes leading zero control. This determines how many zeros are displayed. This flag is off by default, which means that only zeros you enter as digits appear in display fields, as long as these zeros separate other digits higher than zero. (You can't enter a string of zeros if the Z flag is off.)

To toggle this flag on yourself:

**Press:** [F7]-[6]

This executes the zero function (ZER). You'll notice zeros appearing in three of the four notational fields (four in HEX, six in OCTAL, and 16 in BINARY - leading zeros are always suppressed in DECIMAL). You can toggle the flag off by repeating the above command or by setting and clearing flag 3, as described for the following flags.

C       Denotes carry-over. This flag appears whenever a math calculation results in a remainder that can't appear on screen, or when you've shifted or rotated bits beyond the limits of the field. When this flag appears, and you want to toggle it off:

> **Press:** [F7]-[H]-[4]

This executes the clear flag (CF) function for flag 4.

G       Denotes greater-than-the-range. This flag appears whenever the result of a calculation is too large to appear in the display register under conditions imposed by the current word size and complement setting. To clear this flag after it appears:

> **Press:** [F7]-[H]-[5]

This executes the clear flag (CF) function for flag 5.

P       Denotes pending. This flag appears when the calculator presumes it is waiting for more information from you; it is pending more data or commands. To clear this flag:

> **Press:** [F7]-[N]

This executes the clear prefix function (CPX).

Flags are designed to keep you informed of the current status of your current calculation. Whenever they appear, you should check the information you've just entered, as well as the status of current stack and data registers.

## Error Messages

The documentation says there's only one error message in the Programmer's calculator: Illegal digit for this number base.

This is the error you'll probably get most of the time, but you can also get several others, such as Improper mathematical operation and Improper flag number. These are invariably quite specific and self-explanatory.

## Using Registers and Floating Point Precision

You can use two sets of registers in the Programmer's calculator: stack and data. These are essentially the same types of registers as their counterparts in the Financial calculator. All current values in both the stack and data registers will be displayed according to the currently selected notational system.

### The Stack Registers

Five stack registers (X, Y, Z, T, and LSTX) store values which you can see when you press [F4]. These behave the same way as the stack registers in the Financial calculator:

- The selected number in the display register appears in the X register.
- Subsequent values move previous values up the stack to the Y, Z, and T registers in turn.
- When you make a calculation, the number in the X register moves to the LSTX register, should you want to save it.
- The X↔Y procedure switches values in the X and Y registers.
- The R⇓ rolls the value in a specified register down one register.
- The STO and RCL procedures store and recall numbers in specified registers.

There's one unique feature to the stack register in the Programmer's calculator: The R⇑ procedure rolls the value in a specified register up one register.

### The Data Registers

The data registers store values in ten registers, marked R0 through R9, which you can see when you press [F6]. These are identical to the function of the data registers R0-R9 and R.0-R.9 in the Financial calculator, except that you can also roll values up one register using R⇑.

### Floating Point Precision

The term floating point refers to a decimal point that moves (or floats around), depending upon the result of a calculation. For example, look at these two calculations:

4.0 x 4.5 = 18

4.5 x 4.5 = 20.25

The first is actually equal to 18.0, but you probably don't need the 0 after the decimal point. However, if you want to use numbers in the second calculation that all share the same format, you'll have to show them as 4.50 x 4.50 = 20.25.

The first example shows floating-point precision or how many decimal places you want to show turned on; the second shows it turned off. You can specify floating-point precision.

- Typing a period where you want it to appear in a number.
- Using the PRC procedures.

To use the PRC procedure, you type the number of digits after the decimal you want to use and then select the PRC procedure. For example, to set a floating point precision of five decimal places:

**Type:** 5

**Press:** [F7]-[,]

Notice how five zeros appear after the decimal point in the decimal field. Floating point applies to decimal numbers only. If another field is selected when you set floating point precision, the arrow will move to the decimal field.

Notice also how the word size increases to the maximum value of 64 bits. The Programmer's calculator can store up to 18 digits in the maximum word size of 64 bits.

To clear precision, just set the value to 0.

# THE SCIENTIFIC CALCULATOR

The Scientific calculator is designed to emulate parts of the HP-11C calculator.

To open the Scientific calculator, on the Calculators menu:

**Press:** [S]

When the calculator appears, your screen will look like figure 16.17.

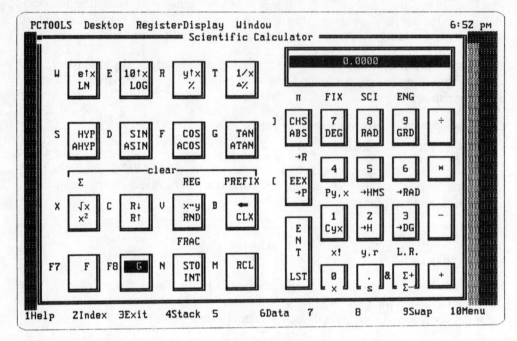

*Figure 16.17. The Scientific calculator screen*

This screen looks less complicated than the Financial calculator, but you might find it a bit harder to work with, if you're not familiar with scientific calculations. Many of us work with financial figures in one form or another every day, but there's not such a common need for scientific calculation.

The only pull-down menu unique to the Scientific calculator is the RegisterDisplay menu, which contains two choices: Stack Registers and Data Registers. The function-key assignments at the bottom of this screen are identical to those in the Financial calculator, except that [F5] for the Financial register is unavailable.

The key display and assigned functions are considerably different from the Financial calculator key display. Table 16.4 shows all the keys and what they do.

*Table 16.4. Key commands in the Scientific calculator*

| Key | Performs | [F7] |
|-----|----------|------|
| W | Raises e to the power of x | |
| E | Raises 10 to the displayed number | |
| R | Raises # in Y register to power of displayed # | |
| T | Computes reciprocal of displayed number | |
| S | Computes hyperbolic sine, cos, or tan in display | |
| D | Computes sine of displayed number | |
| F | Computes cosine of displayed number | |
| G | Computes the tangent of displayed number | |
| X | Computes square root of displayed number | |
| C | Rolls down the stack contents | |
| V | Exchanges contents in X and Y registers | Clears all registers |
| B | Deletes numbers from display | Cancels partial instructions |
| F7 | Activates f functions | |
| F8 | Activates g functions | |
| N | Stores 20 numbers in registers | Displays digits after the decimal |
| M | Recalls stored numbers | |
| ) | Changes sign or exponent of 10 in display | Places value of pi in display |
| ( | Prepares to display number in exponent of 10 | Polar magnitudes in X/Y to rectangular |
| ENT | Enters X register value into Y | |
| . | Inserts comma | Computes sample standard deviation |
| & | Collects statistics of X and Y from R0-R5 | Computes linear regression Σ+ |
| 0 | Inserts 0 | Computes factorial x |
| 1 | Inserts 1 | Computes possible combination sets |
| 2 | Inserts 2 | Converts hours, minutes, secs to decimal |
| 3 | Inserts 3 | Converts degrees to radians |
| 4 | Inserts 4 | |
| 5 | Inserts 5 | |
| 6 | Inserts 6 | |
| 7 | Inserts 7 | Fixes the number of displayed decimals |
| 8 | Inserts 8 | Displays scientific notation |
| 9 | Inserts 9 | Displays grads for trig functions |

| Key | Performs | [F8] |
|-----|----------|------|
| W | Raises e to the power of x | Computes the natural log (LN) |
| E | Raises 10 to the displayed number | Computers the common log of displayed number |
| R | Raises # in Y register to power of displayed # | Computes displayed value % of Y register |
| T | Computes reciprocal of displayed number | Computes % change of Y register value |
| S | Computes hyperbolic sine, cos, or tan in display | Computes the inverse since, cos, or tan of displayed number |
| D | Computes sine of displayed number | Computes the arc sine of displayed number |
| F | Computes cosine of displayed number | Computes the arc cosine of displayed number |
| G | Computes the tangent of displayed number | Computes the arc tangent of displayed number |
| X | Computes square root of displayed number | Computes the square of the displayed number |
| C | Rolls down the stack contents | Rolls up the stack contents |
| V | Exchanges contents in X and Y registers | Rounds the mantissa of 10 digit # in X to match Y |
| B | Deletes numbers from display | Clears contents of X register to zero |
| F7 | Activates f functions | |
| F8 | Activates g functions | |
| N | Stores 20 numbers in registers | Displays digits before decimal point |
| M | Recalls stored numbers | |
| ) | Changes sign or exponent of 10 in display | Returns absolute value of displayed number |
| ( | Prepares to display number in exponent of 10 | Converts rectangular magnitudes in X/Y to polar |
| ENT | Enters X register value into Y | Recalls displayed value before previous function |
| . | Inserts comma | Computes linear/correlation coefficient |
| & | Collects statistics of X and Y from R0-R5 | Subtracts statistics of X and Y from R0-R5 |
| 0 | Inserts 0 | Computes mean average of X and Y using Σ+ |
| 1 | Inserts 1 | Computes possible permutations |
| 2 | Inserts 2 | Converts decimal hrs, min, and sec to standard |
| 3 | Inserts 3 | Converts radians to degrees |
| 4 | Inserts 4 | |
| 5 | Inserts 5 | |
| 6 | Inserts 6 | |
| 7 | Inserts 7 | Changes display to trig functions |
| 8 | Inserts 8 | Displays radians for trig functions |
| 9 | Inserts 9 | Displays engineering notation |

All of the commands assigned to these keys operate as they do in the other calculators, except that you must follow the *reverse Polish* notation method, and not the *infix* method used by the other calculators.

## About Reverse Polish Notation

You can work with various types of calculation systems in the Scientific calculator, such as reverse Polish notation, engineering, and scientific. The default mode is reverse Polish notation. This means that you enter all the numbers for the calculation first, then enter the operators to perform the calculation.

> Reverse Polish notation was devised by Jan Lukasiewicz half a century ago to reorganize numerical calculations so they could be processed by machines. Mr. Lukasiewicz came from Poland, which is where the Polish part of the system's name comes from.

There are various notational systems you can use when making calculations. For the previous three calculators, you've used a method called *infix* notation. This is where you enter numbers and operators in what appears to the human mind to be a logical sequence. For example, in the Algebraic calculator you multiplied 3 x 3 to get 9. Your actual steps were:

**Type:** 3

**Press:** [*]

**Type:** 3

**Press:** [=]

You interspersed numbers with operators, which were processed in a logical order. In reverse Polish notation, you would enter the first 3, then the second 3, and then perform multiplication on the two numbers.

## Scientific Registers

The Scientific calculator provides you with the same five stack registers and 20 data registers as the Financial calculator.

There are an additional six statistical registers, which you can't view, but the calculator uses them for statistical calculations:

**R0**     Number of data points collected

**R1**     $\Sigma x$, the sum of the $x$ values

**R2**     $\Sigma x^2$, the sum of the squares of the $x$ values

**R3**     $\Sigma y$, the sum of the $y$ values

**R4**     $\Sigma y^2$, the sum of the squares of the $y$ values

**R5**     $\Sigma xy$, the sum of the products of the $x$ and $y$ values

You should make sure these registers are clear between each calculation. To clear the statistical registers:

  **Press:** [F7]-[&]

You get the [&] by pressing [Shift]-[7].

## Error Messages

You can run across three error message in the Scientific calculator:

- **ERROR 0** means an impossible calculation.
- **ERROR 1** means no more room in storage registers.
- **ERROR 2** means an incorrect sequence of statistical calculations.

## LOADING A CALCULATOR AUTOMATICALLY

Using program switches, you can load the Desktop Manager and to directly display an often-used specific calculator.

For example, if you're a programmer and you want to use the Programmer's calculator when you load the Desktop Manager:

  **Type:** DESKTOP/CP

If you wanted the Desktop to go resident:

  **Type:** DESKTOP/R/CP

To load the Algebraic calculator, use the /CA switch; the Financial calculator, the /CF switch; and the Scientific calculator, the /CS switch.

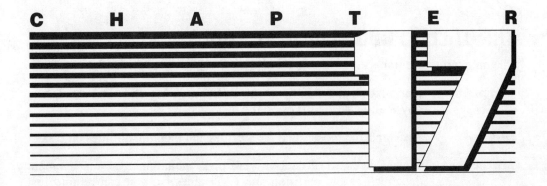

# UTILITY PROGRAMS

I n addition to the PC Shell and the Desktop Manager, there are nine other programs in the PC Tools Deluxe package. These are called *utility* programs because they radically enhance the quality of your work and the security of your files.

## THE UTILITY PROGRAMS IN PC TOOLS

The nine utility programs are:

**Compress**     Optimizes your disk space by unfragmenting and rearranging the physical location of files on the disk.

**Diskfix**      Analyzes, diagnoses, and fixes errors and incompatibilities on disks.

**Mirror**       Creates a record of data on your disk, including DOS management data such as the partition and FAT tables, so you can rebuild lost data and data on damaged disks.

**PC Backup**    Backs up files on a disk, in whole or in part, using a DOS-compatible backup procedure or an alternative high-speed DMA procedure.

**PC Cache**     Creates a memory cache on disk that stores and provides information on files you use most frequently.

**PC Format**    Formats a variety of disks using a nondestructive format that allows you to recover data from formatted disks more easily.

**PC Secure**    Encrypts file data so that only you can access the information.

**Rebuild**      Uses information created and stored by the Mirror program to resurrect data on a damaged disk. If the Mirror information is unavailable, Rebuild tries to resurrect the data as best it can.

**Undelete**     Undeletes accidentally deleted files in a variety of ways.

This chapter describes how you use the first seven of these eight utility files. The Undelete utility program was described in chapter 3.

## COMPRESS

The Compress program optimizes your disk space use. It runs from a file called COMPRESS.EXE. Despite its name, this program does not compress your files; Compress rearranges file segments on the specified disk so they appear in a more logical order for your computer to process.

When you run the Compress program, it does the following:

1. Analyzes the specified disk.

2. Unfragments files.

3. Looks for unmarked errors on the disk and moves file data off these areas.

4. Places your directories at the beginning of a disk.

5. Sorts all directory contents.

The most important procedure is unfragmenting your disk-file data. File fragmentation occurs when you create and save files to disk, and then modify the files several times and add more new files. The first time you create and save a file on an empty disk, it is saved in a continuous block. Your computer continues to save other files as long as contiguous blocks of space are available. When it can't save a file's data in one block, your computer squeezes what data it can into a number of available spaces.

As you continue to add new files, erase old files and modify existing files, fragmentation gets worse and worse. The more a file is fragmented, the longer it takes your disk head to find the data and read it into your computer's memory.

The Compress program solves this program by plowing through the data on a disk cluster by cluster, lifting all the data sections from a single file off the disk and re-recording them in a continuous block. This not only speeds up your disk-head access time, it reduces that chances the you'll encounter lost chains, which happens when DOS loses track of which disk clusters have been erased and which ones contain good data.

You can run Compress from your DOS prompt or from the PC Shell Applications menu, as long as you entered the shell from the DOS prompt.

## Switches with Compress

You can load Compress with the following switches:

**/350**   Loads the program so it can be displayed in VGA mode, with 350 horizontal lines.

**/BW**   Loads the Compress program in back-and-white video mode. This is supposed to give you a better screen display, if you're using a color card with a monochrome screen.

/CC     Runs a full compression and clears all unused sectors. Stands for Compress and Clear.

/CF     Runs a full compress only. Stands for Compression Full.

/CU     Unfragments your hard disk with a minimum of compression. Stands for Compression Unfragment.

*drive*:     The drive letter where you want the Compress program to do its work.

/NM     Prevents the Mirror program from running once Compress has stopped. Mirror will run by default. It's recommended that you run Mirror once you've compressed a disk, so you can update your recovery file. Stands for No Mirror.

/OD     Arranges all files, including subdirectories, in normal DOS order. Stands for Order DOS.

/OO     Arranges files, placing subdirectories first.

/OP     Arranges files so program files (those that end with .COM or .EXE) come first.

/OS     Arranges files using the standard or existing order.

/SA     Sorts file names in ascending order.

/SD     Sorts file names in descending order.

/SE     Sorts file names by extension characters.

/SF     Sorts file names by file name.

/SS     Sorts file names by file size.

/ST     Sorts file names by file time of creation or last save.

These commands fall into several groups marked by the first letter of the switch. The /C group runs various compress options. The /O group controls file order. And the /S group controls sort order.

You can use several of these commands at the same time, as long as you don't use more than one command from each group.

## Loading Compress

To launch Compress from your DOS command line:

**Type:** COMPRESS

**Press:** [C]

When the Compress screen appears, it looks like figure 17.1.

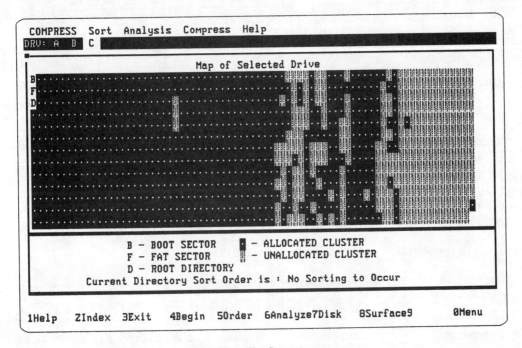

*Figure 17.1. The Compress screen*

The current disk will be highlighted on the left side of the second line from the top, in this case disk DRV C. The most prominent feature on this screen is the cluster map of file data on the selected disk (the map you view will be different from the map shown in figure 17.1).

Five features that appear on the map are listed just below the map:

**Boot Sector**          Contains two DOS files your computer needs to boot or start up.

**FAT Sector**           Contains two copies of the file-allocation table or an assignment of the file sections assigned to each cluster.

**Root Directory**       Contains the information for your root directory. This is the first or topmost directory that you see when you first boot up your computer.

**Allocated Cluster**    A cluster that's been allocated to a valid file, or a file that hasn't been deleted.

**Unallocated Cluster**  A cluster that's not been allocated to a valid file. An unallocated cluster may contain data for an erased file or a file lost by DOS.

The allocated cluster at the very end of the disk, in the lower-right corner of the map, is used by MIRORSAV.FIL. This file is created by the Mirror program and saves information about your boot directory, FAT, and boot record. The Mirror program puts it here because most disk damage occurs at the front end of the disk, especially during an accidental DOS format that is aborted. By placing the file at the end of the disk, the information necessary to rebuild the disk is stored in the least risky position.

You can use four pull-down menus in this screen:

**Sort**        Selects several different ways to sort the files on disk.

**Analysis**    Analyzes the disk three ways.

**Compress**    Compresses the files on the disk according to a variety of settings and issues a report on the compress, if you want one.

**Help**        Opens the help index for Compress.

The Compress pull-down menu map is shown in figure 17.2.

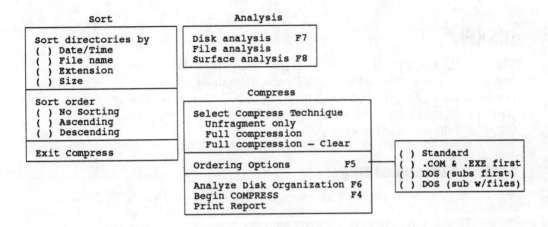

*Figure 17.2. The pull-down menus in Compress*

## The Compress Function Keys

You can use nine function keys in the Compress program:

**[F1] Help**     Opens help for Compress.

**[F2] Index**     Opens the help index for Compress.

**[F3] Exit**     Closes the Compress screen and returns you to the DOS prompt.

**[F4] Begin**     Begins the Compress program according to existing settings in the Sort and Compress pull-down menus. Same as pressing [Alt]-[C]-[B].

**[F5] Order**     Sets the sort option for organizing files on the disk when you run the Compress program. Same as pressing [Alt]-[C]-[O].

**[F6] Analyze**     Performs an analysis of the file organization of the current disk. Same as pressing [Alt]-[C]-[A].

**[F7] Disk**     Performs a full analysis of the current disk. Same as pressing [Alt]-[A]-[D].

**[F8] Surface**     Performs a surface analysis of the current disk. Same as pressing [Alt]-[A]-[S].

**[F10] Menu**     Activates the top menu bar.

Once you've set the sort order and method of analysis, you can start the compression program. Once the program has finished, you should reboot your computer.

# DISKFIX

The Diskfix program is designed to fix common problems you may encounter because of errors recorded to crucial parts of your operating disk. Some of these problems aren't always apparent when they occur, so you can also run the Diskfix program to protect against insidious errors that can grow over time. The program is fully menu-driven and very easy to use.

## Switches When Loading

You can use the following three switches. Only /BW has an effect on performance.

**/?**     Displays switches you can use. Same as /H.

**/H**     Displays switches you can use.

**/BW**   Displays black-and-white attributes on a color monitor.

## Loading the Program

To run Diskfix from the DOS command line:

>   **Type:** DISKFIX

>   **Press:** [Enter]

The program checks the current drive access and then analyzes your partition table. If it finds an error, the program displays a screen telling you this and gives you the option of running REPAIR or proceeding to other work.

If you want to correct the problem in your partition table, you should select REPAIR, insert your DOS system disk in floppy drive A, and reboot your computer:

>   **Press:** [Ctrl]-[Alt]-[Del]

When your A> prompt appears:

>   **Type:** SYS C:

If you have a problem in your partition table or have corrected a partition table problem, Diskfix asks whether you want to repair a disk. If you answer yes, you're given a list of the installed disks on your computer, which looks like figure 17.3.

```
            Select Drive To Analyze
   ┌──────────────────────────────────────────┐
   │   A:       1.2M      Floppy               │
   │   B:       360k      Floppy               │
   │   C:        31M      1st Hard Disk        │
   ├──────────────────────────────────────────┤
   │ Press ENTER or click mouse to continue.   │
   └──────────────────────────────────────────┘
```

*Figure 17.3. The Select Drive To Analyze box*

For this example, highlight C: and press [Enter]. This opens the status analysis screen, which looks like figure 17.4.

```
            Status of Drive C: Analysis
   ┌──────────────────────────────────────────────┐
   │     Areas tested:              Result:        │
   ├──────────────────────────────────────────────┤
   │     DOS Boot Sector            Ok             │
   │     Media Descriptors          Ok             │
   │     File Allocation Tables     Ok             │
   │     Directory Structure        Ok             │
   │     Cross Linked Files         Ok             │
   │     Lost Clusters              ERROR          │
   │     Media Surface                             │
   ├──────────────────────────────────────────────┤
   │ Do you want to check media surface for defects?│
   │          ┌──────┐     ┌──────┐                │
   │          │  NO  │     │ YES  │                │
   │          └──────┘     └──────┘                │
   └──────────────────────────────────────────────┘
```

*Figure 17.4. The Status of Drive C: Analysis box*

The program runs through each of the first six items on the list and checks it with OK or ERROR, depending upon what the program finds. The last item on the list, Media Surface, is an optional test. The ERROR box, shown in in figure 17.5, indicates that there are Lost Clusters in Drive C:

```
================ ERROR ================
113 lost clusters found in 1 chains.

SYMPTOMS:  chkdsk will report lost cluster chains.
You may notice some files are missing.

NOTE:  Space on your disk has been allocated at some
time, but there is no longer any directory information
indicating what file the space belongs to.

Do you want to correct this problem now?
      ┌─────────┐      ┌─────────┐
      │   YES   │      │   NO    │
      └─────────┘      └─────────┘
```

*Figure 17.5. The ERROR box*

When *Yes* is selected, Diskfix gathers together all the lost chains in the single file and assigns them to a file called PCT00000.FIX. If lost chains were found for several files, the resurrected files would be called PCT00000.FIX, PCT00001.FIX, PCT00002.FIX, and so on.

After checking for routine errors, Diskfix asks whether you want to search for lost directories.

The last item for analysis, Media Surface, is optional. Diskfix asks whether you want to check the disk surface for defects. If you select this option, the program checks your DOS file system and then displays a full-screen map of the selected disk. Diskfix will progress over the surface of the disk, checking for errors. If you want to escape from the Media Surface scan, press [Esc] and then [A] for CANCEL.

Once you've checked a disk, you're given the Diskfix Options menu, which looks like figure 17.6.

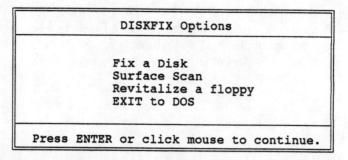

```
        DISKFIX Options

        Fix a Disk
        Surface Scan
        Revitalize a floppy
        EXIT to DOS

Press ENTER or click mouse to continue.
```

*Figure 17.6. The DISKFIX Options box*

These four commands do the following:

**Fix a Disk**            Starts analysis of the selected disk for the six options.

**Surface Scan**          Scans the surface of the selected disk for defects.

**Revitalizes a floppy**  Scans the surfaces of the selected floppy disk and tries to revive the disk from errors.

**EXIT to DOS**           Quits the Diskfix program and returns you to your previous work.

The Diskfix program is very easy to use. Run it periodically as a preventive measure, even when you haven't encountered an obvious problem.

# PC BACKUP

There are two parts to the PC Backup program. The first backs up the data on your hard disk to another storage device, such as a floppy disk or tape. The second part restores this data from the backup media to the original disk. You can backup and restore all or part of your files.

The PC Backup program uses a unique format that squeezes more data onto the backup storage device than usual. This saves you time and trouble when you backup an entire hard disk to a series of floppy disks.

When you run PC Backup, you can use a DOS-compatible backup procedure or an alternative high-speed DMA procedure.

## Switches When Loading

When you load the program, you can use the following 10 switches to change the way it appears or behaves:

/?      Displays a help screen.

/BW     Loads the Backup program in back-and-white video mode. This is supposed to give you a better screen display, if you're using a color card with a monochrome screen.

/DOB    Stands for Deluxe Options Board. This switch turns on automatic detection for this board on. PC Tools Deluxe supports the use of this board, which can dramatically reduce the amount of time it takes to format disks and write information to them.

*drive*:            The drive letter that will write the backup files.

**/filename**       Declares the backup sets of files using the extension .SET.

**/LCD**            Displays the program for the LCD screen usually found in laptop computers.

**/LE**             Switches command assignments between the left and right buttons on your mouse.

**/NO**             Stands for No Overlap. This switch overrides simultaneous DMA (direct memory access) to both floppy and hard disks. On older computers, or computers that are not truly compatible, the Backup program might not perform the way it's supposed to. If you experience problems running Backup, you might want to reload the program using the /NO switch.

**/PS2**            Reconfigures the program on IBM PS/2 computers that fail to control some older models of mouse-input devices.

**/R**              Stands for Restore. This loads the program and starts it out in restore mode. This relieves you of waiting while the program reads the disk directory structure and information about the current files. The first thing it asks you to do is insert the first disk of the series you want to restore.

## Loading the Program

To run PC Backup:

> **Type:** PCBACKUP

> **Press:** [Enter]

If you haven't configured the program for your computer, you'll be walked through two configuration screens. The first is shown in figure 17.7.

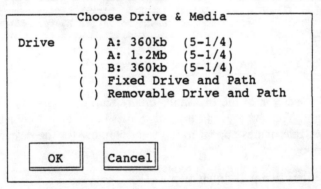

```
┌────Define Equipment────────────────┐
│ Drive A:  ( ) 360kb drive          │
│           ( ) 1.2 meg drive        │
│           ( ) 720kb drive          │
│           ( ) 1.44 meg drive       │
│                                    │
│ Drive B:  ( ) 360kb drive          │
│           ( ) 1.2 meg drive        │
│           ( ) 720kb drive          │
│           ( ) 1.44 meg drive       │
│           ( ) None                 │
│                                    │
│   ┌──────┐   ┌────────┐            │
│   │  OK  │   │ Cancel │            │
│   └──────┘   └────────┘            │
└────────────────────────────────────┘
```

*Figure 17.7. The Define Equipment box*

You should declare the various floppy disk drives you use in this window.

The second screen is shown in figure 17.8.

```
┌────Choose Drive & Media────────────────┐
│ Drive   ( ) A: 360kb  (5-1/4)          │
│         ( ) A: 1.2Mb  (5-1/4)          │
│         ( ) B: 360kb  (5-1/4)          │
│         ( ) Fixed Drive and Path       │
│         ( ) Removable Drive and Path   │
│                                        │
│   ┌──────┐   ┌────────┐                │
│   │  OK  │   │ Cancel │                │
│   └──────┘   └────────┘                │
└────────────────────────────────────────┘
```

*Figure 17.8. The Choose Drive & Media box*

Once you've configured your version of PC Backup, you'll be shown the PC Backup screen, which looks like figure 17.9.

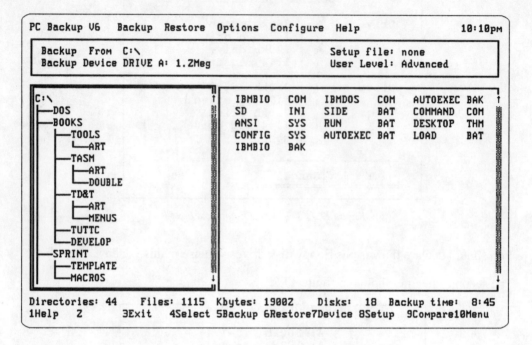

```
 PC Backup V6    Backup  Restore  Options  Configure  Help           10:10PM
 ┌──────────────────────────────────────────────────────────────────────────┐
 │ Backup   From  C:\                        Setup file: none                 │
 │ Backup Device DRIVE A: 1.2Meg             User Level: Advanced             │
 └──────────────────────────────────────────────────────────────────────────┘
 ┌───────────────────────────────┬──────────────────────────────────────────┐
 │C:\                           ↑ │ IBMBIO   COM   IBMDOS   COM   AUTOEXEC BAK↑│
 │ ├─DOS                          │ SD       INI   SIDE     BAT   COMMAND   COM│
 │ ├─BOOKS                        │ ANSI     SYS   RUN      BAT   DESKTOP   THM│
 │ │  ├─TOOLS                     │ CONFIG   SYS   AUTOEXEC BAT   LOAD      BAT│
 │ │  │  └─ART                    │ IBMBIO   BAK                               │
 │ │  ├─TASM                      │                                           │
 │ │  │  ├─ART                    │                                           │
 │ │  │  └─DOUBLE                 │                                           │
 │ │  ├─TD&T                      │                                           │
 │ │  │  ├─ART                    │                                           │
 │ │  │  └─MENUS                  │                                           │
 │ │  ├─TUTTC                     │                                           │
 │ │  └─DEVELOP                   │                                           │
 │ ├─SPRINT                       │                                           │
 │ │  ├─TEMPLATE                  │                                           │
 │ │  └─MACROS                  ↓ │                                          ↓│
 └───────────────────────────────┴──────────────────────────────────────────┘
 Directories: 44    Files: 1115  Kbytes: 19002    Disks:  18  Backup time:  8:45
 1Help    2        3Exit    4Select  5Backup 6Restore7Device 8Setup  9Compare10Menu
```

*Figure 17.9. The PC Backup screen*

This is a modified version of the PC Shell screen, with a tree list on the left and file names on the right. You can press [Tab] and [Shift]-[Tab] to switch activity between the two windows. File names appear in the right window for the directory highlighted in the left window.

The top menu bar has five pull-down menus:

**Backup**        Lets you start the backup procedure, choose the directories you want to back up, and exit the program.

**Restore**        Configures the restore program, starts the restore program, and compares disks.

**Options**        Loads a set-up file, saves a set-up file, and declares many other options that control the way you back up your files.

**Configure**      Allows you to select various options, such as the drive and media you want to use, other special equipment, the backup speed, current user level, and color selection of various features in the program.

**Help**      Opens the basic help screen.

The complete pull-down menu map is shown in figure 17.10.

```
        Backup                              Restore
┌─────────────────────────┐    ┌──────────────────────────┐
│ Start backup        F5  │    │ Start restore        F6  │
│ backup From entry       │    │ start Compare        F9  │
├─────────────────────────┤    │ restore To entry         │
│ cHoose directories  F4  │    ├──────────────────────────┤
├─────────────────────────┤    │ cHoose directories       │
│ Exit                F3  │    └──────────────────────────┘
└─────────────────────────┘
```

```
           Options                              Configure
┌──────────────────────────────────┐   ┌────────────────────────────────┐
│ Load setup           ALT-L        │   │ choose drive and Media      F7 │
│ Save setup           ALT-S        │   │ Define Equipment            F8 │
├──────────────────────────────────┤   ├────────────────────────────────┤
│ Backup Method        (Full)       │   │ Backup Speed     (High Speed)  │
│ Reporting            (None)       │   ├────────────────────────────────┤
│ Compress     (Minimize Time)      │   │ User Level                     │
│ Verify       (When Formatting)    │   │ Color selection                │
│ Format Always                     │   ├────────────────────────────────┤
│ Error Correction                  │   │ Save as default                │
│ Standard Format                   │   └────────────────────────────────┘
├──────────────────────────────────┤
│ Subdirectory inclusion            │
│ Include/exclude files             │
│ Attribute exclusions              │
│ Date range selection              │
├──────────────────────────────────┤
│ Save History                      │
│ Time display                      │
│ Overwrite warning                 │
└──────────────────────────────────┘
```

*Figure 17.10.  The pull-down menus in PC Backup*

The two lines below the top menu bar show the drive you're backing up, the drive your backing up to, the Setup file, and the user level.

The second to bottom line of your screen shows six pieces of information about the disk you want to back up: number of directories, total number of files, disk space occupied by these files, the estimated number of disks you'll need to backup all the files, and approximate time it will take to complete the backup operation.

## Function Keys

You can use nine function keys as shown at the bottom of the screen.

**[F1] Help**     Opens the context-sensitive help screen.

**[F3] Exit**     Closes the PC Backup screen and returns you to the DOS command line. Same as pressing [Alt]-[B]-[X].

**[F4] Select**     Opens the Choose Drive & Media window (shown in figure 17.8), which lets you declare what type of backup device you're using. Same as pressing [Alt]-[B]-[H].

**[F5] Backup**     Starts the backup procedure. You should select this after you've set the various backup options. Same as pressing [Alt]-[B]-[S].

**[F6] Restore**     Runs the restore program, which restores information from backed up disks or tape to the original disk. Same as pressing [Alt]-[R]-[S].

**[F7] Device**     Lets you choose the drive and media you want to back up to. Same as pressing [Alt]-[C]-[M].

**[F8] Setup**     Runs the setup program, which walks you through the two screens you used to configure your version of PC Backup. Same as pressing [Alt]-[C]-[C].

**[F9] Compare**     Starts the disk compare program, which compare backed up files on the backup disk to the files on the original disk. Same as pressing [Alt]-[R]-[C].

**[F10] Menu**     Activates the top menu bar. Same as pressing [Alt].

To back up files, you should set the various conditions you want to use to backup or restore your disk files, make sure your backup media is installed and ready, then begin the backup procedure by pressing [F5].

When you want to restore backed-up file information, make sure you declare the restore settings you want to use, install the backed up media in the proper device, then press [F6].

## Running a Backup

The PC Backup program begins at the top of your directory tree on the left and proceeds to back up each file in the right window. The progress of PC Backup through your disk will be noted at the bottom of your screen. The file being backed up will be highlighted. As one disk fills up, the program will prompt you to replace it with the next disk. *Be sure to number the disks so you can feed them into the restore program in the same order.* This is absolutely necessary, because the backup program will break a file over two disks; the second disk must follow the first or else the program file will be unfinished.

When backing up is complete, the program will write the directory structure to the last disk. When the program is finished, it will display a report screen that resembles figure 17.11.

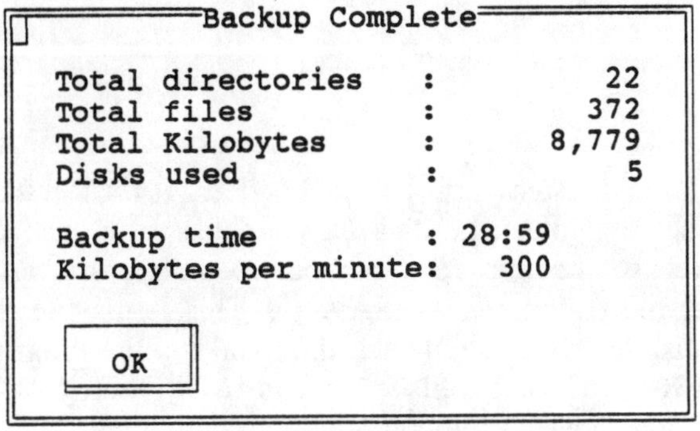

```
┌──────────Backup Complete──────────┐
│                                    │
│   Total directories  :        22   │
│   Total files        :       372   │
│   Total Kilobytes    :     8,779   │
│   Disks used         :         5   │
│                                    │
│   Backup time        : 28:59       │
│   Kilobytes per minute:   300      │
│                                    │
│   ┌──────────┐                     │
│   │   OK     │                     │
│   └──────────┘                     │
└────────────────────────────────────┘
```

*Figure 17.11. The Backup Complete box*

## Using Setup Files

I usually use PC Backup to backup my entire hard disk using the default settings, but I often restore only a single file or a group of files, such as when I restore only those files that have been changed since the last time I backed up the files. To do this, you must create and save special setup files.

To create setup files, declare the options you want to save for special backing up situations using the various menus in the PC Backup program; then press [Alt]-[S] (or [Alt]-[O]-[S]). This opens a screen that lets you type the name you want to give the setup file.

When you want to use the specific setup file, press [Alt]-[L] (or [Alt]-[O]-[L]), type the name of the file, and press [Enter].

## Picking a User Level

Once you've taken a look at the PC Backup program, you may prefer to configure it for your level of skill or confidence. As with the PC Shell, you can use a Beginner, Intermediate, or Advanced user level. Advanced is the default.

To select a user level:

**Press:** [Alt]-[C]-[U]

This opens the Select User Level menu, which lets you pick one of three levels. Press [Tab] to highlight the level you want to use, then press [Enter].

# MIRROR

The Mirror program is the first part of what's called Mirror/Rebuild. These two programs work together to protect the data on your disk from accidental erasure. The Mirror program keeps a backup copy of your root directory, FAT table, and boot record in a special file called MIRORSAV.FIL. This is the file that's stored at the very end of your disk and is updated each time you run the program. When you run PCSETUP, the Mirror command is placed in your AUTOEXEC.BAT file, so the special Mirror file is updated each time you boot your computer.

The Mirror program also creates the PCTRACKR.DEL file that keeps track of file information you've deleted.

## Switches for Loading

The switches you can use when loading Mirror are:

| | |
|---|---|
| /? | Displays a help screen. |
| /1 | Stands for one FAT. This switch saves only the latest directory and FAT information and does not include the backed-up FAT. |
| *drive*: | Specifies the drive that contains the information you want to save. |
| **/PARTN filename** | Creates a copy of your partition file in a text file whose filename you specify and saves it to a disk in drive A, unless you specify another drive after the switch. |

**/TDrive-###**          Stands for delete Tracking option. This switch enables the
delete tracking program. You specify which drive you want
to track and the maximum number **###** of entries you want
to insert in that file (up to a maximum of 999). You can find
more information about the feature later in this section.

There's no screen for the Mirror program. You only run it to update information in
MIRORSAV.FIL and PCTRACKR.DEL.

## Running the Program

To run the Mirror program:

**Type:** MIRROR

**Press:** [Enter]

When you run the program, you'll get the following screen message:

```
C:\>mirror

PC Tools Deluxe - MIRROR  R6
(C) Copyright 1987-1990  Central Point Software, Inc.
Unauthorized duplication prohibited.

Creates an image of the SYSTEM area.

Drive C being processed.

MIRROR successful.

C:\>
```

You can use the various switches to control the way the program behaves. For
instance, to save the partition table information:

**Type:** MIRROR/PARTN

**Press:** [Enter]

When you save partition table information, it will write to a floppy disk in drive A.
You can use two additional switches with the /PARTN switch:

**/L**  Displays the active drive's partition table information on screen.

**/P**  Prints a copy of the active partition table display through your LP1 port.

If you don't want to install the Delete Tracking option, which uses a small amount of your computer's memory:

**Type:** MIRROR /T

**Press:** [Enter]

# REBUILD

The Rebuild program is the second half of Mirror/Rebuild. You should run the Mirror program regularly, but you should only run the Rebuild program when you've accidentally formatted your hard disk or deleted too many files that you want to restore, and the Undelete program can't handle the load.

As with Mirror, the Rebuild program has no screen. It just goes to work when you run it and tries to rebuild lost disk data using the MIRORSAV.FIL and PCTRACKR.DEL files.

You shouldn't run Rebuild unless your hard disk has failed. When you do run Rebuild, you should first reboot your computer from a system disk in drive A. Rebuild can read the data it needs directly from the hard disk.

You can run rebuild in a testing mode with the /J switch.

To test run the program:

**Type:** REBUILD /J

**Press:** [Enter]

As soon as you do this, Rebuild will display the following message:

```
C:\>rebuild c: /j

PC Tools Deluxe - REBUILD  R6
(C) Copyright 1987-1990  Central Point Software, Inc.
Unauthorized duplication prohibited.

Restore the SYSTEM area of your hard drive with
the image file created by MIRROR.

    WARNING !!        WARNING !!
```

```
This should be used ONLY to recover from the inadvertent use
of the DOS 'Format' command or the DOS 'Recover' command.
Any other use of REBUILD may cause you to lose data!  Files modified
since the last use of MIRROR may be lost.  To recover lost or
corrupted files, directories, etc., use PC Tools DISKFIX instead.

Just checking this time.

The LAST time MIRROR was used was at 10:58 on 03-12-90.
The PRIOR time MIRROR was used was at 09:42 on 03-11-90.

If you wish to use the LAST file as indicated
above, press "L". If you wish to use the PRIOR
file as indicated above, press "P". Press ESCAPE
to terminate REBUILD.
```

If you want to stop the test:

**Press:** [Esc]

If you want to continue:

**Press:** [L]

Rebuild will start searching your hard drive for the last file and then display this message:

```
The MIRROR image file has been validated.


The SYSTEM area does NOT agree with the
image file.

C:\>
```

## Switches for Loading

The switches available in Rebuild are:

| | |
|---|---|
| /? | Displays a master help screen when you load the program. |
| *drive*: | Specifies the drive on which to run Rebuild. |
| /J | Compares two existing and different mirror files and lets you pick which one you want to use to rebuild your disk. |

| | |
|---|---|
| /L | Prints a list of every file and directory the program finds. Otherwise, only directory and fragmented file names will appear requiring that you answer queries about each one. You can use the DOS scroll/pause keys [Ctrl]-[S] to pause the scrolling of the list on your screen. You can use this switch with the /P switch for simultaneous screen and printer display. |
| /P | Stands for Printer. This directs all output to your printer so you can monitor the progress of the Rebuild program and saves you the extra steps of printing the disk file information. You can use this switch with the /L switch for simultaneous screen and printer displays. |
| /PARTN | Restores the partition table information you save to a floppy disk. You can specify the floppy disk drive letter after this switch, if the drive is not A. |
| /TEST | Performs a test run of the Rebuild program. |

# PC FORMAT

The PC Format program is intended to be used as a replacement for the DOS file FORMAT.COM.

When you install PC Tools Deluxe using the PCSETUP program, the DOS file FOR-MAT.COM will be renamed FORMAT!.COM. As long as you place the PC Tools directory PCTOOLS on your path, then the PC Format program file FORMAT.COM will be called when you type FORMAT and press [Enter].

## Floppy Disk Switches

You can use the following switches to customize the behavior of PC Format on a floppy disk:

| | |
|---|---|
| /? | Displays a help screen. |
| *drive*: | Specifies the drive to format. |
| /1 | Specifies a format on only one side of a disk. |
| /4 | Specifies a low format (either 360 kilobytes or 180 kilobytes, depending on the disk) in a high format drive (1.2 or 1.44 megabytes). |

| | |
|---|---|
| /8 | Formats a disk for 8 sectors per track, not the standard 9 (for 360-kilobyte diskettes) and 15 (for 1.2-megabyte diskettes). |
| /DESTROY | Formats the disk and then erases it completely. |
| /F | Specifies a full format. You must also use one of these additional switches: /4, /8, or /F###. |
| /F:# | Specifies the size of disk to format. The number you specify (#) can equal 160, 180, 320, 360, 720, 1200, and 1440. |
| /N:# | Specifies the number of sectors per track to format. If you use this switch, you must also use the /T switch. |
| /P | Prints the formatting information you see on your screen through the LP1 port. |
| /Q | Specifies a quick format, which erases the FAT information but not the disk surface data. |
| /R | Specifies the reformatting and rewriting of every track. |
| /S | Copies operating system files to the disk being formatted. |
| /T:# | Specifies the number of tracks to format. If you use the /N switch, you also need to use this switch. |
| /TEST | Simulates a format without actually running a real format, so you can see the results. |
| /V | Adds a volume to the disk being formatted. |

## Hard Disk Switches

You can use the following switches when formatting a hard disk using PC Format:

| | |
|---|---|
| *drive*: | Specifies the hard disk drive you want to format. |
| /P | Prints the formatting information you see on your screen through the LP1 port. |
| /Q | Specifies a quick format, which erases the FAT information but not the disk surface data. |
| /S | Copies the operating system files to the disk being formatted. |

/TEST          Simulates a format without actually running a real format, so you can see the results.

/V             Adds a volume to the disk being formatted.

Most of these switches behave the same way for the original DOS command FORMAT.

# PC SECURE

The PC Secure program is designed to encrypt data files, so only you can decrypt them.

Whenever you use the PC Secure program, you should pay close attention to the password you use. That's your only key to decrypting the files. If you forget the key, Central Point Software can't help you recover the files you've encrypted.

## Switches When Loading

You can use the following nine switches to change the appearance and behavior of the PC Secure program:

/?             Displays a master help screen when you load the program.

/350           Displays the program in VGA mode using 350 horizontal lines.

/BW            Displays the program in black-and-white mode for monochrome display monitors.

/C             Toggles compression off when encrypting.

/D             Decrypts the specified files.

/F             Uses full encryption on the specified files.

/G             Uses the U.S. government's Department of Defense (DOD) encryption standards. This switch is available only on those versions of PC Tools Deluxe that are sold in the United States.

/K*****        Specifies the characters ***** as your masterkey.

/P             Prompts you for a key.

## Loading the Program

PC Secure is a full-screen program with its own menu and command structure. To load the program:

**Type:** PCSECURE

**Press:** [Enter]

PC Secure lets you work with two types of keys: a master key and a password.

To enter PC Secure for the first time, you must create a master key. If you forget this password, you can decrypt you files with the master key; the master key works for all files encrypted with individual passwords. This is called *back door* use.

You can increase your security one more level by overriding the master key and using the expert mode. This requires that you use the individual password for decrypting a file.

For this master key, enter a password:

**Type:** BECKY

Asterisks will appear in place of the characters you type.

**Press:** [Enter]

You're asked to enter the master word a second time for confirmation.

**Type:** BECKY

**Press:** [Enter]

Now you'll enter the PC Secure screen, which looks like figure 17.12.

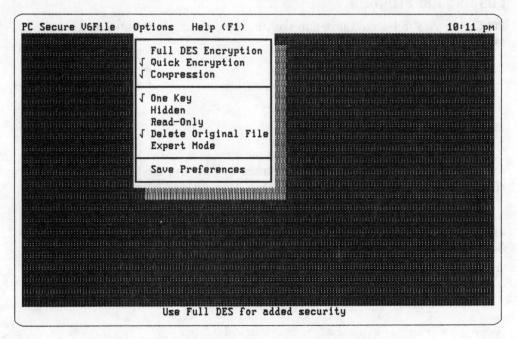

```
PC Secure V6File    Options    Help (F1)                    10:11 PM

                    Full DES Encryption
                  √ Quick Encryption
                  √ Compression

                  √ One Key
                    Hidden
                    Read-Only
                  √ Delete Original File
                    Expert Mode

                    Save Preferences



                Use Full DES for added security
```

*Figure 17.12.  The PC Secure screen with Options menu open*

You won't find much in this screen, except pull-down menus at the top and function-key assignments at the bottom. You can use the two pull-down menus at the top as follows:

**File**         Lets you start encrypting or decrypting files and displaying information about the most recent file you've worked with.

**Options**      Lets you declare various options for encryption or decryption.

The third menu, Help, opens the help index for the PC Secure program.

You can see the pull-down menus specific to PC Secure in figure 17.13.

```
        File                         Options
┌──────────────────────┐   ┌──────────────────────────────┐
│ Encrypt File    F4   │   │ Full DES Encryption          │
│ Decrypt File    F5   │   │ Quick Encryption             │
├──────────────────────┤   │ Compression                  │
│ About                │   ├──────────────────────────────┤
├──────────────────────┤   │ One Key                      │
│ eXit            F3   │   │ Hidden                       │
└──────────────────────┘   │ Read-Only                    │
                           │ Delete Original File         │
                           │ Expert Mode                  │
                           ├──────────────────────────────┤
                           │ Save Preferences             │
                           └──────────────────────────────┘
```

*Figure 17.13. The pull-down menus in PC Secure*

## Function Keys

You can use the five function keys at the bottom as follows:

**[F1] Help**     Opens context-sensitive help information.

**[F2] Index**    Opens the help index for the PC Secure program.

**[F3] Exit**     Closes the PC Secure screen and returns you to the DOS prompt.

**[F4] Encrypt**  Opens the File Selection window for encryption, which lets you select the file you want to encrypt.

**[F5] Decrypt**  Opens the File Selection window for decryption, which lets you select the file you want to decrypt.

## Encrypting a File

To begin encrypting a file:

    **Press:** [F4]

This opens the *File Selection* box for encryption, which looks like figure 17.14.

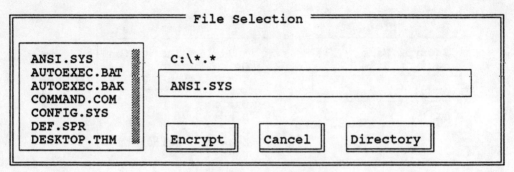

*Figure 17.14. The File Selection box*

The currently selected file name appears in the box below the current path. You can press [Tab] to highlight the various features in this window you want to use. You can either type in a path and file name to encrypt or you can select one from the file list on the left. Once the correct file name appears in the file name field, highlight Encrypt and press [Enter].

For this example, encrypt the file AUTOEXEC.BAT. Make sure that the file name appears in the file name field in the *File Selection* box:

**Press:** [Enter]

This opens the Key Input box, which lets you specify a series of characters for a key word assigned to the file you're about to encrypt. To decrypt the file, you need to specify this key word. For this example, use CAROL:

**Type:** CAROL

Asterisks will appear in place of the characters you type so REMEMBER this key word.

**Press:** [Enter]

You'll be asked to enter the key word a second time, for confirmation:

**Type:** CAROL

**Press:** [Enter]

You have to type the word a second time exactly as you typed it the first time. If they don't match, you start the series over again.

You can use alphanumeric keys or hexadecimal keys for your key words. If you want to use hexadecimal keys, press [F9].

This begins the encryption procedure. You can watch its progress in the Progress window, which looks like figure 17.15.

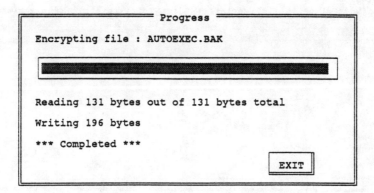

*Figure 17.15. The Progress box*

The results of encryption are quite interesting. Figure 17.16 shows what my file AUTOEXEC.BAK looked like in the PC Shell Text Viewer before encryption.

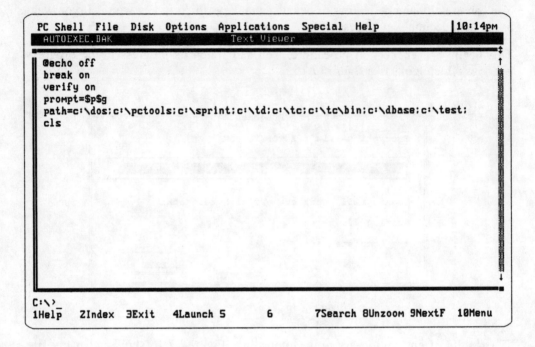

*Figure 17.16.  AUTOEXEC.BAK before encryption.*

Figure 17.17 shows what AUTOEXEC.BAK looks like after encryption.

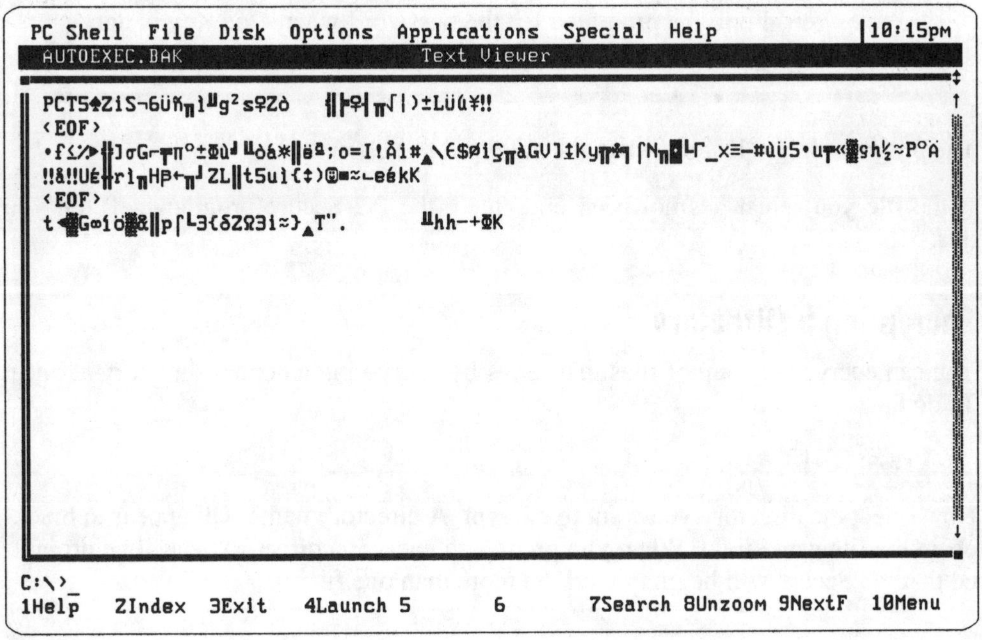

*Figure 17.17. AUTOEXEC.BAK after encryption*

## Decrypting a File

To decrypt the encrypted file AUTOEXEC.BAK:

**Press:** [F5]

This opens the same File Selection window, except the Decrypt command replaces the Encrypt command.

**Type:** AUTOEXEC.BAK

**Press:** [Enter]

**Type:** CAROL

**Press:** [Enter]

> If the command One Key is marked in the Options pull-down menu, you won't be prompted for the password when you try to decrypt a file. You'll only be prompted for the password when One Key is not marked. You can toggle the mark on and off yourself.

The progress box will show when the encryption is complete.

If the file you select has not been encrypted, the PC Secure program will tell you this.

## Encrypting a Directory

You can encrypt a group of files in a series by encrypting an entire directory at once. To do this:

**Press:** [F4]

Now select the directory you want to encrypt. A directory name will appear in brackets in the file name field. When you prepare to encrypt a directory, you'll be prompted that PC Secure will begin to work on more than one file.

## About Compression

You can also compress files while you encrypt them by turning compress on using the Options menu or the /C switch when loading PC Secure.

> The PC Secure program uses the block-adaptive Lempel-Ziv-Welch compression technique.

Some special files, such as dictionaries, will *expand* when compressed with PC Secure.

## Expert Mode

You can turn on the expert mode on the Options pull-down menu, which turns off the effect of a master key. When you do this and try to decrypt the files, you must enter the password assigned to each encrypted file .

# PC CACHE

PC Cache is a memory-resident program that speeds up your access to data on a hard disk. This bypasses your need for a RAM drive and keeps your most frequently used data current in your computer's memory. This program uses both a *read cache* and a *write cache* method.

You should install PC Cache after you've run Mirror, but before you install any other TSR programs. The command to install the program is automatically written into your AUTOEXEC.BAT file, when you run the PCSETUP program.

## Switches When Loading

You can use these switches with PC Cache:

| | |
|---|---|
| **/?** | Displays a help screen. |
| **/EXTSTART=####k** | Specifies the starting location for the cache buffer when you're using extended memory. The ####K value must be larger than 1024 and marks the location above which cache information can be stored. |
| **/FLUSH** | Empties (flushes) the contents of the current cache. |
| **/Id** | Stands for Ignore Drive, where is the drive letter. Normally, PC Cache stores information for up to four hard-disk drives. On a single drive, it will cache all partitions or none. |
| **/INFO** | Displays a table of the available hard-disk drives, their sizes, and the type and size of the current cache on each drive. |
| **/MAX=##** | Sets the maximum limit of sectors that can be saved to the cache from a single read request. This spreads out the files that will be cached, in case information from one particularly large file occupies the entire cache. |
| **/MEASURES** | Displays four measurements gauging the current performance of PC Cache: the number of logical data transfers, the number of data transfers that have occurred for the current application, the number of physical transfers saved, and the percentage of transfers saved. |
| **/PARAM** | Displays the parameters currently in effect for PC Cache. |

| | |
|---|---|
| **/PARAM\*** | Displays all setup information for the current PC Cache. |
| **/PAUSE** | An error checking switch. If you experience problems finding files while PC Cache is active, you should reboot and reload PC Cache using this switch. The program will display certain warning messages when it encounters a problem. |
| **/QUIET** | Disables the display of the sign-on information. Use this switch when you load PC Cache from a batch file. |
| **/SIZE=###k** | Lets you determine how much memory is allocated to PC Cache. The default allocation is 64 kilobytes. The number you use depends upon how much memory you can spare. |
| **/SIZEXP=###k** | Lets you determine how much expanded memory is allocated to PC Cache. The default amount is 256K. The smallest amount is 10K. |
| **/SIZEXT=###k** | Lets you determine how much extended memory is allocated to PC Cache. The default amount is 256 kilobytes. You can only use this switch when working with an 80286, 80386, or 80486 IBM PC or PS/2. |
| **/SIZEXT\*=###k** | Lets PC Cache determine the best method to access extended memory. |
| **/UNLOAD** | Unloads PC Cache from memory if no other TSR programs have been loaded since PC Cache. |
| **/WRITE=##** | Controls the amount of delay in ## seconds before write operations are sent to the disk. |

# INSTALLING THE PROGRAMS

Installing PC TOOLS is easily done. Before you install the program however, you should verify you received everything you paid for. Then you should make back-up or archival copies of the disks that came with the package. This is your best protection against accidental damage to files while working with them.

# WHAT YOU GET IN THE PACKAGE

The PC Tools Deluxe program comes with two sets of disks and three books of documentation.

The two sets of disks cover the sizes of disk media you are most likely to need: six 5.25-inch disks and three 3.5-inch disks. The same files are on both disks; they're just grouped differently in archived files, which you de-archive when you run PC Setup. Disk 1 in both sets contains the PCSETUP.EXE file you'll use to install the program.

The three books of documentation total over 900 pages. They're quite well done as far as documentation goes, but they don't provide many working examples; they presume the reader has a bit of computer knowledge. You have to jump from one book to another to get a clear idea of everything you can do with PC Tools Deluxe. This book will make up for the documentation oversights.

# PROGRAM FILES SUPPLIED ON DISK

There are 20 files supplied on the original disks that come with the PC Tools Deluxe package. The 5.25-inch program disks contain the following files:

### Disk 1

**PC-CACHE.COM**   Program file for running PC Cache.

**PCSECURE.EXE**   Program file for running PC Secure.

**PCSECURE.HLP**   Help text file for the PC Secure program.

**PCSETUP.CFG**   Current information you've declared for your system when you last ran PC Setup.

**PCSETUP.EXE**   Program file for running PC Setup.

**README.TXT**   Last minute text information for your version of PC Tools Deluxe.

### Disk 2

**COMPRESS.EXE**   Program file for running Compress.

**COMPRESS.HLP**   Help text file for the Compress program.

**DISKFIX.EXE**   Program file for running Diskfix.

| | |
|---|---|
| **MI.COM** | Program file for obtaining current memory usage information. |
| **MIRROR.COM** | Program file for running Mirror. |
| **PCFORMAT.COM** | Program file for running PC Format. |
| **REBUILD.COM** | Program file running Rebuild. |
| **UNDELETE.EXE** | Program file for undeleting accidentally deleted files. |

### Disk 3

| | |
|---|---|
| **PCSHELL6.EXE** | Archived file containing the various separate programs that serve to run the PC Shell program version 6. This file will be de-archived when you run PC Setup. You can also de-archive this file yourself as described later in this chapter. |

### Disk 4

| | |
|---|---|
| **SAMPLES.EXE** | A self-extracting archive file that contains all the sample programs you can use with the various Desktop modules and other program files. This file will be de-archived when you run the PC Setup program. |
| **VIEWERS.EXE** | Archived file that contains all the separate viewers you can use while working in PC Shell. This file will be de-archived when you run the PC Setup program. You can also de-archive this file yourself as described later in this chapter. |

### Disk 5

| | |
|---|---|
| **DESKTOP6.EXE** | Archived file that contains all the separate files that comprise the Desktop Manager program for version 6. |

### Disk 6

| | |
|---|---|
| **BACKUP6.EXE** | Archived file that contains all the separate files that comprise the PC Backup program. This file will be de-archived when you run the PC Setup program. You can also de-archive this file yourself as described later in this chapter. |
| **PCTFAX6.EXE** | Program you run when you select *Telecommunications/Send a fax* from the Desktop menu. |

The assortment will differ if you use the 3.5-inch program disks to install the program, but the file name and definitions will remain the same.

You can copy any of the program files yourself from the original (or backup) floppy disk to your hard disk, and it will work just as if it had been installed by your running PC Setup.

# MAKING ARCHIVAL COPIES

You should always make backup copies, also called *archival* copies, of all disks you buy. The software copyright law allows this much.

## Making Copies on a Two-Floppy System

To make copies of the PC Tools Deluxe program disks on a two-floppy disk drive, place the first original disk in drive A and a blank formatted disk in drive B. Now log onto the A drive:

**Type:** A

**Press:** [Enter]

When the A:\> prompt shows on the DOS command line, you can run the DOS program DISKCOPY:

**Type:** DISKCOPY A: B:

**Press:** [Enter]

The program will ask you to insert the disk you want to copy *from* into drive A and the disk that will be copied *to* in drive B. You should have already done this, but you might want to double-check now. When the disks are as they should be:

**Press:** [Enter]

This begins the disk copying process. When the first disk is copied, the program will ask if you want to copy any more:

**Press:** [Y]

**Press:** [Enter]

Next the computer asks you to replace the first original disk with the second original disk in drive A, and insert a new blank formatted disk to receive the copied files. When you've done this:

**Press:** [Enter]

Continue this way until all the disks have been copied. You might want to make several sets of copies just for your own protection.

## Making Copies on a Hard Disk

To make archival copies on a hard disk, first create a temporary directory that can hold each disk's worth of files. Next copy the original disk files to the directory. Begin in your root directory, the one that appears each time you first boot your computer.

**Type:** MD TEMP

**Press:** [Enter]

Next, log into this temporary directory:

**Type:** CD TEMP

**Press:** [Enter]

You're ready to begin the copying once your DOS prompt looks like:

```
C:\TEMP>
```

Place the first original disk in your floppy drive, presumably the A drive.

**Type:** COPY A: *.*

**Press:** [Enter]

This copies all the disk files to the hard disk. When the copying is complete, remove the original disk and replace it with a blank formatted floppy. To copy the files to a new floppy disk:

**Type:** COPY *.* A:

**Press:** [Enter]

When copying is complete, delete the first set of files. Make sure you're still working in the TEMP subdirectory on your hard drive.

>**Type:** DEL *.*

>**Press:** [Enter]

>**Press:** [Y]

Now repeat the procedure for the second original disk and each subsequent original disk. If you want to make several copies of disk sets, do so before you delete the hard disk files.

Remember to mark clearly all disks and the names of the files they contain. Once you've installed the programs, place the original disks and copies in a safe location, preferably in two different locations. Some people put their most important disks in a fire-safe box or in their safety deposit box at the bank.

## READING THE READ.ME FILE

You should read the contents of a simple text file called README.TXT for important new information about several aspects of the PC Tools programs. This file contains information that turned up too late to go into the manuals, or facts discovered about the program more recently.

You can read the file using the Notepads editor screen, unless you haven't yet installed the Desktop Manager. If you can't wait until it's installed, you can either view the file using another printer or word processor or print out the file using the DOS redirection command > PRN:

>**Type:** TYPE READ.ME > PRN

>**Press:** [Enter]

Make sure your printer is turned on and contains paper.

## INSTALLING THE PROGRAM

PC Tools Deluxe provides its own installation program, PCSETUP.EXE. This is a menu driven full-screen program that requires little work on your part except to answer a series of questions. You run this program to copy and configure the various files you might want to use in your version of the PC Tools Deluxe program.

There are several different ways you can install the program, and installation of some files is optional. You can install the PC Tools programs using the default option settings or you can configure them for various modes of operation. If you've never worked with the PC Tools shell or desktop utilities, the default configuration is probably best for you.

The installation program will walk you through over 20 screens, asking you questions to which you reply to guide the configuration. Don't worry if some of the questions don't make sense the first time you use PCSETUP. You can always go back and reconfigure the program to suit your needs any time you want to.

To begin the configuration, place Disk 1 in drive A. To load the program PCSETUP.EXE:

**Type:** PCSETUP

**Press:** [Enter]

If for some reason you want to cancel the installation at any point, press [Esc]. You can always start the program over again and run through the steps quickly.

The first screen that appears looks like figure A.1.

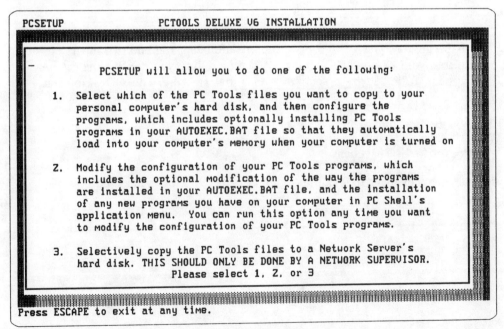

```
 PCSETUP               PCTOOLS DELUXE V6 INSTALLATION


  ─
             PCSETUP will allow you to do one of the following:

        1.   Select which of the PC Tools files you want to copy to your
             personal computer's hard disk, and then configure the
             programs, which includes optionally installing PC Tools
             programs in your AUTOEXEC.BAT file so that they automatically
             load into your computer's memory when your computer is turned on

        2.   Modify the configuration of your PC Tools programs, which
             includes the optional modification of the way the programs
             are installed in your AUTOEXEC.BAT file, and the installation
             of any new programs you have on your computer in PC Shell's
             application menu.  You can run this option any time you want
             to modify the configuration of your PC Tools programs.

        3.   Selectively copy the PC Tools files to a Network Server's
             hard disk. THIS SHOULD ONLY BE DONE BY A NETWORK SUPERVISOR.
                         Please select 1, 2, or 3

 Press ESCAPE to exit at any time.
```

*Figure A.1. The first Install screen*

This first screen lets you select one of three ways for installing the program:

1.  Copy the files selectively (the ones you want to use) to a single personal computer and modify commands in your AUTOEXEC.BAT file.

2.  Change a previous configuration by modifying your AUTOEXEC.BAT. You can use this feature to reconfigure for new applications you've installed on your hard disk, or you can modify the Applications menu on your own (described in chapter 4).

3.  Copy files to a computer on a network facility.

The rest of the program will walk you through similar screens where you can select your install options.

# TEST RUN

To make sure that you've installed the major programs correctly.

Reboot your computer first:

> **Press:** [Ctrl]-[Alt]-[Del]

You might notice this time that it takes a bit longer for your computer to fully boot. This is because two new PC Tools programs are being run and two others are being loaded into your computer's memory. A screen telling you the PC Shell is installed will appear, followed by a second screen that says PC Tools Desktop has been installed.

To open the Desktop menu:

> **Press:** [Ctrl]-[Spacebar]

If your screen changes to look like figure A.2, the Desktop is loaded properly.

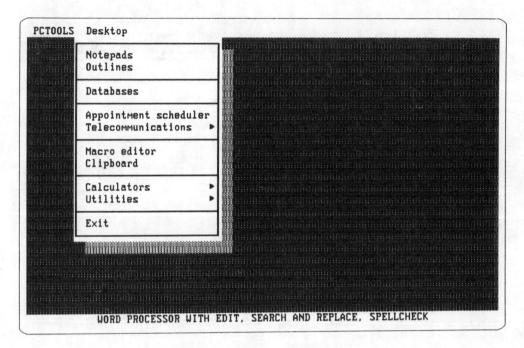

*Figure A.2. The Desktop main menu*

Don't worry if your screen doesn't look exactly like figure A.2.

To return to the DOS prompt:

**Press:** [Esc]-[Spacebar]

To open the PC Shell:

**Press:** [Ctrl]-[Esc]

You should see a message saying the system area is being checked. It takes longer than usual to open the PC Shell screen in resident mode the first time you use it, because the system area has to be read and recorded to the disk file PCSHELL.TRE. When it finally appears, your screen should look something like figure A.3.

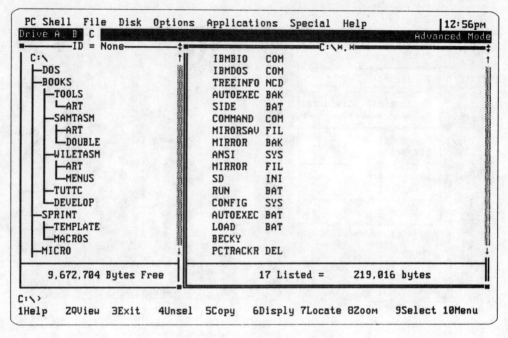

```
 PC Shell  File  Disk  Options  Applications  Special  Help          |12:56PM
 Drive A  B  C                                                  Advanced Mode
 ■────ID = None────────────┊■━━━━━━━━━━━━━━━━C:\*.*━━━━━━━━━━━━━━━━━━━┊
   C:\                        ↑║  IBMBIO    COM                             ↑
   ├─DOS                        ║  IBMDOS    COM
   ├─BOOKS                      ║  TREEINFO  NCD
   │ ├─TOOLS                    ║  AUTOEXEC  BAK
   │ │ └─ART                    ║  SIDE      BAT
   │ ├─SAMTASM                  ║  COMMAND   COM
   │ │ ├─ART                    ║  MIRORSAV  FIL
   │ │ └─DOUBLE                 ║  MIRROR    BAK
   │ ├─WILETASM                 ║  ANSI      SYS
   │ │ ├─ART                    ║  MIRROR    FIL
   │ │ └─MENUS                  ║  SD        INI
   │ ├─TUTTC                    ║  RUN       BAT
   │ └─DEVELOP                  ║  CONFIG    SYS
   ├─SPRINT                     ║  AUTOEXEC  BAT
   │ ├─TEMPLATE                 ║  LOAD      BAT
   │ └─MACROS                   ║  BECKY
   ├─MICRO                      ↓║  PCTRACKR  DEL                           ↓
 ┌───────────────────────────┐║┌───────────────────────────────────────┐
 │    9,672,704 Bytes Free   │║│    17 Listed =      219,016 bytes       │
 └───────────────────────────┘║└───────────────────────────────────────┘
 C:\>
  1Help   2QView  3Exit   4Unsel  5Copy   6Disply 7Locate 8Zoom   9Select 10Menu
```

*Figure A.3. The PC Shell screen*

To close the PC Shell:

   **Press:** [Ctrl]-[Esc]

PC Tools Deluxe should now be properly installed.

**494**

# N

# O